Housing Law: Pleadings in Practice

Christopher Baker
MA (Cantab), LLM (Lond),
Barrister at Arden Chambers

Jonathan Manning
MA (Cantab),
Barrister at Arden Chambers

Jim Shepherd
BA, MCIH
Barrister at Arden Chambers

with contributions from:

Alastair Redpath-Stevens
BSc, MA, MCIH
Barrister at Arden Chambers

Second Edition

ARDEN
A
CHAMBERS

SWEET & MAXWELL

Published in 1997 by Sweet & Maxwell, 100 Avenue Road, London, NW3 3PF,
part of Thomson Reuters (Professional) UK Limited
(Registered in England & Wales, Company No 1679046.
Registered Office and address for service:
Aldgate House, 33 Aldgate High Street, London EC3N 1DL.)

Typeset by YHT Ltd, London
Printed and Bound by
Hobbs the Printers Ltd, Totton, Hampshire
www.hobbs.uk.com

No natural forests were destroyed to make this product;
only farmed timber was used and replanted

**A CIP catalogue record for this book is available from the British
Library**

ISBN 978-0-421-74060-0

Housing Law:
Pleadings in Practice

The University of Law, 2 Bunhill Row, London, EC1Y 8HQ
Telephone: 01483 216371 E-mail: library-moorgate@law.ac.uk

Birmingham ⏐ Bristol ⏐ Chester ⏐ Guildford ⏐ London ⏐ Manchester ⏐ York

Contents

9 Appeals   449

PART I: INTRODUCTION   449

PART II: PRECEDENTS   453

PART III: CHECKLIST   516

Table of Cases

Table of Statutes

TABLE OF STATUTES

Table of Statutory Instruments

Table of Rules

List of Abbreviations

ASBO	Anti-Social Behaviour Order
1997 Regulations	Assured Tenancies and Agricultural Occupancies (Forms) Regulations (SI 1997/194)
CPR	Civil Procedure Rules
CLRA 2002	Commonhold and Leasehold Reform Act 2002
CCA 1974	Consumer Credit Act 1974
CCA 1984	County Courts Act 1984
CCR	County Court Rules 1981
DPA 1972	Defective Premises Act 1972
EPA 1990	Environmental Protection Act 1990
FLA 1996	Family Law Act 1996
HA 1980	Housing Act 1980
HA 1985	Housing Act 1985
HA 1988	Housing Act 1988
HA 1996	Housing Act 1996
LTA 1927	Landlord and Tenant Act 1927
LTA 1985	Landlord and Tenant Act 1985
LTA 1987	Landlord and Tenant Act 1987
LPA 1925	Law of Property Act 1925
LP(R)A 1938	Leasehold Property (Repairs) Act 1938
LVT	Leasehold Valuation Tribunal
1997 Order	Leasehold Valuation Tribunals (Service Charges, Insurance or Appointment of Managers Applications) Order (SI 1997/1853)
LGHA	Local Government and Housing Act 1989
MCR	Magistrates' Courts Rules 1981
PCCA 1973	Powers of Criminal Courts Act 1973
PEA 1977	Protection from Eviction Act 1977
PEA 1990	Protection from Eviction Act 1990
PHA 1997	Protection from Harassment Act 1997
RSL	Registered Social Landlord
RA 1977	Rent Act 1977
R(A)A 1976	Rent (Agriculture) Act 1976
RSC	Rules of the Supreme Court 1965

General Introduction

INTRODUCTION

Much has changed since the first edition of this book appeared in 1994, in terms of both **A**
substantive law and procedure. There have been numerous new statutes (not least the
Housing Act 1996, Human Rights Act 1998 and the Homelessness Act 2002). In addition,
the Civil Procedure Act 1997 brought about the introduction of the new Civil Procedure
Rules (CPR).

Accordingly, the legal landscape in which this second edition appears is considerably
different although, regrettably, this has not resulted in any significant simplification of the
matters with which this book deals, as can be seen from even a cursory reading of this new
edition.

Certain aspects of housing law have, in addition, been the subject of sustained parlia-
mentary scrutiny and activity since the mid 1990s: this is especially true of the allocation of
public housing – particularly to homeless people – and anti-social behaviour. These issues
have served to lengthen this book: the original homelessness chapter has been completely re-
written and its scope extended to cover public sector allocations, and there is now a new
chapter on anti-social behaviour. We have also added a chapter on mortgage possession
proceedings which, it seemed to us, ought properly to fall within the scope of a book on
housing law pleadings. Elsewhere, as may be expected, most of the forms and a good deal of
the legal and procedural sections have required extensive rewriting.

Despite all these changes, however, we have sought to retain the structure of the first
edition, with introductory sections concerning the substantive law and procedural requirements followed by precedents which follow cases through from the letter of claim to close of
pleadings. The fundamental purposes of pleadings and procedure have not changed, after all,
and so although much of the terminology and form is new, the essential substance of a
pleading has, perhaps ironically, been one of the least affected aspects of the CPR revolution.

General Matters

Before considering the particular forms of document and requirements of drafting relevant to **B**
the types of proceedings discussed in the following chapters, it is necessary to observe several
important matters of general application.

Form and forum

Although the introduction of the Civil Procedure Rules has to a large extent standardised the **C**
forms used in the County Court and the High Court, the form of the documents to be
prepared may still be affected by the appropriate venue for proceedings. In most instances,
the County Court will have concurrent jurisdiction with the High Court in housing law

proceedings,[1] apart from applications for judicial review. Where there is concurrent jurisdiction, the County Court will usually be the preferred venue by reason of potential cost sanctions and the risk of strike out. For this reason, where there is a choice of court, the primary emphasis in this book is on County Court proceedings.

The CPR has introduced the generic term "statement of case". This term is used to describe[2]:

a)   claim forms

b)   particulars of claim

c)   defence

d)   defence and counterclaim

e)   reply

f)   defence to counterclaim

g)   Part 20 claim form

h)   particulars of Part 20 claim

i)   Part 20 defence

j)   further information provided under CPR Pt 18

Every statement of case must be verified by a statement of truth (CPR 22.1).

General requirements of originating process

D   In the County Court, housing law proceedings may be brought under CPR Pt 7, CPR Pt 8 or in the case of possession claims under CPR Pt 55.[3] For most cases the claimant will issue a claim form to commence legal proceedings. Under CPR r.16.2(1) a Pt 7 claim form must:

(a)   contain a concise statement of the nature of the claim;

(b)   specify the remedy which the claimant seeks;

(c)   where the claimant is making a claim for money, contain a statement of value in accordance with r.16.3 and

(d)   contain such other matters as may be set out in a practice direction.

If practicable, the particulars of claim should be set out in the claim form (CPR Practice Direction 16, para.3.1). CPR r.16.2(5) confirms that a court may grant a remedy to which the claimant is entitled even if the remedy is not specified in the claim form. The statement of value is dealt with in CPR r.16.3(2). Under this provision the claimant must in the claim form state:

---

[1] Although see CPR 55 PD para.2.1 when a possession claim can only be brought in the High Court in exceptional circumstances.
[2] CPR 2.3(1).
[3] See chapter 6 on possession proceedings. Proceedings may also be brought under CPR 25.4 (application for an interim remedy where there is no related claim).

a) the amount of money which he is claiming;

b) that he expects to recover

    i) not more than £5,000
    ii) more than £5,000 but not more than £15,000; or
    iii) more than £15,000 or

c) that he cannot say how much he expects to recover.

In a personal injury claim, the claimant must state whether he expects to recover not more than £1,000 or more than £1,000 in respect of pain suffering and loss of amenity (CPR 16.3(3)) and if the claim is commenced in the High Court the claim form must state that the claimant expects to recover £50,000 or more.

    Finally, in a claim which includes a claim by a tenant of residential premises against his landlord where the tenant is seeking an order requiring the landlord to carry out repairs or other work in the premises, the claimant must also state in the claim form[4]:

a) whether the estimated costs of those repairs or other work is:

    i) not more than £1,000; or
    ii) more than £1,000; and

b) whether the financial value of any other claim for damages is:

    i) not more than £1,000; or
    ii) more than £1,000.

    Under the CPR there is an alternative procedure for claims. This procedure is dealt with in CPR Pt 8. This procedure should be used whenever a rule or practice direction requires it, or where the claimant seeks the court's decision on a question, which is unlikely to involve a substantial dispute of fact (CPR 8.1). The Pt 8 claim form must state:[5]

a) that Pt 8 applies:

b) (i) the question that the claimant wants the court to decide; or
    (ii) the remedy which the claimant is seeking and the legal basis for the claim to that remedy;

c) if the claim is being made under an enactment, and what the enactment is;

d) if the claimant is claiming in a representative capacity, and what that capacity is;

e) if the defendant is sued in a representative capacity, and what that capacity is.

The Pt 8 procedure contains no statements of case and no defence is required. The defendant is only required to complete an acknowledgement of service form. In this form the defendant can seek an alternative remedy or challenge the use of the Pt 8 procedure. Where the Pt 8 procedure is used, Pt 20 (counterclaims, third party claims and other similar claims) applies except that a party may not make a Pt 20 claim without the courts permission (CPR 8.7).

[4] CPR 16.3(4).
[5] CPR 8.2.

Entitling of documents

E   CPR Practice Direction 7 (paras 4.1 and 4.2) requires the claim form and every other statement of case to be headed with the title of the proceedings. The title should state:

    a)   the number of the proceedings[6]

    b)   the court or Division in which they are proceeding

    c)   the full name of each party

    d)   his status in the proceedings (*i.e.* claimant/defendant)

Formal requirements of particulars of claim and defences

F   CPR Practice Direction 5 requires every document including a statement of case prepared by a party for filing or use at court to be divided into numbered paragraphs and have all the numbers, including dates, expressed as figures (para.2.2).

    By para.14.3 of Practice Direction 16, a party may:

    (1)   refer in his statement of case to a point of law on which his claim or defence, as the case may be, is based,

    (2)   give in his statement of case the name of any witness he proposes to call, and

    (3)   attach to or serve with this statement of case a copy of any document as the case may be (including any expert's report to be filed in accordance with Pt 35).

Particulars of claim

G   Particulars of claim must include a concise statement of the facts on which the claimant relies (CPR 16.4(1)(a)).

    If a claim is based on a written agreement, a copy of the contract or documents should be attached to or served with the particulars of claim (CPR Practice Direction 16, para.8.3).

    Particulars of claim that include a personal injury claim must contain the claimant's date of birth and brief details of the personal injury. The claim must be accompanied by a schedule of details of any past and future losses and by a medical report describing the claimant's injuries.

    If the claimant is seeking aggravated or exemplary damages, the particulars of claim must include a statement to that effect and give the grounds for such a claim (CPR r.16.4(1)(c)).

    In any claim for an injunction in respect of or relating to land or the possession, occupation, use or enjoyment of any land, the particulars of claim must state whether or not the injunction or declaration relates to residential premises, and identify the land (by reference to a plan where necessary (CPR Practice Direction 16, para.8.1).

    If interest is sought, the claimant must include a statement to that effect and must state whether the interest is claimed under the terms of a contract; under an enactment (and if so which); or on some other specified basis (CPR rr.16.4(1)(b) and 16.4(2)). If the claim is for a

---

[6] The number is allocated by the court.

specified amount of money, it must state the percentage rate at which interest is claimed; the date from which it is claimed; the date to which it is calculated (which must not be later than the date on which the claim form is issued); the total amount of interest claimed to the date of the calculation; and the daily rate at which interest accrues after that date (CPR r.16.4(2)).

A claimant who wishes to rely on evidence that someone has been convicted of an offence must state that he intends to do so and give details of the conviction, namely the offence, the date of conviction, the court and the issue in the claim to which the conviction is relevant (CPR Practice Direction 16, para.9.1).

Furthermore a claimant who wishes to rely on any of the following matters in support of his claim must specifically set them out in his particulars of claim:

1) any allegation of fraud

2) the fact of any illegality

3) details of any misrepresentation

4) details of all breaches of trust

5) notice or knowledge of a fact

6) details of unsoundness of mind or undue influence

7) details of wilful default, and

8) any facts relating to mitigation of loss or damage.

Defence

CPR r.16.5 requires the defendant in his defence to state which of the allegations he denies; **H** which he is unable to admit or deny, but which he requires the claimant to prove; and which allegations he admits. Where the defendant denies an allegation, he must state his reason for doing so and if he intends to put forward a different version of events from that given by the claimant he must state that version. A defendant who fails to deal with an allegation but has set out in his defence the nature of his case in relation to the issue to which that allegation is relevant, is taken to require that allegation to be proved. Where the claim includes a money claim, a defendant is taken to require the claimant to prove any allegation relating to the amount of money claimed unless he expressly admits the allegation.

Save for these exceptions, whenever a defendant fails to deal with an allegation he is taken to admit that allegation (CPR r.16.6).

CPR Practice Direction 16 requires defendants to give details of the expiry of any relevant limitation period (para.14.1). In a personal injury claim, the defendant must state, giving reasons, whether he agrees, disagrees, or does not admit knowledge of matters contained in the medical report. He can also attach his own medical report if he has one (para.13.1). The defendant to a personal injury claim must also include a counter schedule of expenses and losses, stating which of the claimant's items he agrees or disagrees with, or has no knowledge of, and supplying alternative figures (para.13.2).

Human rights

I   A party who seeks to rely on any provision of or right arising under the Human Rights Act 1998 or seeks a remedy available under that Act must state that fact in his statement of case, which must also:

   (a)   give precise details of the Convention right which it is alleged has been infringed and details of the alleged infringement;

   (b)   specify the relief sought;

   (c)   state if the relief sought includes:

        i)   a declaration of incompatibility in accordance with s.4 of that Act, or
        ii)   damages in respect of a judicial act to which s.9(3) of that Act applies;

   (d)   where the relief includes a declaration of incompatibility in accordance with s.4 of that Act, give precise details of the legislative provision alleged to be incompatible and details of the alleged incompatibility;

   (e)   where the claim is founded on a finding of unlawfulness by another court or tribunal, give details of the finding; and

   (f)   where the claim is founded on a judicial act which is alleged to have infringed a Convention right of the party as provided by s.9 of the Human Rights Act 1998, the judicial act complained of and the court or tribunal which is alleged to have made it. (CPR Practice Direction 16, para.16.1).

Signature by legal representative

J   Statements of case and other documents drafted by a legal representative should be signed by that representative. If such documents are drafted by a legal representative as a member or employee of a firm, they should be signed in the name of the firm (CPR Practice Direction 5 para.2.1)

Formal requirements of witness statements and affidavits

K   Under the CPR regime, written evidence will be adduced mainly by way of witness statements. At trial the witness statement will stand as the witness's evidence in chief unless the court orders otherwise (CPR r.32.5(2)). At hearings other than trial, evidence should generally be given in the form of a witness statement (CPR r.32.6).
   In certain circumstances an affidavit must be used. CPR Practice Direction 32, para.1.4 states that this is the case in the following instances:

   1)   where sworn evidence is required by an enactment, statutory instrument, rule, order or practice direction.

   2)   in any application for a search order, a freezing injunction, or an order requiring an occupier to permit another to enter his land, and

3) in any application for an order against anyone for alleged contempt of court.

If a party wishes to use affidavit evidence in situations other than those described above, the additional cost of doing so may not be recovered (CPR r.32.15).

The rules on the format of affidavits and witness statements are dealt with in detail in the practice direction to CPR Pt 32. The main rules can be summarised as follows:

a) The affidavit or witness statement should be headed with the title of the proceedings (paras 3.1 and 17.1).

b) At the top right hand corner of the first page (and on the back sheet) there should be clearly written: the party on whose behalf it is made; the initials and surname of the deponent/witness, the number of the affidavit/statement in relation to that deponent/witness; the identifying initials and number of each exhibit referred to and the date sworn/made (paras 3.2 and 17.2).

c) The affidavit/statement must if practicable be in the deponent's/witness's own words. It should be expressed in the first person.

d) The affidavit should commence "I (full name) of (address) state on oath ..." (para.4.1(1)). The witness making the statement should also give his full name (para.18.1(1)).

e) If the deponent/witness is giving evidence in his professional capacity or other occupational capacity he must give the address of his workplace, the position he holds and the name of his employer (paras 4.1(2) and 18.1(2)). He must also give his occupation, or if he has none, his description, and state if he is a party to the proceedings or employed by a party to the proceedings (paras 4.1(3) and (4) and 18.1(3) and (4)).

f) The affidavit/statement must indicate which of the statements made in it are made from the deponent's/witness's own knowledge and which are matters of information and belief and the source for any matters of information or belief (paras 4.2 and 18.2).

g) In the case of an affidavit where the deponent refers to an exhibit he should state "there is now shown to me marked '...' the (description of exhibit)" and if more than one affidavit is sworn the exhibits should run consecutively throughout (para.4.3). In the case of the witness statement the witness should refer to the exhibit by simply stating, "I refer to the (description of exhibit) marked '...'" (para.18.4) and if more than one witness statement is made the numbering of the exhibits should run consecutively (para.18.6).

h) The jurat (statement at the end of the affidavit which authenticates the affidavit) must be signed by all deponents; be completed and signed by the person with whom the affidavit was sworn, whose name qualification and full address must be printed below the signature; and must follow immediately after the text of the affidavit and is not to be put on a separate page (para.5.2).

i) The affidavit/statement should be produced on durable quality A4 paper with a 3.5cm margin; it should be fully legible and normally typed on one side of the paper only; where possible it should be bound securely in a manner which would not hamper filing, or otherwise each page should be endorsed with the case number and should bear the initials of the deponent/witness, and in the former case of the person before whom it was sworn; the pages should be numbered consecutively as a separate document and should be divided into numbered paragraphs; all numbers including dates should be expressed in figures, and the affidavit/statement should give the reference to any document/s mentioned either in the margin or in the bold text in the body of the affidavit (paras 6.1 and 19.1).

j) The affidavit/statement should usually follow the chronological sequence of events or matters dealt with and each paragraph should deal with a distinct area (para.6.2).

k) Any alteration to an affidavit/statement must be initialled by the deponent/witness and in the former case by the person before whom the affidavit was sworn (paras 8.1 and 22.1).

l) Documents used in conjunction with an affidavit/statement should be produced and verified by the deponent/witness, and remain separate from the affidavit/statement (paras 11.1 and 18.2). In the case of an affidavit, the exhibit should also be identified by a declaration of the person before whom the affidavit is sworn. This declaration should be headed in the same way as the affidavit and the first page of each exhibit should be marked in the top right corner as in the affidavit.

m) A witness statement must include a statement of truth (para.20.1).

Style of drafting

L Precision is the key to drafting good statements of case and other documents. Concise expression and the clear use of plain English, which is encouraged under the CPR, are also essential. Consistency of terms is also highly desirable, and it may often be helpful to define certain terms (*e.g.* the "premises") at the outset. Within the basic requirements of the rules and good communication, there is scope for personal style, though many if not most housing law statements of case will in fact follow fairly evident patterns.

Professional standards

M Barristers must pay attention to r.704 of the Code of Conduct of the Bar of England and Wales. This obligation requires counsel, amongst other things, not to make any contention which he does not consider to be properly arguable, and not to allege fraud unless clearly so instructed on reasonably credible material establishing a prima facie case. Also in the Guide to the Professional Conduct of Solicitors (principle 21.01), solicitors are required not to deceive or mislead the court. Aside from this, the sanction of a wasted costs order (under the Supreme Court Act 1981, s.51) could be applied to a legal or other representative who acts improperly in relation to the drafting of documents.

Amendment and further information

N The amendment of statements of case is dealt with by CPR Pt 17. Amendment requires the permission of the court unless the statement of case has not yet been served on any other party, or if all the parties consent (CPR 17.1(1) and (2)(a)), though the court enjoys the power to disallow an amendment where permission was not required (CPR 17.2).

The amended statement of case must be endorsed either (where permission was required) "Amended [*e.g.* Defence] by order of [judge] dated ...", or (where permission was not required) "Amended [*e.g.* Defence] under CPR rule [17.1(1) or 17.2(a)] dated ..." (CPR 17 Practice Direction, para.2.1). The amended statement of case need not show the original text which has been altered, but the court has the power to direct that the amendments be shown either in colour or using a numerical code (CPR 17 Practice Direction, para.2.2). Where colour is used, the same colour must be used both to strike through any deletions and to insert any new text (CPR 17 Practice Direction, para.2.3). Successive stages of amendment in colour are to be in red, green, violet and yellow (CPR 17 Practice Direction, para.2.4). If the original text is not to be shown, it is helpful to begin the amended statement of case by stating that it is in complete substitution for the earlier version.

If the substance of the statement of case is changed by the amendment, a further statement of truth is required (CPR 17 Practice Direction, para.1.4, applicable strictly only to amendments where permission is required, but seemingly of general relevance as well).

Requests and orders for further information of a statement of case may be made under CPR Pt 18. Where further information is given it must be provided in writing, fully headed and identifying the request to which it is a response. It must set out each request in full and then set out the response immediately after each request. Any documents referred to, which are not already in the other side's possession, must be attached. Finally it must be verified by a statement of truth (CPR Practice Direction 18, para.2).

Chapter 1
Homelessness & Allocations

PART I: INTRODUCTION

The duties and remedies in respect of homeless persons, and those seeking an allocation of **1.01** public sector housing, occupy a discrete but fundamental place in housing law. Whereas the following chapters all deal with private law proceedings, this chapter alone is concerned with applications for judicial review or statutory appeals on a point of law in which judicial review principles are applied. The circumstances in which a private law claim could or would be brought will be rare.

Legislative Outline

Homelessness

The provisions governing local authorities' duties to homeless persons are contained in the **1.02** Housing Act 1996, Pt VII (as amended by the Homelessness Act 2002). In addition, the Secretary of State for Transport Local Government and the Regions (now the Deputy Prime Minister) has published a Code of Guidance to which authorities must have regard.

Under Pt VII there is a series of duties which may fall to be considered and performed by the authority. Some involve the making of enquiries as to the circumstances of an applicant for assistance, making decisions as to what if any duties are owed, and notifying applicants of those decisions and the reasons for them. Other duties involve the furnishing of advice and assistance and securing the provision (or continuation) of accommodation, whether on an interim basis (*i.e.* pending the completion of enquiries and the making of a decision on the application) or on a longer term basis after a decision has been made in favour of the applicant. There is also a duty to protect personal property. Statutory powers exist, moreover, to refer a homeless applicant to another housing authority with whom the applicant has a connection.

Authorities who have secured interim accommodation for an applicant while they are making their enquiries also have power (but are not obliged) to continue such accommodation pending a review of or appeal against an adverse decision on the application (see further below).

Challenging homelessness decisions

An applicant who has received an adverse decision on most aspects of a homelessness **1.03** application, has a right to seek a review of that decision (1996 Act, s.202(1)). A request for a review must be made within 21 days of the applicant being notified of the decision (s.202(3)). The procedure on review is governed by the Allocation of Housing and Homelessness (Review Procedures) Regulations 1999, SI 1999/71.

Appeals to the County Court

1.04 By s.204(1) of the 1996 Act, an applicant who is dissatisfied with a decision on review, or who is not notified of such a decision within the prescribed time, may appeal to the county court on any point of law arising from the decision on review (or, if not notified, the original decision).

The appeal must be brought within 21 days of the appellant being notified of the decision on review (or the date by which he should have been notified – normally eight weeks from the date of the request: reg.9).

Section 204A of the Housing Act 1996 (inserted by s.11 of the Homelessness Act 2002) provides a right of appeal to the county court against a refusal, by an authority, to continue interim accommodation pending the outcome of a s.204 appeal. The right of appeal does not extend to a refusal to continue such accommodation pending an internal review under s.202 of the 1996 Act (see CPR Practice Direction 52, para.24.2).

Appeal procedure

1.05 The appeal to the county court is governed by the CPR Pt 52 procedure (see r.52.1 and Practice Direction 52, paras 17 and 24.2). The Pt 52 procedure is discussed in more detail at Chapter 9. In most cases, a modified form of procedure will apply, with the authority being required to plead some kind of formal "Answer" to the Appellant's Notice and to provide evidence in the form of a witness statement explaining their position. In this sense, the procedure is very similar to that applicable under CPR Pt 54, in relation to judicial review proceedings (see below).

Judicial review

1.06 Given the existence of the right of appeal referred to above in relation to most aspects of an authority's decision under Pt VII of the 1996 Act, there is very little scope for challenge by way of judicial review, particularly given the general requirement of judicial review that before bringing such proceedings, a claimant must exhaust all his or her alternative remedies. Accordingly, in the context of homelessness decisions, the availability of judicial review as a remedy will be restricted to those limited situations in which there is no right to seek a review or thereafter to appeal to the county court. This will principally arise where an authority refuse to continue interim accommodation pending a review of an adverse decision under s.202 of the 1996 Act. Even in such cases, however, the court will only rarely intervene: see *R v Camden LBC Ex p. Mohammed* (1998) 30 H.L.R. 315, *R v Newham LBC Ex p. Lumley* (2001) 33 H.L.R. 11, *R v Brighton and Hove Council Ex p. Nacion* (1999) 31 H.L.R. 1095, CA.

Allocations

1.07 Part VI of the Housing Act 1996, as amended by s.14 of the Homelessness Act 2002, governs the allocation of public housing, both to new applicants and to pre-existing tenants seeking to transfer to different accommodation. Authorities are obliged to have, and publish details of, an allocation scheme for determining the priority each applicant has for an allocation of housing. Allocations must be made in accordance with that scheme (1996 Act, s.167 (as amended)).

Challenging allocation decisions

Unlike homelessness cases, Pt VI of the Housing Act 1996 confers no right of appeal against allocation decisions. Accordingly the only means by which the allocation scheme itself or any decision made under it can be challenged is by way of judicial review, in accordance with the procedure set out in CPR Pt 54.   **1.08**

Judicial review procedure

Pre-action protocol

Before bringing proceedings, claimants must comply with the Judicial Review Pre-Action Protocol, save in cases which are urgent or where the body under challenge has no power to change its decision (not applicable in allocations cases). The protocol generally requires that a detailed letter before claim be sent to the authority setting out the basis of the challenge and the action which the authority will need to take to avoid legal proceedings. The letter should also state whether there is any form of alternative dispute resolution which the Claimant can propose as an alternative to litigating the dispute (see *R(Cowl) v Plymouth CC* [2001] EWCA Civ 1935; [2002] 1 W.L.R. 803).   **1.09**

The defendant authority should generally be given 14 days to respond to the pre-claim letter. The protocol prescribes a procedure for defendants to respond, and warns of costs (and other) potential consequences if both parties have not followed the procedures provided by the protocol in cases in which the court considers they ought to have done.

Commencement of proceedings

The judicial review procedure is contained in CPR Pt 54. The application is made in Form N461, which must contain amongst other things, a pleaded statement of facts relied on, the relief sought (including any interim relief) and the grounds on which the claim for review is based. There is no longer any formal requirement for a witness statement by the Claimant, but this may still be useful, particularly in cases where the Claimant's case is based on his or her specific treatment by the authority, or where matters of fact are important or there is or may be some factual dispute. The relevant documents must be included with the application (whether or not exhibited to a witness statement)   **1.10**

Urgent cases

Where permission and/or interim relief are required urgently, an additional application form must be completed (N463) stating the reason for the urgency, the order the court is asked to make and the timescale within which a decision by the court is required. The form and the judicial review claim form must be sent to the Defendant (usually by fax) prior to the issue of the proceedings.   **1.11**

Alternative remedies

1.12   It is a principle of judicial review that a claimant must exhaust all alternative remedies available before seeking judicial review, unless there is a particular reason why either such alternative remedies are not suitable for the challenge or judicial review is the most appropriate remedy for a specific reason or series of reasons. This means that if there is a statutory right of review and appeal or even if an authority operates an internal appeals or review or complaints procedure, the Claimant would normally be expected to utilise such remedies before seeking judicial review. To fail to do so would risk the court refusing permission or relief and/or costs (see *e.g. Cowl* (above); *R v Chief Constable of Merseyside Police Ex p. Calveley* [1986] QB 424, CA; *R v Birmingham City Council Ex p. Ferrero* [1993] 1 All E.R. 530).

If an alternative remedy exists but has not been pursued, this should be stated and explained in the claim form.

Time Limits

1.13   Judicial review proceedings must be commenced promptly and in any event within three months of the date when the grounds for seeking review first arose, generally the date on which the Claimant was informed of the decision under challenge (CPR r.54.5). It is important to recognise that the Claimant does not "have" three months in which to bring a challenge. The primary requirement of the rules is that the challenge be brought promptly – the three month limit is simply a backstop.

Claimants can be refused permission to proceed (see below) and/or refused any relief at the end of the proceedings if the court considers that they have delayed unduly. If the claim is brought after three months, an extension of time will be required (see CPR r.3.1(2)(a)).

Where there has been delay, the claim form should state this and explain the reasons for the delay.

Service and acknowledgement of service

1.14   The Claimant must serve the judicial review papers on the Defendant and any other interested party within seven days of having issued them (CPR r.54.7). The Defendant (and interested parties if any) then have 21 days to file an acknowledgement of service with the court, setting out whether any part of the claim is to be defended and, if so, a summary of the grounds for defending it. The acknowledgement must be served within seven days of it being filed. If an acknowledgement is not filed, the Defendant (or interested party) will not be permitted to take part at the permission stage (see below) without the permission of the court (CPR rr.54.8 and 54.9).

The permission decision

1.15   The permission of the court is required before a judicial review claim can proceed to a final hearing. This permission decision is the first hurdle for the Claimant to overcome and will in the first instance be made on the papers, *i.e.* without an oral hearing. If permission is refused, the parties will be informed of the reasons for refusal and the Claimant is entitled to ask for the decision to be reconsidered at an oral hearing (CPR rr.54.11 and 54.12). If permission is still refused, the Claimant may appeal to the Court of Appeal, utilising the CPR Pt 52 procedure, slightly modified for the process (CPR r.52.15).

Ancillary orders on the grant of permission

On the grant of permission, the court may also give directions (CPR r.54.10). Common **1.16** directions include the abridgement of the defendant's time for filing its evidence in reply (see below) and ordering that the hearing of the claim should be expedited. The court has power to make any case management directions it sees fit, including ordering disclosure, the attendance of witnesses for cross examination and, of course, the grant of interim relief.

After the grant of permission

If permission is granted, the Defendant has 35 days to file its evidence and detailed grounds **1.17** of defence (CPR r.54.14). An application to set aside the grant of permission may not be made under the rules (CPR r.54.13) but the court has an inherent jurisdiction to set aside an order made on an urgent basis, where the Defendant had no opportunity to put its case to the court before the permission decision was made (see *R(Webb) v Bristol City Council* [2001] EWHC Admin 696).

Amendments

The court's permission is required to rely on additional grounds other than those for which **1.18** permission was given. If permission is only granted on some grounds, the grounds on which permission was rejected may not normally be raised unless the Claimant appeals requests an oral hearing of the permission application and thereafter successfully appeals the refusal of permission in relation to those grounds to the Court of Appeal. If this course is not taken, the claimant is likely to be unable to raise such grounds at the substantive hearing unless, on the basis of a real justification, the judge came to the conclusion that there was a good reason for allowing the additional grounds to be realised: *R (Smooth) v Parole Board* [2003] EWCA Civ 1014 and see CPR r.54.15.

The court may also give permission for additional witness statements to be filed. This may frequently be sought, for example, by claimants who wish to respond to defendants' evidence.

Reconsideration of the merits

If permission is granted, the Claimant's advisers are under a duty to reconsider the strength **1.19** of their claim (and hence whether or not to proceed with the challenge) on receipt of the Defendant's evidence, regardless of whether the Claimant is publicly funded.

Preparation for the hearing

The detailed provisions for the preparation of skeleton arguments and chronologies etc., and **1.20** the lodging of bundles may be found in Practice Direction 54, paras 15–16.

Settlement

1.21   If the parties agree terms before the hearing, a consent order must be filed with the court setting out the proposed order together with a statement of reasons, justifying the making of the order sought. Copies of any relevant statutory provisions and authorities should also be included. (Practice Direction 54, para.17). If the court assents to the order, it will pronounce it in open court without the need for the parties to attend; otherwise the matter will be listed for the attendance of the parties.

Costs

1.22   Generally, costs will follow the event, but the courts have indicated a greater willingness to penalise the successful party in costs where the litigation has not been conducted reasonably, for example, because of a refusal to consider alternative dispute resolution, or if the hearing was unreasonably extended due to the raising of a large number of grounds which were ultimately unsuccessful. The courts may be willing, in such circumstances, to decide costs on an issue by issue basis rather than make the loser pay all the winner's costs (see CPR r.44.5(3) and *e.g. Cowl* (above), *Dunnett v Railtrack plc* [2002] EWCA Civ 303; [2002] 1 W.L.R. 2434; *R(Bateman) v Legal Services Commission* [2001] EWHC Admin 757, [2002] ACD 29).

Where the case has settled, the most likely outcome is that there will be no order for costs, unless either party can demonstrate some unreasonable conduct on the part of the other, or that they would clearly have been successful in the claim had it proceeded to a contested hearing (see *R (Boxall) v Waltham Forest LBC* (2000) 4 CCLR 258, QBD.

Relief in judicial review claims

1.23   As stated above, relief in judicial review claims is discretionary and may be refused for any number and combination of reasons. Aside from this, the courts recognise that public authorities generally respect the law and will reconsider a decision that the courts have ruled to have been unlawfully arrived at. This has an effect on the relief that the courts will routinely grant. Some of the orders described below are rarely awarded in practice (such as mandatory and prohibiting orders) on the basis that they are unnecessary. Quashing orders and declarations are by far the most common orders made in judicial review proceedings.

A quashing order (formerly known as an order of *certiorari*) is the remedy required to quash any decision, and will generally be the primary form of order which is sought.

A mandatory order (*mandamus*) is the order by which the court orders the defendant to do something. In general, it will not be possible to obtain a final order that the defendant must do the substantive act which the claimant desires (such as afford an application for housing greater priority). The courts are not usually willing to make such an order, but will leave the authority to reconsider the matter in the light of the court's decision that the previous decision was unlawful. The court will not normally be in a position to know whether the claimant is entitled to any substantively greater rights than those which have been accorded him, albeit in an unlawful manner. In general, a mandatory order, if granted, will order no more than that the defendant must reconsider the application according to the law. Such an order, however, has no significant advantages over a declaration.

A prohibiting order (*prohibition*) prevents the public authority from continuing to act in a way which the court considers to be unlawful. As with mandatory orders, these are rarely granted.

Declarations can often usefully be claimed in order to establish a legal entitlement or state of affairs. In particular, a declaration may be necessary to provide a foundation for a claim in damages.

The court also has power to award damages on an application for judicial review (Supreme Court Act 1981, s.31(4) and Human Rights Act 1998, s.8). The claim must be made on the claim form, but will be recoverable only if either the court is satisfied that the Claimant could have been awarded damages if he or she had proceeded by way of a private law action. If the court awards damages, it may assess them itself or may, instead, transfer the case to a master or county court for assessment. The latter course is more usual save in human rights cases.

It is of course impossible to set out rules as to when each type of remedy should be pleaded. As relief is discretionary, however, advisers should not be afraid of pleading remedies in the alternative, assuming they are remedies the court has power to order.

Nature of Challenge

A statutory appeal to the county court against a homelessness decision and an application for judicial review are very similar in nature. The Court of Appeal has confirmed in *Nipa Begum v Tower Hamlets LBC* [2000] 1 W.L.R. 306, (1999) 32 H.L.R. 445 that the county court, on a homelessness appeal applies judicial review principles. Although it does have power to "vary" the decision as well as the more conventional powers to quash or confirm it, a variation would probably only be possible if the court has sufficient information before it and does not entitle the court, in effect, to re-make for itself the substantive decision appealed. Neither judicial review nor appeal on a point of law give rise to an appeal on the merits; rather they provide a means by which the legality of the decision can be challenged.   **1.24**

Generally, grounds for challenging decisions might include: a misdirection of law; taking into account irrelevant considerations or failing to take account of relevant ones; reaching a decision unsupported by any evidence; irrationality; deciding an application on the basis of an inflexible rule or policy; applying an unlawful policy (taking account of an irrelevant consideration); or procedural unfairness.

Although in the vast majority of cases (and in those demonstrated below) the challenge is made by individual applicants, and under s.204, only the applicant can appeal, the judicial review procedure is not restricted to such challenges, so that (for example) occasionally one authority may seek a review of another's decision.

Effect of Challenge

A successful challenge will, as stated above, generally result in the authority being required only to reconsider the application and take the decision again, this time lawfully, in the light of the court's judgment. The impact of this can range, however, from the requirement simply to make further enquiries (on a homelessness appeal) to an effective reversal of the original decision. The grant of relief, which is always discretionary, can sometimes also result in substantive and substantial benefits.   **1.25**

Human Rights

1.26   In *Chapman v United Kingdom* (2001) 33 E.H.R.R. 18, the European Court of Human Rights confirmed that Art.8 of the European Convention on Human Rights (Human Rights Act 1998, Sch.1, Art.8) which requires respect to be shown, *inter alia*, for a person's home, private and family life does not entitle a person to be provided with a home. Accordingly, Art.8 will only have limited effect in relation to the subjects under discussion in this chapter. In *R (Bernard) v Enfield LBC* [2002] EWHC Admin 2282, the court was prepared to find a breach of Art.8 where an authority had refused to provide the claimant with properly adapted accommodation under s.21 National Assistance Act 1948, causing her to remain in grossly unsuitable temporary accommodation for almost two years, and awarded damages as just satisfaction for that breach.

Article 6, it is submitted, will give equally limited scope for challenge, given the decision of the House of Lords in *Begum (Runa) v Tower Hamlets LBC* [2003] UKHL 5; [2003] 2 W.L.R. 388, that the scheme of review and statutory appeal in homelessness cases (in ss.202–204 of the 1996 Act) was compliant with Art.6.

PART II: PRECEDENTS

Form 1

N161: Appellant's Notice   1.27

Appellant's Notice

Notes for guidance are available which will help you complete this form. Please read them carefully before you complete each section.

In the   Sweetslurrie County Court

(Seal)

For Court use only	
Appeal Court Reference No.	
Date filed	

Section 1   Details of the claim or case

Name of court	Sweetslurrie County Court	Case or claim number	

Names of claimants/ applicants/ petitioner	Elizabeth Jane Glennslurrie	Names of defendants/ respondents	Sweetslurrie District Council

In the case or claim, were you the
(tick appropriate box)

☐ claimant   ☐ applicant   ☐ petitioner

☐ defendant   ☐ respondent   ☑ other *(please specify)* Homeless applicant

---

Section 2   Your (appellant's) name and address

Your (appellant's) name   Elizabeth Jane Glennslurrie

Your solicitor's name   Yevgeny Yevtush & Co   *(if you are legally represented)*

Your (your solicitor's) address

17-19 Strawberry Boulevard Smokestack FR0 0TY	reference or contact name	Gary Goodlad YY/GG/EG-1
	contact telephone number	01789 873670
	DX number	20 Smokestack

1

Section 3	Respondent's name and address

Respondent's name   Sweetslurrie District Council

Solicitor's name   Director of Legal Services   *(if the respondent is legally represented)*

Respondent's (solicitor's) contact address

Sweetslurrie Legal Services Sweetslurrie District Council Bumblebee House Bunny Close Smokestack SM4 5EL	reference or contact name	Barry Badboy
	contact telephone number	01789 666666
	DX number	19 Smokestack

Details of other respondents are attached   ☐ Yes   ☑ No

Section 4	Time estimate for appeal hearing

Do not complete if appealing to the Court of Appeal

	Days	Hours	Minutes
How long do you estimate it will take to put your appeal to the appeal court at the hearing?	1		

Who will represent you at the appeal hearing?   ☐ Yourself   ☐ Solicitor   ☑ Counsel

Section 5	Details of the order(s) or part(s) of order(s) you want to appeal

Was the order you are appealing made as the result of a previous appeal?   Yes ☐   No ☑

Name of Judge	Date of order(s)
Decision of Sweetslurrie District Council	April 18, 2002

If only part of an order is appealed, write out that part (or those parts)

N/A

Was the case allocated to a track?   Yes ☐   No ☑

If Yes, which track was the case allocated to?   ☐ small claims track   ☐ fast track   ☐ multi-track

Is the order you are appealing a case management order?   Yes ☐   No ☑

2

Section 6	Permission to Appeal

Has permission to appeal been granted?

Yes ☐   complete box A   No ☑   complete box B

if you are asking for permission or it is not required

A

Date of order granting permission _____

Name of judge _____

Name of court _____

B

☒ I do not need permission

☐ I _____

appellant('s solicitor) seek permission to appeal the order(s) at **section 5** above.

Are you making any other applications?   Yes ☐   No ☑
If Yes, complete section 10

Is the appellant in receipt of legal aid certificate or a
community legal service fund (CLSF) certificate?   Yes ☑   No ☐

Does your appeal include any issues arising from the Human Rights Act 1998?   Yes ☐   No ☑

Section 7	Grounds for appeal

I (the appellant) appeal(s) the order(s) at **section 5** because:

See attached grounds

Section 8	Arguments in support of grounds

My skeleton argument is:-

☐ set out below   ☑ attached   ☐ will follow within 14 days of filing this notice

I (the appellant) will rely on the following arguments at the hearing of the appeal:-

See attached

Section 9	What decision are you asking the appeal court to make?

I (the appellant) am (is) asking that:-

(tick appropriate box)

☐ the order(s) at **section 5** be set aside

☑ the order(s) at **section 5** be varied and the following order(s) substituted :-

> The Court is asked to allow the appeal and vary the decision dated April 18 2002 to record that the Appellant is not intentionally homeless, and that accordingly the Respondents are under a full housing duty pursuant to s.193 of the Housing Act 1996.
>
> Alternatively, the Court is requested to quash the decision and remit it back to the Respondents for re-determination

☐ a new trial be ordered

☐ the appeal court makes the following additional orders :-

5

Section 10	Other applications

I wish to make an application for additional orders   ☐ in this section

☐ in the Part 23 application form (N244) attached

Part A
I apply (the appellant applies) for an order (a draft of which is attached) that :-

because :-

Part B
I (we) wish to rely on :

☐ evidence in Part C
☐ witness statement (affidavit)

Part C
I (we) wish to rely on the following evidence in support of this application:-

Statement of Truth

I believe (the appellant believes) that the facts stated in Section 10 are true.

Full name _____

Name of appellant's solicitor's firm _____

signed _____ position or office held _____

Appellant ('s solicitor)   (if signing on behalf of firm or company)

7

Section 11	Supporting documents

If you do not yet have a document that you intend to use to support your appeal, identify it, give the date when you expect it to be available and give the reasons why it is not currently available in the box below.

Please tick the papers you are filing with this notice and any you will be filing later.

☑ Your skeleton argument *(if separate)*

☑ A copy of the order being appealed

☐ A copy of any order giving or refusing permission to appeal together with a copy of the reasons for that decision

☑ Any witness statements or affidavits in support of any application included in this appellant's notice

☑ A copy of the legal aid or CLSF certificate *(if legally represented)*

☑ A bundle of documents for the appeal hearing containing copies of your appellant's notice and all the papers listed above and the following:-

    ☐ a suitable record of the reasons for the judgment of the lower court;

    ☐ any statements of case;

    ☐ any other affidavit or witness statement filed in support of your appeal;

    ☐ any relevant transcript or note of evidence;

    ☐ any relevant application notices or case management documents;

    ☐ any skeleton arguments relied on by the lower court;
    relevant affidavits, witness statements, summaries, experts' reports and exhibits;

    ☐ any other documents ordered by the court; (give details)

    _____

    ☐ in a second appeal, the original order appealed, the reasons given for making that order and the appellant's notice appealing that original (first) order

    ☑ if the appeal is from a decision of a Tribunal, the Tribunal's reasons for that decision, the original decision reviewed by the Tribunal and the reasons for that original decision

Reasons why you have not supplied a document and date when you expect it to be available:-

Signed _____ Appellant ('s Solicitor)

Elizabeth Glennslurrie v Sweetslurrie DC   *Claim No.*

GROUNDS FOR APPEAL (SECTION 7)

1. The Authority have misdirected themselves in law and/or taken into account an irrelevant consideration in concluding that the Appellant made herself intentionally homeless by virtue of the act of her husband in causing the destruction of their home.

    The Respondent failed to consider whether the Appellant was party to, or acquiesced in, her husband's deliberate act of tampering with the gas supply at their home, which is relied on by the Respondent as the deliberate act founding their conclusion that the Appellant is intentionally homeless. Unless the Appellant was party to or acquiesced in the conduct of her husband, his acts cannot in law render her intentionally homeless.

    > "If ... at the end of the day because of material put before the housing authority by the wife, the housing authority are not satisfied that she was a party to the decision, they would have to regard her as not having become homeless intentionally" *R v North Devon DC Ex p. Lewis* [1981] 1 W.L.R. 328, *per* Woolf J. at 333G.

    The Appellant, at her interview with the Respondent's housing officer, informed him that she had not realised either that her husband was serious about manufacturing whisky at their home, nor that he was attempting to modify the gas supply to the house for that purpose. She further informed the housing officer that if she had realised his true intentions, she would have attempted to stop him from doing so.

    The Respondent appear to have taken no account whatsoever of this information in making the decision. The material part of the letter on review reads as follows:

    > "I have found you to be intentionally homeless because of a deliberate act or omission by yourself which caused the loss of your accommodation which you have now ceased to occupy. The accommodation was available to you and it was reasonable for you to continue to occupy it. However, your husband tampered with the gas supply to your house causing an explosion which demolished your property; an act which caused the loss of your accommodation."

    In the premises, the Respondent has misdirected itself in law and failed to have regard to a relevant consideration.

2. In the alternative, if the Respondent has taken account of the information referred to in ground 1 above, and have concluded that the Appellant did acquiesce in the acts of her husband, such conclusion was entirely contrary to the evidence and unreasonable in the *Wednesbury* sense: *Associated Provincial Picture Houses v Wednesbury Corporation* [1948] 1 KB 223, CA.

3. Further, or alternatively, the Respondent's decision is contrary to the principles of natural justice.

If the Respondent did take the information referred to above into account, at no time did they indicate to the Appellant that they did not believe her or otherwise rejected her contentions, nor did they ever give her an opportunity to answer any concerns – or contrary information – they may have had: see *R v Tower Hamlets LBC Ex p. Rouf* (1989) 21 H.L.R. 405; *R v Poole BC Ex p. Cooper* (1995) 27 H.L.R. 605.

4. In the alternative, the Respondent has, in any event, failed to consider whether the acts of the Appellant's husband were acts done in good faith by him for the purposes of s.191(2) of the Housing Act 1996.

    The Appellant's husband, in tampering with the gas supply to the premises, was not aware of a relevant fact, namely that he had failed to make safe the gas supply – by turning it off – before starting work on the gas pipes. Accordingly, he was wholly unaware of any danger involved in the work he was carrying out.

5. Further or alternatively, if the Respondent did take proper account of, and properly consider, the matters set out at paras 1 and 4 above, the reasons given for their decision are defective in that they do not explain the conclusions reached in relation to those matters, nor do they give the Appellant any or any proper indication of why her evidence was not believed or why her application was unsuccessful.

    Accordingly, the reasons provided pursuant to s.203(4) of the Housing Act 1996, were not adequate, proper and intelligible and did not deal with the substantial issues raised, in order to allow consideration of those reasons so that the parties should know why they won or lost and whether the decision could be challenged, as required by law: *Re Poyser & Mills Arbitration* [1964] 2 QB 467; *Westminster CC v Great Portland Estates plc* [1985] 1 A.C. 661, HL, *per* Lord Scarman at 673, approving *Poyser* above.

                                                                              Vere Ecross

Form 2 1.28

Appellant's skeleton argument

IN THE SWEETSLURRIE COUNTY COURT Claim No.

B E T W E E N

ELIZABETH JANE GLENNSLURRIE **Appellant**

and

SWEETSLURRIE DISTRICT COUNCIL **Respondent**

SKELETON ARGUMENT ON BEHALF OF THE APPELLANT

BACKGROUND

1. The Appellant is a married woman with three children: Gordon (6), Mincie (5) and Chesney (3). In about April 1999, she and her husband purchased a three bedroom house at 27 Moonbeam Alley, Smokestack (the "property").

2. On January 10, 2002, the Appellant's husband attempted to modify with the gas supply pipes to the house, in the cellar, causing an explosion which destroyed the house.

3. Approximately six weeks prior to the explosion, on November 31, 2001, a gas fitter employed by Imperial Gas had attended the property and moved the gas meter from its previous location under the stairs to a new location in a meter box attached to the exterior of the property. He did not, however, remove the old meter, informing the Appellant that someone else would come to the property for this purpose. No-one ever did and the old meter remained in-situ.

4. The Appellant had been at home when the gas meter was moved, although the gas fitter had attended the property without warning, but her husband was not there and knew nothing about it. The Appellant did not tell her husband that the meter had been moved because, once the gas fitter had left, she forgot about it.

5. Accordingly, on January 10, 2002, whereas the Appellant's husband believed he had turned off the gas at the meter before he began his modifications to the gas pipes, in fact he had not because he had not been aware that the pipework and meter under the stairs were redundant.

6. The Appellant's husband had attempted to modify the gas pipework to the property for the purpose of installing a whisky still in the cellar. He had for many years

mentioned to the Appellant that he wanted to be a distiller, but the Appellant always believed that this was just a pipe-dream, and never believed that he was serious about it or intended to do anything about it. The Appellant paid very little attention to him. At no time prior to the explosion on January 10, 2002, did the Appellant have any knowledge or belief that her husband intended to construct a whisky still in the cellar or interfere with the gas pipes to the property. Had she realised that he intended to do so, she would have done everything in her power to prevent it.

7. On January 11, 2002, the Appellant and her husband applied to the Respondent as homeless, pursuant to Pt VII of the Housing Act 1996. They were provided with temporary accommodation and told to report back to the office on January 20, 2002 at 4pm to be interviewed further.

8. At their interview, the Appellant specifically informed the Respondent's officer, Mr Marlowe, of the matters set out above, particularly those at para.6 above. The Appellant's husband also informed Mr Marlowe of the matters set out at para.5 above.

9. Mr Marlowe informed the Appellant and her husband, however, that if they had blown up their house, they could not expect the council to give them another one and that they were intentionally homeless, handing them a decision letter under s.184 then and there (*Bundle* pp.33–34).

10. On January 27, 2002, the Appellant requested a review of the Respondent's decision and submitted further representations to the Respondent (*Bundle* pp.35–39). On April 18, 2002, the Appellant received the decision on the review, signed by a Mrs Sands (*Bundle* pp.40–41).

THE DECISION ON REVIEW

11. The material part of the decision on review reads as follows:

"I have found you to be intentionally homeless because of a deliberate act or omission by yourself which caused the loss of your accommodation which you have now ceased to occupy. The accommodation was available to you and it was reasonable for you to continue to occupy it. However, your husband tampered with the gas supply to your house causing an explosion which demolished your property; an act which caused the loss of your accommodation."

LEGAL FRAMEWORK

12. By s.191(1) and (2) of the Housing Act 1996:

"(1) A person becomes homeless intentionally if he deliberately does or fails to do anything in consequence of which he ceases to occupy accommodation which is available for his occupation and which it would have been reasonable for him to continue to occupy.
    (2) For the purposes of subs.(1) an act or omission in good faith on the part of a person who was unaware of any relevant fact shall not be treated as delibrate."

13. Section 184 of the Housing Act 1996 (the "1996 Act") provides, so far as material:

> "(3) On completing their inquiries the authority shall notify the Applicant of their decision and, so far as any issue is decided against his interests, inform him of the reasons for their decision."

14. By s.202 of the 1996 Act, an applicant has the right to request a review of any decision of an authority as to what if any duty is owed to him under, *inter alia*, s.190–193 of the Act: s.202(1)(b). The request for a review must be made within 21 days of the Applicant receiving notification of the authority's decision under s.184(3) above.

15. By s.203(4) of the 1996 Act, on conclusion of the review, if the authority's decision is:

> "(a) to confirm the original decision on any issue against the interests of the Applicant...
>
> they shall also notify him of the reasons for that decision."

16. In *R v North Devon DC Ex p. Lewis* [1981] 1 W.L.R. 328, QBD, Woolf J. held that an authority must consider whether an Applicant who did not personally perform the acts which caused the homelessness was a party to those acts or acquiesced in them, and cannot find her to be intentionally homeless unless they are satisfied that this was the case.

17. In *R v Tower Hamlets LBC Ex p. Rouf* (1989) 21 H.L.R. 405, it was held that an authority's failure to put matters to an applicant and give her the chance to comment on them before deciding them against her amounted to a breach of the principles of natural justice (see also *R v Tower Hamlets LBC Ex p. Nadia Saber* (1992) 24 H.L.R. 611 – where decisive issues ought to have been but were not put to the applicant and *R v Poole BC Ex p. Cooper* (1995) 27 H.L.R. 605 – where information ought still to have been put even though it had been provided on a "confidential" basis).

18. Where there is a statutory obligation to give reasons, such reasons must be adequate, proper and intelligible, dealing with the substantial issues raised, to allow consideration of those reasons so that the parties should know why they won or lost and whether the decision could be challenged: see *Rev Poyser & Mills Arbitration* [1964] 2 QB 467, approved in *Westminster CC v Great Portland Estates plc* [1985] 1 A.C. 661, HL (esp *per* Lord Scarman at 673). This has been confirmed in numerous cases in the context of homelessness, including *R v Croydon LBC Ex p. Graham* (1993) 26 H.L.R. 286. A failure to give proper reasons is itself sufficient reason for a decision to be quashed: *R v Westminster CC Ex p. Ermakov* (1996) 28 H.L.R. 819, CA.

SUBMISSIONS

Grounds 1 and 4
19. The Respondent relies on the Appellant's husband's act of tampering with the gas

pipes to their home as the deliberate act which gave rise to their intentional homelessness. It has, however, failed to give any consideration whatsoever to whether the Appellant was party to, or acquiesced in, that deliberate act of her husband. Accordingly, they have given no proper or lawful consideration to her application (see also the Code of Guidance, paras 7.25–7.26). Unless the Appellant was party to or acquiesced in the conduct of her husband, his acts cannot in law render her intentionally homeless.

20. The Respondent, moreover, has failed to take any account of the information provided by the Appellant at her interview, where she specifically informed the Housing Officer that she had not realised either that her husband was serious about manufacturing whisky at their home, nor that he was attempting to modify the gas supply to the house for that purpose, and that if she had realised his true intentions, she would have attempted to stop him from doing so. None of these matters is referred to anywhere in the decision letter on review (see above).

21. In addition, the Respondent has, in any event, failed to consider whether the acts of the Appellant's husband were acts done in good faith by him for the purposes of s.191(2) of the Housing Act 1996.

22. The Appellant's husband, in tampering with the gas supply to the premises, was not aware of a relevant fact, namely that he had failed to make safe the gas supply – by turning it off – before starting work on the gas pipes. Accordingly, he was wholly unaware of any danger involved in the work he was carrying out. At the very lowest, these circumstances are capable of rendering the Appellant's husband's acts acts done in good faith for the purposes of s.191(2). The Respondent has, however, failed even to consider this aspect of the case.

23. Accordingly, the Respondent has misdirected itself in law and failed to have regard to a relevant consideration.

Ground 2

24. If the information referred to in ground 1 above, was taken into account, and the Respondent nevertheless concluded that the Appellant did acquiesce in the acts of her husband, such a conclusion was entirely unsupported by, indeed was wholly contrary to, the evidence and unreasonable in the *Wednesbury* sense: *Associated Provincial Picture Houses v Wednesbury Corporation* [1948] 1 KB 223, CA.

Ground 3

25. If the Respondent was proposing to reject the Appellant's account that she did not realise that her husband was serious in his intentions to interfere with the gas pipes, it was under a clear obligation to put it to her that they did not believe her or rejected her contentions for some other reason, and give her the opportunity to comment on any concerns or contrary evidence they may have had (see para.17 above). Their failure to do so renders their decision in breach of the principles of natural justice, for which reason it should be quashed.

Ground 5

26. If the Respondent did take proper account of, and properly consider, the matters

set out above, the reasons given for their decision are wholly defective in that they give no real explanation at all of the conclusions reached in relation to those matters. There is no explanation, for example, of whether they disbelieved the Appellant's contentions that she was unaware of her husband's intentions, and considered her to be party to his acts, or whether they believed it but for some other reason rejected her contention that she did not acquiesce in his conduct. No reference whatsoever to the issue of acquiescence is made anywhere in the letter.

27. Similarly, as to the issue of good faith, there is no explanation of whether the Respondent concluded that the Appellant's husband knew that the gas was not turned off, or did not know but ought to have known, or that it made no difference whether he knew or not. No reference to s.191(2) is made in the decision letter and it is quite impossible to discern from the letter what conclusion (if any) the authority reached on this point. Accordingly, the reasons provided did not comply with the requirements of s.203(4) of the Housing Act 1996, and for that reason alone should lead to the quashing of the decision.

28. For all of the above reasons, the decision of the Respondent in this matter was unlawful and should be quashed.

Vere Ecross

1.29 <u>Form 3</u>

Appellant's witness statement[1]

Appellant
E. J. Glennslurrie
First statement
Made: 20/4/02
Filed: 25/4/02
Exhibits: "EJG-1" – "EJG-2"

IN THE SWEETSLURRIE COUNTY COURT   Claim No.

B E T W E E N

ELIZABETH JANE GLENNSLURRIE   **Appellant**

and

SWEETSLURRIE DISTRICT COUNCIL   **Respondent**

WITNESS STATEMENT OF ELIZABETH JANE GLENNSLURRIE

I, ELIZABETH JANE GLENNSLURRIE, of 14 Hyacinth Way, Smokestack, unemployed, WILL SAY as follows:

1. I am the Appellant in this case and I make this statement in support of my appeal against the decision of the Defendant, notified to me on April 18, 2002, that I am intentionally homeless. In so far as the facts and matters I set out below are within my own knowledge, they are true; to the extent that they are not within my own knowledge, their source is indicated and I sincerely believe them to be true.

2. I have been married to my husband, Yorrick, for seven years. Ever since I first knew him he used to joke about becoming a whisky distiller one day. I never took any notice as it never occurred to me that this was anything other than a joke.

3. In about April 1999, we purchased a three bedroom house at 27 Moonbeam Alley, Smokestack. We then had two children, Gordon who was three and Mincie who was almost two. In March 2001, we had our third child, Chesney.

4. Shortly after this, my husband began talking again about becoming a distiller and began to make drawings of what was apparently a still. He said he wished to make us all rich. I still did not believe that he seriously intended to do anything about it, however, and I paid very little attention to him. He seemed to be spending large

amounts of time in the cellar, but I assumed he was just looking at his magazines and keeping out the way of the baby.

5. On November 31, 2001, while my husband was out, a man from Imperial Gas called and said he had come to replace our gas meter which was quite old. He set up the new meter in a box on the outside of the house, as he said this was more convenient than putting it back under the stairs, where the old meter had been. He connected it all up and left. He said someone else would call to remove the old meter, but no-one ever did. By the time my husband returned home, I had forgotten all about this and so I did not tell him what had happened.

6. On January 10, 2002, my husband told me that he was going to have to adapt the gas supply pipes if he was going to make his whisky still work. Then he went down to the cellar. I told him to stop being stupid. It never crossed my mind that he was serious or that he was sufficiently stupid to tamper with the gas supply pipes, and I thought no more about it. It still did not register with me that the gas meter had been moved and that the old one was not connected to anything any more, or that he did not know about it. I went out into the garden where the children were playing and about 15 minutes later there was an enormous explosion and the house collapsed.

7. The next day, we went to Honeypot House, the Council's housing office, and applied to them for assistance as a homeless person. We were provided with temporary accommodation at 14 Hyacinth Way, Smokestack, ST7 1EN, and were told to report back to the office on January 20, 2002 at 4pm to be interviewed further.

8. We attended the interview on that day and explained what had happened. I particularly told the officer, Mr Marlowe, that I had never approved of my husband's schemes and that had I thought he was serious about doing this, or about tampering with the gas supply, I would certainly have done everything within my power to dissuade or prevent him from doing so.

9. My husband also told him that he thought he had turned off the gas supply before he had started work on the pipes, being wholly unaware that he now had to do so from the box outside the house and not under the stairs. Accordingly, he was totally unaware that there was any danger in what he was doing.

10. Mr Marlowe just said, however, that if we had blown up our house, we could not expect the council to give us another one and that we were intentionally homeless. He left us in the interview room for about five minutes and then came back with a letter which said the same thing. I refer to a true copy of this letter, which I now produce at exhibit "EJG-1".

11. On January 27, 2002, my solicitor, Mr Yevtush, requested a review of this decision and made submissions to the Council on our behalf. On April 18, 2002, following a number of letters from my solicitor to the Council, chasing them up, we received the decision letter on the review, signed by a Mrs Sands. I refer to a bundle of documents comprising true copies of all the correspondence referred to in this paragraph, which I now produce at exhibit "EJG-2".

12. I believe that the decision contains errors of law which render it unlawful, not least because the Council have failed to consider whether or not I acquiesced in my husband's conduct but have simply concluded that I am intentionally homeless because he blew up our home.

13. Nor do I really have any idea what the Council thought about the points that I and Mr Yevtush put to them. I do not even know whether they believed me or, if not, why not. There is just no real explanation of the decision in the letter, just a statement that we are intentionally homeless because my husband blew up the house.

14. I would therefore respectfully request the court to allow my appeal.

STATEMENT OF TRUTH

I believe that the contents of this witness statement are true.

[END AS IN FORM 22]

---

[1] There is no formal requirement in CPR Pt 52 for a witness statement on the part of the Appellant, but it can sometimes be very helpful, particularly where the Appellant wishes to assert certain facts.

Form 4   1.30

Respondent's Answer[2]

IN THE SWEETSLURRIE COUNTY COURT   Claim No.

B E T W E E N

ELIZABETH JANE GLENNSLURRIE   **Appellant**

and

SWEETSLURRIE DISTRICT COUNCIL   **Respondent**

ANSWER

---

1. As to ground 1, the Respondent did not fail to consider the issue of acquiescence. It is denied that the Appellant, at her interview or at any other time prior to the making of the original decision or during the review process informed the Respondent that she had not realised that her husband was actually intending to distil whisky in their home and to tamper with the gas supply to the house for that purpose. The Appellant did not inform the Respondent that had she realised his true intentions, she would have attempted to stop her husband from carrying them out.

2. The Respondent was entitled to decide that the Appellant must have been aware of her husband's actions, which took place over a period of time, and that she was therefore party to those actions.

3. As to ground 2, the Respondent's decision was neither contrary to the evidence nor unreasonable in the *Wednesbury* or any other sense.

4. The Respondent's decision was not contrary to the principles of fairness or natural justice. There was no requirement upon the Respondent to put any further matters (or matters in any greater detail) to the Appellant before making a decision. In particular, at no stage in her application to the Respondent did the Appellant raise the points of fact which she now asserts as to her state of knowledge or intentions. Accordingly, there were no matters which could have been put to the Appellant prior to the making of the Respondent's decision.

5. As to ground 4, the issue of whether the Appellant's husband's acts were done in good faith and in ignorance of a relevant fact did not arise. The Appellant did not at any stage in her application assert that this was or may have been the case.

6. In any event, the Appellant's husband plainly intended to do the acts which led to

the family becoming homeless. The claim that he did not appreciate the danger of those actions does not make out ignorance of any relevant facts and is in any event not credible.

7. The reasons given for the decision were lawful and adequate, especially given that none of the matters now relied on were raised before the Respondent.

[CONCLUDE AS IN FORM 19]

[2] This is not a document required by, or even referred to in CPR Pt 52, but is sometimes ordered by the court in order to assist with an early understanding of what will be the Repondent's position on the appeal.

<u>**Form 5**</u>   **1.31**

<u>**Defendant's evidence**</u>

Respondent
E. T. Sands
First statement
Made: 21/6/02
Filed: 23/6/02
Exhibits: "ETS-1"

<u>**IN THE SWEETSLURRIE COUNTY COURT**</u>   **Claim No. SW991002**

B E T W E E N

ELIZABETH JANE GLENNSLURRIE   <u>**Appellant**</u>

and

SWEETSLURRIE DISTRICT COUNCIL   <u>**Respondent**</u>

WITNESS STATEMENT OF EGON TAMARA SANDS

I EGON TAMARA SANDS of Honeypot House, Forget-Me-Not Lane, Smokestack, Local Government Officer, WILL SAY as follows:

1. I am an Assistant Director of Housing in the full-tine employment of the Respondent Authority. I am duly authorised to make this witness statement on behalf of the Respondent, resisting the Appellant's appeal against the decision of April 18, 2002 that she is intentionally homeless. The facts and matters contained in this statement are either within my own knowledge, in which case they are true, or they are derived from the Respondent's files, in which case I sincerely believe them to be true.

2. I am the person who conducted the s.202 review in this case and made the decision against which this appeal is brought. I should like to make the following comments about the matters raised by Mrs Glennslurrie in her Appellant's Notice and witness statement.

3. It is simply not the case that I failed to take into consideration whether or not the Appellant acquiesced in the conduct of her husband. From the file, and the notes of interview, which Mrs Glennslurrie signed as an accurate record of interview, I can see that Mrs Glennslurrie clearly told Mr Marlowe, the officer who interviewed her – and does not deny in her witness statement – that she had known all along of her

husband's plan to distil whisky in their house. She knew that he was making a still and indeed that he intended to tamper with the gas supply.

4. At the interview, from the note, Mrs Glennslurrie never claimed to have tried to dissuade him from taking that course of action: nor does the note record her as having stated that she did not think her husband would be stupid enough to actually attempt to carry out his plans, not even when Mr Marlowe specifically asked her whether she had said or done anything to stop him. In reaching my decision on review, I did not accept that she could have lived in the same house as her husband while he was building a still in the cellar and not have realised what he was doing, as she now claims.

5. I believe, on the facts of this case, I was quite entitled to find that Mrs Glennslurrie was a party to her husband's actions and that she is therefore intentionally homeless. I do not accept that there was anything unreasonable in the *Wednesbury* or any other sense about such a decision.

6. As to the second point which is made, namely that these were acts done in good faith and in ignorance of a relevant fact, it seemed to me that for an act to be deliberate, for the purposes of a finding of intentional homelessness, it need only have been intended to do the act itself. It does not have to have been deliberate in the sense of intended to result in homelessness. It is beyond doubt (indeed it is not denied) that Mr Glennslurrie intended to tamper with the gas supply. I simply do not accept that such an act can have been done in good faith and in ignorance of the relevant fact claimed – that the gas had not, as he believed, been turned off at the meter. There are two reasons for this.

7. First, I concluded that if Mr and Mrs Glennslurrie were unaware of any danger, they were simply shutting their eyes to the obvious: that if a person tampers with the domestic gas supply with a blow torch to weld on new lengths of pipe and without any training or experience of what he is doing, he may well cause an explosion. Indeed, the fact that the Appellant now says that she did not believe her husband would actually do something so stupid implies that she is well aware of the gravity of the risk involved in tampering with the gas supply. The fact that it may not have been their desire to blow up their home cannot be relevant.

8. Secondly, and in any event, neither the Appellant nor her husband has ever raised this contention at any time before this appeal has been brought. They certainly did not raise it at interview. It was not, therefore, information before me when I came to make my decision and so it cannot be a matter which the Appellant is entitled to criticise me for failing to take into account. For the reasons I have set out above, however, I do not believe it would have made any difference to my decision had it been raised before me.

9. As to the contention that I took account of matters which had never been put to the Appellant, as I have said above, it is clear from the interview notes of Mr Marlowe that he specifically asked Mrs Glennslurrie whether she had done anything to persuade her husband to desist from his plans, or to stop him. She simply replied "Well I tried" to this question, but despite further questioning, did not indicate anything she had actually done or said to her husband. I therefore reject the

contention, contained in ground 3 of the Grounds of Appeal that these matters were not put to the Appellant. First, as stated above, she did not raise the arguments she is now relying on; secondly, she was given every opportunity to explain her own actions. It was her total inability to give any satisfactory answers to these questions that led to my conclusion that she was in fact a party to and jointly responsible for her husband's deliberate act. I do not accept that there was any further need to put matters to the Appellant.

10. For all of the above reasons, I am advised and believe that my decision was lawful and correct and I would therefore respectfully request this court to dismiss the Appellant's appeal. I now produce a bundle of documents which comprise true copies of all the information before the Respondent when the decision on appeal was made, marked "ETS-1".

[END AS IN FORM 22]

Form 6

1.32   Letter Before Claim

Well & Greens
Solicitors
9 Kirra Street
Surfsup
SU9 9AY

Tel: 07099-3334456
Fax: 07099-333457
Email: enquiries@wellangreens.com
DX: 44 Surfsup 1

Our ref: AG_Narley.002

March 24, 2003

Mrs Patricia Jenkins
Director of Law and Things
Surfsup Council
The Water Offices
Surfsup SU8 8ER

Dear Mrs Jenkins

Narley Wave – Proposed Claim for Judicial Review
Your reference: HousApp1/03/no

We act in this matter for Ms Narley Wave, who has received from the Housing Department of your authority (the "authority") a notification from the authority's Head of Housing Need, Mr Kerr, dated February 24, 2003, of the decision to accept her application for accommodation under Pt VI of the Housing Act 1996 (the "1996 Act"), but (a) to place her application in the inactive section of the authority's housing list because of her refusal of a property at 539 Jeffrey's Bay Towers, offered under Pt VII of the 1996 Act, and (b) that once this period of suspension has passed, her application will be listed on the active part of the register along with all the other applicants in date order of application, and given no priority other than that which she may acquire by virtue of waiting time.

This letter is to inform you that we consider this decision to be unlawful for the reasons set out below and are instructed by Ms Wave, and have been granted public funding, to commence judicial review proceedings against you, subject to your agreeing to the proposals set out in this letter by 4pm on April 7, 2003.

For your convenience, the remainder of this letter will follow the format set out at Annex A to the Judicial Review Pre-Action Protocol. In accordance with that protocol, a copy of this letter has been sent to Mr Kerr.

The Claimant
Ms Narley Wave
c/o 32 Stoke Court
Surfsup SU9 9NY

Reference Details
See above

Details of the matter being challenged
The decisions of the authority, notified to the claimant by letter of February 24, 2003, to list her application for accommodation under Pt VI of the 1996 Act in the inactive section of the authority's waiting list for 12 months and, thereafter, to accord it priority only on the basis of waiting time.

The Issues
We believe these decisions to be unlawful for the following, principal reasons:

1. It is irrational to have placed Ms Wave's application on the inactive part of the list given that:

   (a) although she refused an offer of accommodation under Pt VII, your authority has a discretion not to impose the 12 month suspension (see para.32 of your allocations scheme which only states that it will "normally" be imposed);

   (b) in this case, there are very strong reasons why no such suspension should be imposed, namely that:

      (i) the offer of accommodation refused, although not appealed due to our client not receiving legal advice at that time, was so plainly unsuitable that it would clearly have been withdrawn and should never have been made. We have already sent you, under cover of our letter of March 1, 2003, a copy of an expert surveyor's report following an inspection he has made of the property;

      (ii) the Claimant and her four children are currently sharing a bedsit with the Claimant's father which is wholly unsuitable for their needs and is causing considerable hardship to the Claimant's father. In particular, the landlord has threatened to forfeit the lease of the flat, because the Claimant's father is in breach of its terms in that he has caused the flat to become statutorily overcrowded by permitting the claimant and her children to stay with him;

      (iii) on receipt of Mr Kerr's decision letter, the Claimant attempted to take her own life. We have sent you, also under cover of our March 1 letter, a report from the consultant psychiatrist whose care she is now under and a letter from a team leader in your authority's social services department (children and families team) which both state that the Claimant's need for appropriate accommodation is urgent, failing which her mental state will continue to be so low that another attempt on her life is very probable.

(c) there is no indication in the decision letter that the authority even considered exercising the discretion not to impose a suspension in the claimant's favour. If this was not considered, that amounts to a clear error of law. If it was and a decision was made to impose a suspension nevertheless, we consider that decision to be unreasonable in the *Wednesbury* sense.

2. The authority's allocations scheme, a copy of which we have seen, is dated March 2001 and therefore does not address s.167(2) of the 1996 Act as amended by s.16 of the Homelessness Act 2002. For this reason it is unlawful.

3. The policy is also unlawful because, even in the "active" or "hyperactive" sections of the waiting list, the only means by which an application can be accorded priority is by waiting time and/or the residual discretion referred to at para.43. The scheme is, accordingly, incapable of conferring the statutory preferences required by s.167(2) of the 1996 Act whether in its original form or as amended. It is also incapable of taking account of multiple categories of need. The use of discretion as the sole means of rectifying these defects is also unlawful. We would refer you to the following cases: see *R(A) v Lambeth LBC* [2002] EWCA Civ 1084; [2002] H.L.R. 57; *R v Islington LBC Ex p. Reilly and Mannix* (1998) 31 H.L.R. 651, QBD; *R v Westminster CC Ex p. Al-Khorsan* (1999) 33 H.L.R. 77, QBD.

4. In any event, you have failed to apply your allocations scheme properly in accordance with its terms, in that you have failed even to consider whether or not to exercise the discretion contained at para.43 in the Claimant's favour. This in itself is unlawful, and given the matters referred to above and in the enclosed reports and letter (referred to above) we consider that it would be irrational not to exercise that discretion so that an offer of accommodation is made urgently to the Claimant.

Action to be taken
We shall issue an application for judicial review without further notice to you unless, by 4pm on April 7, 2003, you have confirmed to us that you have reconsidered our client's application and exercised your discretion so as to lift the supension currently applied to it, place her application on the active part of the waiting list and accorded it sufficient priority that an offer of accommodation will be made on an urgent basis.

Claimant's legal advisers
The solicitor with conduct of this case on behalf of the Claimant is Ann Greens who can be contacted using the details at the head of this letter. Please use our ref: AG_Narley.002

Interested parties
None

Information sought

Please supply, pursuant to s.7 of the Data Protection Act 1998, a copy of the Claimant's housing and homelessness files. We enclose a signed permission from the claimant for this purpose, and agree to be responsible for your reasonable photocopying charges.

Necessary documents

If the March 2001 edition of your allocation scheme is not the most up to date version of the scheme, please inform us of this and let us have a copy of the relevant edition.

Address for reply and service of court documents

Please use the address at the head of this letter.

Proposed reply date

4pm on April 7, 2003.

Yours sincerely,

Well & Greens
Solicitors

cc. Mr Don Kerr
Head of Housing Need
Surfsup Council
The Water Offices
Surfsup SU8 8ER

1.33 Form 7

Reponse to letter before claim

From the Director of Law and Things

Directorate of Law & Things
(Director: Patricia Jenkins)
Surfsup Council
The Water Offices
Surfsup SU8 8ER

d/l: 07099-444999
d/f: 07099-444000
e: patricia@surf.gov.uk
DX: 007 Surfsup 1

Our ref: housapp/1/03/no
Your ref: AG_Narley.002
April 9 2003

Dear Sirs,

Your client: Ms Narley Wave

Thank you for your letter of March 24, 2003, which I have read with interest and discussed with the relevant officers in the Housing Department. I apologise for not meeting your deadline of April 7, but it seemed preferable to take a little more time in order to let you have a full response, rather than send an incomplete reply. I trust that you will overlook my not having sent a holding reply.

Although it seems somewhat repetitive and unnecessary, this letter will follow the suggested format of Annex B to the Judicial Review Pre-Action Protocol.

Claimant
Ms Narley Wave
c/o Well & Greens
9 Kirra Road
Surfsup SU9 9AY

From
Mrs Patricia Jenkins
Director of Law and Things
Surfsup Council
The Water Officers
Surfsup SU8 8ER

Reference Details
Yours: AG_Narley.002
Ours: housapp/1/03/no

I have been handling this matter personally with Mr Don Kerr, the Defendant's Head of Housing Need.

Details of challenge

I have considered your proposed grounds of challenge, as set out in your letter before claim, and would make the following preliminary comments. I refer to my previous letter of March 13, 2003, which set out detailed reasons for the decision made in your client's case. In particular, the suspension of your client's housing register application was due to her refusal of the property at 539 Jeffrey's Bay Towers property. Once her period of suspension has passed, her application will be accorded priority in the normal way and an offer made as soon as she is eligible for one.

I am sure you are well aware of the acute shortage of accommodation in the local area, and indeed of the large number of applicants in a position similar to or worse than that of your client and who have been waiting considerably longer than she has for an appropriate offer.

Mr Kerr and I have both studied the new evidence you have put before us from your client's doctor, social worker and surveyor, but note that (a) your client gave no reason for refusing the property at 539 Jeffrey's Bay Towers, and certainly did not refer to any of the matters suggested by the surveyor; and the comments of the doctor and social worker do not materially alter the authority's understanding of your client's medical and welfare needs. As I have said, these are unfortunately similar to all of those applicants who will be above your client on the register, once her period of suspension has been served.

Response to the proposed claim

I have made the authority's position clear by my letter of March 13 and in the foregoing part of this letter.

I would add that any challenge to the authority's allocation scheme is long out of time, the policy having been adopted in March 2001. You have suggested no reason why your client did not seek to challenge the legality of the policy at that time, rather than waiting until it has been in force for two years. I would refer you to the provisions of s.31(6) of the Supreme Court Act 1981 and CPR r.54.5 with regard to the need for promptness in judicial review proceedings.

Leaving the issues of strict legal principle aside, however, I am willing to make a proposal to your client in the hope that her dispute with the authority can be resolved in another manner, thus hopefully eliminating the need for the courts to become involved in this matter at all, especially bearing in mind that both your client and the authority are publicly funded.

I would be willing to accept your letter before claim as a reference to the authority's Corporate Complaints Conduit ("CCC") This is a three stage complaints procedure which, if your client's complaint is accepted as justified, could lead to her application being given additional priority as a means of remedying the complaint. I enclose a leaflet about CCC which explains in more detail how it works.

Alternatively, I shall arrange for 539 Jeffrey's Bay Towers to be re-offered to your client (exceptionally) under Pt VII of the 1996 Act. If your client now accepts that offer, no period of suspension will be applicable to her Pt VI application.

This seems to me to be by far the most sensible way forward for your client, particularly given that the authority is in the process of overhauling its allocations scheme in the light of the Homelessness Act 2002 and of the authority's modernisation agenda and commitment to continuous improvement of services. Accordingly, any ruling the court may make in your favour would be likely to turn out to be a somewhat pyrrhic victory, as we expect to have the new scheme in place early in 2004.

Other interested parties
I do not consider there to be any.

Address for correspondence/service of documents
Please use the address at the head of this letter, quoting our reference. We do not accept service by fax or email.

Yours sincerely,

Patricia Jenkins
Director of Law and Things

Form 8   1.34

Judicial Review Application

Judicial Review
Claim Form

| In the High Court of Justice |
| Administrative Court |

Notes for guidance are available which explain how to complete the judicial review claim form. Please read them carefully before you complete the form.

Seal

For Court use only	
Administrative Court Reference No.	
Date filed	

SECTION 1 Details of the claimant(s) and defendant(s)

Claimant(s) name and address(es)

name
NARLEY WAVE

address
C/O 32 STOKE COURT
SURFSUP SU9 9NY

| **Telephone no.** 07099-333456 | **Fax no.** n/a |
| **E-mail address** n/a | |

Claimant's or claimant's solicitors' address to which documents should be sent.

name
ANN GREENS

address
WELL & GREENS
9 KIRRA STREET
SURFSUP SU9 9AY

| **Telephone no.** 07099-333457 | **Fax no.** 07099-333458 |
| **E-mail address** ann.greens@wellandgreens.co.uk | |

Claimant's Counsel's details

name
VERE ECROSS

address
SMOKIN' CHAMBERS
59 BLOODBOILER STREET
LONDON EC5A 3PY

| **Telephone no.** 020-7090 9999 | **Fax no.** 020-7090 9998 |
| **E-mail address** vereecross@smokin.com | |

1st Defendant

name
SURFSUP COUNCIL

Defendant's or (where known) Defendant's solicitors' address to which documents should be sent.

name
MRS PATRICIA JENKINS

address
DIRECTOR OF LAW & THINGS
SURFSUP COUNCIL
THE WATER OFFICES
SURFSUP SU8 8ER

| **Telephone no.** 07099-444567 | **Fax no.** 07099-444568 |
| **E-mail address** patricia@surf.gov.uk | |

2nd Defendant

name
n/a

Defendant's or (where known) Defendant's solicitors' address to which documents should be sent.

name

address

| **Telephone no.** | **Fax no.** |
| **E-mail address** | |

SECTION 2 Details of other interested parties

Include name and address and, if appropriate, details of DX, telephone or fax numbers and e-mail

name
n/a

name

address

address

Telephone no.

Fax no.

Telephone no.

Fax no.

E-mail address

E-mail address

SECTION 3 Details of the decision to be judicially reviewed

Decision:

Defendant's decision to place the Claimant's Part VI application for accommodation on the inactive part of the waiting list for 12 months, and thereafter to afford it priority only by reference to the date on which it was accepted.

Date of decision:

February 24, 2003

Name and address of the court, tribunal, person or body who made the decision to be reviewed.

name

SURFSUP COUNCIL

address

THE WATER OFFICES
SURFSUP SU8 8ER

SECTION 4 Permission to proceed with a claim for judicial review

I am seeking permission to proceed with my claim for Judicial Review.

Are you making any other applications? If Yes, complete Section 7.	☑ Yes	☐ No
Is the claimant in receipt of a Community Legal Service Fund (CLSF) certificate?	☑ Yes	☐ No
Are you claiming exceptional urgency, or do you need this application determined within a certain time scale? If Yes, complete Form N463 and file this with your application.	☑ Yes	☐ No
Have you complied with the pre-action protocol? If No, give reasons for non-compliance in the space below.	☑ Yes	☐ No

Does the claim include any issues arising from the Human Rights Act 1998? If Yes, state the articles which you contend have been breached in the space below.	☐ Yes	☑ No

SECTION 5 Detailed statement of grounds

☐ set out below   ☑ attached

SEE ATTACHED

SECTION 6 Details of remedy (including any interim remedy) being sought

1.) A quashing order to quash the decision of February 24, 2003

2.) Further, a quashing order to quash the Defendant's allocations scheme dated March 2001.

3.) Further or alternatively, a declaration that the Defendant's said allocations scheme is unlawful in that it is incapable of affording the statutory preferences required by section 167(2) of the Housing Act 1996 as amended by section 16 of the Homelessness Act 2002;

4.) An order that the time for the Defendant to file its acknowledgement of service be abridged to 48 hours;

5.) An order that, if permission is granted, this case is suitable for an early hearing and that the Defendant's time for filing evidence in response and its detailed grounds of defence be abridged to 7 days from the date of receipt of the Judge's reasons.

6) Further or other relief;

7) Costs.

SECTION 7 Other applications

I wish to make an application for:-

an extension of time, should one be required, pursuant to CPR Rule 3.1(2)(a) to challenge the Defendant's allocations scheme, dated March 2002.

The Claimant will rely on paragraphs 42-47 of her Grounds for seeking review and paragraphs 7 and 8 of her witness statement dated 1 May 2003, in support of this application.

SECTION 8 Statement of facts relied on

SEE ATTACHED

Statement of Truth

I believe (The claimant believes) that the facts stated in this claim form are true.

Full name ANN GREENS

Name of claimant's solicitor's firm   WELL & GREENS

Signed _____   Position or office held PARTNER _____

Claimant ('s solicitor)   (if signing on behalf of firm or company)

4 of 5

SECTION 9 Supporting documents

If you do not have a document that you intend to use to support your claim, identify it, give the date when you expect it to be available and give reasons why it is not currently available in the box below.

Please tick the papers you are filing with this claim form and any you will be filing later.

☑ Statement of grounds	☐ included	☑ attached
☑ Statement of the facts relied on	☐ included	☑ attached
☑ Application to extended the time limit for filing the claim form	☑ included	☑ attached
☐ Application for directions	☐ included	☐ attached

☑ Any written evidence in support of the claim or application to extend time

☐ Where the claim for judicial review relates to a decision of a court or tribunal, an approved copy of the reasons for reaching that decision

☑ Copies of any documents on which the claimant proposes to rely

☑ A copy of the legal aid or CSLF certificate *(if legally represented)*

☑ Copies of any relevant statutory material

☑ A list of essential documents for advance reading by the court *(with page references to the passages relied upon)*

Reasons why you have not supplied a document and date when you expect it to be available:-

Signed _____ Claimant ('s Solicitor) ANN GREENS _____

1.35

R(Narley Wave) v Surfsup Council

STATEMENT OF FACTS AND GROUNDS FOR SEEKING JUDICIAL REVIEW

FACTS

1. The Claimant is a 37 year old woman, and a single mother with 4 children: Henry (aged 11), Bobby (aged 9), Cnutt (aged 4) and Jodie (aged 2). She is unable to work due to a suffering severe pains in her legs as a result of an accident at work suffered in 1998.

2. On February 18, 2003, she applied to the Defendant for accommodation under Pt VI of the Housing Act 1996 ("Pt VI" and the "1996 Act", respectively). The background to this application is as follows.

BACKGROUND

3. In October, 2002, the Claimant and her children left the accommodation at 32 Sandringham Close, Surfsup, which she had shared with her partner, due to domestic violence. She took the children to stay with her father and applied to the Defendant for assistance as a homeless person under Pt VII of the 1996 Act ("Pt VII"). The Defendant accepted her application and that she was owed a duty under s.193(2) of the 1996 Act.

4. The claimant applied for benefit at the same time as she applied to the Defendant under Pt VII, but these applications are still being processed by the Benefits Agency. She and the children are currently living on her child benefit and £50 per week which her former partner pays towards the upkeep of the children. Her total weekly income is £99.80

5. On 22 December, 2002, the Defendant secured an offer of accommodation to the Claimant, in purported discharge of its duty to her under Pt VII of the 1996 Act, of a licence of a property situate at and known as flat 539 Jeffrey's Bay Towers, Surfsup, a three bedroom flat on the fifth floor of a 21 storey block of flats. This was short-life accommodation in a block scheduled for demolition in 2005. The Defendant had granted a licence of the block to a Liberian registered company: Suitable Homes for Lodgers Ltd, which company made the offer of the flat to the Claimant.

6. The Claimant viewed and refused the offer on the basis that it was unsuitable because it was too small, almost derelict and on too high a floor for her to be able to manage there by herself, given the age of her children and her problems with her legs.

7. Accordingly, the Claimant formally rejected the property on January 4, 2003. She

was not at that time in receipt of legal advice and she did not seek a review of the suitability of the offer, nor did she exercise her right of appeal to the county court (ss.202–204, 1996 Act). Accordingly, the Defendant formally discharged its duty to her.

8. The Claimant and her children remained (and remain) living with her father. This accommodation is a studio flat in warden controlled retirement accommodation. The accommodation is wholly unsuitable for the following reasons:

(a) It is precarious. Permitting the claimant and her children to stay there is in breach of the Claimant's father's lease as it renders the accommodation statutorily overcrowded. On March 23, 2003, the landlord served a notice on the Claimant's father under s.146 of the Law of Property Act 1925, requiring him to evict the Claimant and her children by April 20, 2003. Proceedings for forfeit the lease were issued on April 28, 2003 and are due to be heard on May 24, 2003;

(b) It is overcrowded. There are two adults and four children (one over the age of ten) sleeping in one bedsitting room measuring 4m × 3.7m. This breaches both the room and the space standards specified by s.325 and 326 of the Housing Act 1985 and renders the flat statutorily overcrowded;

(c) It is wholly unsatisfactory for a family of five to be sharing one room with an elderly relative. In particular, the Claimant's mental health has deteriorated significantly, and she attempted suicide on February 25, 2003.

THE DEFENDANT'S ALLOCATIONS SCHEME

9. By para.32 of the Defendant's allocations scheme dated March 2001:

"32. If a person:
(a) – (c)...
(d) refuses an offer of accommodation under Pt VII of the 1996 Act;
(e) – (g)...
her or his Part VI application will be accepted but normally be held on the 'inactive' part of the register for a period of 12 months from the date of the application."

10. Paras 41 to 43 of the scheme state:

"41. The active part of the register is divided into 2 sections. The first is the "active" section. Applicants in the active section will receive active consideration for an offer of accommodation. The second is the "hyperactive" section. Applicants in the hyperactive section will also receive active consideration for an offer of accommodation.
42. Applications will be listed in over all priority by date order of the acceptance of their application into the active or hyperactive section, regardless of which of these sections their application is in. As both sections are listed together, it makes little difference which section the application is listed in and so the council will only rarely agree to move an application from one to the other.
43. The council has an absolute discretion to list an application in a different order from the date order order if it chooses to do so in its absolute discretion. This might be because

of an unusual factor in relation to a particular application rendering it illegal to list the application in date order."

THE PART VI APPLICATION

11. On February 24, 2003, the Defendant wrote to the Claimant, informing her that her application for accommodation had been accepted but that it would be treated as "inactive" on the basis that she had refused suitable accommodation offered under Part VII. She was informed that her application would remain inactive until the first anniversary of her application, namely February 18, 2004.

12. On her release from hospital, on March 1, 2003, the Claimant sought legal advice. On the same date, the Claimant's solicitor wrote to the Defendant setting out the facts pleaded above (paras 3–8) and requesting that the Defendant reconsider their treatment of the Claimant's application as "inactive" on the basis of the exceptional circumstances of her case, namely:

    (a) that she had left her accommodation with her former partner for a good reason;

    (b) that she and her children (and her father) were living in grossly unsuitable and precarious accommodation which may be lost as a result of her living there rendering her father also in need of accommodation;

    (c) that the offer of accommodation which she had refused under Pt VII of the 1996 Act was plainly wholly unsuitable and ought never to have been offered. The offer could not lawfully have been maintained on review or on appeal had the Claimant utilised these remedies: her failure to do so was attributable to her fragile mental state and lack of legal advice;

    (d) the medical evidence demonstrated that the Claimant required an urgent offer of accommodation.

13. Under cover of this letter, the Defendant's solicitors sent to the Defendant three supporting letters. The first was from the consultant psychiatrist under whose care the Claimant was placed following her unsuccessful attempt to take her own life. That letter included the following comment:

> "It follows from the three sessions I have had with Ms Wave that I consider her mental state to be extremely fragile. She feels she is clinging on to life by a thread but that there is little point in her continuing to do so. She stated that if she were dead, the council would have to look after her children. Ms Wave's feelings are clearly due in very large measure to her current living conditions, and I cannot overstate the urgency of her need to move to appropriate accommodation for herself and her children. If such accommodation is not made available urgently, I am sure that she will make a further attempt on her life."

14. The second letter was from the a team leader in the Defendant's social services department was to the same effect. The third letter was from an independent surveyor, concluding that flat 539 Jeffrey's Bay Towers (which he had been permitted to inspect internally by Suitable Homes for Lodgers Ltd) was unfit for habitation

under s.604 of the Housing Act 1985 and constituted a statutory nuisance under s.79 of the Environmental Protection Act 1990, on the basis that there was no operational toilet or bath in the flat, that the entire flat suffered from penetrating dampness and that there was a large hole in the living room wall measuring approximately 1m × 75cms, rendering the room exposed to the elements and causing a serious risk of injury to the Claimant and her children.

15. On March 13, 2003, the Defendant's Director of Law & Things responded to the Claimant's solicitors, stating that the Defendant had no power to consider the matters raised in the Claimant's solicitor's letter as, by s.167(1) of the 1996 Act, the Defendant was obliged to allocate properties in accordance with their allocation scheme, and the Defendant's allocation scheme contained no provisions entitling the Defendant to ignore the Claimant's refusal of the Part VII accommodation.

16. The letter continued that in any event, even if the Claimant's application were activated, it would still be a number of years before she would be made an offer of accommodation since the order of applicants on the waiting list was entirely based on the length of time they had been waiting for an offer of accommodation. Accordingly, the Claimant would still be 107th and last on the list and could expect to wait at least five years for an offer of five person accommodation.

17. On March 23, 2003, the Claimant was granted public funding to make this application. On March 24, 2003, the Claimant's solicitors sent a letter before claim to the Defendant, stating that these proceedings would be brought unless the Defendant agreed to implement its allocations policy in a lawful manner, activate the Claimant's application and accord it the statutory preferences to which the Claimant was entitled under s.167(2) of the 1996 Act as amended by s.16 of the Homelessness Act 2002. The Defendant was given until April 7, 2003 (*i.e.* 14 days) to respond.

18. On April 9, 2003, the Defendant's Director of Legal Services responded stating that she was satisfied that the decision had been lawful, but that in the interests of avoiding litigation, she was prepared either to (a) re-offer a licence of flat 539 Jeffrey's Bay Towers under Pt VI of the 1996 Act; or (b) permit the Claimant to utilise the Defendant's complaints procedure.

19. By letter of April 10, 2003, the Claimant's solicitor rejected the offer of 539 Jeffrey's Bay Towers and asked for clarification as to the complaints procedure, including in particular how long it would take and what it could achieve.

20. The Defendant's Director of Law and Things responded on April 15, 2003, stating that the complaints procedure was in three stages, each of which would take approximately two months, and that the Claimant could, if ultimately successful achieve a discretionary reconsideration of her priority on the list once she had served her one year suspension for refusing the Part VII offer. If her complaint was unsuccessful, her application would be subject to a further year's suspension for failure to accept the offer of Flat 539 Jeffrey's Bay Towers for a second time.

21. By letter of April 16, 2003, the Claimant's solicitor rejected the offer of the complaints procedure and informed the Defendant that unless it agreed by return to

reconsider the imposition of the suspension and the Claimant's priority on the list within 14 days, these proceedings would be issued.

22. No response has been received to this letter.

LEGAL FRAMEWORK

23. Section 167(2) of the 1996 Act as amended by s.16 of the Homelessness Act 2002 provides as follows:

> "(2) As regards priorities, the scheme shall be framed so as to secure that reasonable preference is given to:
>
> (a)   people who are homeless (within the meaning of Part 7);
> (b)   people who are owed a duty by any local housing authority under s.190(2), 193(2) or 195(2) (or under s.65(2) or 68(2) of the Housing Act 1985) or who are occupying accommodation secured by any such authority under s.192(3);
> (c)   people occupying insanitary or overcrowded housing or otherwise living in unsatisfactory housing conditions;
> (d)   people who need to move on medical or welfare grounds; and
> (e)   people who need to move to a particular locality in the district of the authority, where failure to meet that need would cause hardship (to themselves or to others).
>
> The scheme may also be framed so as to give additional preference to particular descriptions of people within this subsection (being descriptions of people with urgent housing needs).
>
> (2A) The scheme may contain provision for determining priorities in allocating housing accommodation to people within subs.(2); and the factors which the scheme may allow to be taken into account include:
>
> (a)   the financial resources available to a person to meet his housing costs;
> (b)   any behaviour of a person (or of a member of his household) which affects his suitability to be a tenant;
> (c)   any local connection (within the meaning of s.199) which exists between a person and the authority's district.
>
> (2B) Nothing in subs.(2) requires the scheme to provide for any preference to be given to people the authority have decided are people to whom subs.(2C) applies.
>
> (2C) This subsection applies to a person if the authority are satisfied that:
>
> (a)   he, or a member of his household, has been guilty of unacceptable behaviour serious enough to make him unsuitable to be a tenant of the authority; and
> (b)   in the circumstances at the time his case is considered, he deserves by reason of that behaviour not to be treated as a member of a group of people who are to be given preference by virtue of subs.(2).
>
> (2D) Subsection (8) of s.160A applies for the purposes of subs.(2C)(a) above as it applies for the purposes of subs.(7)(a) of that section.
>
> (2E) Subject to subs.(2), the scheme may contain provision about the allocation of particular housing accommodation –
>
> (a)   to a person who makes a specific application for that accommodation;
> (b)   to persons of a particular description (whether or not they are within subs.(2))."

GROUNDS

Ground 1 – Unlawful Policy

24. The Defendant has misdirected itself in law and taken account of an irrelevant consideration – namely its unlawful allocations policy – in reaching its decision about the treatment of the Claimant's case.

25. The Claimant falls into more than one of the reasonable preference categories listed in s.167(2) of the HA 1996 as amended (see para.23 above). For example:

    (a) she and her family are living in overcrowded conditions which are also "otherwise unsatisfactory" for the reasons stated above (para.8);

    (b) they need to move on medical and welfare grounds;

    (c) they are homeless within the meaning Pt VII of the 1996 Act.

26. The Defendant's allocation policy does not address the issue of reasonable preference either under s.167(2) of the 1996 Act in its original form or in its current form as amended by the Homelessness Act 2002. Accordingly, the policy is for that reason, if no other, unlawful.

27. The policy is incapable, moreover, of providing any such reasonable preference (or indeed the discretionary additional preference) because the only criterion for priority is the date order of acceptance onto the active part of the waiting list. For this additional reason, it is therefore unlawful (see *R(A) v Lambeth LBC* [2002] EWCA Civ 1084; [2002] H.L.R. 57, in particular *per* Collins J. at [18]–[19]; and *per* Pill L.J. at [40]).

Composite assessment

28. Further, the scheme for determining priorities ignores the possibility of multiple categories of need and, as such, fails to provide for a rational or composite assessment of housing need. In *R. v Islington LBC Ex p. Reilly and Mannix* (1998) 31 H.L.R. 651, QBD, a policy which awarded a set number of points for a medical priority without regard, subject to a residual discretion, to cumulative needs was held to be unlawful (see especially at p.666, *per* Richards J.).

29. In *R. v Westminster CC Ex p. Al-Khorsan* (1999) 33 H.L.R. 77, QBD, Latham J. held, applying *Reilly*, that the authority's scheme was unlawful in that, if the applicant was homeless, the scheme precluded consideration of any of the other categories to which reasonable and additional preference had to be given (see p.81).

30. The Authority's scheme not only fails to take make provision for a composite assessment, it also fails to take account of need in a way that *could* secure a preference for the more needy applicants.

Discretion

31. The only provision for progression up the list within such a group (other than by waiting time) is the Defendant's residual discretion to afford greater priority (if such discretion actually exists). Following *A* and *Reilly* (above), this is not a rational means by which to assess need.

32. According to the Defendant's response to the letter before claim, however, no such discretion actually exists within the policy. If this is the correct construction of the policy, then it is unlawful for this additional reason, namely that it amounts to an over-rigid and inflexible policy and an unlawful fetter on the Defendant's discretion: see *Reilly* and *Al Khorsan* (above).

Additional preference

33. The Defendant has failed even to consider whether, and if so how, to address the issue of the discretionary additional preference. For this additional reason, the policy is unlawful.

Ground 2 – Policy applied unlawfully

34. In the alternative, if the policy itself is lawful, no proper application of it has taken place in relation to the Claimant's application. In particular, if a discretion exists to increase the priority given to an application in particular in cases where to fail to do so would be unlawful, the Defendant has failed even to consider exercising such a discretion in favour of the Claimant, apparently believing that no such discretion exists (*Bundle* pp.44–45).

35. In this case, it is unlawful to fail to give any proper priority to the Claimant's claim (policy, para.42, *Bundle* p.63), not least because to do so requires her to remain in statutorily overcrowded accommodation, and because the matters referred to above render the decision unlawful.

36. The Defendant has also improperly failed to consider the exercise of its discretion not to impose a 12 month suspension of her application on the basis that she refused accommodation offered under Pt VII of the 1996 Act. The allocations scheme only states that such a refusal will "normally" result in a 12 month suspension, not that it will inevitably do so. (It would be unlawful in any event to fail to retain some discretion not to apply the policy).

37. In the Claimant's case, there were compelling factors which ought to have led to an exercise of discretion in her favour: namely the matters set out at para.12 above.

38. The Defendant has misunderstood its powers, believing no discretion to exist (see its letter of March 13, 2003. In the alternative, it has failed properly to consider the exercise of its discretion.

Ground 3 – Perversity

39. Further, or alternatively, the Defendant's policy, and the treatment which the Defendant has given to the Claimant's application are both unreasonable in the *Wednesbury* sense.

40. In particular, its continued assertion that it enjoys no discretion in the matter in direct contradiction of the wording of its own policy is perverse to a point that borders on bad faith.

ALTERNATIVE REMEDIES

41. The complaints procedure proposed by the Defendant is not an appropriate means of resolving the dispute in this case. The court should not require the Claimant to attempt to utilise that procedure before bringing these proceedings, for the following principal reasons:

    (a) by adopting that route, the Claimant would run the risk of having an additional unlawful and/or irrational penalty imposed on her should her complaint be unsuccessful – that of another year's suspension. Even if successful, she would have to wait until the end of her current period of suspension until any discretionary increase in her priority would take effect;

    (b) the Claimant has no confidence in the Defendant's ability to carry out a fair and appropriate complaints procedure;

    (c) the Claimant's primary challenge is to the legality of the Defendant's policy. That is a matter which requires the involvement of the court. The complaints procedure would not be able to rule on or otherwise deal with that central issue. Accordingly, the result of any complaints procedure, even if in the Claimant's favour, would still leave an unlawful policy in place governing the position (and, as stated above, would still leave the claimant suspended for at least a year);

    (d) the Claimant's need for accommodation is urgent and the proposed complaints procedure is likely to take at least six months;

    (e) the Defendant has rejected the Claimant's suggestions concerning resolving this dispute, namely that it considers the use of its powers expressly conferred by the policy, on the irrational and factually incorrect grounds that no such powers exist;

    (f) as a publicly funded client, the Claimant would be forced to argue points of law without legal representation before a non-qualified body: *R. v Sutton LBC Ex p. Tucker* [1998] 1 C.C.L.R. 251, QBD.

DELAY

42. Although the Defendant introduced the allocations scheme in March 2001, the Claimant could not be expected to have challenged it at this date because, until February 2003, she did not know, and could not reasonably be expected to have known, about it or the matters concerning its illegality now raised on her behalf; and (b) she was not affected by it prior to making her application under Pt VI.

43. The matters complained of amount, moreover, to continuing breaches of duty by the Defendant, in their continuing failure to allocate accommodation under Pt VI in accordance with a lawful policy and their continuing failure to accord to the Claimant's application the priority to which she is statutorily entitled.

44. The Claimant is not seeking any retrospective remedy in relation to decisions that have already been made in accordance with the policy. She simply seeks to quash it

prospectively and to have her own application dealt with lawfully: see *R v Rochdale BC Ex p. Schemet* [1994] ELR 89 *per* Roch J. at 100–101 citing Nicholls L.J. in *R v Westminster CC Ex p. Hilditch* June 14, 1990 (unreported) transcript p.17.

45. There is, further, a public interest in the bringing of this claim bearing in mind the importance of the issues, the number of people affected and the continuing nature of the breaches of duty alleged.

46. Since learning of her right to challenge the continuing breaches and the policy itself, the Claimant has acted promptly.

47. If the Claimant has been guilty of delay, the circumstances are set out in her witness statement and the Claimant's request the court to extend time for this challenge and/or not to refuse relief if the substantive grounds are made out, given the reasons for such delay and the public importance of the challenge.

Vere Ecross

LIST OF ESSENTIAL READING

Document	Bundle page no.
Application Notice and Grounds	1–12
Urgency Notice	13–14
Claimant's statement	15–16
Defendant's letter 24/2/03	17
Claimant's letter 1/3/03	18–19
Defendant's letter 13/3/03	20–22
Claimant's letter before claim 24/3/03	23–25
Defendant's response 9/4/03	26–27
Claimant's letter 10/4/03	28
Defendant's letter 15/4/03	29
Claimant's letter 16/4/03	30
Report of Mr Smith (paras 9 and 10)	42–43
Defendant's allocation scheme	44–48; 51–59

Form 9 1.36

Urgency form – N463

Judicial Review
Application for urgent consideration

This form must be completed by the Claimant or the Claimant's advocate if exceptional urgency is being claimed and the application needs to be determined within a certain time scale.

The claimant, or the claimant's solicitors must serve this form on the defendant(s) and any interested parties with the N461 Judicial review claim form.

To the Defendant(s) and Interested party(ies)
Representations as to the urgency of the claim may be made by defendants or interested parties to the Administrative Court Office by fax - 020 7947 6802

In the High Court of Justice	
Administrative Court	
Claim No.	CO/
Claimant(s) *(including ref.)*	NARLEY WAVE
Defendant(s)	SURFSUP COUNCIL
Interested Parties	N/A

SECTION 1 Reasons for urgency

1.   The Claimant and her 4 children are currently staying with the claimant's father in his studio flat. They are statutorily overcrowded. Accordingly, the Claimant's father is committing a criminal offence. There are, in addition, forfeiture proceedings pending against the Claimant's father, based on his breach of his lease by causing the flat to become statutorily overcrowded by permitting the Claimant and her family to stay with him. These proceedings are due to be heard on 24 May, 2003.

2.   In addition, the Claimant has attempted suicide due to her current circumstances, including her housing circumstances, and her consultant psychiatrist considers her to be at very high risk of a second attempt unless some adequate accommodation is provided for her as a matter of urgency.

SECTION 2 Proposed timetable *(tick the boxes and complete the following statements that apply)*

[✓] a) The N461 application for permission should be considered within 3 days _____ hours/days

[✓] b) Abridgement of time is sought for the lodging of acknowledgements of service

[✓] c) If permission for judicial review is granted, a substantive hearing is sought by May 24, 2003 _____ (date)

SECTION 3 Interim relief *(state what interim relief is sought and why in the box below)*

A draft order must be attached.

> 1.   The Claimant seeks abridgement of the Defendant's time for lodging its acknowledgement of service to 48 hours from the service of this application.
>
> 2.   The Claimant further seeks, if permission be granted, an abridgment of time for the Defendant to lodge its detailed grounds for defence and evidence to 7 days from the date of the receipt of the Judge's reasons.
>
> 3.   The Claimant seeks an expedited hearing by May 24, 2003.

SECTION 4 Service

A copy of this form of application was served on the defendant(s) and interested parties as follows:

Defendant	**Interested party**
☒ by fax machine to time sent	☐ by fax machine to time sent
Fax no. 07099-444568 time 15.53	Fax no. time
☐ by handing it to or leaving it with	☐ by handing it to or leaving it with
name	name
☐ by e-mail to	☐ by e-mail to
e-mail address	e-mail address
Date served	Date served
Date 1/5/03	Date

Name of claimant's advocate	Claimant (claimant's advocate)
name VERE ECROSS	Signed

Form 10 1.37

Draft Order

IN THE HIGH COURT OF JUSTICE
ADMINISTRATIVE COURT   CO/

THE QUEEN

on the application of

NARLEY WAVE   **Claimant**

and

SURFSUP COUNCIL   **Defendants**

---

draft/ORDER

Before Mr Justice....................

On reading the Claimant's application for permission to apply for judicial review; application for urgent consideration of the permission application and the Claimant's statement dated 1/5/03.

IT IS ORDERED THAT

1. Permission granted

2. The Defendant's time for lodging and serving its detailed grounds of defence and evidence be abridged to seven days;

3. The hearing of this application be expedited and heard, if possible, by May 24, 2003;

4. The Defendant shall have permission to apply to the court to vary or discharge paras 2 and/or 3 of this Order

5. There be an assessment of the Claimant's publicly funded costs.

1.38   Form 11

Claimant's Statement

> Claimant
> N Wave
> First Statement
> Date: 1/5/03
> Lodged: 1/5/03
> Exhibits "NW-1" – "NW-3"
>
> CO/1354/2003
>
> **IN THE HIGH COURT OF JUSTICE**
> **ADMINISTRATIVE COURT**
>
> THE QUEEN
>
> on the application of
>
> NARLEY WAVE
>
> and
>
> SURFSUP COUNCIL
>
> _____
>
> **WITNESS STATEMENT OF THE CLAIMANT**
>
> _____
>
> I, NARLEY WAVE, currently of 32 Stoke Court, Surfsup, unemployed, WILL SAY AS FOLLOWS:
>
> 1. I am the Claimant in this matter and I make this statement in support of my application for judicial review of the Defendant's decision of February 24, 2003, to suspend my housing application under Pt VI of the Housing Act 1996 for 12 months and then to give my application no priority at all save for what I may acquire by means of waiting time alone. The facts stated in this statement are within my own knowledge and they are true.
>
> 2. I refer to a paginated and indexed bundle of documents, containing true copies of the decision letter referred to above, together with all the correspondence mentioned in the Statement of Facts and Grounds between my solicitor and the Defendant, marked "NW-1". I also refer to a copy of the Defendant's allocations scheme dated March 2001, marked "NW-2".

3. Finally, I refer to a further indexed and paginated bundle of documents, marked
    "NW-3", which contains: (a) a report from Mr Arthur Smith my consultant psy-
    chiatrist, (b) a letter from Carol Singer, a team leader in the Defendant's social
    services department and (c) a report from Robert Ampillage, a chartered surveyor.
    These are the documents which were sent to the Defendant under cover of my
    solicitor's letter of March 1, 2003.

REJECTION OF 539 JEFFREY'S BAY TOWERS

4. I should like to explain what happened about the property I refused, because it has
    been said that I gave no reasons for this. When I viewed this property on January 3,
    2003, I could not believe that anyone could be expected to live in such conditions,
    which were the same as are described in the report of Mr Ampillage. In addition,
    moreover, the lifts of the block both had out of order notices on them, and I was
    told by a lady who was walking past that they had been out of order for the last five
    months and that the landlords had sent a note round to the residents saying that as
    the block was soon to be demolished, the lifts would not be repaired. I have bad
    legs and four children under 12; I could not see how I could manage using just the
    stairs.

5. When I got back to the Defendant's housing office, I said that I did not like the
    property. The woman behind the desk just carried on reading her magazine and
    said "Whatever". Then she asked for the keys back, took out a big file, opened it
    and ripped out a page. She handed me the page and asked me if I wanted it as a
    souvenir. I saw that the page contained the details of my homelessness application.
    I did not know what to say and did not take the page. After a minute the woman
    screwed up the page and threw it in the bin, saying "too late".

6. I asked if there was somewhere I could record my reasons for refusing the property
    and tried to tell her what they were, but she just said "Talk to the hand – you're
    history, you loser. No-one cares about your excuses. Just tell us where you'll be so
    we can come and take the kids". I was very upset and asked her for her name, but
    she just laughed and said "My name's Mrs Your Worst Nightmare". Then she
    went back to her magazine.

DELAY

7. I should now like to explain the reasons for my not seeking to challenge the
    Defendant's allocation scheme in March 2001, when it came into force. At that
    time I was living in a house which was owned by my long term partner with my
    partner and our children, and had no intention of ever leaving owner-occupied
    accommodation. I had no idea at that time what an allocations scheme was nor
    that the Defendant had one. I was certainly not concerned with the detailed pro-
    visions of the scheme – it had nothing to do with me then.

8. It is only since my circumstances have changed so dramatically that I have found
    myself obliged to apply to the Defendant for accommodation. The way in which
    the allocations scheme operates is now of critical importance to me and to my

children – and my father, for the reasons set out in my application. I have no wish to re-open allocation decisions made by the Defendant on the basis of the scheme going back two years, none of which decision have anything to do with me. All I want is for my application to be dealt with fairly and lawfully on the basis of a lawful policy which gives me the priority to which I am entitled under s.167(2) of the Housing Act 1996.

9. That is why I wish to challenge the legality of the allocations scheme itself and why I would respectfully contend I should not be penalised for not having attempted to challenge the scheme back in 2001. I suspect that if I had tried to challenge it then, as a person living in owner-occupied accommodation, the Defendant would have tried to argue that I did not have standing to bring a judicial review challenge. I am advised by my solicitor that it is very unlikely I would have been granted public funding to bring a challenge then, because I would have had nothing personally to gain by bringing such a challenge.

10. For these reasons, I would respectfully request the court to grant permission to apply for judicial review on all the bases set out in my application notice.

[CONCLUDE WITH STATEMENT OF TRUTH ETC, AS IN FORM 22 ABOVE]

Form 12 1.39

Acknowledgement of Service

Judicial Review
Acknowledgment of Service

In the High Court of Justice	
Administrative Court	

Name and address of person to be served

name
ANN GREENS

address
WELL & GREENS
9 KIRRA STREET
SURFSUP SU9 9AY

Claim No.	CO/1354/2003
Claimant(s) (including ref.)	NARLEY WAVE
Defendant(s)	SURFSUP COUNCIL
Interested Parties	N/A

SECTION A

Tick the appropriate box

1. I intend to contest all of the claim ☑
2. I intend to contest part of the claim ☐ } complete sections B, C, D and E
3. I do not intend to contest the claim ☐ complete section E
4. The defendant (interested party) is a court or tribunal and **intends** to make a submission. ☐ complete sections B, C and E
5. The defendant (interested party) is a court or tribunal and **does not intend** to make a submission. ☐ complete sections B and E

Note: If the application seeks to judicially review the decision of a court or tribunal, the court or tribunal need only provide the Administrative Court with as much evidence as it can about the decision to help the Administrative Court perform its judicial function.

SECTION B

Insert the name and address of any person you consider should be added as an interested party.

name	name
N/A	
address	address
Telephone no. Fax no.	Telephone no. Fax no.
E-mail address	E-mail address

SECTION C

Summary of grounds for contesting the claim. If you are contesting only part of the claim, set out which part before you give your grounds for contesting it. If you are a court or tribunal filing a submission, please indicate that this is the case.

DECISION LAWFUL

1.   The Defendant's decision is lawful and cannot be challenged, for the following reasons. The Claimant refused an offer of 539 Jeffrey's Bay Towers made under Part VII of the Housing Act 1996. The Defendant's allocation scheme lawfully suspended her application for 1 year from the date of her Part VI application (scheme para 32).

2.   Such a policy is lawful in accordance with section 167(2B) and (2C) of the Housing Act 1996 as amended by the Homelessness Act 2002, in that the behaviour of the Claimant in rejecting the offer of accommodation is unacceptable and serious enough for the Defendant to have concluded that she was not a person suitable to be a tenant of the Defendant for a period of 12 months and that, by reason of that behaviour, she deserved to be treated as a person not entitled to a statutory preference.

3.   In addition, the affording of a reasonable preference does not mean that an authority cannot withdraw that preference on account of matters personal to the particular applicant such as rent arrears and/or the refusal of a suitable offer of accommodation: see the decision of the Court of Appeal in R v Wolverhampton BC ex p Watters (1997) 29 HLR 931.

4.   The Defendant's allocation scheme is also lawful and capable of affording the necessary statutory preferences. The housing waiting list is divided into two parts: the active part and the inactive part. All those applicants whose cases are listed on the active part (whether the active or hyperactive section) have such similar needs (not necessarily the same needs, but equally pressing ones) that the requisite statutory preferences are afforded by the placing of them in that part of the waiting list. The further prioritisation by way of date order is only a question of seeking to fine-tune that prioritisation and is lawful: see R(A) v Lambeth LBC [2002] EWCA Civ 1084; [2002] HLR 57.

5.   The Defendant's scheme amounts to the banding of applicants with similar needs and prioritising between them on the basis of waiting time, which is one of the models suggested by the Secretary of State's Code of Guidance, para 5.4(a).

ALTERNATIVE REMEDIES

6.   The Claimant should be required to exhaust her alternative remedies before troubling this court with an application for permission. The Defendant operates a comprehensive complaints procedure which it has offered to the Claimant in this case to carry out a discretionary reconsideration of the decisions challenged. The Claimant's interest in this case relates only to her own case. If she is entitled to additional priority and achieves that by means of an alternative remedy, it is of no consequence to her whether the Defendant's policy is quashed or not.

7.   An alternative remedy cannot be ignored simply because it may not offer all the same relief that this court could grant. It should be attempted even if it would only deal with part of a claimant's grievances: R(Cowl) v Plymouth CC [2001] EWCA Civ 1935; [2002] 1 WLR 803, per Lord Woolf CJ at [11] - [14].

DELAY

8.   The Claimant is out of time to challenge the legality of the Defendant's allocations scheme. The scheme was adopted in March 2001 and the Claimant ought to have challenged it promptly and in any event within 3 months of that adoption.

CHALLENGE FUTILE

9.   In any event, the Defendant is currently in the process of updating its scheme in accordance with the requirements of the Homelessness Act 2002 and the amendments it has made to section 167 of the Housing Act 1996. It is envisaged that a new policy will be in place some time during 2004. The Defendant cannot move any more quickly to replace its existing policy than this whatever rulings the court may make on this application. The Claimant should wait for the adoption of the new policy and challenge that within 3 months of its adoption if she believes that she has grounds for so doing.

NORA-LEIGH PHUSSED

SECTION D

Give details of any directions you will be asking the court to make, or tick the box to indicate that a separate application notice is attached.

N/A

SECTION E

*delete as appropriate

*(I believe)(The defendant believes) that the facts stated in this form are true.

*I am duly authorised by the defendant to sign this statement.

(if signing on behalf of firm or company, court or tribunal)

Position or office held

DIRECTOR OF LAW AND THINGS

(To be signed by you or by your solicitor or litigation friend)

Signed

Date

2/5/03

Give an address to which notices about this case can be sent to you

name

PATRICIA JENKINS

address

DIRECTOR OF LAW AND THINGS
SURFSUP COUNCIL
THE WATER OFFICES
SURFSUP SU8 8ER

Telephone no.

07099-444567

Fax no.

07099-444568

E-mail address

patricia@surf.gov.uk

If you have instructed counsel, please give their name address and contact details below.

name

NORA-LEIGH PHUSSED

address

HEYDOODE CHAMBERS
CALMER STREET
LONDON EC5A 1AH

Telephone no.

020-7000 8712

Fax no.

020-7000 8715

E-mail address

nlp@heydoode.com

Completed forms, together with a copy, should be lodged with the Administrative Court Office, Room C315, Royal Courts of Justice, Strand, London, WC2A 2LL, within 21 days of service of the claim upon you, and further copies should be served on the Claimant(s), any other Defendant(s) and any interested parties within 7 days of lodgement with the Court.

3 of 3

1.40   Form 13

Renewed application for permission – Form 86B

IN THE HIGH COURT OF JUSTICE   CO Ref No: CO/1354/2003
QUEEN'S BENCH DIVISION
ADMINISTRATIVE COURT

In the matter of a claim for Judicial Review

The Queen on the application of

NARLEY WAVE

versus

SURFSUP COUNCIL

Notice of RENEWAL of claim for permission to apply for Judicial Review (CPR 54.12).

1. This notice must be lodged in the Administrative Court Office and served upon the Defendant (and interested parties who were served with the claim form) within seven days of the service on the Claimant or his solicitor of the notice that the claim for permission has been refused.

2. If this form has not been lodged within seven days of service (para.1 above) please set out the reasons for delay:

3. Set out below the grounds for renewing the application:

    1. The learned Judge was wrong to state that the application had no prospects of success. The Claimant relies on the matters pleaded in the claim form and the contents of the Claimant's witness statement.

    2. The learned judge was also wrong to state that the application was now academic as the Claimant has now received an offer of rehousing by the Defendant. This is not the case. The Defendant has simply re-offered the accommodation at 539 St Jeffrey's Bay Towers, which is the accommodation that the Claimant reasonably rejected in January 2003, and which is the subject of the expert report of Mr Ampillage, included in the *Bundle* at pp.60–69. Such an offer does not render the application academic.

4. Please supply

COUNSEL'S NAME: Vere Ecross
COUNSEL'S TELEPHONE NUMBER: 020-7090 9999

Signed
Dated   7/5/03
Claimant's Ref No.   AG_Narley.002
Tel No.   07099-333456
Fax No.   07099-333457

Form 86B

1.41   Form 14

Defendant's evidence

Defendant
D Kerr
First Statement
Date: 10/5/03
Lodged: 10/5/03
Exhibits "DK-1"

CO/1354/2003

IN THE HIGH COURT OF JUSTICE
ADMINISTRATIVE COURT

THE QUEEN

on the application of

NARLEY WAVE

and

SURFSUP COUNCIL

WITNESS STATEMENT OF DON KERR

I, DON KERR, of The Water Offices, Surfsup SU8 8ER, Local Government Officer,
WILL SAY AS FOLLOWS:

1. I am in the full time employment of the Defendant Council (the "Authority") as its
    Head of Housing Need and am duly authorised by it to make this statement in
    support of its defence of this claim for judicial review of its decision of February 24,
    2003, in relation to the Claimant's application for accommodation under Pt VI of
    the Housing Act 1996 ("Pt VI" and the "1996 Act" respectively), and of the
    Defendant's Housing Allocation Policy dated March 2001. The facts and matters
    contained in this statement are either within my own knowledge or else are derived
    from the authority's files, and I sincerely believe them to be true.

2. I made the decision in this case as to the treatment of the Claimant's housing
    application. It was quite clear – indeed she accepts – that she rejected accom-
    modation which the authority had arranged to be offered to her at 539 St Jeffrey's

Bay Towers, Surfsup, in discharge of its obligations to her under Pt VII of the Housing Act 1996.

SUSPENSION OF THE CLAIMANT'S APPLICATION

3. I have read her witness statement concerning the circumstances of that rejection. I now refer to a copy of the refusal form which she filled in, dated January 4, 2003, where she states that she rejected the property because the landlord of the property had a no pets policy and she was considering buying a dog for the children. The form does mention any of the other factors she now relies on. Her witness statement does not mention this form, indeed its very existence is wholly inconsistent with the account she gives in that statement. Nor were any such allegations made in correspondence by the Claimant's solicitors at any time prior to the issue of proceedings.

4. I am personally familiar with all the reception staff at the Defendant's homelessness office. Indeed, I was personally involved in training most of them when I was in my previous post with the authority. I would be astonished and horrified if any of them ever behaved in a way even approaching the allegations made by the Claimant.

5. For these reasons, I would invite the court to reject this account of what allegedly took place at the homelessness office on January 2003, and accept the account which the Claimant herself recorded on the refusal form.

6. On the basis of the reasons for refusal given in that form, I would respectfully submit that I was amply justified in applying the suspension of the Claimant's application for the normal 12 month period referred to in para.32 of the allocations scheme.

7. Nor do I accept that the authority has ever said that it did not have discretion under the policy not to impose such a suspension. I discussed the contents of that letter with Mrs Jenkins, and what it was intended to point out was that there was no basis for exercising that discretion in her favour given the reasons she gave for refusing the property.

DATE ORDER AND STATUTORY PREFERENCES

8. I am well aware of the provisions of the Homelessness Act 2002, s.16 and of the changes that these provisions have made to s.167 of the 1996 Act. At present the authority are in the process of revising their allocations scheme to give effect to those changes as well as other changes arising from the authority's ambitious modernisation agenda and its commitment to the continuous improvement of its services. I shall return to this point below.

9. The active part of the authority's housing register contains 107 applicants including the Claimant. Of those 72 are homeless and owed a full duty by the authority; 84 have young children living in unsatisfactory accommodation. (29 of those 84 are living with relatives; 35 in hotel or hostel accommodation; and 14 are what is known as "homeless at home" – i.e. it is not considered reasonable for them to

continue to occupy their current accommodation. Most of these people are also occupying precarious accommodation). Thirty seven have no adequate washing facilities or are sharing those facilties with people not in their own household. Nine are statutorily overcrowded. One hundred and three have medical needs requiring them to move and all have welfare needs for accommodation.

10. In these circumstances, it would be invidious for the authority to seek to choose between the various needs of the applicants, all of which can be characterised as urgent and all of whom have multiple needs (and most of whom are families with such needs). The preference to which applicants are entitled is, by s.167(2) only a "reasonable preference" not an absolute entitlement to an offer of accommodation before any other given applicant.

11. Before we introduced the date order policy, our previous means of prioritising need was by points. However, this had the disadvantages that (a) most of out applicants had approximately the same number of points and so very minor fluctuations in the number of points allotted to an individual application could cause an applicant to move up or down the list by as many as 60 places; and (b) no applicant could be given any realistic assessment of when they would be made an offer – an applicant waiting for years could find themselves permanently stuck at third or fourth on the register as other applicants continually overtook them. This did not seem fair to us or to reflect the actual levels of need of those applicants on the register accurately or adequately.

12. In these circumstances, bearing in mind the factors I have set out above, we decided that a date order priority system was the fairest we could devise which, while not perfect, was considerably fairer and more certain than a points based system. I would respectfully submit that the policy is therefore lawful and takes account of multiple needs. Where any additional priority is required, the authority has discretion to move an applicant up the register, but this is rarely necessary. I do not consider it appropriate to increase the Claimant's priority – although this is not strictly relevant for another nine or so months as her application is currently suspended.

NEW POLICY

13. As stated above, we are currently working on a new policy. A draft will be ready for consultation in July 2003. It will then go out for statutory consultation until the end of October 2003. Once any responses have been considered, we expect to be in a position to adopt the new policy (with any revisions) and have the new scheme up and running on our computer system by about April 2004.

14. Whatever the court may decide in relation to the current policy, we are working as quickly as we can towards the new policy in any event, and could not adopt a new one according to any quicker timescale than that which I have identified.

RELIEF

15. For all of these reasons. I would invite the court to dismiss this application or to refuse any relief.

16. The Defendant offered to invoke its Compaints procedure, which would be concluded long before the new policy is in effect and indeed long before the 12 month suspension of the Claimant's application has expired. The Claimant rejected this suggestion and brought her claim to court. For this additional reason I would invite the court to refuse relief, even if it finds any of her grounds of challenge made out.

17. In addition, the quashing of the policy would only serve to cause administrative inconvenience, in that the Defendant would not be able to allocate any properties at all, including to the Claimant, because by s.167(1) of the 1996 Act, authorities can only allocate in accordance with their allocations scheme. If our scheme is quashed, we will not have an allocations scheme until the new one is ready to be brought into force, and so will not be able to allocate any properties for up to a year.

18. That would not serve any purpose for the Claimant, nor for any of the other applicants waiting on the register with urgent needs of their own, nor for the Defendant which will have a number of empty properties and be unable to let them leading to numerous housing management problems such as loss of rent, difficulties in balancing the ringfenced Housing Revenue Account and unlawful occupation.

[CONCLUDE WITH STATEMENT OF TRUTH, AND THEN AS IN FORM 22]

1.42　Form 15

<u>Defendant's detailed grounds of defence</u>

CO/1354/2003

IN THE HIGH COURT OF JUSTICE ADMINISTRATIVE COURT

THE QUEEN

on the application of

NARLEY WAVE

and

SURFSUP COUNCIL

DEFENDANT'S DETAILED GROUNDS FOR CONTESTING THE CLAIM

DECISION LAWFUL

1. The Defendant's decision of February 24, 2003, as to the claimant's case was lawful, rational and reasonable.

2. The Claimant refused an offer of 539 Jeffrey's Bay Towers made under Pt VII of the Housing Act 1996. The Defendant's allocation scheme therefore suspended her application from active consideration for 12 months from the date of his or her Part VI allocation (scheme para.32).

3. This is wholly lawful and reasonable. The courts have upheld such policies since the governing legislation was ss.21 and 22 of the Housing Act 1985 (see *e.g. R v Wolverhampton MBC Ex p. Watters* (1997) 29 H.L.R. 931).

4. This has now been put on a statutory footing (first in ss.159–161 of the Housing Act 1996 (the "1996 Act")) and now in ss.167(2B) and (2C) of the 1996 Act, inserted by s.16 of the Homelessness Act 2002. Those new subsections provide (as the court of appeal held in *Watters*) that the requirement to give reasonable preference to an applicant does not apply if:

   "(2C) ... the authority are satisfied that:

   (a) [the applicant], or a member of his household, has been guilty of unacceptable behaviour serious enough to make him unsuitable to be a tenant of the authority; and

    (b)   in the circumstances at the time his case is considered, he deserves by reason of that behaviour not to be treated as a member of a group of people who are to be given preference by virtue of subsection (2)."

5.   It is submitted that this statutory formulation is sufficiently wide to apply to the situation in this case. The Claimant's behaviour in rejecting the accommodation offered at 539 St Jeffrey's Bay Towers for a plainly frivolous reason (to do with the landlord's policy towards a pet she did not even possess) was unacceptable, and sufficiently serious enough for the Defendant to have concluded that she was not a person suitable to be a tenant of the Defendant for a period of 12 months and that, by reason of that behaviour, she deserved to be treated as a person not entitled to a statutory preference.

6.   In any event, even if s.167(2B) and (2C) do not apply, it is settled law that the affording of a reasonable preference only requires the giving of a "head start" to those entitled to it, and does not mean that that head start may not be lost or reduced or suspended on account of matters personal to the particular applicant which the authority is entitled to take account in deciding how preferences are to be awarded, such as rent arrears and/or the refusal of a suitable offer of accommodation: see again the decision of the Court of Appeal in *Watters* especially at pp.936–937.

7.   The Defendant's allocation scheme is lawful and capable of affording the necessary statutory preferences. The housing register is divided into two parts: the active part and the inactive part. All those applicants whose cases are listed on the active part (whether the active or hyperactive section) have such similar needs and multiple categories of need (not necessarily the same needs, but equally pressing ones) that the requisite statutory preferences are afforded by the placing of them in that part of the waiting list. The Defendant relies on the witness statement of Mr Kerr at paras 9–12, particularly the analysis of the active part of the register which he sets out at para.9.

8.   The further prioritisation by way of date order is a legitimate, fair and lawful way of choosing between those applicants all of which are receiving their statutory preferences by virtue of being in the active part of the register: see *e.g. R(A) v Lambeth LBC* [2002] EWCA Civ 1084; [2002] H.L.R. 57, esp *per* Collins J. at [22].

9.   The Defendant's scheme amounts to a system of banding applicants with similar needs and only prioritising between those who have similar needs on the basis of waiting time, which is one of the models suggested by the Secretary of State's Code of Guidance, para.5.4(a). The hyperactive part of the list would be capable of affording any further preference that was required on the facts of a particular applicant's case.

ALTERNATIVE REMEDIES

10. The Claimant should be required to exhaust her alternative remedies before resort to litigation. The Defendant operates a comprehensive complaints procedure (its "Corporate Complaints Conduit", or "CCC") which it has offered to the Claimant in this case to carry out a discretionary reconsideration of the decisions challenged. The Claimant's interest in this case relates only to her own case. If she were entitled to additional priority and achieved that by means of an alternative remedy, it is of no consequence to her whether the Defendant's policy is quashed or not. This is particularly so given that the Defendant is currently in the course of revising and replacing the allocations scheme under challenge with a new scheme, due to come into operation in about April 2004.

11. An alternative remedy cannot be ignored simply because it may not offer all the same relief that this court could grant. It should be attempted even if it would only deal with part of a claimant's grievances. This was made clear by the Court of Appeal in *R(Cowl) v Plymouth CC* [2001] EWCA Civ 1935; [2002] 1 W.L.R. 803, *per* Lord Woolf C.J. at [11]–[14].

DELAY

12. The Claimant is out of time to challenge the legality of the Defendant's allocations scheme. The scheme was adopted in March 2001 and the Claimant ought to have challenged it promptly and in any event within three months of that adoption.

13. It is no answer to this point to state that the Claimant was not interested in the allocations scheme at that time because she was an owner occupier. The strict time limits imposed by s.31(6) if the Supreme Court Act 1981 and CPR r.54.5 are intended to protect public authorities from the prejudice and administrative chaos caused by Claimants who do not have any interest in challenging a decision or a policy until perhaps – as in this case – years after the event.

CHALLENGE FUTILE

14. In any event, as stated above, and in the witness statement of Mr Kerr, the Defendant is currently in the process of updating its scheme in accordance with the requirements of the Homelessness Act 2002, the Defendant's modernisation agenda and its commitment to continuous improvements in its services.

15. It is envisaged that the new allocations scheme will be in place some time during 2004. The Defendant cannot move any more quickly to replace its existing policy than this, whatever rulings the court may make on this application. The Claimant should wait for the adoption of the new policy and challenge that within three months of its adoption if she believes that she has grounds for so doing.

16. No relief should be granted, in ant event, for the reasons set out above and at paras 16–18 of Mr Kerr's witness statement.

NORA-LEIGH PHUSSED

Consent Order

CO/1354/2003

IN THE HIGH COURT OF JUSTICE
ADMINISTRATIVE COURT

THE QUEEN

on the application of

NARLEY WAVE

and

SURFSUP COUNCIL

_____

CONSENT ORDER

_____

On the parties coming to terms in this application
BY CONSENT, it is ORDERED:

1. that the Claimant's application for judicial review be dismissed;

2. that the Defendant shall pay the Claimant's costs of and incidental to this application, to be subject to detailed assessment if not agreed.

3. that there be a detailed assessment of the Claimant's publicly funded costs.

The reason for the making of this order is that this application has now been rendered academic in that the Defendant has offered to the Claimant, and the Claimant has accepted, accommodation which is appropriate to her needs. There is therefore no longer any need for the court to adjudicate on the issues raised in this claim, which may be dismissed.

Signed   Signed
Vere Ecross   Nora-Leigh Phussed
Counsel for the Claimant   Counsel for the Defendant
May 23, 2003   May 23, 2003.

1.44   PART III: CHECKLIST

1.   Identify the decision(s) or failure(s) giving rise to the challenge. In a homelessness case, it will be unusual to seek judicial review, given the statutory right of appeal, though this might arise, for example where a full duty has been accepted but no accommodation offered for a protracted period of time, or in a clearly wrong case of a refusal to provide interim accommodation pending review.

2.   In judicial review cases, have all alternative remedies or means of alternative dispute resolution been exhausted; if not, can the failure to do so be adequately explained?

3.   Has there been delay? Has any time limit expired? If so, is there an adequate explanation?

4.   Claimant: prepare and send a letter before claim, giving as much detail as possible. If you are missing important documents, seek to obtain these: the letter before claim can be used to request information and documents *e.g.* under s.7 of the Data Protection Act 1998, but these documents may be more sensibly requested in earlier correspondence.

5.   Defendants: reply to the letter before claim within the timescale allowed, even if only by way of a holding letter proposing a longer timescale and explaining why this is necessary.

6.   Draft pleadings carefully: all permission decisions are now taken initially on the papers, so the quality of paperwork is more important than ever. Claimants will require an extension of their funding certificate for a renewed application to be made.

7.   If permission is refused altogether or on some grounds following a renewed oral application, the time for appealing to the Court of Appeal is not the usual 14 days, but only seven days. If you do not appeal the refusal of permission on some grounds, you may not be able to rely on them at the substantive hearing.

8.   Defendants: check the time periods for drafting pleadings and evidence and prepare papers accordingly. In particular, check the court order granting permission – time to file evidence and detailed grounds of defence may have been abridged.

9.   Claimants: after receipt of the Defendant's evidence and detailed grounds of defence, reconsider the grounds and the merits of the claim. This is an obligation required by the court, independent of any separate obligation to the Legal Services Commission in funded cases.

10. Claimants: after receipt of the Defendant's evidence and detailed grounds of defence, consider also whether any further evidence is necessary or new grounds available.

11. Is any interim application necessary, such as disclosure or cross-examination?

12. Claimants: prepare, lodge and serve documents for the full hearing: a full bundle, a chronology, a list of issues, a skeleton argument and a list of persons referred to in the court papers. This must all be filed in the Administrative Court Office at least 21 *working* days prior to the substantive hearing.

13. Defendants, skeleton arguments must be lodged and served at least 14 *working* days prior to the substantive hearing.

Chapter 2
Disrepair and Statutory Nuisance

PART I: INTRODUCTION

Causes of action

The causes of action which make up the body of law governing housing conditions are **2.01** extremely diverse and wide ranging, and are not always easy to identify. Some are statutory, others are contractual, yet others derive from the common law rights of occupiers of land. Some are actionable in the civil courts, others only in the criminal courts. Some may be enforced by local authorities against private landlords, but are unable to be used against a local authority landlord.

In order to bring some semblance of comprehensibility to this chapter, it is proposed to identify, briefly, each possible cause of action and the use which may be made of it. This chapter will deal with civil actions for what is generally called "disrepair", and that term will be used as a generic term to cover both all the relevant causes of action, and the conditions in respect of which an action is being brought.

Contract

Express terms

Most residential leases and tenancy agreements make express provision for those repairs **2.02** which the landlord covenants to undertake (*e.g.* structural and exterior repairs) and those which are the responsibility of the tenant (*e.g.* decorating and damage caused by the tenant). If either party fails to carry out the obligations he has covenanted to perform, the other will have a straightforward action for breach of contract.

Several cases have illustrated the potential breadth of express repairing obligations. In *Johnson v Sheffield CC* (1994) August Legal Action 16 the tenancy agreement provided that the landlord would keep the dwelling "fit to live in". The landlord was therefore liable for severe condensation and mould growth not involving structural or external disrepair. See also *Welsh v Greenwich LBC* (2001) 33 H.L.R. 40, CA.

Statutorily implied terms

Whatever the express terms of the contract may or may not provide, statute will imply into **2.03** most residential tenancy agreements, whether or not the tenant enjoys security of tenure, certain repairing obligations on the part of the landlord.

Section 11 Landlord and Tenant Act 1985

2.04	Section 11 LTA 1985, (formerly the Housing Act 1961, s.32) creates the most important of the landlord's implied obligations: namely to keep in repair the structure and exterior of the dwelling-house and to keep in repair and proper working order various installations within the dwelling-house. Section 11 applies to all tenancies for less than seven years (this includes periodic tenancies), which were granted on or after October 24, 1961 (s.13(1)).

Section 11 does not apply to licensees (*Bruton v London & Quadrant Housing Association* [2000] 1 A.C. 406; (1999) 31 H.L.R. 902, HL). Similarly, where a tenant has been permitted to remain in occupation as a "tolerated trespasser", there is no tenancy during this "limbo period" and so no implied repairing covenant. If the tenancy is subsequently revived, however, liability under the repairing covenant will also revive retrospectively and so extend to cover the limbo period (*Lambeth LBC v Rogers* (1999) 32 H.L.R. 361, CA). The Human Rights Act 1998, Sch.1, art.8, may be relevant to the courts' exercise of their discretion in deciding an application to revive the tenancy (*Clements v Lambeth LBC* [2000] J.H.L. D80). Even during the limbo period, the tenant may sue the former landlord in nuisance, for instance if the property suffers from infestation (*Pemberton v Southwark LBC* [2000] 1 W.L.R. 1672, CA).

In any event even if s.11 applies, the duties it imposes are not as extensive as, may, at first sight, appear to be the case.

Repair and improvement

2.05	First, the duty to "repair" does not include any liability to effect improvements. In order to discover whether proposed works constitute repairs or improvements the following guidelines have been given by the courts (*Ravenseft Properties Ltd v Davstone Holdings Ltd* [1980] QB 12, QBD; *Elmcroft Developments Ltd v Tankersley-Sawyer* (1984) 15 H.L.R. 63, CA):

(*a*)	what was the intention of the parties at the time of the letting?

(*b*)	what is the cost of the repairs as a whole as compared to the value of the property as a whole?

(*c*)	are repairs or alterations required to the whole or substantially the whole of the structure or just a part?

(*d*)	would the repairs produce a building of a wholly different character from that unrepaired?

Note that where the remedy of a particular defect amounts to an improvement rather than a repair, allegations of nuisance and/or breach of the covenant of quiet enjoyment will not afford a remedy by other means (*Southwark LBC v Mills and Others* and *Baxter v Camden London Borough (No.2)* [2001] 1 A.C. 1.

Structure and exterior

2.06	Only disrepair *to* the structure or exterior is actionable under s.11. This means that damage which is not structural will not be covered, for instance black mould (*Quick v Taff Ely BC* [1986] QB 809, CA). In addition, defects of the structure (inherent defects) resulting from bad design, such as condensation dampness caused by a design defect, will not be covered (*Quick* (above); *Stent v Monmouth DC* (1987) 19 H.L.R. 269, CA). The Quick Construction of s.11 is not incompatible with the European Convention on Human Rights, Art.8 (*Lee v Leeds CC*; *Ratcliffe v Sandwell MBC* [2002] EWCA Civ 6; (2002) H.L.R. 17).

"Exterior" for the purposes of s.11, is the outside or external parts of a dwelling, but does not include items such as outside paving, garden walls and gates etc. While "structure" covers more than structural defects, in the sense of those which hold the dwelling together, it does not include purely decorative items nor probably those such as internal plaster, skirting boards, internal doors etc (*Irvin v Moran* (1992) 24 H.L.R. 1, QBD), although these may well be affected by other items of disrepair and, if so, will be caught by the duty to make good.

Flats

Until the introduction of common parts liability, determining the structure and exterior of **2.07** flats was much more difficult. In order to take action on parts not included in the dwelling itself, it was necessary to rely on the common law concepts of, in particular, nuisance, negligence and derogation from grant.

Now, however, as to flats, s.11(1A) implies the same obligations to any part of the building, and any installation serving the dwelling-house and forming part of the building, in which the dwelling-house is contained in which the landlord has an interest. This provision applies only to tenants whose leases were entered into on or after January 15, 1989.

Notice

A landlord is not in breach of any repairing covenant until he has had notice of the disrepair **2.08** complained of and until a reasonable time has elapsed, from the date of such notice, for him to have carried out any necessary works (*O'Brien v Robinson* [1973] A.C. 912, HL; see also *McGreal v Wake* (1984) 13 H.L.R. 107, CA and more recently *British Telecommunications plc v Sun Life Assurance Society plc* [1996] Ch. 69, CA) unless the disrepair in question is not within the demised premises but in land retained in the landlord's own possession and control (*British Telecommunications* (above) and *Passley v Wandsworth LBC* (1996) 30 H.L.R. 165, CA), in which case the landlord may be liable immediately after a defect occurs.

Notice, in this context, means actual knowledge, and so it need be in no specific form; may be written or oral, although written notice will be easier to prove; nor need it give any particular information. It may be given to an agent of the landlord and, in short, must simply constitute sufficient information to put a reasonable man upon inquiry as to whether works of repair are needed.

Standard of repair

The dwelling must be put and kept in a reasonable state of repair. The obligation to keep **2.09** premises in repair is a lower standard than that sometimes found in leases to keep the premises in "good repair". By s.11(3), the standard of repair is determined having regard to the age, character and prospective life of the dwelling.

Landlord's rights of access

The landlord has an implied right, on giving 24 hours notice, to enter the premises in order to **2.10** view the condition of the premises and the state of repair (s.11(6)). In addition to this statutory provision, a right or duty to repair carries with it an implied licence to enter and do the works involved, for such reasonable time as they may take (*Saner v Bilton* (1878) 7 Ch D 815). A tenant who refuses permission to enter to his landlord will be unable to take legal action in respect of the breach (*Granada Theatres v Freehold Investment (Leytonstone)* [1959] 1 W.L.R. 570. The landlord's right is enforceable by a mandatory injunction (*Minja Properties v Cussins Property Group plc and others* [1998] 2 E.G.L.R. 52.

Tenant's responsibilities

2.11 Section 11(2) excludes from the implied covenant responsibility for damage arising by virtue of the tenant's failure to use the premises in a "tenant-like manner". Responsibility for such damage is that of the tenant (see *Warren v Keen* [1954] 1 QB 15, CA). In a modern context, however, the tenant's duties do not extend to tasks such as disconnecting a gas fire, removing the back plate and cleaning the chimney of any blockages (*Churchill v Nottingham CC* (2001) January Legal Action 25).

Gas Inspections

2.12 In addition to their s.11 obligations, landlords also have statutory obligations of inspection and maintenance of gas fittings and flues in their properties: Regulation 36 of the Gas Safety (Installation and Use) Regulations 1998, SI 1998/2451. No express right of access to carry out such inspections/works is however provided by the Regulations.

Section 8 Landlord and Tenant Act 1985

2.13 Section 8 LTA 1985 implies a term that the house is and will be kept fit for human habitation. However, this section is of extremely limited value as it applies only to lettings at low rents, and the rent limit, never having been raised, is now so low as to exclude almost all tenants from its ambit.

Terms implied by common law

2.14 Certain terms will be implied at common law, although only if they can satisfy the ordinary test of "business efficacy" (*The Moorcock* (1889) 14 PD 64) or that of the so-called "officious bystander" (*Shirlaw v Southern Foundries* (1926) Ltd [1939] 2 KB 206 at 227 (affirmed [1940] A.C. 701). Hence covenants for quiet enjoyment, and against derogation from the grant, will be implied unless an express covenant exists. The latter type of covenant may impose some limited obligation to keep common parts in repair.

   The courts have also been prepared to find terms not expressed in the contract, on the slightly different basis that they are not implying such a term, but rather that the parties have not "themselves fully stated the terms"; so that the court is merely establishing "what the contract is", and in this sense only, searching for what must be implied (*Liverpool City Council v Irwin* [1977] A.C. 239, HL). Accordingly, it has been held that the essential means of access to a property must be kept in repair – although as regards tenancies commencing after January 15, 1989 (see above) such a term will be largely unnecessary.

   In addition, a furnished letting must be fit for human habitation at the time of the letting.

   Further, given that repair covenants clearly envisage repairs to be done where premises are not in a state of repair (see s.17 of the LTA 1985), it is likely that terms may be implied into the tenancy agreement concerning the carrying out of such works, *e.g.* that reasonable skill and care will be used. This may be important, procedurally and in the context of damages, as to which see below. There is no basis in Common Law for implying a term to keep premises in "good condition" as to do so would make for the parties a bargain which they had not themselves made (*Lee v Leeds CC*; *Ratcliffe v Sandwell MBC* [2002] EWCA Civ 6; (2002) H.L.R. 17).

Tort

Nuisance

In some cases, the tort of nuisance may be of assistance where the express or implied repair **2.15** covenants will not give rise to any cause of action, as is likely to be the position in the case of infestations. It seems clear that an infestation cannot amount to "disrepair", properly so called, ie a breach of a repairing covenant. It is, however, by no means automatic that an infestation will amount to a common law nuisance, as the ordinary common law principles will apply. Accordingly, it will be necessary to show that the nuisance originated on neighbouring land under the control of the defendant, and was caused by the defendant's unreasonable user of that land. In the case of a "tolerated trespasser" although there will be no repairing obligation during the limbo period, the occupier may still maintain an action in nuisance (*Pemberton v Southwark LBC* (above)).

Negligence

The applicability of liability in negligence, in relation to the disrepair claims, will be dictated **2.16** by the general principles of such liability. In other words, it will be necessary to establish a duty of care, and a breach which has caused sufficiently proximate damage.

In this context, however, it is important to remember, first, that in general there is no liability for negligent omissions; secondly, that the courts have severely restricted the situations in which a duty of care will be held to arise where the parties' relationship is otherwise regulated by contract and/or statute; thirdly, that there is generally no liability for the negligence of independent contractors who have not been appointed negligently; and, lastly, that the measure of damages in contract and tort is different, and it is likely that the contractual measure will be more advantageous in most situations (see below: Damages).

Accordingly, it seems likely that any liability in negligence will be residual, given the existence of the Defective Premises Act 1972 (see below), and the existence of contractual remedies. It may be of use, however, in specific situations such as badly carried out works or defective common parts in relation to a tenancy which pre-dates January 15, 1989, especially where the landlord has designed and/or constructed the premises (*Rimmer v Liverpool CC* [1985] QB 1.

Breach of statutory duty

The Defective Premises Act 1972, imposes various duties with regard to the condition of **2.17** accommodation, in particular by s.4, which imposes the duty to take reasonable care to see that persons who might reasonably be expected to be affected by defects in the state of the premises are kept reasonably safe from personal injury or damage to their property caused by a "relevant defect" (see also s.3). It is important to note that this is not a duty to prevent personal injury or damage to property, but only a duty of care. Moreover, it is not a duty to take care to keep such persons reasonably safe from damage or injury caused by anything other than a "relevant defect". The term "relevant defect" is defined in s.4(3) to have the same meaning as under s.11 of the LTA 1985, and so, if there is no duty to remedy the defect under the implied repair covenant, there will be no liability under this section (*McNerny v London Borough of Lambeth* (1988) 21 H.L.R. 188, CA).

However, the requirement that the lessor must have actual notice of any defect is not replicated by s.4. Liability may be established in respect of defects of whose existence he knew or ought to have known (*Smith v Bradford City Council* (1982) 4 H.L.R. 86, CA). Accordingly, where a landlord has reserved a right of entry to inspect and/or repair the demised premises, s.4 may be a useful provision if there are difficulties proving the tenant actually informed the landlord of the defect(s) in question.

The landlord is expected to take positive steps to inspect for hidden defects when he is aware that there might be a problem. He is not, however, expected to inspect for unforeseeable dangers (*Morley v Knowsley Borough Council* (1998) May Legal Action 22).

The Defective Premises Act may enable members of the tenant's family, or guests, to have a right of action in personal injury cases. They will need to be joined to the action as Claimants (*C (a minor) v Hackney LBC* [1996] 1 All E.R. 973).

Remedies

Specific performance/injunction

2.18 Section 17 of the LTA 1985 expressly confers upon the court power to make an order for specific performance of the repair covenants, thereby compelling the landlord to comply with his obligations. The court, however, retains a discretion in the matter, the language of the section being permissive rather than mandatory.

The power under s.17 does not supersede the court's common law power to grant mandatory injunctions. This common law power may be important where the breach complained of is not of a repairing covenant, for instance where a breach of s.4 of the DPA 1972 is alleged. In such a case an injunction may be obtained (*Barrett v Lounova (1982) Ltd* (1988) 20 H.L.R. 584, CA).

In addition, if there is disrepair which immediately threatens damage to health or property an interim injunction requiring the landlord to do urgent works may be sought before the case goes to trial.

Damages

2.19 Compensation in damages falls into two main categories: special damages and general damages.

Special damages are the amounts awarded by the court for specific losses *e.g.* damaged clothes, damaged furniture and decorations, extra heating bills, loss of earnings, cost of alternative accommodation (if premises are uninhabitable), cost of eating out (*e.g.* if food storage or cooking facilities have been damaged).

The amount awarded for items damaged beyond repair is their second-hand value.

General damages is the amount given for the loss of the value of the tenancy to the tenant, (*Calabar Properties v Stitcher* [1984] 1 W.L.R. 287, CA and *Wallace v Manchester CC* (1998)

30 H.L.R. 1111, CA). The level of damages can be assessed in various different ways including:

(a) a notional deduction in rent to reflect the fact that the tenant is receiving less from the landlord than he bargained for. In *Calabar* the Court of Appeal held that more than 100% of the rent may be awarded under this head,

(b) a global award for discomfort (*Calabar; Personal Representatives of Chiodi v De Marney* (1988) 21 H.L.R. 6, CA), or

(c) a combination of the two (*Sturolson & Co v Maroux* (1988) 20 H.L.R. 332, CA).

Damages should not be assessed separately under the heads of both diminution in value and discomfort because those heads are alternative ways of expressing the same thing (*Wallace*).

It may, additionally, be possible to obtain specific damages for injury to health, but this must be pleaded as in any other personal injury action.

Compensation may only be awarded in respect of foreseeable loss or damage: where a tenant claimed damages for falling on a staircase that she was only using because the lift did not work, it was held that the injury was not reasonably foreseeable (*Berryman v Hounslow LBC* (1996) 30 H.L.R. 567, CA. *cf Marshall v Rubypoint* (1996) 29 H.L.R. 850, where the landlord had failed to carry out repairs to door lock at the premises allowing burglars to enter. The tenant was entitled to damages for items stolen).

Landlord's rights

In the case of most long leases, there will be an express covenant obliging the tenant to keep **2.20** the demised property in repair during the term of the lease and to deliver it up in good repair at the expiration of the term. If the tenant fails to comply with the obligation, the landlord will, in the ordinary way have a right of action in contract, either for an injunction or damages or both.

However, the Landlord and Tenant Act 1927 has intervened to impose an upper limit to the quantum of damages which landlords may recover in this situation. By s.18(1) of the LTA 1927, damages are in no case to exceed the amount, if any, by which the value of the reversion in the premises is diminished owing to the tenants' breach of covenant.

In the usual case, at the expiration of the term, damages are awarded by reference to the cost of the necessary repairs. However, where the lessor does not intend to carry out any repairs, but instead to sell the reversion, the measure of damages is likely to be the difference in the market value of the reversion. The measure of damages, in an action during the currency of the term, is usually the depreciation to the market value of the reversion by the premises being out of repair.

The Leasehold Property (Repairs) Act 1938, imposes more substantial restrictions to the landlord's right to bring an action for damages during the currency of the term. If more than three years of the lease remain unexpired, the lessor may not bring a claim for damages for breach of a tenant's repair covenant without first serving a notice under s.146 of the LPA 1925, not less than one month before the commencement of the action.

If notice is served, the tenant is then entitled, within 28 days of the service of the notice upon him, to serve a counter-notice claiming the benefit of the 1938 Act. If a counter-notice is served, the lessor cannot take any proceedings, by action or otherwise, whether for forfeiture or for damages for the breach of covenant, without the leave of the court (s.1(3) of the LP(R)A 1938).

The court may not grant leave unless one of the following is proved:

(a) that the immediate remedying of the breach is necessary to prevent substantial damage to the value of the reversion or that such damage has already occurred;

(b) that the immediate remedying of the breach is necessary, in essence, to give effect to the purposes of any enactment or court order;

(c) where the lessee is not in occupation of the whole premises, that the immediate remedying of the breach is necessary in the interests of the occupier of the premises or of part of them;

(d) that the expense of remedying the breach immediately would be relatively small in comparison with the much greater expense which would be occasioned by post-poning the necessary work; or

(e) special circumstances which, in the opinion of the court, make it just and equitable for leave to be given (s.1(5) of the LP(R)A 1938).

In addition, if a counter-notice is served, the lessor is not entitled to the benefit of s.146(3) of the LPA 1925 (costs and expenses of the lessor in relation to the breach) unless the lessor applies to the court for leave to proceed, in which case by s.2 of the LP(R)A 1938 the court may direct whether and to what extent the lessor shall have the benefit of s.146(3) of the LPA 1925.

Procedure under the Civil Procedure Rules

2.21   The CPR, which must be complied with in all cases, affect disrepair proceedings in a number of specific ways.

Pre-action protocols

2.22   Failure to comply with the pre action protocols for disrepair (when it is finally promulgated) and personal injury claims is likely to result in adverse cost consequences if proceedings are issued which may have been unnecessary (CPR r.44.3(5)(a)). Whilst the Pre-Action Protocol for Disrepair is likely to apply only to claims and not extend to counterclaims, the court will expect to see reasonable pre-action behaviour applied in all cases [Draft Pre-Action Protocol REF] for Housing Disrepair cases prepared by the Housing Disrepair Protocol Working Party, May 2003.

If the claim principally relates to disrepair but includes an element of personal injury, it is not necessary to comply with the personal injury protocol as well as the disrepair protocol, although the personal injury element should be clearly identified in the letter of claim. If however there is a personal injury claim, which is sufficiently serious to be dealt with sepa-rately, the personal injury protocol should be followed, with necessary modifications (Draft Pre-Action Protocol above).

In cases not covered by an approved protocol (*e.g.* a straightforward disrepair case with no personal injury element, prior to the coming into effect of the disrepair protocol), the court still expects the parties, in accordance with the overriding objective, to act reasonably in exchanging information relevant to the claim and, generally, in attempting to avoid the necessity for the proceedings to be commenced (CPR Practice Direction Protocols para.4).

Part 36 Offers

Before a disrepair case comes to court, the claimant or the defendant may choose to make a **2.23** Pt 36 offer of settlement. (See CPR Pt 36). If the offer is accepted the claim will be stayed on the terms of the offer and the claimant will be entitled to his costs up to service of the acceptance (CPR 36.13 and 36.14). If the parties are unable agree the level of costs, the court will decide the issue (CPR 36.15).

If the claimant's offer is not accepted and the claimant subsequently gets a higher award of damages at trial he may be entitled to indemnity costs and interest at 10% above base rate from the date when the offer could have been accepted, unless the court considers that this would be unjust (CPR 36.21).

If, however, the claimant fails to do better than the defendant's Pt 36 offer he will be ordered to pay the defendant's costs incurred after the last date for acceptance of the offer, unless this would be unjust (CPR 36.20).

Allocation

A disrepair claim will generally be a CPR Pt 7 claim commenced using prescribed Form N1. **2.24** Disrepair claims will normally be allocated to the small claims track if the value of the claim is less than £5000 (CPR 26.6(3)). However if the claim includes a claim for specific performance and the estimated cost of the necessary work is more than £1000 or the financial value of any other claim for damages is more than £1000 the claim will be allocated to the fast track (CPR 26.6(1)(b)).

The fast track will also be the appropriate track where the claim includes an element of personal injury, which is valued at over £1000 (CPR 26.6(1)(a)).

If the disrepair claim is valued at over £15,000 or if the trial is likely to last longer than a single day it will be allocated to the multi-track (CPR 26.6(4), (5) and (6)).

Experts

The CPR lay down a number of strict requirements for the use of experts, which may be **2.25** summarised as follows:

- A party requires permission from the court to rely on expert evidence (CPR r.35.4).

- The court will only order that the expert attends and gives oral evidence at a fast track trial if it is in the interests of justice to do so (CPR r.35.5)

- The court can direct that expert evidence be given by a single expert (CPR r.35.7).

- A party may put written questions to the other side's expert (CPR r.35.6) and the court can direct a without prejudice meeting of the experts (CPR r.35.12).

- An expert's first duty is to the court (CPR r.35.3) and any report s/he produces must contain a statement that s/he understands and has complied with this duty. (CPR r.35.10 and Practice Direction 35, para.1.2(7)). The expert must also state in the report the substance of all of his instructions (CPR r.35.10(3)).

- The report that the expert produces should be addressed to the court and not to the party from whom the expert has received his instructions (CPR Practice Direction 35, para.1.1).

- The report should conclude with a statement of truth in the form set out at CPR Practice Direction 35, para.1.4.

An employee of the landlord can properly act as an expert witness, provided s/he is properly qualified and understands her/his overriding duty to the court (*Field v Leeds CC* (1999) 32 H.L.R. 618, CA).

Statutory nuisance

2.26   The statutory provisions relating to statutory nuisance, are contained in Pt III of the Environmental Protection Act 1990. Proceedings are by way of criminal prosecution in the Magistrates' Court rather than by civil action.

Where "any premises are in such a state as to be prejudicial to health or a nuisance" (s.70(1)(a)) a statutory nuisance exists. These provisions apply both to public and private sector housing, apparently whether or not they are occupied at the time. Premises may be "in such a state" as to amount to a statutory nuisance even though the origin of the nuisance is outside the premises, *e.g.* dampness. The premises must be "prejudicial to health or a nuisance ..." *i.e.* they need not be both prejudicial to health and a nuisance.

Prejudicial to health is defined as "injurious or likely to cause injury to health" (s.79(7)). This includes actual and potential ill health, and mental as well as physical health. However, mere interference with comfort is not enough. Whether premises are prejudicial to health is to be determined objectively, rather than by reference to the needs of the particular occupants (*Cunningham v Birmingham CC* (1997) 30 H.L.R. 158 DC. It is sufficient if the premises are so defective as to cause actual or potential detriment to the health of occupiers.

It will not, however, suffice that the premises are in such a state that there is a likelihood of an accident causing personal injury (*R. v Bristol CC Ex p. Everett* (1999) 31 H.L.R. 1102, CA) and direct evidence will be required to establish the link between the state of the premises and injury to health, although the evidence of a medically qualified person is not generally required (*Southwark LBC v Simpson* (1998), 31 H.L.R. 725 and *O'Toole v Knowsley Metropolitan Council, The Times,* May 21, 1999).

In *Oakley v Birmingham City Council* [2001] 1 A.C. 617, the House of Lords held that the positioning of a WC (containing no wash hand basin) on one side of the kitchen with the bathroom on the other side was not sufficient to render the house in a "state" so as to be prejudicial to health, notwithstanding the potential for cross-infection. The prejudice to health arose, rather, from the failure to wash hands or use the sink, not from the position of the rooms.

A nuisance, for these purposes is either a public nuisance which affects the comfort or quality of life of the public generally or a private nuisance where the actions of the owner or occupier of a neighbouring property interferes with the use and enjoyment of the subject premises.

Any "person aggrieved" may commence proceedings directly against his landlord, by s.82. This applies to private sector, local authority and housing association tenants. Moreover, a person aggrieved may be not only a tenant or licensee, but also other occupiers such as family members and lodgers (s.82(1)). Proceedings are brought against the person responsible for the nuisance or, where the defects are structural or the person responsible cannot be found, against the owner (s.82(4)).

Although s.82 speaks of proceedings being commenced by "complaint", it is established that such proceedings are criminal in nature, and therefore should be commenced by information (*R v Newham Justices Ex p. Hunt* [1976] 1 W.L.R. 420). The complainant, in such cases, is not required first to serve an abatement notice (as is the case where a local authority decides to start proceedings under s.80). However, by s.82(6), a complainant is required to give notice in writing of his/her intention to bring proceedings and to specify the matter(s) complained of. The requisite period of notice is 21 days, except in the case of a nuisance falling within 79(1)(g) (noise pollution). The notice must provide reasonable details of the allegations but need not be comprehensive or set out what remedial works are required (*East Staffordshire Borough Council v Fairless* (1999) 31 H.L.R. 677 and *Pearshouse v Birmingham CC* [1999] EHLR 140).

The Magistrates' Court has a variety of options when hearing such claims. If satisfied of the existence of a statutory nuisance it must make a nuisance order requiring abatement of the nuisance and, if necessary, order the execution of works for this purpose. If satisfied that the nuisance has been abated but is likely to recur it must, again, make a nuisance order, and may order any works necessary to prevent its recurrence. It may also, or alternatively, impose a fine. By s.82(3), where the court is satisfied that the nuisance exists and renders the premises unfit for human habitation the court may prohibit use of the premises until rendered fit.

If the order is not complied with "without reasonable excuse" further proceedings may be taken and defaulters may be repeatedly fined (s.82(8)), although it is a defence for the defendant to prove that the best practicable means to abate the nuisance have been taken (s.82(9)). *Carr v London Borough of Lambeth* (1995) 28 H.L.R. 747 concerned whether a nuisance, having been abated, was likely to recur, and–if so–whether the defendant was the person responsible for the likely recurrence of the nuisance. The authority successfully argued that since the tenant had refused them access to the premises (for the purpose of ensuring the nuisance would not recur), the authority was not responsible for any recurrence.

It is for the magistrates to decide whether a statutory nuisance existed, whether it has been abated, whether it is likely to recur and, if not abated, or if likely to recur, the necessary steps to remedy the situation. It is critical to obtain expert evidence as the court cannot substitute its own general knowledge of nuisance for that of an expert. If a court is faced with the expert's report of a complainant, establishing a nuisance, and with no report on behalf of the defendant it will be bound to convict. Where an abatement notice has been served under s.80, the relevant date on which the justices are to consider whether a nuisance exists or, if abated, is likely to recur, is the date of the service of the abatement notice (*SFI Group plc v Gosport Borough Council* [1999] Env. L.R. 750, CA). Where a prosecution is brought under s.82, however, (and arguably also under s.81), the relevant date is the date of the hearing of the information, which presumably means the date the magistrates make their findings: *Coventry CC v Doyle* [1981] 1 W.L.R. 1325, DC.

Proceedings are brought primarily against "the person responsible for the nuisance" (s.82(4)(a)), which means the person to whose act, default or sufferance the nuisance is attributable (s.79(7)). However, where the nuisance arises from any defect of a structural character, proceedings must be brought against the owner of the premises (s.82(4)(b)). In *Network Housing Association Ltd v Westminster CC* (1994) 27 H.L.R. 189, QBD, it was decided that a housing association, the owner of a property converted into flats, was the "person responsible" for noise nuisance which had resulted from a lack of sound proofing in the construction. Where the person responsible for the nuisance cannot be found, proceedings must be brought against the owner or occupier of the premises (s.82(4)(c)).

Service should be effected in accordance with s.160 of the Environmental Protection Act **2.28** 1990 (*Baker and Others v Birmingham CC and Others* (1999) 31 H.L.R. 1079). The service requirements of s.160 have, however, been held to be directory rather than mandatory so that where a defendant was aware of an allegation of nuisance, there was no prejudice occasioned by service of the notice having been effected at an address other than the registered business address (*Hewlings v McLean Homes East Anglia Ltd* [2001] 2 All E.R. 281; *Hall v Kingston upon Hull CC* (1999) 31 H.L.R. 1079). In the case of service on a secretary or clerk of a body corporate, as required under s.160(3), it is not however sufficient to address a notice to someone else in the body's employment (*Leeds v Islington LBC* (1998) 31 H.L.R. 545 QBD).

Compensation may also be awarded by a Magistrates' Court, either on the application of the complainant or of its own motion, for damage resulting from a statutory nuisance. This power arises not under the EPA 1990, but under the court's more general powers to award compensation for any personal injury, loss or damage resulting from an offence of which a defendant has been convicted (Powers of Criminal Courts Act 1973, s.35 (as amended)). Compensation can be ordered in addition to the other penalties outlined above (*Herbert v London Borough of Lambeth* (1991) 24 H.L.R. 299 and *Botross v London Borough of Hammersmith and Fulham* (1994) 27 H.L.R. 179). The maximum award under such an order is £5000 for each offence (Magistrates' Courts Act 1980 (as amended)).

The principles for calculating the sums on which such compensation orders are based are not set out in detail in the legislation but have been added to and expanded by case-law. In *R. v Liverpool CC. Ex p. Cooke* (1996) 29 H.L.R. 249 QBD, it was held that compensation could only be made in relation to the period of the nuisance indicated in the summons. In *R v Vivian* [1979] 1 All E.R. 48, it was held that the loss must be actually suffered. However, it is not necessary to show that the landlord would have been liable in civil proceedings (*R v Chappell* [1984] Crim LR 574). If a claim is made for personal injury, full details should be provided (*R v Cooper* [1982] Crim LR 308). Injury may include fear and anxiety (*Bond v Chief Constable of Kent* [1983] 1 E.R. 456).

If compensation is to be awarded, the loss or damage in relation to which the order is made must result from the offence in relation to which the order is made. Thus the order cannot deal with matters which were not the subject of the proceedings in the magistrates' court. In this context therefore, it is only loss or damage which is attributable to the statutory nuisance which may be compensated, not broader matters which might arise in cases of disrepair or other types of civil proceedings. In *Herbert* it was considered that it would not be an appropriate use of the powers under s.35 of the PCCA 1973 for a Magistrates' Court to award compensation for damages which can loosely be described as personal injury. If compensation for that sort of injury is to be awarded, it is preferable that it should be dealt with in the course of the civil proceedings in the county court.

2.29   In determining whether loss or damage resulted from the offence, it has been stated that the usual, strict rules as to causation are not to be adopted, but the court must ask itself whether the loss or damage can fairly be said to have resulted from the relevant offence, (*R v Thomson Holidays* [1973] QB 592).

In *Davenport v Walsall MBC* (1995) 28 H.L.R. 754, the Divisional Court reviewed the principles to be applied to questions of compensation and costs. It was held that the court does not have to hear evidence before deciding whether or not a compensation order is appropriate; compensation orders should be confined to simple and straightforward cases and the absence of a civil remedy did not automatically mean that a compensation order should be made although it may be important in the exercise of discretion.

In *R. v Dudley Borough Council Ex p. Hollis* (1997) 30 H.L.R. 902 QBD it was held that Magistrates should not adjourn proceedings where the person responsible had indicated a willingness to carry out the works, but was unable to do so within the time specified in the notice because the effect of such an adjournment would be to deprive the complainant of the right to compensation under the PCCA 1973.

A Defendant who has been ordered to pay compensation may appeal to the Court of Appeal, which has wide powers to vary or annul the compensation order. A compensation order can also be reviewed by the court which made it after the time for appealing has passed if the injury, loss or damage in respect of which the order was made has been held in civil proceedings to be less than it was taken to be for the purposes of the compensation order.

A Defendant can also appeal against conviction or sentence to the Crown Court, which takes the form of a rehearing. However, the court remains confined to considering the matters as they were at the date of the Magistrates' Court hearing. Finally, either party may appeal to the Divisional Court on a point of law, by way of case stated.

As to costs, where the court is satisfied that the alleged statutory nuisance existed at the date the information was laid then, irrespective of whether the nuisance has since been abated or is unlikely to recur, the court is obliged under s.82(12) of the Act to order the Defendant to pay such amount as the court considers reasonably sufficient to compensate the complainant for any expenses properly incurred by them in the proceedings. The court does not have a discretion to refuse costs on the basis that the person responsible has indicated a willingness to carry out the work but was unable to do so within the time specified in the notice (*R. v Dudley Borough Council Ex p. Hollis* (above)). If a summons is dismissed, the Defendant will usually apply for costs from central funds (Prosecution of Offences Act, 1985, s.16).

Community funding is not available for representation at trial. Previously, *British*   **2.30** *Waterways Board v Norman* (1994) 26 H.L.R. 232 had held that a contingency fee arrangement was contrary to public policy and accordingly a successful complainant who was represented under such an arrangement could not recover costs (see also *Thai Trading Co v Taylor* (1998) 2 W.L.R. 893 and *Hughes v Kingston upon Hull Council* (1998) 31 H.L.R. 779).

Section 27(1) of the Access to Justice Act 1999, however, amends the Courts and Legal Services Act 1990 to permit conditional fee arrangements in respect of proceedings under s.82 of the EPA 1990.

The test for making an award of costs, under s.82(12) of the 1990 Act, is whether those costs were properly incurred. Accordingly, even where a claim for a compensation order failed it did not follow that the application had been improper, and costs could still be awarded (*Davenport v Walsall MBC* (1995) 28 H.L.R. 754 DC).

Enforcement of orders

As to the enforcement of orders obtained from the court, see the introduction to Chapter 5.   **2.31**

PART II: PRECEDENTS

2.32   Form 17

Letter before action *(in the form recommended by the draft Pre-Action Protocol for Housing Disrepair Cases as at May 2003)*

Dear Sirs

Our Client – Emily Spunge

We are instructed by Ms Spunge, who is a tenant of your authority, at 150 Comfy House, Flurry Street, Cuddington Estate, Poynton, Snackshire. We are providing our client with advice and assistance under the Community Legal Service Legal Help Scheme. We are using the housing disrepair pre-action protocol, and enclose a copy of the protocol for your information.

We write further to our letter to your letter of October 13, 2001 concerning the appalling condition of our client's flat, and requesting you to remedy the situation to which we still have not had the courtesy of a reply from you.

Repairs
Since the commencement of her tenancy in 1992, Ms Spunge's flat has suffered from serious disrepair. In particular she has had no hot water supply, her hall ceiling has been damaged and is now in imminent danger of collapse, her bath was impossible to empty until June 1998 and since 1994 as a result of works carried out by your authority, water has poured through her lounge and bedroom ceilings every time it rains.

You have had notice of this disrepair because our client has informed you of it on numerous occasions by telephone and in person at the estate office. Further your surveyor Peter Davidson was told about the hall ceiling on April 26, 1995.

As a result of the disrepair, our client has suffered reactive depression and anxiety, which is affecting her work and home life. Medical reports will be provided in due course. The premises are dangerous and unpleasant to live in and our client is embarrassed to have guests home with her. Also our client and her new-born baby were forced to sleep on her brother's floor for a total of nine months as a result of the state of the premises.

Urgent works
Please ensure that the work to rectify the penetrating dampness, lack of hot water and danger from the hall ceiling is commenced immediately. If this work is not commenced within seven days we will seek an interim injunction requiring you to do so.

Disclosure
Please provide within 20 days a full schedule of the works you propose to carry out to remedy the remaining defects at the premises and the anticipated date for completion of the works.

Please also provide within 20 days the following:

All records or documents in any file relevant to the disrepair claim including:

  (i)   copy of the tenancy agreement including tenancy conditions

  (ii) tenancy file

  (iii) documents relating to notice given, disrepair reported, inspection records or
        repair works to the Property

  (iv) computerised records

We enclose a signed authority from our client for you to release this information to
ourselves and a cheque in the sum of £10.

We also enclose copies of relevant documents from our client.

Expert
If agreement is not reached about the carrying out of repairs within 20 days, we propose
that we should jointly instruct a single joint expert (Mr William Bough of Messrs
Noggin and Nogbad) to carry out an inspection of the property and provide a report.
We enclose a copy of his CV, plus a draft letter of instruction. Please let me know if you
agree to their appointment. If you object please let me know your reasons within 20
days.

If you do not object to the expert being instructed as a single joint expert, but wish to
provide your own instructions, you should send those directly to Messrs Noggin and
Nogbad within 20 days of this letter. Please send us a copy of your instruction letter. If
you do not agree to a single joint expert we will instruct Noggin and Nogbad to inspect
the premises in any event. In these circumstances, if you wish to instruct your expert to
attend at the same time please let us and Messrs Noggin and Nogbad know within 20
days.

Claim
We take the view that you are in breach of your repairing obligations under the tenancy
agreement and under s.11 of the Landlord and Tenant Act 1985, and have been negligent in carrying out the roof repairs mentioned above. Please provide us with your
proposals for compensation. Our client also requires compensation for special damages
she has suffered. We attach a schedule of special damages claimed.

Finally we also attach a schedule of our costs incurred to date.

Yours faithfully,

Fred Fudge & Co

2.33   Form 18

Letter instructing expert (in the form recommended by the Draft Pre-Action Protocol for Housing Disrepair Cases – as at May 2003)

Dear Mr Gough

Our client – Emily Spunge

We act for Ms Emily Spunge who is the tenant of Pighole District Council, living at 150 Comfy House, Flurry Street, Cuddington Estate, Poynton, Snackshire. This is a flat on the fifth and top floor of Comfy House. We are using the housing disrepair protocol. We enclose a copy of the protocol for your information.

Ms Spunge has legal funding to obtain an expert's report for the purposes of commencing proceedings against the Council for disrepair in relation to her flat.

Please carry out an inspection of the above property by (date) and provide a report covering the following points:

(a) Whether you agree that the defects are as claimed;

(b) Whether any of the defects are structural;

(c) The cause of the defects

(d) The age, character and prospective life of the property.

Access will be available on the following dates and times (list dates and times as appropriate).

You are instructed as a single joint expert. The landlord is (landlord's name and details).

Please provide the report within 10 working days of the inspection. Please contact us immediately if there are any works, which require an interim injunction.

[*If not a joint expert*] The landlord will contact you to confirm that their expert will attend at the same time as you in order to carry out a joint inspection. If the case proceeds to court, your report may be used in evidence. In order to comply with court rules we would be grateful if you would insert above your signature a statement that the contents are true to the best of your knowledge and belief. We refer you to Pt 35 of the Civil Procedure Rules, which specifies experts' responsibilities, the contents of any report and the statements experts must sign.

Yours sincerely

Fred Fudge & Co

Particulars of Claim

Claim No. P10001582

IN THE WEST POYNTON COUNTY COURT

B E T W E E N

EMILY SPUNGE <u>**Claimant**</u>

and

POYNTON DISTRICT COUNCIL <u>**Defendants**</u>

PARTICULARS OF CLAIM

---

1. On March 11, 1992 the Claimant was granted, by the Defendants, the secure tenancy of the property known as and situate at 150 Comfy House, Flurry Street, Cuddington Estate, Poynton, Snackshire (hereinafter referred to as "the dwelling"), at a weekly rent of £436, to commence on March 23, 1992 (hereinafter referred to as "the tenancy"). A copy of the said agreement is annexed hereto.[1] The dwelling is a one bedroom flat on the fifth and top floor of the said block of flats and comprises a bedroom, bathroom, toilet, living room and kitchen.

2. At all material times since about April 10, 1992 the dwelling has been occupied by the claimant and, since about April 17, 1994, by the claimant and her daughter, Suede (born April 15, 1994).

3. The terms of the tenancy and the respective rights and duties of the Claimant and Defendants were set out in a document entitled "Your Tenancy Agreement" (hereinafter referred to as "the Agreement").

4. Further, s.11 of the Landlord and Tenant Act 1985 applies to the tenancy.

5. By clause 1.2(a) of the Agreement, it was, *inter alia*, an express term of the tenancy that the Defendants would keep in repair the structure and exterior of the dwelling together with the structure and exterior of the building in which the dwelling is situated.

6. Further, by clause 1.2(b) of the Agreement, it was, *inter alia*, an express term of the tenancy that the Defendants would keep in repair and proper working order the installations in the dwelling for the supply of water, gas and electricity and for

sanitation and refuse disposal and the installations which directly or indirectly serve the dwelling with a supply of water, gas and electricity and for sanitation or for space heating and water heating.

7. Further, by clause 1.2(d) of the Agreement, it was, *inter alia*, an express term that the Defendants would carry out repairs within a reasonable time giving priority to urgent repairs. The Claimant will refer to the Agreement at trial for its full terms and legal effect.

8. Further, or alternatively, it was an implied term of the Agreement that the Defendants would keep in repair the structure and exterior of the dwelling and keep in repair and proper working order the installations therein for the supply of water, gas and electricity, and for sanitation, space heating and heating water.

9. Further or alternatively, it was an implied term of the Agreement that the Defendants would carry out their said obligations as pleaded hereinabove, with skill, care and competence.

10. Further or alternatively, the Defendants owed to the claimant and her family, a duty to take care to ensure that in repairing the roof and/or guttering of the said Comfy House, rain water would not penetrate the dwelling.

11. Further, or alternatively, by s.4 of the Defective Premises Act 1972, the Defendants owed to the claimant and to any other person who may be affected by any defect in the dwelling, a duty to take care to prevent any such defect causing personal injury to, or damage to the property of, any such person.

12. On or about 24 and April 25, 1994 the Defendants, their servants or agents were in the course of repairing the roof and/or roof parapet gutter to the said Comfy House, directly above the dwelling.

13. The Defendants have been in breach of the express and/or implied terms of the tenancy agreement pleaded hereinabove under paragraphs 3–10 inclusive.

PARTICULARS OF BREACH OF CONTRACT

a) on April 25, 1994, the claimant discovered rain water pouring through the bedroom and living room ceilings across their full length, and running down the inside of the external wall of the living room from the ceiling to the window cill. The Claimant further discovered a patch of dampness on the said living room wall, beneath the said window. On each and every occasion that it has rained, since the said date, rain water has poured through the said ceilings and down the said living room wall;

b) from the commencement of the tenancy until about June 1998, the wastepipe to the bath in the dwelling was blocked so that it took more than 48 hours for water used for bathing by the Claimant and/or her baby to drain fully from the bath in the dwelling, rendering the said bath unusable;

c) since the commencement of the tenancy there has been no hot water supply to the bathroom of the dwelling;

d) since the commencement of the tenancy, the roof void access hatch frame, in the hallway ceiling, has been detached at its rear right hand corner causing the ceiling to become cracked and appears now to be in imminent danger of collapse;

e) the Defendants failed, in carrying out the said repairs to the roof and/or guttering of the said Comfy House, to protect the roof parapet gutter or ensure the same was protected sufficiently or at all during the replacement of the said gutter;

f) the Defendants have failed to remedy the defects pleaded under sub-paragraphs a) to e) inclusive herein above within a reasonable time or to accord them any or any sufficient priority in view of their urgency;

g) the Defendants have failed to take any or any sufficient other precautions to prevent water from penetrating the dwelling;

h) in the premises, the Defendants have failed to effect the said repairs with any or any due skill, care or competence.

14. Further or alternatively, the matters pleaded under para.13 hereinabove were caused by the negligence of the Defendants, their servants or agents.

PARTICULARS OF NEGLIGENCE

a) the Claimant repeats sub-paragraphs f)-h) inclusive of para.13 hereinabove;

b) Further or alternatively, the Claimant will rely upon the fact, as evidence of negligence, that during the course of repairs to the said roof and/or roof parapet gutter carried out by the Defendants, their servants or agents, rain water poured through the ceiling of the bedroom and living room of the dwelling;

c) failing, in the premises, to take any or any proper precautions to prevent rain water penetrating the dwelling.

15. The Claimant further relies on the matters particularised in the report, schedule and photographs of Messrs Noggin & Nogbad, dated April 8, 2000, a copy of which is annexed hereto.

16. The Defendant has, at all material times, had notice of the matters complained of.

PARTICULARS

a) the defect referred to in para.13a) hereinabove was reported to a servant or agent of the Defendants by the Claimant by telephone on April 25, 1994, and in person to one Peter Davidson, one of the Defendants' surveyors, at the Defendants' estate office, on April 26, 1994;

b) the matters complained of in para.13b) to d) inclusive hereinabove have been reported to the Defendants by the Claimant since the commencement of the tenancy, by telephone and in person at the Defendants' estate office on occasions too numerous to particularise;

c)   further, the Claimant's solicitor notified the Defendants' estate office of the matters complained of by letter dated October 13, 2001, and sent to the Defendants' estate office a copy of the said report, schedule and photographs of Messrs Noggin & Nogbad under cover of a letter dated April 16, 2001

17. By reason of the matters complained of, the Claimant and her daughter have suffered personal injury, distress, inconvenience, loss and damage.

PARTICULARS OF PERSONAL INJURY[2]

The Claimant was born on August 15, 1964. She is employed as a secretary. The Claimant is continuously depressed and bursts into tears easily. Her weight has increased by approximately two stones. Her concentration is poor and she is unable to read or watch television except for short periods. She believes that her performance in her job has suffered. She has suffered and continues to suffer from Reactive Depression and Anxiety in the result of the matters complained of. The Claimant will rely on the contents of the report of Mr Alun Bingley, dated February 18, 2001, which is annexed hereto.[3]

PARTICULARS OF DISTRESS AND INCONVENIENCE

a)   the property is and has been dangerous and unpleasant to live in. The Claimant spends as little time there as she can and is too embarrassed to invite guests home with her;

b)   the Claimant repeats the particulars of personal injury above as further particulars of distress and inconvenience.

PARTICULARS OF SPECIAL DAMAGE

c)   the Claimant's carpets, curtains, furniture and clothing have been damaged by water. A full schedule of all such losses will be provided on discovery herein.

d)   the value of the tenancy to the Claimant has been diminished;

e)   because of the ingress of water from the roof and dampness, the dwelling has been damp and unsightly.

f)   because of the said ingress of water and dampness, the Claimant who had just given birth to her daughter, was unable to live in the dwelling from April 25, 1994, until about June 1994, and from about October 1994, until about May 1995 during which times she was obliged to stay with her brother and to sleep on the floor;

g)   during the said stays with her brother, the Claimant paid to him £50 per week in respect of her living expenses;

    h)   the Claimant's daughter was born April 15, 1994. Until about June 1998, the Claimant when living in the dwelling, was unable to bathe herself or her baby in the bath, due to the failure of the water to drain therefrom;

    i)   the Claimant has suffered stress in the result of the matters particularised hereinabove;

    j)   further, the Claimant has suffered stress in the result of her having been obliged, at the time of the birth of her baby, to make numerous visits and telephone calls to the Defendants, and to move from the premises;

18. Further, the Claimant claims interest on any sums found to be due to her, pursuant to s.69 of the County Courts Act 1984, at such rate and for such periods as the Court deems just.

AND the Claimant claims

    (1) an order for specific performance of the Defendants' said obligations pursuant to s.17 of the Landlord and Tenant Act 1985;

    (2) further, or alternatively, an injunction compelling the Defendants to comply with their said obligations;

    (3) damages for breach of contract and/or negligence in excess of £5000 but less than £15,000;

    (4) the aforesaid interest, pursuant to s.69 of the County Courts Act 1984, to be assessed.

STATEMENT OF TRUTH

- (I believe) (The Claimant believes) that the facts stated in these Particulars of Claim are true.

- I am duly authorised by the Claimant to sign this statement.

Full name...

Name of Claimant's solicitor's firm..

Signed............................ Position or office held...........................

- (Claimant)   (if signing on behalf of firm or company) (Claimant's solicitor)

- delete as appropriate

Dated this 12th day of May, 2002

Fred Fudge & Co, 167 Saxby Road, Poynton, solicitors for the Claimant who will accept service at this address.

TO the District Judge

AND TO the Defendants

---

[1] CPR Practice Direction 16, para.7.3.
[2] *ibid.*, para.4.1.
[3] *ibid.*, para.4.3.

Defence and Part 20 Claim (claim for possession on the grounds of rent arrears)

Claim No. SM000184

IN THE SMEARSBY COUNTY COURT

B E T W E E N

THE BLOOMSBURY PROPERTY
CORPORATION PLC   **Claimant**

and

ARNOLD SPROUT
Defendant/Part 20 Claimant

DEFENCE AND COUNTERCLAIM

DEFENCE

1. Save that it is denied that the Claimant is entitled to possession of the premises, paras 1 and 2 of the Particulars of Claim herein [averments of landlord's title and of the letting] are admitted.

2. Save that it is admitted that there is rent in arrears, para.3 [particulars of arrears of rent] is not admitted and the Claimant is put to strict proof thereof.

3. Further, or alternatively, the Defendant is entitled to set off the sums counterclaimed herein in diminution or extinction of any sums found to be due to the Claimant.

COUNTERCLAIM

4. By a tenancy agreement in writing, dated January 31, 1996, annexed hereto, (hereinafter referred to as the "Agreement"), the Defendant was granted, by the Claimant, the assured tenancy of the property known as and situate at 42 Willow Towers, Dogtrack Walks, Smearsby, (hereinafter referred to as "the dwelling"), at a monthly rent of £548 (hereinafter referred to as "the tenancy"). The dwelling is a flat on the eighteenth floor of a block of flats and comprises three bedrooms, a living room, kitchen, bathroom and WC.

5. The only means of access to the dwelling is provided by two electric lifts, one of which stops at the even numbered floors and the other of which stops at the odd

numbered floors, or by a communal stairway, situated within the common parts of the said block.

6. At all material times, since January 31, 1996, the dwelling has been occupied by the Defendant, his wife and their two daughters, Beattie (aged ten) and Paula (aged six) pursuant to the terms of the Agreement.

7. Section 11 of the Landlord and Tenant Act 1985 applies to the tenancy.

8. It was an implied term of the Agreement that the Claimant would keep in repair the structure and exterior of the dwelling and the building in which the dwelling is situated, and keep in repair and proper working order the installations therein for the supply of water, gas and electricity, and for sanitation, space heating and heating water, and such installations as directly or indirectly serve the dwelling house and form part of any part of a building in which the Defendant has an estate or interest, or which are owned by or under the control of the Claimant.

9. Further or alternatively, it was an implied term of the Agreement that the Claimant would keep the common parts of the building and the essential means of access to the dwelling in repair and in a reasonable state of efficiency.

10. Further, or alternatively, it was an implied term of the Agreement that the Claimant would not derogate from its grant of the dwelling to the Defendant.

11. The Claimant is in breach of the said implied terms, pleaded under paras 8 and 10 hereinabove:

PARTICULARS

a) in about June 1999, all the panes of glass in the windows in the communal hallway directly outside the dwelling fell out, causing the floor of the said communal hallway to become slippery and dangerous when it rains, and causing wind and rain to enter the dwelling, through gaps beneath and to the side of the dwelling's front door;

b) since the commencement of the tenancy, the lifts or one of them have frequently broken down and been inoperative for several days at a time:

   (i) without prejudice to the generality of the foregoing, both lifts were inoperative between August 15 and September 2, 1999,
   (ii) the lift serving the even numbered floors was inoperative between 6 September and November 15, 1999;

c) since the commencement of the tenancy, the lights serving the said communal staircase have been inoperative;

d) since about January 2000, water has been cascading through the ceiling of the communal hallway on the seventh floor, and down the communal staircase from the seventh floor to the ground floor.

12. At all material times during the tenancy, the dwelling has been infested with cockroaches, entering the dwelling from the common parts of the said Willow Towers, retained by the Defendant.

13. By reason of the matters pleaded under sub-paras (b)-(d) inclusive of para.11 the Claimant has derogated from its grant.

14. At all material times, the Claimant has had notice of the matters complained of:

PARTICULARS

a) on June 30, 1999, the Defendant's wife attended the Claimant's Property Maintenance Department at its registered office situate at and known as 989, Pasta Place, Smearsby, there informed one Arthur Grummit, a servant of the Claimant, of the defect to the window, particularised under sub-para.(a) of para.11 hereinabove, and completed a pro forma complaints form supplied to her for the purpose, by the said Grummit;

b) on occasions, too numerous to particularise, the Defendant, alternatively his wife, alternatively, numerous other tenants in the said Willow Towers, complained to servants of the Claimant at the said Property Maintenance Department, of the inoperability of the, or one of the, said lifts and/or completed pro forma complaints forms supplied to them for the purpose by servants of the Claimant;

c) without prejudice to the generality of sub-para.(b) herein above, by letters dated August 20, 1999, August 23, 1999, August 28, 1999, September 1, 1999, September 8, 1999, October 19, 1999 and November 5, 1999 the Defendant informed the Claimant of the inoperability of the said lifts;

d) since the commencement of the tenancy, on occasions too numerous to particularise, the Defendant, alternatively his wife, has informed the Claimant by letter and by telephone of the defect to the lights on the communal staircase particularised under sub-para.(c) of para.11 hereinabove;

e) on or about January 16, 2000, the Defendant attended the Claimant's said Property Maintenance Department and informed a servant of the Claimant who identified himself only as "Badger" of the water cascading down the communal staircase, particularised under sub-para.(d) of para.11 hereinabove, but was informed by the said "Badger" that he was not permitted to complete a complaints form as to the said complaint.

15. Further or alternatively, the matters complained of under para.11 hereinabove constitute a nuisance for which the Claimant is responsible.

16. By reason of the matters complained of, the Defendant has suffered loss and damage:

PARTICULARS

a) the value of the tenancy to the Defendant has been diminished;

b) since about June 1999, the dwelling has been cold and damp in the result of the said windows in the communal hallway having fallen out;

c) on numerous occasions, the Defendant and his wife have been obliged to walk up 18 flights of stairs with their children and with heavy shopping, sometimes in the dark and with water cascading down the said stairs;

d) the Defendant and his family have suffered from coughs, colds and stress in the result of the matters complained of;

e) cockroaches have rendered the dwelling unpleasant to occupy. The Defendant and his family have, on occasion, found cockroaches in their food, beds and on their toothbrushes. Further, the Defendant has, on occasion, awoken in the night to find a cockroach in his mouth;

f) by reason of the condition of the dwelling, the Defendant and his family have been too embarrassed to invite friends to their home.

PARTICULARS OF SPECIAL DAMAGE

a) two front doormats, ruined by rain and broken glass @ £10 each: £20

b) for three weeks between about mid August 1999, and the September 3, 1999, the Claimant and his family were unable to reside in the dwelling, but were obliged to stay in a hotel @ £90 per week: £270

c) three pairs of men's shoes @ £30 each, and two pairs of women's shoes @ £35 each, ruined by water while climbing the said communal stairs when the said lifts have been inoperative: £195

d) dry cleaning charges for clothes soaked by water while climbing the said stairs: £47.59

e) cockroaches have ruined clothes, furnishings and food belonging to the Claimant and his family. A full schedule of such losses will be served in early course.

17. Further the Defendant claims interest upon any sums adjudged to be due to him, pursuant to s.69 of the County Courts Act 1984, at such rate and for such periods as the court may deem just.

AND the Defendant counterclaims:

(1) an order for specific performance of the Claimant's obligations pursuant to s.17 of the Landlord and Tenant Act 1985;

(2) further or alternatively, an injunction compelling the Claimant to comply with its said obligations;

(3) damages in excess of £5000 but less than £15,000

(4) the aforesaid interest, pursuant to s.69 of the County Courts Act 1984, to be assessed.

STATEMENT OF TRUTH

- (I believe) (The Defendant believes) that the facts stated in this Defence are true.

- I am duly authorised by the Claimant to sign this statement.

Full name...

Name of Defendant's solicitor's firm...

Signed............................ Position or office held...........................

- (Defendant)   (if signing on behalf of firm or company) (Defendant's solicitor)
- delete as appropriate

Dated this 10th Day of February 2001

Bunsen & Honeydew of The Big House, Smearsby, solicitors for the Defendant, who will accept service at this address.

[CONCLUDE AS IN FORM 19]

2.36   Form 21

Interim application

THE SMEARSBY COUNTY COURT

General form of application for an injunction[4]

Notes on completion	
Tick whichever box applies and specify legislation where appropriate	☐ By application in pending proceedings ☐ Under statutory provisions This application raises issues under the Human Rights Act 1998 ☐ Yes ☐ No
(1) Enter the full name of the person making the application	The Defendant[1] **Arnold Smith** applies to the court for an injunction order in the following terms:
(2) Enter the full name of the person the injunction is to be directed to	**The Claimant[2]** be forbidden (whether by himself or by instructing or encouraging any other person)[3] **N/A**
(3) Set out here the proposed restraining orders (if the defendant is a limited company delete the wording in brackets and insert whether by its servants, agents, officers or otherwise)	
(4) Set out here any proposed mandatory orders requiring acts to be done	And that the Claimant The Bloomsbury Property Corporation plc Do[4] a) **restore the lighting to the communal staircase of Willow Towers, Dogtrack Walks, Smearsby, within seven days hereof:** b) **carry out such works as are necessary to prevent water leaking through the ceiling of the communal hallway on the seventh floor, and down the communal staircase from the seventh floor to the ground floor**
(5) Set out here any further terms asked for including provision for costs	And that[5] **(1) The Claimant do pay the costs of this application.**
(6) Enter the names of all persons who have made witness statements or sworn affidavits in support of this application	**The grounds of this application are set out in the witness statement(s) of the Defendant dated February 10, 2000.** **This statement is served with this application.**

(7) Enter the names and addresses of all persons upon whom it is intended to serve this application	The application is to be served upon[7] **The Bloomsbury Property Corporation plc of 989 Pasta Place, Smearsby**
(8) Enter the full name and address for service and delete as required	This application is filed by[8] **Bunsen & Honeydew** **(the Solicitors for) the Defendant whose address for service is** **The Big House Smearby**
	Signed **Dated**
*Name and address of the person this application is directed to	*This section to be completed by the court* **To*** **Of** **This application will be heard by the (District) Judge** **At** **on** **the** **day of** **2000 at** **o'clock** **If you do not attend at the time shown the court may make and injunction order in your absence.** *If you do not fully understand this application you should go to a Solicitor, Legal Advice Centre or a Citizens' Advice Bureau.*

The Court Office at
is open 10am to 4pm Mon-Fri. Where corresponding with the court, please address all forms and letters to the Court Manager and quote the claim number.

---

[4] County Court Prescribed Form N16A which has been retained under the Civil Procedure Rules.

2.37   Form 22

Witness Statement[5] in support

Defendant
Arnold Sprout
First statement
Dated February 11, 2001

Claim No. SM0000184

IN THE SMEARSBY COUNTY COURT

B E T W E E N

THE BLOOMSBURY PROPERTY
CORPORATION PLC   **Claimant**

and

ARNOLD SPROUT   **Defendant**

WITNESS STATEMENT OF ARNOLD SPROUT

I, ARNOLD SPROUT, of 42 Willow Towers, Dogtrack Walks, Smearsby, Hair Consultant, will say as follows:

1. I am the Defendant in these proceedings, and I make this statement in support of my application for an interim injunction, obliging the Claimant to repair the common parts of the block of flats in which I live with my family. In so far as the facts and matters herein are within my own knowledge, they are true; in so far as they are not within my own knowledge, their source is indicated and I believe them to be true.

2. I have been the assured tenant of 42 Willow Towers, Dogtrack Walks, Smearsby, and have lived there with my family, since January 31, 1996. Our flat is on the 18th floor.

3. There are two lifts in the block, one of which serves the even numbered floors and the other of which serves the odd numbered floors. There is also a communal staircase. These are the only two means of obtaining access to our flat.

4. Immediately outside our flat, there is a communal hallway with a large window containing 16 individual panes of glass. Since the beginning of the tenancy, the panes have all seemed loose. We have never done anything about this, as it was not

causing us any problems. However, in about June 1999, one of the panes fell out, and crashed on to the ground, 18 floors below. Over the next two or three weeks, all the other panes fell out as well. Since then, every time it rains, water comes into the communal hallway and, as the floor is on a slight slope down towards our flat, it seeps under our front door, drenching our hall carpet and the bottom of the walls. In addition, when the wind is blowing in a particular direction, it blows through the open windows and into our flat, through the gaps at the bottom of and around the front door, making the flat cold and difficult to keep warm, although we keep the internal doors shut as much as possible.

5. In addition, ever since we moved in, there have been problems with the lifts, which frequently break down. Most weeks, at least one of them does so. When this happens, they are usually out of action for at least a couple of days, but sometimes for weeks. While they are not working, we have no alternative but to walk up and down the 18 flights of stairs.

6. There are neon type light fittings on all the communal stair landings, and on the walls going up the stairs, but from the time our tenancy commenced, none of these lights have ever worked. This means that at night, and on winter afternoons, we are forced to walk up and down the stairs, with our young children, pushchairs, shopping etc, in the dark. We often trip on the stairs, although, fortunately, so far none of us has suffered any injury or damage.

7. In addition, since about the first week of January 2000, water has been pouring through the ceiling of the landing on the seventh floor, and cascading down the stairs, all the way down to the ground floor. This has made walking up and down the stairs extremely hazardous, quite apart from the fact that our clothes and shoes get drenched every time we have to do so.

8. There is now produced and shown to me marked "AS-1" a true copy of an inspection report compiled by Messrs. Noggin & Nogbad, dated April 16, 2000, which verifies the matters I am complaining of.

9. On June 30, 1999, I attended the Claimant's Property Management Department, at 989 Pasta Place, Smearsby, where I reported the fact that the windows had fallen out to the man on duty, who identified himself to me as Arthur Grummit. I filled in one of the Claimant's standard form complaints forms, and he told me that someone would come round to see what needed to be done. To the best of my knowledge, no-one has ever done so.

10. My wife and I have both reported the lack of lighting to the Claimant on numerous occasions during our tenancy, either by attending the office of the Property Maintenance Department and filling in forms, or by letter. However, the lights have never worked and, so far as I am aware, the Claimant has never even sent anyone round to rectify the problem.

11. In addition, on January 16, 2000, I attended the Claimant's Property Maintenance Department and reported the water cascading down the communal staircase to the man who was on duty there, who told me his name was "Badger". He informed me, however, that I could not fill in a complaints form about it. He would give me no reason why I was not permitted to do so.

12. There is now produced and shown to me, marked "AS-2" a bundle of documents comprising true copies of various letters we have written and complaints forms we have filled in.

13. The problems I have mentioned above are becoming intolerable and the Claimant has made no effort whatsoever to remedy them. Whenever it rains, the floor outside my flat becomes very slippery and dangerous and my flat gets wet. My family and I frequently have to climb 18 flights of stairs in the dark and with water pouring down the stairs. We frequently slip over as a result of the water both outside our flat and on the stairs.

14. It is still winter, getting dark very early in the afternoons and raining most days, and I fear that unless something is done about these problems soon, one of my family will be injured or our property damaged.

15. Accordingly, I respectfully request this Honourable Court to grant the interim relief I seek.

STATEMENT OF TRUTH

- I believe that the contents of my Witness Statement are true.

Full name ....

Signed ....

Date ....

---

[5] Evidence will normally be given by witness statement (CPR 32.6(1)) unless the Court Practice Direction or other enactment requires otherwise.

Form 23   **2.38**

Draft minute of order

[Heading as in Form 20 above]

UPON hearing Counsel for the Claimant and for the Defendant, and upon reading the witness statement of Arnold Sprout filed on February 11, 2001;

AND UPON the Defendant undertaking to abide by any Order this Court may make for the payment of damages in case this Court shall hereafter find that the Claimant has sustained any loss or damage by reason of this Order;

IT IS ORDERED

1. that the Claimant does carry out the works specified in para.1 of the Schedule hereto within seven days of the date hereof;

2. that the Claimant does carry out the works specified in para.2 of the Schedule hereto within 28 days of the date hereof;

3. that the costs of this application be in the cause;

4. that there be detailed assessment of the Defendant's costs payable by the Legal Services Commission.

To the Bloomsbury Property Corporation, plc, 989 Pasta Place, Smearsby.[6]

TAKE NOTICE that if you fail to obey this order you will be guilty of contempt and may be sent to prison.

[6] See *R v Wandsworth CC and Another, Ex p. Munn* (unreported) March 2, 1994, QBD. A director of the Defendant can be named in the Penal Notice if this is thought necessary, although this should only be done by the Judge and not by the court office of its own motion. In any event, the failure to name an officer of the company does not prevent a committal application being made in respect of an officer, provided the officer it is sought to commit was served with a copy of the order at the time it was made.

2.39   Form 24

Undertakings (N117)

N. 117
General Form of Undertaking

General Form of Undertaking

B E T W E E N

The Bloomsbury Property Company PLC	**Claimant** ~~Applicant~~ ~~Petitioner~~	**In the Smearsby County Court**
and		**Claim Number** *Always quote this* SM0000184
Arnold Sprout	**Defendant** ~~Respondent~~	**Claimant's Ref**
		Defendant's Ref

This form is to be used only for an undertaking not for an injunction

On the 14th day of May 2001   (Seal)

[Bloomsbury Property Company]
[~~appeared in person~~] [was represented by ~~Solicitor~~/Counsel] and gave an undertaking to the Court promising

1. to carry out the works specified in para.1 of the Schedule hereto within seven days of the date hereof;

2. to carry out the works specified in para.2 of the Schedule hereto within 28 days of the date hereof;

And to be bound by these promises until [*Give the date and time or event when the undertaking will expire*]
The Court explained to [*Name of the person giving undertaking*] the meaning of his undertaking and the consequences of failing to keep his promises
And the Court accepted his undertaking [*The judge may direct that the party who gives the undertaking shall personally sign the statement overleaf*] [and *if so ordered* directed that [*Name of the person giving undertaking*] should sign the statement overleaf].
And the Court ordered that the Claimant should pay the Defendant's costs of and incidental to this application in any event.

Dated

IMPORTANT NOTICE

To [*Name of the person giving undertaking*]
of [*Address of the person giving undertaking*]

- You may be sent to prison for contempt of court if you break the promises that you have given to the court.

- If you do not understand anything in this document you should go to a Solicitor, Legal Advice Centre or a Citizens' Advice Bureau.

The Court Office at
is open from 10am to 4pm Mon–Fri. When corresponding with the court, address all forms and letters to the Chief Clerk and quote the Claim number.

The court may direct that the party who gives the undertaking shall personally sign the statement below.

STATEMENT

I understand the undertaking that I have given, and that if I break any of my promises to the court I may be sent to prison for contempt of court.

Signed

To be completed by the court

Delivered:
☐ by posting on:
☐ by hand on:
☐ through solicitor on:

Officer:

2.40   Form 25 (In the form of a Part 23 application on form N244)

Application for an Order for Committal

Claim No. SM0000184

IN THE SMEARSBY COUNTY COURT

THE BLOOMSBURY PROPERTY
CORPORATION PLC   **Claimant**

and

ARNOLD SPROUT   **Defendant**

PART A

I, Bob Stopper solicitor on behalf of the Defendant intend to apply for an order that:

(1) the Director of Property Management, Bloomsbury Property Corporation plc of 989 Pasta Place, Smearsby be committed to prison for disobeying the order of the court made on May 14, 2001

because

On May 14, 2001 the said Director of Property Management gave an undertaking on behalf of the Claimant as follows:

1. that the Claimant would carry out the works specified in para.1 of the Schedule thereto within seven days of the date thereof;

2. that the Claimant would carry out the works specified in para.2 of the Schedule thereto within 28 days of the date thereof;

3. The Claimant has breached the undertaking by:

    (1) failing to carry out any works at all in compliance with paras 1 and 2 of the Order;

    (2) further, by refusing to re-glaze the window in the common parts directly outside the Defendant's dwelling as required by para.2 of the Order, unless the Defendant pay for such works.

4. The Defendant further relies on his affidavit, which is filed and served with this application notice.

5. Unless the Claimant is punished for his actions it will continue to disobey the orders.

PART B

I wish to rely on my statement of case and on the attached affidavit

Signed B. Stopper   **Position or office held** Solicitor

IMPORTANT NOTICE

The court has power to send you to prison and to fine you if it finds that any of the allegations made against you are true and amount to a contempt of court.

<u>You must attend court</u> on the date shown on the front of this form. It is in your own interest to do so. You should bring with you any witnesses and documents which you think will help you put your side of the case.

If you consider the allegations are not true you must tell the court why. If it is established that they are true, you must tell the court of any good reason why they do not amount to a contempt of court, or, if they do, why you should not be punished.

If you need advice you should show this document at once to your solicitor or go to the Citizens' Advice Bureau.

Address to which documents about the case should be sent
Fred Fudge and Co
Chester House,
Lungly Road,
Smearsby

STATEMENT OF TRUTH

The Applicant believes that the facts stated in this application are true

Signed B. Stopper   **Position or office held** Solicitor
Date

2.41 Form 26

Affidavit in support of an Application to Commit[7]

[HEADING AS IN FORM 22]

I, ARNOLD SPROUT, of 42 Willow Towers, Dogtrack Walks, Smearsby, Hair Consultant, MAKE OATH and say as follows:

1. I am the Defendant herein and I make this affidavit in support of my application for the Claimant's Director of Property Management to be committed to prison for contempt of this Honourable Court.

2. On May 14, 2001, this Honourable Court ordered the Claimant to carry out such works as were necessary to stop the water pouring through the ceiling of the common parts on the seventh floor of Willow Towers, and running down the communal stairs to the ground floor, and restoring the lighting to the communal stairs in the block within seven days of the date of the order. The court also ordered the Claimant to re-glaze the window outside my flat within 28 days of the date of the Order. A true copy of the Order is now produced and shown to me marked "AS-1".

3. I do not know whether or not anyone has attended or attempted to stop the water leaking through the ceiling or to restore the lighting. However, the water is leaking as badly as it ever did, and the lights on the communal staircase still do not work.

4. I have telephoned the Claimant's Property Maintenance Department on several occasions, but no-one has answered the telephone.

5. On June 1, 2001, someone called at my front door, and said he had come to re-glaze the window outside my flat, but that I would have to pay him for doing so. I informed him that the Claimant was responsible for the cost of the works, but the man said that he did not know anything about that, that he would not carry out the work unless I agreed to pay him and I would have to reclaim the money from the Claimant if the Claimant was responsible for the cost of the work.

6. I refused to pay for the work and so the man went away. I have attempted to inform the Claimant of this by telephone, but again, no-one ever answers.

7. Accordingly, I am advised and verily believe that the Claimant is in breach of the Order of the court and I respectfully request this court to grant me the relief I seek.

Sworn by
at
this   day of   2001
Before me,

A Solicitor/Commissioner for Oaths

---

[7] Under CPR Sch.1 PD 52, para.3.1 written evidence in support of a committal application must be given by affidavit.

Form 27   **2.42**

<u>**Application to Discharge Order**</u>

Claim No. SM0000184

<u>**IN THE SMEARSBY COUNTY COURT**</u>

THE BLOOMSBURY PROPERTY
CORPORATION PLC

<u>**Claimant**</u>

and

ARNOLD SPROUT   <u>**Defendant**</u>

<u>**PART A**</u>

I, Gary Sidebotham solicitor on behalf of the Claimant intend to apply for an order that:

(1) Valerie Dude, Director of Property Management, Bloomsbury Property Corporation plc of 989 Pasta Place, Smearsby be released from the undertakings given by her on May 14, 2001

(2) the costs of this application be the Defendant's in any event

because

On May 14, 2001 the said Director of Property Management gave an undertaking on behalf of the Claimant as follows:

(a) That the Claimant would carry out the works specified in para.1 of the Schedule thereto within seven days of the date thereof;

(b) That the Claimant would carry out the works specified in para.2 of the Schedule thereto within 28 days of the date thereof;

The Defendant has prevented the Claimant from carrying out the works.

The Claimant further relies on his witness statement, which is filed and served with this application notice.

PART B

I wish to rely on my statement of case and on the attached witness statement.

Signed G. Sidebotham   **Position or office held** Solicitor

Address to which documents about the case should be sent
Pickering, Flock and Co Solicitors
Gorgon House,
Dangledale,
Smearsby

STATEMENT OF TRUTH

The applicant believes that the facts stated in this application are true.

Signed G. Sidebotham   **Position or office held** Solicitor
Date

Witness Statement in support

[HEADING AS IN FORM 27]

I, VALERIE DUDE, of 989 Pasta Place, Smearsby, Company Director, will say as follows:

1. I am the Claimant company's Property Management Director, and I am authorised by the Claimant to make this Statement on the company's behalf. The facts and matters which I set at below are within my own knowledge and are true.

2. On May 17, 2001, I attended Willow Towers, with a contractor engaged by the Claimant for the purpose of carrying out the repairs to the block in accordance with the Claimant's undertakings given to this court on May 14, 2001. With us, we brought a number of panes of glass, with which to reglaze the window outside the Defendant's flat.

3. I knocked at the Defendant's door, to inform him that the works were being carried out. However, to my surprise, the Defendant picked up a large baseball bat from somewhere within his flat, came into the common parts and smashed every one of the new panes of glass. I then informed him that because of his actions, we would require him to pay for the glass he had ruined. He became very abusive and threatening, and told me that the court had ordered us to glaze the window, that he was not prepared to pay for anything and that we would just have to find some more glass.

4. I informed Mr Sprout that in my view we had done our best to comply with the order, but that if he wanted us to make any further attempt to repair the window, I would require him to pay for the broken glass. I then informed him that the contractor and myself would be going downstairs to see about the lighting to the common parts and the water leaking down the stairs.

5. At this point, the Defendant threatened us with his baseball bat and said that if we did not leave the building then and there he would beat us with the bat. I could not expect the contractor to take the risk of injury, as Mr Sprout was genuinely menacing, and accordingly, we left the block.

6. On or about May 23 I returned to the block with a different contractor to attend to the common parts of the block. However, when we entered at ground floor level, we encountered Mr Sprout again, this time carrying what looked like a shot gun. Mr Sprout pointed his gun at us and told us that we were to leave and that he would not warn us again: next time he would just start shooting.

7. I would respectfully assure the court that the Claimant has sought to comply with the terms of the undertakings. However, I do not see that we should be required to risk possibly serious harm at the hands of the Defendant, in order to carry out the works. In addition, I cannot expect the Claimant's contractors to undertake such risks.

8. Accordingly, as the Defendant has prevented us from carrying out the works, I would respectfully request this Honourable Court to release the Claimant from the undertakings given on May 14, 2001.

[CONCLUDE AS IN FORM 22]

Form 29   **2.44**

Application for an Access Injunction – Particulars of Claim

Claim No. P10001600

IN THE WEST POYNTON COUNTY COURT

B E T W E E N

POYNTON DISTRICT COUNCIL   **Claimants**

and

EMILY SPUNGE   **Defendant**

PARTICULARS OF CLAIM

1. At all material times:

   a) the Claimants are and have been freehold owners of premises situate at and known as 150 Comfy House, Flurry Street, Cuddington Estate, Poynton, Snackshire (hereinafter referred to as the "dwelling");

   b) since March 23, 1992 the Defendant is and has been the secure tenant of the Claimants in the dwelling.

2. The Defendant's said tenancy was granted by an agreement in writing, dated March 11, 1992 (hereinafter referred to as the "tenancy agreement") upon the terms, conditions and covenants contained therein. The Claimant will refer to the tenancy agreement at trial for its full terms and legal effect.

3. By clause 2.7 of the tenancy agreement, the Defendant is obliged, upon 24 hours notice from the Claimants to give access to the dwelling to the Claimants, their officers and/or agents for the purposes of inspecting the condition of the same and/or carrying out works therein or thereto.

4. Further or alternatively, it was an implied team of the Defendant's tenancy that the Claimants, their officers or agents, would be granted access to the dwelling, for the said purposes, upon the giving of reasonable notice to the Defendant.

5. On May 12, 2002 the Defendant commenced proceedings against the Claimants, in the West Poynton County Court, in relation to alleged disrepair affecting the dwelling.

6. On May 17, 2002, the Claimants by their Housing Officer, Will Porker, informed the Defendant by telephone that the Claimants required access to the dwelling on May 22, 2002 in order to undertake works to the roof of the said Comfy House directly above the dwelling, to restore the hot water supply to the premises and to repair the roof void access hatch frame in the hallway of the dwelling.

7. Further, by letters dated May 24, 28, 30 and June 8, 2002 the Claimants requested access for the said purposes.

8. In breach of clause 2.7 of the tenancy agreement, alternatively, in breach of the said implied term, the Defendant has refused to allow any access to the Claimants their officers or agents.

PARTICULARS

a) on May 22 the Claimant's construction workers attended the dwelling and were informed by the Defendant that she would not allow them entry because it was not convenient;

b) on May 26 the Defendant attended the Claimants' estate office and informed the Claimant Estate Manager, one Brian Piglett, that she was not prepared to allow access to the Claimant until the Defendant's said litigation against the Claimant was resolved.

7. In the premises, the Claimant claim an injunction requiring the Defendant to grant access to the Claimant, their officers and/or agents for the purpose of effecting the said works, at 9.00am on Tuesday July 19, 2002, or at such other time(s) as the court may require.

AND the Claimant's claim

1. A mandatory injunction requiring the Defendant to grant access to the dwelling to the Claimant its servants or agents at 9.00am on Tuesday July 19, 2002, or at such other time(s) as the court may require.

[CONCLUDE AS IN FORM 19]

Form 30   **2.45**

Application for access information

THE WEST POYNTON COUNTY COURT

General form of application for an injunction

Notes on completion	
Tick whichever box applies and specify legislation where appropriate	☐ By application in pending proceedings ☐ Under statutory provisions This application raises issues under The Human Rights Act 1998 ☐ Yes ☐ No
(1) Enter the full name of the person making the application	The Claimants[1] **Poynton District Council** apply to the court for an injunction order in the following terms:
(2) Enter the full name of the person the injunction is to be directed to	The Defendant[2] **Emily Spunge** be forbidden (whether by herself or by instructing or encouraging any other person)[3] **N/A**
(3) Set out here the proposed restraining orders (if the defendant is a limited company delete the wording in brackets and insert whether by its servants, agents, officers or otherwise)	
(4) Set out here any proposed mandatory orders requiring acts to be done	And that the Defendant, Emily Spunge Do[4] **Allow access to the dwelling situate at and known as 150 Comfy House, Flurry Street, Cuddington Estate, Poynton, Snackshire, to the Claimants, their officers and/or agents at 9am on Tuesday July 19, 2002 or at such other times as the court may require.**
(5) Set out here any further terms asked for including provision for costs	And that[5] **The Claimant do pay the costs of this application.**
(6) Enter the names of all persons who have made witness statements or sworn affidavits in support of this application	**The grounds of this application are set out in the witness statement(s) of the Claimant dated June 29, 2002.** **This statement is served with this application.**
(7) Enter the names and addresses of all persons upon whom it is intended to serve this application	The application is to be served upon[7] **Emily Spunge** 150 Comfy House Flurry Street Cuddington Estate Poynton Snackshire

(8) Enter the full name and address for service and delete as required	This application is filed by[8] **Snout, Truffle and Co** **(the Solicitors for) the Claimants whose address for service is:** **The Penn,** **Poynton,** **Snackshire** **Signed Dated**
*Name and address of the person this application is directed to	*This section to be completed by the court* **To*** **Of** **This application will be heard by the (District) Judge** **At** **on the day of 2002 at o'clock** **If you do not attend at the time shown the court may make and injunction order in your absence.** *If you do not fully understand this application you should go to a Solicitor, Legal Advice Centre or a Citizens' Advice Bureau.*

The Court Office at
is open 10am to 4pm Mon-Fri. Where corresponding with the court, please address all forms and letters to the Court Manager and quote the claim number.

Form 31   **2.46**

<u>Witness Statement in support</u>

Claimants
Brian Pollard
First Statement
Dated 29 June 2002

Claim No. PI0001600

IN THE WEST POYNTON COUNTY COURT

B E T W E E N

POYNTON DISTRICT COUNCIL   **Claimants**

and

EMILY SPUNGE   **Defendant**

WITNESS STATEMENT OF BRIAN POLLARD

I, BRIAN PIGLETT, of Estate Office, Snuggly Street, Cuddington Estate, Poynton, Snackshire, Local Government Officer, will say as follows:

1. I am employed by the Claimants as Estate Manager of Cuddington Estate, Poynton and have been in this position since about 1987. I am authorised to make this witness statement on their behalf, in support of their application for an interim injunction, requiring the Defendant to grant access to her flat to the officers and agents. In so far as the facts and matters herein are within my own knowledge, they are true; in so far as they are not within my own knowledge, their source is indicated and I believe the same to be true.

2. On May 12, 2002, I was served with proceedings which had been commenced in this court by Ms Spunge, the Defendant to this application, against the Claimants in respect of the condition of her flat. This was the first complaint I had ever received from Ms Spunge about the state of her property, except for a complaint which, I see from the property file, was made on June 12, 1998 about a blockage to the bath, and which was remedied on June 14, 1998. The action sheet, upon which any such complaints would be recorded (and on which the complaint I have referred to is recorded) is now produced and shown to me marked "BP-1".

3. Upon receipt of the proceedings, I immediately contacted one of the Housing

Department's surveyors, Barry Trotter, and asked him to make arrangements to ensure that any necessary works were swiftly attended to. Mr Trotter telephoned me on April 30, and informed me that he would be available to attend Ms Spunge's flat with some construction workers on May 5 to see what needed doing and begin the works.

4. Accordingly, on the same day, I telephoned Ms Spunge and asked her if Mr Trotter and the workmen could attend on that date at 9.00am, and she said that that would be fine.

5. I am informed by Mr Trotter, and verily believe, that he did attend the Defendant's flat at 9.00am on May 5, with two construction workers but when Ms Spunge answered the door, she informed him that she was not prepared to let him in because that day was not convenient, and that he would have to make a new appointment.

6. Because of this, I wrote letters to Ms Spunge, informing her that under her tenancy agreement the Claimants had the right to access to undertake inspections and carry out works on giving her reasonable notice, and that I considered that the notice we had given her of the May 5 appointment was reasonable and that, in any event, she had agreed to the Plaintiff's workers attending on that day. I also asked her to telephone me in order to arrange a new appointment.

7. I wrote these letters on May 24, 28, 30 and June 8, 2002 and a bundle comprising true copies of these letters is now produced and shown to me marked "BP-2".

8. I heard nothing from the Defendant at all until, on May 26, she came in to the estate office and told me that she was not prepared to allow the Claimants to carry out any works until her disrepair action was concluded as she did not wish to prejudice any of her rights.

9. On May 27 I wrote to Ms Spunge's solicitors, stating that their position was unacceptable to the Claimants and that we expected to be granted access to carry out the works, failing which we would make an application to this court. On June 10 I received a reply from them, stating that they were taking instructions. However, despite chasing letters sent by me on 18 and June 24 I have had no further reponse. A bundle comprising true copies of all these letters is now produced and shown to me marked "BP-3".

10. We are being proceeded against in respect of the premises, and urgently need access to inspect them and to carry out any necessary works, both for the purpose of putting the premises into satisfactory condition (if they are not, which we will not know until we can gain access) and in order properly to defend this action.

11. Accordingly, I respectfully request this Honourable Court to grant the relief sought.

[CONCLUDE AS IN FORM 22]

Form 32   2.47

Defence and Part 20 Claim

[HEADING AS IN FORM 19]

DEFENCE AND PART 20 CLAIM

DEFENCE

1. Paragraph 1 of the Particulars of Claim herein is admitted.

2. Paragraph 2 is not admitted.

3. Paragraphs 3–8 inclusive are admitted.

4. No admissions are made as to paras 9–11 inclusive.

5. Paragraph 12 is admitted.

6. Paragraph 13 is denied. Without prejudice to the generality of the foregoing denial, by clause 2.7 of the Agreement, the Claimant covenanted to allow the Defendant's officers and contractors access to inspect the condition of her premises and/or to undertake any necessary repairs therein or thereto.

7. The Claimant has failed and/or refused to allow the Defendant any access to her dwelling.

PARTICULARS

a) on May 17, 2002 the Claimant and the Defendant's Estate Manager, one Brian Piglett, arranged an appointment for May 22, for a surveyor and construction workers to inspect the dwelling. On May 22, the said surveyor, one Barry Trotter and the said workers attended the dwelling but were sent away by the Claimant.

b) on 26 May, the Claimant informed the said Piglett at the Defendant's estate office that she would not allow access to the Defendants until her disrepair proceedings had been resolved.

c) by letter dated May 24, 28, 30 and June 8, 2002, the Defendant's Estate Manager informed the Claimant's solicitor that access was required for the purposes of inspection of the dwelling, but no substantive reply to the said letters has been received.

8. Paragraph 14 is denied. It is denied that the Defendants have been negligent as alleged or at all. The Defendants have been refused access to the premises by the

Claimant and have therefore been unable to carry out the works or take the precautions described in paras 13 and 14 of the Particulars of Claim or indeed carry out any works or take any precautions at all. Further it is not admitted that any negligence on the part of the Defendants (which is denied) has caused or contributed to any distress, inconvenience, loss or damage (which is not admitted) to the Claimant.

9. Further or alternatively, any distress, inconvenience, loss or damage which the Claimant may have suffered (which is not admitted) has been wholly caused or contributed to by her own negligence.

PARTICULARS

a) failing to allow access to the Defendant's surveyors and/or contractors to enable the Defendant to undertake any necessary works as pleaded under para.7 hereinabove.

10. Save as has been expressly denied or admitted hereinabove, no admissions are made as to the physical state of the dwelling.

11. As to para.15, the Defendant admits receipt of the Claimant's expert's report. Save that it is denied that items 2.3, 2.4, 2.5, 3.1, 3.4 or 4.7 fall within the scope of any repairing covenant owed by the Defendants to the Claimant (which is verified by the Defendant's own export report), no admissions are made as to its contents of the said report.

12. Save that

a) it is admitted that the Defendant had notice on June 12, 1998 that there was a blockage to her bath, which blockage was remedied by the Defendants on June 14, 2000, and

b) it is admitted that the report of Messrs Noggin and Nogbad was sent to the Defendant by the Claimant's solicitor under cover of a letter dated April 16, 2002, which was misaddressed and only received by the Defendant on April 27, 2002;

paragraph 16 is not admitted and the Claimant is put to strict proof thereof.

13. No admissions are made as to the alleged or any distress, inconvenience, loss or damage.

14. Further, or alternatively, the alleged causes of action, prior to May 12, 1996, did not arise within six years before the commencement of this action and to that extent the Claimant's claims are barred by ss.2 and 5 of the Limitation Act 1980.

15. Further or alternatively, the alleged cause of action for personal injury, prior to

May 12, 1999, did not arise within three years before the commencement of this action and to that extent the Claimant's claim is barred by s.11 of the Limitation Act 1980.

16. Save as is expressly admitted or denied herein the Defendant is unable to admit or deny the allegations contained in the Particulars of Claim and requires the Claimant to prove them.

17. Further, the Defendant claim to be entitled to set off the sums counter-claimed hereinbelow in diminution or extinction of the Claimant's claim.

PART 20 CLAIM

18. Paragraphs 1 and 3 of the Defence hereinabove are repeated. It is averred that the Defendant is the freehold owner of the dwelling and that since March 23, 1992, the Claimant has been the tenant of the Defendant in the dwelling at a weekly rent of £436.

19. The Claimant has failed to pay the said weekly rent to the Defendant as it has fallen due.

PARTICULARS

436[×]418 weeks (23/3/92–14/4/00) = £182,248.[8]

20. In the premises, the Claimant is indebted to the Defendant in the sum of £182,248.

21. Further, the Defendant claims interest on the said sum, pursuant to s.69 of the County Courts Act 1984, at 15% until April 1, 1993 and thereafter at 8% amounting to £205,937.04 at the date hereof and continuing at the daily rate of £39.94.

22. On February 25, 2002, notice seeking possession was served upon the Claimant, informing her that proceedings for possession would not be taken against her before March 27, 2002.

AND the Defendant counterclaims

(1) Possession of the dwelling;

(2) Judgment in the sum of £182,248;

(3) The aforesaid interest pursuant to s.69 of the County Courts Act 1984, amounting to £205,937.04 at the date hereof and continuing at the daily rate of £39.94;

(4) Rent at the weekly rate of £436 until the date of judgment herein;

(5) interest on the said rent pursuant to s.69 of the County Courts Act 1984 to be assessed;

(6) Mesne profits from the date of judgment to the date upon which possession is obtained at the weekly rate of £436.

STATEMENT OF TRUTH

- (I believe) (The Defendant believes) that the facts stated in this Defence are true.

- I am duly authorised by the Defendant to sign this statement.

Full name ....

Name of Defendant's solicitor's firm ....

Signed...Position or office held ....

- (Defendant)   (if signing on behalf of firm or company)
  (Defendant's solicitor)

- delete as appropriate

[CONCLUDE AS IN FORM 19]

---

[8] Under s.19 of the Limitation Act 1980, a claim for rent is statute-barred after six years, so that if the claimant here were to raise this by way of defence to the counterclaim, the amount recoverable will be restricted proportionately.

Form 33   2.48

Defence

Claim No. PI0101582

IN THE WEST POYNTON COUNTY COURT

B E T W E E N

EMILY SPUNGE   **Claimant**

and

PIGHOLE DISTRICT COUNCIL   **Defendant**

DEFENCE

---

1. Paragraphs 1–10 of the Particulars of Claim are admitted. It is denied, however, that the Claimant can rely on any of the said express or implied tenancy terms because the Claimant's legal status in the premises is that of a mere tolerated trespasser.

PARTICULARS

a) On September 23, 1995 at West Park County Court the Defendant was granted a suspended possession order in respect of the Claimant's property. The Claimant had outstanding rent arrears of £335. The order required the Claimant to pay the current rent plus £5 per week.

b) On October 1, 1995 the Claimant failed to make the first payment of current rent plus £5 as required by the order. Accordingly the Claimant's tenancy dated March 11, 1991 was thereafter at an end and her legal status was that of a tolerated trespasser who has no recourse or claim under the previous tenancy.

c) The rent arrears on the Claimant's account now stand at £3800 because the Claimant has persistently failed to make payments.

2. Further or alternatively if, which is denied, the Claimant's tenancy has not ended, the Defendant denies that it is in breach of the express and or implied terms either in the manner alleged by the Claimant or at all. In particular the Defendant will state the following:

a) The Defendant denies that the Claimant gave the Defendant any notice at all of the alleged rain water penetration to the premises. The Defendant's own sur-veyor, Peter Davidson discovered that the roof was leaking when he carried out a routine maintenance check. Despite persistent efforts to contact the Claimant Mr Davidson has been unable to determine whether any damage has been caused to the premises. Mr Davidson has written to the Claimant on numerous occasions and has also visited the premises almost every other week. Despite this the Claimant has not been in contact with the Defendant at all since the suspended possession order was granted.

b) The Defendant does not admit that the waste-pipe in the bath was blocked in the manner alleged and that the bath took 48 hours to drain and that the bath was unusable. The Claimant is put to strict proof of these matters. If which is not admitted the bath was so blocked the Defendant will maintain that this is the result of the Claimant blocking the bath with her hair and other debris which should have been removed by the Claimant in line with her duties as a reasonable tenant.

c) The Defendant has had no notice at all of the alleged lack of hot water supply to the dwelling.

d) It is denied that the ceiling in the premises is in imminent danger of collapse. The Defendant's own housing officer, Jake Robinson inspected the ceiling during an arrears visit. The Claimant was not in attendance but her boyfriend, Trevor was. There is a large dent in the ceiling, which Trevor admitted was caused when his shoe hit the ceiling when he was re-enacting Geoff Hurst's winning goal in the 1966 World Cup. Other than the dent there is no damage to the ceiling.

e) It is denied that the Defendant's contractors failed to protect the roof during the roofing works. The contractors, Fred Felt and Sons erected a temporary roof, which was in place throughout the works.

f) It is denied that the roofing works were not carried out within a reasonable period. Peter Davidson discovered the defect in April 1993 and the roof works were satisfactorily completed by July 1993.

g) It is further denied that the Defendants failed to take precautions to prevent water penetrating the dwelling and that the repairs were effected without due care or competence and that the Defendant's contractors have been negligent in any way. The roofing contractors erected a "Seal It" temporary roof which was in place throughout the roofing contract in 1993. The "Seal It" roof ensured that no water was allowed to penetrate. Mrs Wiggins who lives at 151 Comfy House, which is also on the top floor has not complained of any water penetration and when asked about the issue said that her flat was "bone dry".

3. The Defendant denies that the Claimant has had any notice of the alleged disrepair from the Claimant. Indeed the Claimant has remained un-contactable since the suspended possession order was granted against her. In particular it is denied that the Claimant made the phone-call alleged on April 25, 1993 or spoke in person to Mr Davidson on April 26, 1993. The Defendant's can be sure of this because on

April 25, 1993 the Defendant's offices were closed due to industrial action and on April 26, 1993 Mr Davidson was away from work at a long weekend in Amsterdam.

4. It is also denied that the Claimant's solicitors have notified the Defendants of the matters complained of. The letter dated October 13, 2001 stated only "Dear Sirs – we enclose a report from Messrs Noggin and Nogbad" no report was enclosed. The report of Messrs Noggin & Nogbad was sent on April 16, 2002, but the report itself is confused, irrelevant and incomprehensible. Further the Defendant will maintain that Bill Noggin is not an appropriate expert to give evidence in a disrepair case as ...ardening.

...daughter have suffered in the manner alleged ...d there is disrepair at the premises it is denied ...ry alleged. It is noted that the report of Alun ...ween the disrepair and the Claimant's alleged ...paragraph Mr Bingley states "In my opinion ...king, drink less, pull herself together and get

...terms of distress and inconvenience or special ...trict proof of these alleged losses. In particular ...ced to decant from the premises as alleged and ...at trial that the Claimant was seen living at the

...Claimant is entitled to the relief claimed or to

...ieves) that the facts stated in this Defence are

...efendant to sign this statement.

....
....
...........Position or office held ....
...behalf of firm or company)

...DE AS IN FORM 19]

2.49   **Form 34**

Landlords' remedies – Particulars of Claim

Claim No. HC002020

IN THE HIGH COURT OF JUSTICE
CHANCERY DIVISION

B E T W E E N

BRICK PROPERTIES LIMITED   **Claimant**

and

BILLY BRICK   **Defendant**

PARTICULARS OF CLAIM

---

1.   At all material times, the Claimant has been the freehold owner of the property situate at and known as Brick House, 22 Morcabe Street, Legsley, Armshire (hereinafter referred to as "the property").

2.   By a lease dated January 21, 1970, the Claimant demised the property to the Defendant for a term of 30 years commencing January 24, 1970 in consideration of £30,000 and an annual ground rent of £50.

3.   By clause 4 of the agreement, the Defendant covenanted with the Claimant, *inter alia*:

   a)   to put and keep the property, externally and internally, in good repair at all times during the continuance of the term;

   b)   in the 4th, 8th, 12th, 16th, 24th and 28th years of the term, to paint or varnish, using two coats of good quality paint or varnish, all the external surfaces of the property which were painted or varnished at the commencement of the term, and to do the same to the interior in the 6th, 12th, 18th, 24th and last years of the term;

   c)   to deliver up to the Claimant at the determination of the said lease, the property in a state of good repair and decorative order.

4.   The term determined by effluxion of time on January 23, 2000.

5.   The Defendant is in breach of his said covenants.

PARTICULARS

   a) the property is derelict, having no roof, no external doors, no windows and, in places, no floors to the upper storey;

   b) dampness and rainwater has penetrated all the rooms, the electricity supply is no longer functional and part of the gas installation and pipes have been removed;

   c) the bath and lavatories have been smashed to pieces, fireplaces and internal doors smashed and removed, and internal walls holed and part demolished.

6. The Claimant will further rely on the defects set out in the report of Messrs Edsan Jackson, Chartered Surveyors, dated February 24, 2000, a copy of which is annexed hereto.

7. The matters complained of have caused the Claimant to suffer loss and damage.

PARTICULARS

   a) Cost of works to repair property to the standard required by the said covenants
                                                                              £104,031

8. Further, the Claimant claims interest, pursuant to s.35A of the Supreme Court Act 1981, on any sums found to be due at such rate and for such period as the court thinks just.

AND the Claimant claims

   (1) Damages for breach of covenant

   (2) The aforesaid interest, pursuant to s.35A of the Supreme Court Act 1981, to be assessed.

Sidney Boggle[9]

STATEMENT OF TRUTH

   • (I believe) (The Claimant believes) that the facts stated in these Particulars of Claim are true.

   • I am duly authorised by the Claimant to sign this statement.

Full name ....

Name of Claimant's solicitor's firm ....

Signed...Position or office held ....

- (Claimant)   (if signing on behalf of firm or company)
  (Claimant's solicitor)

- delete as appropriate

Served this 29th day of March 2000, by Messrs Eitzan Miller, of 242 Nose House, Langley, Armshire. Solicitors for the Claimant.

To: Nathan Nowz & Co, 3A Gum Place, Langley, Armshire, Solicitors for the Defendant.

---

[9] CPR Chancery Guide Appendix 1 – if solicitors or counsel drafted the statement of case, their name should appear at the end.

Form 35   **2.50**

Defence

[HEADING AS IN FORM 34]

DEFENCE

---

1. For the purposes of this action alone, the Defendant admits liability to the Claimant herein.

2. As to para.7 of the Particulars of Claim herein, it is denied that the Claimant is entitled to recover damages on the basis of the cost of repair works necessary to put the property in the condition required by the covenants.

3. The Claimant intends to sell the property to Brick Realisations plc for the purpose of office development (for which the site has planning permission) for the sum of approximately £1,500,000.

4. In the premises, the Claimant is entitled only to claim from the Defendant the difference between the market value of the reversion with the property in good repair and the market value of the reversion with the property in its current state.

5. In the result of the matters pleaded under para.3 hereinabove, the said difference in market value of the reversion is nil, and it is accordingly denied that the Claimant has suffered any loss or damage as claimed or at all.

6. Save as is expressly admitted or denied herein the Defendant is unable to admit or deny the allegations contained in the particulars of claim and requires the Claimant to prove them.

Arthur Montifiore

STATEMENT OF TRUTH

-   (I believe) (The Defendant believes) that the facts stated in this Defence are true.

-   I am duly authorised by the Defendant to sign this statement.

Full name ....

Name of Defendant's solicitor's firm ....

Signed...Position or office held

- (Defendant)   (if signing on behalf of firm or company)
  (Defendant's solicitor)

- delete as appropriate

[CONCLUDE AS IN FORM 19]

Notice pursuant to s.82(7) EPA 1990

Law and Administration Department,
Armsley District Council,
Footham Road,
Armsley,
Legshire LG3 0AR

Dear Sirs,

Re: Michael Hartley – 278, Mitsley Court, Handfield Place, Armsley, Legshire.

We are instructed by Mr Michael Hartley, who is the secure tenant of the above address. We attach a report compiled by Messrs Kneesan Towers, which sets out numerous defects to the property as a result of which Mr Hartley's property constitutes a statutory nuisance.

He hereby gives you formal notice that unless the said defects are remedied within 21 days of the date of this notice, Mr Hartley will make complaint against the Armsley District Council before the North Street Magistrates' Court, stating that he is a person aggrieved by a nuisance within the meaning of s.79 of the Environmental Protection Act 1990.

Yours faithfully,

2.52 Form 37

Summons[10]

IN THE LEGSHIRE AREA AND POLICE DISTRICT

BEFORE the NORTH STREET Magistrates' Court

The 29th day of July 2000

To: Armsley District Council
      Law and Administration Department
      Footham Road,
      Armsley,
      Legshire LG3 0AR

INFORMATION HAVING THIS DAY BEEN LAID BEFORE ME, THE
UNDERSIGNED, By Michael Leonard Hartley, 278 Mitsley Court, Handfield Road,
Armsley, Legshire,

THAT HE IS A PERSON AGGRIEVED BY THE EXISTENCE OF A STATU-
TORY NUISANCE AS DEFINED BY SECTIONS 79 AND 82 OF THE ENVIR-
ONMENTAL PROTECTION ACT 1990, IN THAT THE PROPERTY SUFFERS
FROM CONDENSATION MOULD GROWTH AND COCKROACH INFESTA-
TION (AND OTHER MATTERS AS TO WHICH SEE ATTACHED SCHEDULE)

AND THAT YOU ARE THE PERSON RESPONSIBLE FOR THE STATUTORY
NUISANCE.

YOU ARE HEREBY SUMMONED TO APPEAR BEFORE THE NORTH STREET
MAGISTRATES' COURT, 91 NORTH STREET, ARMSLEY, LEGSHIRE, ON
12–8–00 AT THE HOUR OF 2.00 IN THE AFTERNOON TO SHOW CAUSE WHY
AN ORDER SHOULD NOT BE MADE REQUIRING YOU TO ABATE THE
SAID NUISANCE AND TO EXECUTE ANY WORKS NECESSARY TO THE
PURPOSE AND WHY A FINE SHOULD NOT BE IMPOSED AND COMPEN-
SATION PAID TO THE COMPLAINANT AS SET OUT IN THE PROVISIONS
OF THE ABOVE ACT AND THE POWERS OF THE CRIMINAL COURTS ACT
1973.

Justice's Clerk.

---

[10] In order to cause the Magistrates' Court to issue the summons, it will be necessary to lay on information before the court, as to which see pp.237–238 and 264.

1. It is important to ensure that, as far as possible, the relevant pre-action protocols have been complied with before proceedings are commenced. Failure to do so may result in costs sanctions later on.

2. It is important to send a proper letter of instruction to the expert to inform him or her of what exactly is required for the purposes of the action and of any particular important points which need to be dealt with.

3. The expert should be asked to provide a properly priced schedule of works. Apart from anything else, this information will assist in decisions as to track allocation. The schedule will also assist in determining whether any of the works are urgent and require an application for interim relief. Finally in statutory nuisance cases, the schedule is required in order to inform the court of the works the complainant is asking to be undertaken.

4. Sometimes a claim for aggravated or exemplary damages may be made in the claim. It is necessary for such a claim to be pleaded in the body of the Particulars in addition to the prayer.

5. The Defendant's advisers should remember to plead any relevant limitation period in their defence. If the claim *includes* a claim for personal injury the limitation period for the whole case, *i.e.* even including non-personal injury claims is only three years from the date of injury or, if later, knowledge (Limitation Act 1980, s.11). Otherwise the limitation period is likely to be six years.

6. If interim relief is sought, the Defendant's adviser should seek the traditional undertaking in damages, even if, in the event, it may prove worthless. Moreover, if the Defendant is prepared to offer temporary rehousing, it may be possible to avert the grant of an interim injunction.

7. As to the costs of an unsuccessful interim application, if the Claimant is Legal Services Commission funded, it may be possible, as an alternative to the usual order – costs not to be enforced without leave – for a Defendant to obtain an order that the costs be set off against any damages or costs to which the Legal Services Commission funded party was, or may become, entitled in the action (*Lockley v National Blood Transfusion Service* [1992] 1 W.L.R. 492, CA).

8. Where the Defendant wishes to make a Pt 36 offer, the sum offered will have to be paid into court (CPR 36.3). If the claim includes a claim for specific performance as well as damages, the Defendant should make the payment in *and* make a Pt 36 offer in relation to the specific performance claim (CPR 36.4). Furthermore, the Pt 36 payment notice must identify the document which sets out the Pt 36 offer and state that if the Claimant gives notice of acceptance of the Pt 36 payment he will be treated as giving notice of acceptance of the Pt 36 offer in relation to the specific performance claim.

9. Potential Claimants should always check the express repairing terms in the tenancy agreement. These may be wider than the statutorily implied terms (see *Johnson v Sheffield CC* (1994) August Legal Action 16).

Chapter 3
Rent and Service Charges

PART I: INTRODUCTION

Recovery of rent at common law

At common law, rent is recoverable by action in the same way as any other debt. **3.01**

At common law the covenant to pay rent runs with the land, and so assignees of the reversion are generally entitled to take proceedings even in respect of amounts falling due before the assignment. The original tenant will generally remain liable in contract, on his covenant to pay, for rent falling due after the date of his assignment of the term. Where the assignment relates to a tenancy granted after January 1, 1996, however, the right to sue for arrears of rent in existence at the date of the assignment remains with the assignor of the reversion unless expressly assigned to the assignee, and in the case of an assignment by the tenant, the original tenant is automatically released unless the assignment is made in breach of covenant or takes effect by operation of law: see Landlord and Tenant (Covenants) Act 1995, s.11. Generally, the assignee of the term will only be liable for rent falling due after the date of the assignment.

The county court and High Court have concurrent jurisdiction in respect of rent claims (CCA 1984, s.15, as amended by the Courts and Legal Services Act 1990). Where the claim is for less than £15,000 however, the action must be instituted in the county court. Where the amount claimed is in excess of £15,000, the matter may be tried in the High Court, unless the claim is commenced in the county court and the county court considers it unnecessary to transfer it to the High Court (see generally, the High Court and County Courts Jurisdiction Order 1991 (SI 1991/724) as amended by the High Court and County Courts Jurisdiction (Amendment) Order 1999 (SI 1999/1014) and CPR Pt 30). A claim with an estimated value of less than £50,000 will generally be transferred to a County Court: see CPR Practice Direction 29, para.2.2.

Matters which the court must have regard to in deciding whether to transfer the matter include the financial value of the claim and the amount in dispute if different and the complexity of the facts, legal issues, remedies or procedures involved: see CPR r.30.3(2).

Statutory rent control

The strict control of private sector rents contained in the Rents Acts, was abolished subject to **3.02** transitional provisions, in respect of all tenancies created after January 15, 1989 (Housing Act 1988) and the rent payable in respect of new private sector tenancies reflects an entirely different philosophy.

The Rent Acts

3.03   The Rent Act 1977 is still extremely important, as its provisions remain in force in respect of all those tenancies to which it applied prior to its replacement.

In brief, a tenant or a landlord–or both–is entitled to apply to the Rent Officer to register a fair rent, defined in s.70. What renders the level of fair rents below that of market rents is the fact that scarcity is expressly left out of account: by s.70(2), it shall be assumed that the number of persons seeking tenancies of similar dwelling-houses in the locality on similar terms is not substantially greater than the number of such dwelling-houses which are available for letting on such terms.

For the purposes of registering a fair rent, the country is divided into registration areas (s.62), each with a rent officer (s.63) who keeps the register of fair rents for that area (s.66). The tenant, the landlord, or both of them, may apply in the prescribed form for a rent to be registered, whether for the first time or for reregistration (see s.67 as amended by Housing Act 1980, s.60(1)). The forms prescribed for the purpose are set out in the Rent Regulation (Forms etc) Regulations (1980) SI 1980/1697.

By s.44(1), once a fair rent has been registered, it becomes the contractual rent limit from the date of registration (s.72) and any contractually agreed excess becomes irrecoverable from the tenant (s.44(2)). If the registered rent is higher than the contractual rent, the higher rent cannot be charged until the contractual tenancy has been determined. This is generally brought about by the service of a statutory notice of increase (s.49), which has the effect of a notice to quit (s.49(4)) if the date of increase it shows is later than the date upon which a valid notice to quit could bring the tenancy to an end.

Housing Act 1988

Assured tenancies

3.04   The rent regime of the Housing Act 1988, which replaced protected tenancies with assured and assured shorthold tenancies, is fundamentally different. Assured tenancies are at market rents, not fair rents, the rent being that agreed between the parties, subject to a reference to a Rent Assessment Committee, which may be made by the tenant in limited circumstances.

Section 13 concerns rent increases in relation to periodic tenancies. If a landlord wishes to retain power to increase the rent of a fixed term assured tenancy, this must be provided for by a clause in the lease.

By s.13(2) a landlord may, on Form 4B prescribed for the purpose by the Assured Tenancies and Agricultural Occupancies (Forms) (Amendment) (England) Regulations 2003 SI 2003/260 propose a new rent to take effect at the beginning of a new period of the tenancy, specified in the notice, which period may not be earlier than the "minimum period" after the service of the notice. The minimum period is, in the case of a yearly tenancy, six months; in the case of a periodic tenancy where the period is less than one month, one month; and in all other cases, the period of the tenancy (s.13(3)). In most cases, a notice may not propose a new rent to take effect earlier than the first anniversary of the commencement of the tenancy, or the first anniversary of the last rent increase, whether under s.13(2) or s.14 (reference to a Rent Assessment Committee).

By s.13(4), the tenant has the right to refer a notice under s.13(2) to a Rent Assessment Committee, by application in the form (Form 5) prescribed by the Assured Tenancies and

Agricultural Occupancies (Forms) Regulations 1997, SI 1997/194 (the "1997 Regulations") and, if he does so, the rent is determined by the Committee.

The factors by reference to which the Committee determines the rent are set out in s.14. In essence, they are the same as those under s.70 of the RA 1977 save for one critical difference. There is no equivalent to RA 1977, s.70(2) to be found in the 1988 Act: it is not to be assumed that the supply of dwellings is equal to the demand. Scarcity is, therefore, taken into account in assessing rent levels.

It is important to note that the right to refer the rent to a Committee does not arise in relation to the rent agreed on the initial grant of the tenancy, but only to subsequent attempts by the landlord to increase the rent, and that nothing in ss.13 or 14 prevents rent increases by agreement between the parties (s.13(5)).

Assured shorthold tenancies

By s.22, the assured shorthold tenant has a limited right, in effect on one occasion only, to apply in the form prescribed by the 1997 Regulations (Form 6) to the Rent Assessment Committee for the determination of a rent.

3.05

By s.22(1), the tenant may apply to a committee unless a reference has been made previously (s.22(2)(a)) or the fixed period of the tenancy has already expired and the tenancy continues simply as a periodic tenancy (s.22(2)(b) and s.20(4)).

By s.22(3), the Committee "shall not" make a determination unless they consider both that there is a sufficient number of similar dwelling houses in the locality let on assured tenancies (whether shorthold or not) and that the rent payable under the shorthold tenancy in relation to which the reference has been made, is "significantly higher" than that which the landlord might reasonably be expected to be able to obtain under the tenancy, having regard to the level of rents payable under the similar dwelling houses let on assured tenancies referred to above.

By s.22(4), the determination shall have effect from the date the committee directs, which may not be earlier than the date of the application, and if the determined rent is lower than the rent otherwise payable under the tenancy agreement, the excess is irrecoverable from the tenant. In addition, no notice may be served by the landlord under s.13(2) (proposal for a new rent–see above) until the first anniversary of the date on which the determination takes effect.

Where an assured shorthold tenancy continues as a statutory periodic tenancy, the landlord or the tenant may, no later than the first anniversary of the former fixed term tenancy coming to an end, serve a notice in the prescribed form (under the Assured Tenancies and Agricultural Occupancies (Forms) Regulations 1988, SI 1988/2203) proposing new tenancy terms different from those implied by HA 1988, s.5(3)(e) and proposing an adjustment of the rent to take account of them.

By s.6(3)(a), within three months of the date of being served, the party may, by an application in the prescribed form, refer the notice to a rent assessment committee. Otherwise, with effect from the date in the notice, which must not be within the three month period after service, the proposed terms take effect: s.6(3)(b).

Public sector tenancies

3.06　Local housing authorities are under a duty to prevent a debit balance on the Housing Revenue Account (LGHA 1989, s.76) and must set rent levels accordingly. Although this may be done by imposing a general rental income, rather than tailoring individual rents, it necessarily impacts on the levels of rent. Furthermore s.24 of the HA 1985 states that local housing authorities may make such reasonable charges as they may determine for the tenancy or occupation of their houses, that they shall from time to time review their rents and make such charges as the circumstances require, and that they should have regard in particular to the principle that the rents of houses of any class or description should bear broadly the same proportion to private sector rents as the rents of houses of any other class or description: *i.e.* if, in the private sector, the rent for a three-bedroom house is twice that of a three-bedroom flat, then the authority should have particular regard to the principle that their own three-bedroom houses should fetch twice as much as their three-bedroom flats.

Housing association tenancies

3.07　Until January 15 1989, when HA 1988 came into force, the provisions of RA 1977 applied to housing association tenancies. Such tenancies were either protected, in which case the provisions applied in any event, or secure, in which case the provisions were applied with some variations. The rent officer registered rents on essentially the same basis as described above; there were different provisions relating to statutory notices of increase of rent where the rent registered exceeded the previously charged rent (s.93).

　　Since January 15, 1989, housing association tenancies are assured tenancies under HA 1988. The Housing Corporation has, however, given guidance as to rent levels for their tenants (the "Housing Corporation Regulatory Code[1] and the 'Charter for housing association applicants and residents'").

Housing benefit

3.08　The local authority which administers the Housing Benefit regime enjoys limited discretion as to the amount of housing benefit payable in relation to tenancies. While, in theory at least, this does not affect the contractual rent, it is likely to have a significant practical effect.

　　Regulation 7 of the Housing Benefit (General) Regulations (1987) SI 1987/1971 (as amended) obliges authorities to treat certain arrangements—essentially devices—as if they created no liability to make payments. Regulation 11 obliges, the authority to restrict the amount of benefit payable by means of a "maximum rent" formula applied to figures produced by the Rent Officer which are intended to indicate the rent at which similar (or, at least, suitable) properties in the area are generally available to let. The local authority has limited power to pay benefit in excess of the maximum rent, in cases of exceptional hardship (reg.61(3)). Regulation 12 applies the same powers to rent increases. In most cases, authorities are obliged to refer the claims to the rent officer to assess a reasonable market rent (reg.12A).

---

[1] "The way forward: Our approach to regulation."

Recovery of overpaid rent

Common law

There is a general right to recover money paid under a mistake of fact or law, subject to any **3.09** defence which may be available under the law of restitution: see *Kleinwort Benson v Lincoln City Council* [1999] 2 A.C. 349, HL. In *Nurdin & Peacock plc v D B Ramsden & Co Ltd (No.2)* [1999] 1 W.L.R. 1249, Ch D it was held that overpayments of rent made under a mistaken belief that they were due and owing could be recovered as money paid by mistake, whether the mistake was one of fact or law.

If the tenant pays under duress, he may recover the excess rent paid, even though there was no mistake of fact or law (*Maskell v Horner* [1915] 3 KB 106, CA).

The Rent Act 1977

Section 57

Section 57 provides two remedies for a private sector tenant who has paid sums in excess of **3.10** the rent which is recoverable by the landlord, by virtue of Pt III of the 1977 RA. The first is that the tenant may recover such sums (s.57(1)), and the second is that the tenant may deduct the excess from future payments of rent, without prejudice to any other method of recovery (s.57(2)). There is a special limitation period, however, of one year, where rent is recoverable by virtue of a failure to comply with the procedural provisions of s.51, and two years in any other case.

It seems that this provision, referring to the "tenant who paid it" as the person entitled to recover, precludes an assignee of the tenancy from recovering under the section. This is not the case if recovery is possible at common law.

Section 94

The provisions of s.94, in relation to public sector tenants, are almost identical to those under **3.11** s.57. The limitation period is two years for all purposes.

The Housing Act 1988

There is no analogous provision in the new assured regime. The rent payable is that con- **3.12** tractually agreed, as increased by notice, other agreement, or determination by a rent assessment committee.

Sections 47 and 48, Landlord and Tenant Act 1987

Sections 47(1) and 48 of the Landlord and Tenant Act 1987, impose requirements upon **3.13** landlords to give notice of their address to their tenants.

Section 47

3.14 Section 47(1) provides:

Where any written demand is given to a tenant of premises to which this Part applies, the demand must contain following information, namely –

(a) the name and address of the landlord, and

(b) if that address is not in England and Wales, an address in England and Wales at which notices (including notices in proceedings) may be served on the landlord by the tenant.

Section 48

3.15 Section 48(1) is worded differently. By its terms, the landlord must, in addition to his obligations under s.47:

"(1) ... by notice furnish the tenant with an address in England and Wales at which notices (including notices in proceedings) may be served on him by the tenant."

It is important to remember that these statutory provisions apply not only to periodic tenancies or short leases of premises let as a separate dwelling, but to any such tenancy not falling within Pt II of the Landlord and Tenant Act 1954 – *i.e.* any such tenancy which is not a business tenancy including premises, such as an agricultural holding, which include a dwelling: *Dallhold Estates (UK) PTY Ltd v Lindsey Trading Properties Inc* [1994] 17 E.G. 148, CA.

The sanction for failure to comply is that any rent or service charge otherwise due from the tenant shall be treated as not being due "for all purposes" until such information is furnished. Accordingly, if a landlord has not complied with the requirement, then any proceedings instituted before service of a proper notice will not be founded upon a completed cause of action see *Dallhold* (above).

Although the notice must be in writing, the statutory obligation will be fulfilled where the address of the landlord in England or Wales is stated without qualification in a written tenancy agreement or a rent book. In such cases there is no need to serve a separate notice unless, *e.g.* the landlord changes address or indeed, there is a change of landlord: see *Rogan v Woodfield Building Services Ltd* (1994) 27 H.L.R. 78, CA. A notice served under s.20 of the Housing Act 1988, was held to be sufficient in *Marath v MacGillivray* (1995) 28 H.L.R. 484, CA. In *Drew-Morgan v Hamid-Zadeh* [1999] 26 E.G. 156, CA, it was held that the requirements of s.48 were satisfied even if the notice did not expressly state that the address was one at which notices could be served. In that case, a notice under the Housing Act 1988, s.21, which stated the landlord's address, was sufficient.

Deductions from and set offs against rent

3.16 Where the landlord is obliged, but fails, to make payments, and such failure would interfere with the tenant's possession of the demised property, the tenant is entitled to make the payments himself and deduct them from his rent, treating them, in effect, as part payments.

Where lawful deductions have been made, they will also provide the tenant with a defence by way of set off, should the landlord attempt to recover the full rent from him.

In general, a breach of covenant will not entitle a tenant to make deductions from the rent. If a landlord fails to comply with, for instance, his repairing obligations under a lease, the tenant will remain obliged in law to pay the full rent. However, should the tenant fail to do so, the landlord's breach of covenant will also give rise to a right of set-off in equity, amounting to a defence to the landlord's claim to the extent of the tenant's right to damages.

Where, however, a lease requires the rent to be paid without deduction or set off, it appears that the right of set-off is precluded (*Electricity Supply Nominees v IAF Group Ltd* [1993] 1 W.L.R. 1059), although a requirement that the rent be paid simply "without deductions" has been held to be too narrow to exclude the equitable right of set-off (*Connaught Restaurants Ltd v Indoor Leisure Ltd* [1994] 1 W.L.R. 501, CA).

Rent and possession

This topic is dealt with in detail in Chapter 5. Failure to pay rent constitutes a breach of **3.17** covenant which gives rise to a ground upon which a landlord may claim possession under each of the forms of statutory protection contained in the Rent Acts, and the Housing Acts 1985 and 1988.

In relation to tenancies which enjoy no statutory protection, the normal contractual principles apply. Most leases contain re-entry clauses: if the rent remains unpaid for a specified period, usually 21 days, the landlord will be entitled to forfeit the lease and re-enter the property, even if no prior formal demand has been made. Where forfeiture is claimed for failure to pay rent, it is not necessary to serve a notice under s.146 of the LPA 1925.

In this respect, if service charges have been reserved expressly as rent within the lease, they are thereby invested with the character of rent for the purposes of the law of forfeiture. Section 81 of the HA 1985, however, restricts the ability to forfeit for failure to pay service charges unless the amount of such charges has been agreed, admitted or determined by the county court or an arbitral tribunal.

For this purpose service charges are defined as an amount payable by a tenant of a dwelling as part of or in addition to the rent, which is payable, directly or indirectly, for services, repairs, maintenance, improvements or insurance or the landlord's costs of management, and the whole or part of which varies or may vary according to the relevant costs. The relevant costs are the costs or estimated costs incurred or to be incurred by or on behalf of the landlord, or a superior landlord, in connection with matters for which the service charge is payable: see s.18 of the LTA 1985, as amended by the Commonhold and Leasehold Reform Act 2002 ("CLRA 2002").

The relevant principles, in the country court, are now set out in s.138 of the CCA 1984.

In brief, where the lease has been forfeited and possession proceedings have been commenced, solely on the grounds of rent arrears, if the full sum in arrear and the costs of the action are paid into court, or to the lessor, not less than five clear days before return day, the action shall cease and the original lease shall continue (s.138(2) of the CCA 1984).

If the action continues and the court, at trial, is satisfied that the lessor is entitled to enforce **3.18** the right of re-entry or forfeiture, the court must order possession of the land at the expiration of a period of time, which may not be less than for weeks, unless within that time the lessee pays into court or to the lessor all the rent in arrear and the costs of the action (s.138(3) of the CCA 1984). By s.138(4) of the CCA 1984, the court has power further to extend the time before possession has been recovered, and if the lessee complies with the order, the original lease continues.

Where possession is recovered pursuant to an order of the Court under s.138(3) of the CCA 1984 the lessee may again apply for relief from forfeiture at any time within six months from the date on which possession was recovered.

Distress

3.19   Despite calls for its abolition the right to levy distress – *i.e.* the seizure of chattels on the land belonging to the tenant – for the recovery of rent in arrear remains a remedy open to the landlord, albeit that in modern conditions it is no longer generally regarded as appropriate or convenient. There are substantial restrictions on the use of distress, and where security of tenure attaches to a dwelling under the R(A)A 1976, RA 1977 or HA 1988 the leave of the county court must be obtained.

In order for distress to be available, the relationship of landlord and tenant must arise both when the rent fell due and when the distress is levied, although there is no need for a formal tenancy agreement. Moreover, distress is only available, in the absence of express agreement in the lease, in respect of rent: there is no common law right of distress in relation to other charges save that where a service charge has been expressly reserved as rent then once agreed or otherwise ascertained, it may properly be the subject of distraint: *Concorde Graphics v Andromeda Investments SA* (1983) EG 386. The rent must also be in arrear before distress may be levied.

Before levying distress, a landlord is well advised to take care that there are no claims available to the tenant by way of equitable set-off against the outstanding rent, *e.g.* an overpayment of rent. The human rights implications should be in the forefront of the landlord's mind before levying distress, so that he is satisfied that doing so would be in accordance with law: see *Fuller v Happy Shopper Markets Ltd and another* [2001] 1 W.L.R. 1681, Ch D.

Recovery of service charges

The position at common law

3.20   Most modern leases will include provision for the tenant to contribute to the cost of services provided, such as repairs and maintenance to common parts, cleaning and insurance. At common law the ascertainment of which sums are recoverable, including the extent to which any discounts, obtained by the landlord, *e.g.* by negotiating bulk insurance deals, must be passed to the tenant, will generally be a matter of the construction of the lease in question: see *Williams v Southwark LBC* (2001) 33 H.L.R. 224, Ch D. However, there are some general common law principles concerning recovery.

As a general rule, interest on money borrowed by the landlord to finance the provision of the services will not be recoverable in the absence of clear words to that effect in the lease: see *Boldmark v Cohen* [1986] 1 EGLR 47; (1987) 19 H.L.R. 135, CA. The same is true in respect of the cost of employing managing agents, except where the lease permits recovery of the total cost of providing certain services, in which case it has been held that the management costs of providing those services alone will be recoverable (*Lloyds Bank v Bowker Orford* (1992) 2 EGLR 44). The cost of collecting rent is not recoverable as part of a management charge (*Woodtrek v Jezek* (1982) 261 EG 571). Even where a lease permits recovery of professional fees, the right of recovery will be limited to such fees expended on items themselves recoverable under the clause.

In the absence of clear words, the cost of legal and other professional fees incurred in taking legal proceedings against defaulting tenants will not be recoverable as service charge. Whether the costs of legal proceedings are contractually recoverable from the defaulting tenant will be a question of construction of the lease.

In the absence of a clause limiting recovery to amounts reasonably expended, a term to the effect that the charge must be fair and reasonable will generally be implied (*Finchbourne v Rodrigues* [1976] 3 All E.R. 581). This does not oblige the landlord necessarily to choose the cheapest method of carrying out his obligations. In the absence of clear words, a landlord will not be entitled to any profit element in carrying out the services specified.

Some leases contain wide clauses, intended to include within the scope of recovery, items not specifically referred to. Such clauses are restrictively construed, unless there are clear words indicating that expenditure of a particular class was contemplated.

Statutory intervention as to service charges

The two main statutory sources, limiting the recovery of service charges, are the Landlord and Tenant Act 1985 (as amended by the LTA 1987, and the CLRA 2002), ss.19 and 20 and the Housing Act 1985, s.125A–E. **3.21**

The Landlord and Tenant Act 1985

Section 19

Section 19 provides that service charges (defined in s.18)[2] are only recoverable to the extent that they are reasonably incurred and, where they are incurred in the provision of services or the carrying out of works, if the services or works are of a reasonable standard.[3] A further limit may apply if a landlord, when required, fails to consult tenants about work to be done. Furthermore, in certain circumstances, a tenant may withhold payment of a service charge.[4] **3.22**

An agreement by the tenant of a dwelling (other than a post-dispute arbitration agreement) is void in so far as it purports to provide for a determination in a particular manner, or on particular evidence, of any question whether costs incurred for services, maintenance, insurance or management were reasonably incurred, whether services or works for which costs were incurred are of a reasonable standard, or whether an amount payable before costs are incurred is reasonable (s.19(3)). Accordingly a provision in a lease purporting to make a certificate by the landlord's surveyor conclusive as to the reasonableness of a service charge is void, unless it is made pursuant to a post-dispute arbitration agreement.

By s.29A(1) a tenant by whom, or a landlord to whom, a service charge is alleged to be payable may apply to a LVT for a determination whether a service charge is payable, including the amount to be paid and the date and method of payment. An application may also be made for a determination whether, if costs were incurred for services, repairs, maintenance, improvements, insurance or management, a service charge would be payable,

[2] See para.3.17, above.
[3] See para.3.26, below.
[4] See para.3.28, below.

and if so the amount and date and method of payment: s.27A(3). This jurisdiction applies whether or not any payment has been made.[5]

This type of application is applicable where, for example, the landlord has produced estimates for works in accordance with s.20 which the tenants considers warrant an examination of what a reasonable amount might be before any costs are incurred. In appropriate cases a court has jurisdiction to grant an injunction restraining a landlord from carrying out work prior to a determination by the LVT: see *Bounds v Camden LBC* [1999] 6 C.L. 423. Where in proceedings before a court there falls for determination a question which falls within the LVT's jurisdiction, the court may transfer that part to the LVT and dispose of the remaining matters, or adjourn the disposal pending a determination by the LVT (s.31C(1)).[6] The court may give effect to any determination of the LVT by order.[7]

3.23   By s.27A(4), no application under subs.(1) or (3) may be made in respect of a matter which has been agreed or admitted by the tenant, or has been, or is to be, referred to arbitration under a post-dispute arbitration agreement, or has been the subject of a determination by a court or, in the case of a post-dispute arbitration agreement, an arbitral tribunal. In this context, the mere fact that a tenant makes a payment does not amount to an admission by him of any matter.

Any application must contain the information prescribed by the Leasehold Valuation Tribunals (Procedure) (England) Regulations 2003, SI 2003/2099 ("The 2003 Procedure Regulations").

The following information must be included in any application:

- the address of the premises to which the application relates;
- the name and address of:
  ○ the applicant;
  ○ the respondent;
  ○ any landlord or tenant of the premises; and,
  ○ the secretary of any recognised tenants' association;
- a statement that the applicant believes that the facts stated in the application are true; and,
- a copy of the lease.

A fee is payable unless the applicant is entitled to a waiver or reduction.[8]

Costs

3.24   Where an applicant's application has been dismissed because it is frivolous or vexatious or an abuse of process or, in relation to the proceedings, he has acted in such a manner or otherwise unreasonably, the LVT may order him to pay the other party's costs, limited to a prescribed amount.[9] Otherwise, and subject to any other statutory provision, no person can be required

---

[5] LTA 1985, s.27A(2), reversing the decision in *R v London Leasehold Valuation Tribunal, Ex p. Daejan Properties Ltd* [2001] EWCA Civ 1095, (2001) 29 E.G. 122.
[6] CLRA 2002, s.174 and Sch.12, para.3(1).
[7] *ibid.*, para.3(2).
[8] Leasehold Valuation Tribunals (Fees) (England) Regulations 2003, SI 2003/2098.
[9] Currently £500: CLRA 2002, Sch.12, paras 7 and 10 and the 2003 Procedure Regulations, reg.11.

to pay the costs of another incurred before the LVT.[10] In addition, a tenant may make an application for an order that all or any of the costs incurred, or to be incurred, by the landlord in connection with proceedings before a court or LVT, or the Lands Tribunal, or in connection with arbitration proceedings, are not to be regarded as relevant costs to be taken into account in determining the amount of any service charge payable by the tenant or any other person or persons specified in the application.[11]

Appeals from the LVT

An appeal from the LVT is to the Lands Tribunal with the permission of the LVT or the **3.25** Lands Tribunal. An application for permission must be made to the tribunal within the period of 21 days starting on the date on which the tribunal's written decision was sent to that party by the tribunal: see reg.20 of the 2003 Procedure Regulations.

The LVT, or the Lands Tribunal, may, if a request is made before the 21 days are up, allow a single extension to the period of time in which an application may be made: reg.24.

By s.19(5), if a person takes proceedings in the High Court, in pursuance of any of the provisions of the Act relating to service charges, which he could have taken in the county court, he shall not be entitled to recover any costs.

Section 20

Where the cost of qualifying works[12] and/or those which will be incurred under a qualifying **3.26** long term agreement[13] in any given accounting period,[14] exceed an appropriate amount,[15] then unless the landlord has complied with the prescribed consultation requirements, or they have been dispensed with,[16] any additional costs, over and above the appropriate amount, cannot be recovered.

The consultation requirements differ, depending on whether the landlord intends:

- to enter into a long term agreement;

- to carry out qualifying works under an existing agreement (whether or not it is a qualifying agreement); or,

---

[10] CLRA 2002, Sch.12, para.10(4).

[11] The LVT has absolute discretion, however, and is not obliged to accede to the application, even where the tenant has succeeded in the substantive claim: *Tenants of Langford Court (El Sherbani) v Doren Ltd* [2002] 5 J.H.L. D8.

[12] Defined as "works on a building or other premises": LTA 1985, s.20ZA(2).

[13] Defined as "an agreement entered into, by or on behalf of the landlord or a superior landlord, for a term of more than twelve months", subject to the Service Charges (Consultation Requirements) (England) Regulations 2003, SI 2003/1987 ("the 2003 Consultation Regulations"), reg.3, which provides that the following are not qualifying long term agreements: an agreement for a term of more than twelve months entered into before October 31, 2003, or which provides for the carrying out of qualifying works for which public notice has been given before October 31, 2003; a contract of employment; a management agreement made between a local housing authority and a tenant management organisation or a body established under s.2 of the Local Government Act 2000; where the parties are a holding company and one or more of its subsidiaries, or two or more subsidiaries of the same holding company; and an agreement for a term not exceeding five years which when entered into relates to buildings or other premises which are not tenanted.

[14] If the landlord accounts on a yearly basis, the relevant accounting period starts on the new accounting year which first begins after October 31, 2003, or if the accounts are not prepared annually, then starting on October 31, 2003, and in both cases, twelve-monthly thereafter: the 2003 Consultation Requirements, reg.4.

[15] Currently £250 for qualifying works and £100 for a qualifying long term agreement: the 2003 Consultation Requirements, regs 6 and 4(1).

[16] If satisfied that it is reasonable to do so, the LVT, or on appeal, the Lands Tribunal, may dispense with the requirements: LTA, ss.20(1)(b) and 20ZA(1).

- simply to carry out qualifying works.

In the first and third cases, a further distinction is made where public notice must be given in the Official Journal in order to comply with EU procurement rules. In all cases, the landlord must given written notice of his intention to each tenant and, where relevant, to any recognised tenants' association, containing information prescribed by Regulations.[17]

Section 20B

3.27   If any "relevant costs" (*i.e.* the costs of qualifying works) were incurred more than 18 months before the demand for service charge relating to them was made, those costs are not recoverable, unless, within the period of 18 months following the incurring of the relevant costs, the tenant was notified in writing that they had been incurred and that he would be required under the terms of his lease to contribute to them by payment of a service charge.

Sections 21–30

3.28   These sections are concerned with the right of tenants to a regular statement of account, certified by a qualified accountant, together with a summary of their rights and obligations in relation to service charges.[18] Such a summary must also accompany any demand for the payment of a service charge.[19] Where the landlord fails to provide and, or any proper, documentation, the tenant may withhold service charges.[20] By s.26, most public sector tenants are excluded, as are some Rent Act protected tenants (s.27).

The Leasehold Reform, Housing and Urban Development Act 1993

3.29   Part 1, Chapter V of the Act creates, for certain qualifying tenants, a right to a management audit, to ascertain the extent to which the landlord's obligations in relation to his management functions are being carried out, and the extent to which service charges are being applied, in an efficient and effective manner.

The Housing Act 1985

3.30   Where public sector tenants exercise their right to buy, the Housing Act 1985, s.125A–E, inserted into the Act by Housing and Planning Act 1986, s.4(2), and Sch.6, impose limitations on the amount of service charge recoverable what is known as the "reference period", usually for the first five years after the transfer.[21]

Sections 125A and 125B

3.31   By s.125A and B, the landlord must give information and estimates about the level of service charge and the costs of works which may be incurred during the "reference period" (defined

---

[17] The 2003 Consultation Requirements, Schs 1-4.
[18] LTA 1985, s.21, inserted by CLRA 2002, s.152.
[19] LTA 1985, s.21B, inserted by CLRA 2002, s.153.
[20] LTA 1985, ss.21A and 21B(3) set out the amounts which may be withheld, and the circumstances under which they become payable.
[21] Housing Act 1985, s.125C. See also para.3.31 below.

in s.125C as essentially the first five years after a date not more than six months from the date of the notice).

By paras 16A–C of Sch.6 to the 1985 Act, the tenant cannot, in general, be required to pay sums in excess of the estimates given.

Limitation

Rent falling due more than six years prior to the institution of proceedings will be time barred **3.32** and irrecoverable by the landlord (Limitation Act 1980, s.19).

Overpayments of rent which are recoverable at common law have the same limitation period. Payments recoverable in equity are not subject to statutory periods of limitation, but their recovery may be barred by laches, acquiescence or waiver after substantial delay. Overpayments which are recoverable under the Rent Acts, have the limitation periods specified above, either one or two years.

So far as service charges are concerned, by the Landlord and Tenant Act 1985, s.20B, the limitation period is eighteen months from the date the relevant costs were incurred.

PART II: PRECEDENTS
Form 38
3.33 **Form No. 4B**

FORM No. 4B

Housing Act 1988 s.13(2), as amended by the Regulatory Reform (Assured Periodic Tenancies) (Rent Increases) Order 2003

Landlord's Notice proposing a new rent under an Assured Periodic Tenancy of premises situated in England
The notes over the page give guidance to both landlords and tenants about this notice.

To:		*[Tenant(s)]*
of:		*[Address of the premises subject to the tenancy]*
From:		*[Landlord(s)] [Landlord's Agent]* *
		**delete as appropriate*
		[Address for correspondence]
		[Contact telephone number]

1. This notice affects the amount of rent you pay. Please read it carefully.

2. The landlord is proposing a new rent of **£** . . . .
per[week][month][year]*, in place of the existing one of £ . . . . per [week][month][year]*

* *delete as appropriate*

3. The first rent increase date after 11th February 2003 is . . . . (see note 10 over the page)

4. The starting date for the new rent will be . . . . (see notes 13 to 17 over the page)

5. Certain charges may be included and separately identified in your rent. (See note 11 over the page.) The amounts of the charges (if any) are:

Charges	Amount included and separately identified *(enter "nil" if appropriate)*	
	In the existing rent	In the proposed new rent
Council tax	£	£
Water charges	£	£
Fixed service charges	£	£

6. If you accept the proposed new rent, you should make arrangements to pay it. If you do not accept it, there are steps you should take before the starting date in paragraph 4 above. **Please see the notes over the page for what to do next.**

Signed: . . . . [Landlord(s)][Landlord's Agent]* (see note 12 over the page)

* *delete as appropriate*

Date:. . . . .

Please read these notes carefully.

Guidance notes for tenants
What you must do now

1. This notice proposes that you should pay a new rent from the date in paragraph 4 of the notice. **If you are in any doubt or need advice about any aspect of this notice, you should immediately either discuss it with your landlord or take it to a citizens' advice bureau, a housing advice centre, a law centre or a solicitor.**

2. If you accept the proposed new rent, please make arrangements to pay it. If you pay by standing order through your bank, you should inform them that the amount has changed. You should also notify your Housing Benefit office if you are claiming benefit. If you are worried that you might not be able to pay your rent, you should seek advice from a citizens' advice bureau or housing advice centre.

3. If you do **not** accept the proposed new rent, and do not wish to discuss it with your landlord, you can refer this notice to your local rent assessment committee. **You must do this before the starting date of the proposed new rent in paragraph 4 of the notice.** You should notify your landlord that you are doing so, otherwise he or she may assume that you have agreed to pay the proposed new rent.

4. To refer the notice to the local rent assessment committee, you must use the form *Application referring a notice proposing a new rent under an Assured Periodic Tenancy or Agricultural Occupancy to a Rent Assessment Committee.* You can obtain this from a rent assessment panel, housing advice centre or legal stationer (details can be found in the telephone directory).

5. The rent assessment committee will consider your application and decide what the maximum rent for your home should be. In setting a rent, the committee must decide what rent the landlord could reasonably expect for the property if it were let on the open market under a new tenancy on the same terms. The committee may therefore set a rent that is higher, lower or the same as the proposed new rent.

Guidance notes for landlords on how to complete the notice
6. You can complete this notice in ink or arrange for it to be printed.

7. This notice should be used when proposing a new rent under an **assured periodic**

tenancy (including an assured shorthold periodic tenancy) of premises situated in England. There is a different notice (Form No. 4C – *Landlord's or Licensor's Notice proposing a new rent or licence fee under an Assured Agricultural Occupancy of premises situated in England)* for proposing a new rent or licence fee for an assured agricultural occupancy of premises situated in England.

8. Do not use this notice if the tenancy agreement contains a term allowing rent increases, or there is some other basis such as a separate agreement with the tenant for raising the rent. Any provision you rely on needs to be binding on the tenant. Legal advice should be sought if there is any doubt on this score.

9. You need to use a different form to propose a rent increase for a statutory periodic tenancy (the first exception mentioned in note 16) if you are seeking to adjust rent solely because of a proposed change of terms under s.6(2) of the Housing Act 1988. Seek legal advice if you think this may apply to you. You can obtain the form headed *Notice proposing different terms for a Statutory Periodic Tenancy* from a rent assessment panel or a legal stationer.

10. Unless the tenancy is a new one, or one of the exceptions mentioned in note 16 applies, you must insert in paragraph 3 of the notice the first date after 11th February 2003, on which rent is proposed to be, or was, increased under this statutory notice procedure. That date determines the date that you can specify in paragraph 4 of the notice. See also note 15.

11. You should enter in each of the boxes in the second and third columns of the table in paragraph 5 either "nil" or the amount of the existing or proposed charge. You should only enter amounts for council tax and water charges where the tenant does not pay these charges directly. You should only enter fixed service charges which are payable by the tenant in accordance with a term or condition which specifies that these charges will be included in the rent for the tenancy. Only enter an amount for service charges where the tenant has agreed to pay a **fixed** sum. Do **not** include in the table any **variable** service charge, *i.e.* a service charge within the meaning of s.18 of the Landlord and Tenant Act 1985, where the whole or part of the sum payable by the tenant varies or may vary according to costs.

12. You or your agent (someone acting on your behalf) must sign and date this notice. If there are joint landlords, each landlord must sign unless one signs on behalf of the rest with their agreement. The signature does not have to be hand-written if, for instance, the form is being printed or if you wish to use a laser or autosignature.

When the proposed new rent can start
13. The date in paragraph 4 of the notice must comply with the three requirements of section 13(2) of the Housing Act 1988, as amended by the Regulatory Reform (Assured Periodic Tenancies) (Rent Increases) Order 2003.

14. The **first requirement,** which applies in **all** cases, is that a minimum period of notice must be given before the proposed new rent can take effect. That period is:

- one month for a tenancy which is monthly or for a lesser period, for instance weekly or fortnightly;

- six months for a yearly tenancy;

- in all other cases, a period equal to the length of the period of the tenancy - for example, three months in the case of a quarterly tenancy.

15. The **second requirement** applies in **most** cases (but see note 16 for two exceptions):

> (a) the starting date for the proposed new rent must not be earlier than 52 weeks after the date on which the rent was last increased using this statutory notice procedure or, if the tenancy is new, the date on which it started, **unless**

> (b) that would result in an increase date falling one week or more before the anniversary of the date in paragraph 3 of the notice, in which case the starting date must not be earlier than 53 weeks from the date on which the rent was last increased.

This allows rent increases to take effect on a fixed day each year where the period of a tenancy is less than one month. For example, the rent for a weekly tenancy could be increased on, say, the first Monday in April. Where the period of a tenancy is monthly, quarterly, six monthly or yearly, rent increases can take effect on a fixed date, for example, 1st April.

16. The two exceptions to the second requirement, which apply where a statutory tenancy has followed on from an earlier tenancy, are:

- where the tenancy was originally for a fixed term (for instance, 6 months), but continues on a periodic basis (for instance, monthly) after the term ends; and

- where the tenancy came into existence on the death of the previous tenant who had a regulated tenancy under the Rent Act 1977.

In these cases the landlord may propose a new rent at once. However, the first and third requirements referred to in notes 14 and 17 must still be observed.

17. The **third requirement,** which applies in **all** cases, is that the proposed new rent must start at the beginning of a period of the tenancy. For instance, if the tenancy is monthly, and started on the 20th of the month, rent will be payable on that day of the month, and a new rent must begin then, not on any other day of the month. If the tenancy is weekly, and started, for instance, on a Monday, the new rent must begin on a Monday.

3.34 Form 39

Application referring rent increase to a Rent Assessment Committee

---

FORM No. 5

Housing Act 1988, s.13(4)

Application referring a Notice proposing a new rent under an Assured Periodic Tenancy or Agricultural Occupancy to a Rent Assessment Committee

• Please write clearly in black ink • Please tick boxes where appropriate and cross out text marked with an asterisk (*) that does not apply. • This form should be used when your landlord has served notice on you proposing a new rent under an assured periodic tenancy, including an assured shorthold periodic tenancy	• This form may also be used to refer a notice proposing a new rent or licence fee for an assured periodic agricultural occupancy. In such a case references to "landlord"/"tenant" can be read as references to "licensor"/"licensee" etc. • This form must be completed and sent to your local rent assessment panel - with a copy of the notice served on you proposing the new rent - before the date it is proposed that the new rent will take effect.

1. Address of premises:

_____
_____
_____

2. Name(s) of landlord(s)/agent*:

_____
_____

Address of landlord(s)/agent*:

_____
_____
_____
_____

3. Details of premises:

    (a) What type of accommodation do you rent?
    Room (s)   Flat   Terraced House
    Semi-Detached House   Fully Detached House
    Other (*Please specify*)

    (b) If it is a flat or room(s) what floor(s) is it on?

       Ground   First   Second   Other   (*Please specify*)

(c) Give the number and type of rooms, *e.g.* living room, bathroom etc.

_____

_____

(d) Does the tenancy include any other facilities, *e.g.* garden, garage or other separate building or land?

      Yes   No

(e) If yes, please give details:

_____

_____

(f) Do you share any accommodation with

(i) the landlord?	Yes	No
(ii) another tenant or tenants?	Yes	No

(g) If yes to either of the above, please give details:

_____

_____

4. When did the present tenancy begin?

_____

5. (a) Did you pay a premium?

      Yes   No

- a premium is a payment which is additional to rent and is equivalent to more than two months rent. It may give you the right to assign the tenancy (pass it on to someone else) unless the tenancy agreement states or implies otherwise.

(b) If yes, please give details:

_____

_____

_____

6. Services

(a) Are any services provided under the tenancy (*e.g.* cleaning, lighting, heating, hot water or gardening)?

      Yes   No

(b) If yes, please give details:

_____

_____

(c) If yes, is a separate charge made for services, maintenance, repairs, landlord's costs of management or any other item?

Yes   No

(d) What charge is payable?	£	per
	(e.g. week, month, year)	

(e) Does the charge vary according to the relevant costs?

Yes   No

(f) If yes, please give details:

_____
_____
_____

7. (a) Is any furniture provided under the tenancy?

Yes   No

(b) If yes, please give details. Continue on a separate sheet if necessary or attach a copy of the inventory:

_____
_____
_____

8. Improvements
(a) Have you, or any former tenant(s) carried out improvements or replaced fixtures, fittings or furniture for which you or they were not responsible under the terms of the tenancy?

Yes   No

(b) If yes, please give details. Continue on a separate sheet if necessary:

_____
_____
_____

9. What repairs are the responsibility of:
(a) the landlord?

_____
_____
_____

(b) the tenant?

_____

_____

_____

10. (a) Is there a written tenancy agreement?

Yes   No

(b) If yes, please attach the tenancy agreement (with a note of any variations). It will be returned to you as soon as possible.

11. Do you have an assured agricultural occupancy?

Yes   No

12. (a) I/we* attach a copy of the notice proposing a new rent under the assured periodic tenancy and I/we* apply for it to be considered by the rent assessment committee.

Signed	*Date*
_____	_____
_____	

To be signed and dated by the tenant or his agent. If there are joint tenants each tenant or the agent must sign unless one signs on behalf of the rest with their agreement.

Please specify whether: tenant   joint tenants   tenant's agent

(b) Name and address of tenant(s) referring to the rent assessment committee.

Name(s) (Block Capitals)

_____

_____

_____

Address

_____

_____

_____

Telephone – Daytime

3.35 **Form 40**

<u>Application to a Rent Assessment Committee for a Determination of a rent under an assured shorthold tenancy</u>

FORM No. 6

Housing Act 1988 s.22(1) as amended by s.100 of the Housing Act 1996

Application to a Rent Assessment Committee for a determination of a rent under an Assured Shorthold Tenancy

- Please write clearly in black ink.
- Please tick boxes where appropriate and cross out text marked with an asterisk (*) that does not apply.
- This form should be used by a tenant with an assured shorthold tenancy which began (or for which a contract had been made) before February 28, 1997, to apply to the local rent assessment committee, during the fixed term of the original tenancy, to have the rent reduced.

- This form should also be used by a tenant with an assured shorthold tenancy which began on or after February 28, 1997 (unless a contract had been made before that date), to apply to the rent assessment committee within six months of the beginning of the original tenancy, to have the rent reduced.
- This form cannot be used in the cases specified at the end of this form.
- When you have completed the form please send it to your local rent assessment panel.

1. Address of premises:

_____

_____

_____

2. Name(s) of landlord(s)/agent*

_____

Address of landlord(s)/agent*

_____

_____

_____

3. Details of premises

    (a) What type of accommodation do you rent?

    Room (s)   Flat   Terraced House

    Semi-Detached House   Fully Detached House

    Other (*Please specify*)

    (b) If it is a flat or room(s) what floor(s) is it on?

    Ground   First   Second   Other   (*Please specify*)

(c) Give the number and type of rooms, *e.g.* living room, bathroom etc.

_____

(d) Does the tenancy include any other facilities, *e.g.* garden, garage or other separate building or land?

      Yes   No

(e) If yes, please give details:

_____
_____
_____

(f) Do you share any accommodation with:

(i) the landlord?	Yes	No
(ii) another tenant or tenants?	Yes	No

(g) If yes to either of the above, please give details:

_____
_____
_____

4.(a) What is the current rent?	£	per
	(e.g. week, month, year)	
(b) Does the rent include council tax?	Yes	No
(c) If yes, the amount that is included for council tax is:	£	per
	(e.g. week, month, year)	
(d) Does the rent include water charges?	Yes	No
(e) If yes, the amount that is included for water charges is:	£	per
	(e.g. week, month, year)	

5. (a) When did the present tenancy begin?

_____

  (b) When does the present tenancy end?

_____

(c) Does the tenancy replace an original tenancy?   Yes   No

If yes, when did the original tenancy begin

_____

6. (a) If the tenancy began before February 28, 1997, please confirm by ticking the box that you received a notice saying that the tenancy was to be an assured shorthold tenancy before

the agreement was entered into.

(b) Attach a copy of the notice, if available. It will be returned to you as soon as possible.

7. (a) Did you pay a premium?

         Yes   No
- a premium is a payment which is additional to rent and is equivalent to more than two months rent. It may give you the right to assign the tenancy (pass it on to someone else) unless the tenancy agreement states or implies otherwise.

(b) If yes, please give details:

_____
_____
_____

8. Services.

(a) Are any services provided under the tenancy (e.g. cleaning, lighting, heating, hot water or gardening)?

         Yes   No

(b) If yes, please give details:

_____
_____
_____

(c) Is a separate charge made for services, maintenance, repairs, landlord's costs of management or any other item?

         Yes   No

(d) If yes, what charge is payable?	£	per
	(e.g. week, month, year)	

(e) Does the charge vary according to the relevant costs?

         Yes   No

(f) If yes, please give details:

_____
_____
_____

9. (a) Is any furniture provided under the tenancy?

        Yes   No

(b) If yes, please give details. Continue on a separate sheet if necessary or provide a copy of the inventory.

_____
_____
_____

10. What repairs are the responsibility of:

(a) the landlord. Continue on a separate sheet if necessary:

_____
_____
_____

(b) the tenant. Continue on a separate sheet if necessary:

_____
_____
_____

11. (a) Give details (if known) of the other terms of the tenancy, *e.g.* whether the tenancy is assignable and whether a premium may be charged on an assignment. (Continue on a separate sheet if necessary).

_____
_____
_____

(b) Is there a written tenancy agreement?
        Yes   No

(c) If yes, please attach the tenancy agreement (with a note of any variations). It will be returned to you as soon as possible.

12.

(a) I/We* apply to the rent assessment committee to determine a rent for the above mentioned premises.

Signed	Date

To be signed and dated by the tenant or his agent. If there are joint tenants each tenant or the agent must sign unless one signs on behalf of the rest with their agreement.

Please specify whether: tenant   joint tenants   tenant's agent

      (b) Name and address of tenant(s) referring to the rent assessment committee.

Name(s) (*Block Capitals*)

_____

_____

_____

Address

_____

_____

_____

Telephone – Daytime

_____

Cases where this form should not be used
• An application cannot be made if –
      (a) the rent payable under the tenancy is a rent previously determined by a rent assessment committee; or
      (b) the tenancy is a replacement tenancy and more than six months have elapsed since the beginning of the original tenancy. A replacement tenancy is an assured shorthold tenancy that came into being on the ending of a tenancy which had been an assured shorthold of the same, or substantially the same, property and the landlord and tenant under each tenancy were the same at that time.
• The rent assessment committee cannot make a determination unless it considers –
      (a) that there is a sufficient number of similar properties in the locality let on assured tenancies (whether shorthold or not) for comparison; and
      (b) that the rent payable under the shorthold tenancy in question is significantly higher than the rent which the landlord might reasonably be expected to get in comparison with other rents for similar properties let on assured tenancies (whether shorthold or not) in the locality.

Form 41   **3.36**

Tenant's application to the Leasehold Valuation Tribunal of the liability to pay a service charge

---

APPLICATION TO THE LEASEHOLD VALUATION TRIBUNAL

Tenant's application for a determination of liability to pay a service charge (s.27A) Landlord and Tenant Act 1985

Property: The Garden Flat, Cecily Court, Bunbury, BN1 2PZ ("the property")

Determination Applied For:	The Applicant hereby applies for a determination as to the reasonableness of the items of expenditure listed in the schedule to this Application. The disputed items of expenditure relate to the 2000; 2001 and 2002 service charge years.
	The said items are challenged on the basis that the costs were unreasonably incurred, and/or were unreasonable in amount and/or that the standard of works/services to which the sums relate were not of a proper or reasonable standard.
Applicant:	Sebastian Melmoth, The Retreat, Bunbury, BN2 3PZ
Applicant's Representative:	Renters and Co, Solicitors, 2 The Cottages, Bunbury, BN3 4PZ.
Respondent's Name and Address:	Queensbury Holdings Ltd, whose nominated address for service under s.48 of the Landlord and Tenant Act 1987 is c/o Boxer, Blow and Co, Solicitors, 2 The Forte, Bunbury, BN4 5PZ.
Landlord's Name and Address (if different)	N/A
Reduction/waiver of fees:	The Applicant is not liable to pay any fee as he is in receipt of income-based jobseeker's allowance within the meaning of the Jobseekers Act 1995.
Recognised Tenant's Association:	The name and address of the secretary to the recognised tenant's association is:
	Ms. L. Bracknell The Salon Flat, Cecily Court, Bunbury, BN1 2PZ
Statement of Reasons/ Evidence:	The Applicant relies on the witness statement attached to this Application and the witness statement served by the Applicant in response to the landlord's application for a determination as to the reasonableness of the 2003

service charge expenditure ("the Landlord's Application").

Service Charge Demands: Copies of all service charge demands received from 2000 to 2003, inclusive, are attached hereto.

Service Charge Accounts: The Applicant attaches the service charge accounts for 2000, the hand-written copy of the 2001 accounts that were placed on the Notice Board in the communal hallway to the property. The Applicant has not received a copy of the 2002 accounts, or a hard copy of the 2001 accounts that remain affixed to the notice board.

Other parties liable to pay the service charge: The Applicant believes that in addition to the property, there are three other dwellings in respect of which the same or substantially the same service charge is payable. Other than Ms. Bracknell (whose details are given herein above) the Applicant does not know the names and/or addresses of the other leaseholders who are liable by way of service charge for any part of the expenditure which is included in the service charge.

Relevant Leases: A specimen occupational long lease and the under lease held by Queensbury Management Limited ("Queensbury") are attached to the Applicant's witness statement in response to the Landlord's Application.

Application for an order under section 20C The Applicant also applies for an order under s.20C of the Landlord and Tenant Act 1985 debarring the landlord and/or the Management Company from including the costs of these proceedings as additional service charges.

This application is dated February 14, 2003

RONALD RODD

Signed: ROBBIE ROSS

Renters and Co, 2 The Cottages, Bunbury, BN3 4PZ, Solicitors to the Applicant

....

I believe that the facts stated in this application are true.

Signed: SEBASTIAN MELMOTH

Form 42   3.37

Particulars of Claim (debt action)

IN THE BOLSWITCH COUNTY COURT   **Claim No. B0145000**

B E T W E E N

CARL CRENOLINE

and   **Claimant**

SARAH BUZZCOCK

Defendant

PARTICULARS OF CLAIM

---

1. The Claimant is and has been, at all material times, the freehold owner of the premises situate at and known as 18 Baldry Mews, Bolswitch, Greater Cirencester ("the premises").

2. By an agreement in writing dated August 24, 1998 between the Claimant and the Defendant ("the agreement"), the Claimant let to the Defendant, the premises, on a weekly tenancy commencing August 29, 1998, at the rent of £120 per week ("the rent"), payable in advance each Monday.

3. In breach of the agreement, between about March 7, 2001 and about August 15, 2001, inclusive, the Defendant has failed and/or refused to pay any part of the rent. In the premises, the Defendant is indebted to the Claimant in the sum of £2760.

PARTICULARS OF INDEBTEDNESS

£120 × 23 weeks = £2740.

4. Further, the Claimant claims interest pursuant to s.69 of the County Courts Act 1984, at the rate of 8 per cent, upon the said sum, amounting to £53 at the date hereof and continuing until judgment or sooner payment at the daily rate of £0.58.

AND the Claimant claims

1) £2740;

2) interest,

Ann DaLucia

Dated the 30th day of August 2001.

Signed............................

Jackson & Nelson
23 Bolswitch Road
Bolswitch
Cirencester
Solicitors for the Claimant

STATEMENT OF TRUTH

- (I believe) (The Claimant believes) that the facts stated in these Particulars of Claim are true.

- I am duly authorised by the Claimant to sign this statement.

Full name ....

Name of Claimant's solicitor ....

Signed.................................... Position or office held ....
Date

Form 43   **3.38**

Particulars of Claim (recovery of overpayment)

IN THE BOLSWITCH COUNTY COURT   **Claim No. B0145001**

B E T W E E N

GRAHAM CRASS

and   **Claimant**

THE GRANITE PROPERTY CORPORATION PLC

Defendant

PARTICULARS OF CLAIM

1. At all material times, the Defendant has been the freehold owner of the premises situate at and known as 13B Scrag End, Bolswitch, Greater Cirencester ("the premises") and the Claimant has been the protected tenant of the Defendant in the premises.

2. By an agreement in writing dated January 14, 1988, the Defendant let to the Claimant, the premises, on a weekly tenancy at the rent of £56 per week, payable each Monday in advance. The provisions of the Rent Act 1977 have, at all material times, applied to the tenancy.

3. On March 31, 1995, the Rent Officer for the Bolswitch area registered a new fair rent for the premises of £46 per week.

4. The Claimant never received any notification of the said registration, and has continued to pay to the Defendant £56 per week by way of rent.

5. In the premises, the Claimant is entitled to recover the overpayments he has made to the Defendant.[22]

PARTICULARS OF OVERPAYMENT

£10 × 335 weeks = £3350

6. Further, the Claimant claims interest, pursuant to s.69 of the County Courts Act 1984, upon the said sum, at such rate and for such periods as the court thinks just.

AND the Claimant claims

1) £3350

2) interest

[CONCLUDE AS IN FORM 42]

[22] The fact that part of the claim is statute barred under the Rent Act and at common law does not prevent the tenant from pleading an entitlement to recover all sums overpaid. Limitation is a defence for the landlord to raise if he chooses to do so.

Form 44   3.39

Particulars of Claim (recovery of service charge)

IN THE BOLSWITCH COUNTY COURT   **Claim No. B01430000**

B E T W E E N

MICHAEL BROWN

and   **Claimant**

KEITH ANDERSON

Defendant

PARTICULARS OF CLAIM

---

1. The Claimant is, and has been at all material times, the freehold owner of premises known as and situate at 34 Romney Road, Bolswitch, Cirencester ("the property").

2. By a lease dated June 23, 1989, ("the lease") the Claimant demised to the Defendant the premises situate at and known as Flat 4, in the property ("the flat"), for a term of 67 years from June 24, 1989, at an annual rent of £48, payable quarterly in advance, in equal instalments on the usual quarter days.

3. By clause 4(1) of the lease, the Defendant convenanted to pay to the Claimant, by way of service charge, quarterly in arrears, on the same quarter days, one quarter of the sums expended by the Claimant in respect of the cleaning and general maintenance of the common parts of the property, together with one quarter of the sums expended by the Claimant complying with his obligations under clauses 5(1) and 5(2) of the lease.

4. By clause 5(1) of the lease, the Claimant covenanted to arrange and pay any premium in respect of building insurance for the property and to pay the quarterly charges for electricity, gas and water to the common parts thereof.

5. By clause 5(2) of the lease, the Claimant covenanted to keep the structure and exterior and common parts of the property in good repair and decorative order.

6. The Defendant has failed to pay the following charges which have been demanded in accordance with the terms of clause 5(1) of the lease.

PARTICULARS

25.3.98	£	45
24.6.98	£	698
29.9.98	£	451
25.12.98	£	97
25.3.99	£	386
TOTAL	£	1677

7. On June 14, 1998, the Claimant notified the Defendant in accordance with s.20 of the Landlord and Tenant Act 1985, that works were required to be undertaken to the roof of the property ("the works") to the cost of which the Defendant would be required to contribute in the sum of approximately £7,484.16. Three estimates from independent contractors were attached to the notice and the Defendant was informed that his comments should be received by July 16, 1998.

8. No comments were received from the Defendant and the works were carried out.

9. On December 25, 1998, the Claimant demanded payment of the Defendant's contribution to the cost of the said in the sum of £7490.87 ("the sum").

10. In breach of the terms of the lease, the Defendant has failed and/or refused to pay any, or any part of the sum to the Claimant.

11. In the premises, the Defendant is indebted to the Claimant in the sum of £9167.87.

12. Further, the Claimant claims interest on the sum of £1677, pursuant to s.69 of the County Courts Act 1984. from April 1, 1999 at the rate of 8 per cent, amounting to £324.56 at the date hereof and continuing at the daily rate of £0.37 until judgment or sooner payment.

13. Further, the Claimant claims interest on the sum of £7490.87, pursuant to s.69 of the County Courts Act 1984 from April 1, 1999 at the rate of 8 per cent, amounting to £1597.51 at the date hereof and continuing at the daily rate of £1.64 until judgment or sooner payment.

AND the Claimant claims

1) £1677

2) £7490.87

3) interest, under para.12 amounting to £324.56 at the date of the claim and continuing at the daily rate of £0.37 until judgment or sooner payment

4) interest, under para.13 amounting to £1597.51 at the date of the claim and continuing at the daily rate of £1.64 until judgment or sooner payment.

[CONCLUDE AS IN FORM 42]

Form 45   3.40

Defence (section 48 LTA 1987)

IN THE BOLSWITCH COUNTY COURT   **Claim No. B0145000**

B E T W E E N

CARL CRENOLINE

and   **Claimant**

SARAH BUZZCOCK

Defendant

DEFENCE

---

1.   Paragraphs 1 and 2 of the Particulars of Claim herein are admitted.

2.   Save that it is admitted that the Defendant has not paid certain amounts to the Claimant, para.3 is denied. Without prejudice to the generality of the foregoing, it is denied that the Defendant is indebted to the Claimant in the sum alleged or any sum. The Claimant has failed to give any notice to the Defendant of his address for the service of notices, including notices in proceedings, pursuant to s.48 of the Landlord and Tenant Act 1987 and, in the premises, no rent is due from the Defendant.

Cathy Lonia

Dated the 15th day of September 2001

Signed ....

Belson & Broome
23 The Avenue
Bolswitch
Cirencester
Solicitors for the Defendant

STATEMENT OF TRUTH

- (I believe) (The Defendant believes) that the facts stated in this Defence are true.

- I am duly authorised by the Defendant to sign this statement.

Full name ....

Name of Defendant's solicitor ....

Signed... Position or office held ....

Date

Form 46   3.41

Defence and Counterclaim (declaration as to service charges)[23]

IN THE BOLSWITCH COUNTY COURT

CLAIM No. B0143000

B E T W E E N

MICHAEL BROWN

and   **Claimant/Part 20 Defendant**

KEITH ANDERSON

Defendant/Part 20 Claimant

DEFENCE AND COUNTERCLAIM

DEFENCE

1. Paragraphs 1–5 inclusive of the Particulars of Claim herein are admitted.

2. Save that it is admitted that the sums pleaded under para.6 of the Particulars of Claim herein have not been paid, para.6 is denied, and it is denied that the Defendant Part 20 Claimant (the "Defendant") is indebted to the Claimant Part 20 Defendant ("the Claimant") in the sum of £1677 or at all.

3. Without prejudice to the generality of the foregoing, the Defendant avers as follows.

4. On the following dates, the Defendant paid the following sums to the Claimant:

25.3.93	£ 358
24.6.93	£ 228
29.9.93	£ 76
25.12.93	£ 277
25.3.94	£ 66

5. The sums claimed by the Claimant under para.6, constitute amounts which the Defendant is not liable to pay under the terms of the lease in that the sums were not reasonably incurred.

PARTICULARS

  a) The sums all relate to cleaning and maintenance charges for the common parts of the property. The Claimant employed his mother to carry out such works, who charged for her services at the extortionate rate of £90 per hour.

  b) The sums paid by the Defendant to the Claimant pleaded under para.4 hereinabove, included payment for such services at the rate of £5 per hour.

6. As to paras 7 and 8 of the Particulars of Claim herein, it is denied that any such notice was received by the Defendant at any time, for which reason no comments as to any such works or estimates were made by the Defendant. In the premises, it is denied that the requirements of s.20 of the Landlord and Tenant Act 1985 have been complied with by the Claimant.

7. Save that no admissions are made as to the works carried out as alleged under para.8. Save as aforesaid, paras 7 and 8 are denied.

8. Save as follows paras 9 and 10 are denied, and it is denied that the Defendant is liable to the Claimant in the sum claimed or any sum. It is admitted that on December 25, 1993, the Claimant demanded payment from the Defendant in the sum of £7490.87. It is further admitted that the Defendant has refused to pay such sum in full.

9. It is denied that the Defendant has refused to pay any sum to the Claimant. Under cover of a letter dated January 12, 1994, the Defendant tendered to the Claimant a cheque in the sum of £250, which cheque was returned to the Defendant by the Claimant on January 13, 1994.

10. Further or alternatively, it is denied that such works as were carried out, which are not admitted, were of a reasonable standard.

PARTICULARS

  a) Since about December 27, 1993, following the completion of works carried out by the Claimant the Defendant's flat, which is situate on the top floor of the property, has suffered from severe ingress of water in all rooms through the roof.

  b) The Defendant's flat, prior to the said date, had at no time during the currency of the Defendant's tenancy, suffered from any water ingress whatever.

11. In the premises, the Defendant denies that he is liable to the Claimant as claimed or at all, and avers that his maximum liability to the Claimant if any, which is denied, in respect of such works, which are not admitted, is £250, being one quarter of the maximum recoverable from those tenants liable to contribute to the cost of such works, which are not admitted, absent compliance with s.20 of the said Act.[24]

12. Paragraph 11 of the Particulars of Claim is denied.

COUNTERCLAIM

13. Paragraphs 1, 5, 6, 7, 8, and 10 above are repeated.

AND the Defendant counterclaims

1) A declaration that the charges claimed in para.6 of the Particulars of Claim herein were not reasonably incurred and are irrecoverable from the Defendant;

2) A declaration that the Claimant has failed to comply with the requirements of s.20 of the Landlord and Tenant Act 1985 as to matters pleaded under paras 7 to 10 inclusive of the Particulars of Claim herein and that the charge claimed in relation thereto is irrecoverable from the Defendant in excess of £500;

3) A declaration that, in any event, the charges pleaded under paras 7 to 10 inclusive of the Particulars of Claim are irrecoverable from the Defendant by reason of the works in relation to which the said charges are claimed not being works of a reasonable standard.

Dated the 8th day of September 2001

Signed ....
Faber Holmes Solicitors
Bonart Gardens
Polaris
nr Manchester
Solicitors for the Defendant

STATEMENT OF TRUTH

- (I believe) (The Defendant believes) that the facts stated in this Defence and Counterclaim are true.

- I am duly authorised by the Defendant to sign this statement.

Full name ....

Name of Defendant's solicitor ....

Signed................................... Position or office held ....
Date

---

[23] It is perfectly proper to counterclaim for such a declaration, albeit that this falls within the jurisdiction of one leasehold valuation tribunal. The court would order that it be transferred to the tribunal for determination by them, and that the matter be adjourned pending that determination.
[24] For the appropriate amounts from October 31, 2003, see para.3.26 and fn.14 above.

3.42   **Form 47**

Defence and Counterclaim (deductions/set off)

[HEADING AS IN FORM 46]

DEFENCE AND COUNTERCLAIM

DEFENCE

1. Paragraphs 1 and 2 of the Particulars of Claim herein are admitted.

2. Save that it is admitted that the Defendant/Part 20 Claimant ("the Defendant") is in arrear with her rent, para. 3 is denied. Without prejudice to the generality of the foregoing, the Defendant avers that she was entitled to deduct the following sum:

    on about April 24, 1994, the Defendant paid to one Brian Clash, the superior landlord of the Claimant/Part 20 Defendant ("the Claimant") the sum of £1768, having been required to do so by the said Clash in order to avoid the said Clash levying distress against the premises on account of arrears of rent due to him from the ("the Claimant").

3. Further, or alternatively, the Defendant is entitled to set off the sums counter-claimed herein in diminution or extinction of any sums found to be due to the Claimant.

COUNTERCLAIM

4. Paragraphs 1 to 3 of the Defence inclusive are repeated.

5. Section 11 of the Landlord and Tenant Act 1985 applies to the tenancy.

6. By clause 3(4) of the said agreement, the Claimant covenanted with the Defendant to keep in repair the structure and exterior of the premises and to keep in repair and proper working order the installations therein for the supply of water, gas and electricity, and for sanitation, space heating and heating water, and such installations as directly or indirectly serve the premises ("the covenant").

7. Further or alternatively, the covenant was an implied term of the agreement.

8. Further, or alternatively, by s.4 of the Defective Premises Act 1972, the Claimant owed to the Defendant and to any other person who may be affected by any defect in the dwelling, a duty to take care to prevent any such defect causing personal injury to, or damage to the property of, any such person.

9. The Claimant is in breach of the express and/or implied term, pleaded under paras 6 and 7, and/or in breach of his said duty of care, pleaded under para.8 and/or has been negligent:

PARTICULARS

a) Since the commencement of the tenancy the central heating and hot water supply to the premises have failed to operate.

b) Since the commencement of the tenancy, all three bedrooms have been severely affected by penetrating dampness and have been unusuable.

c) The Defendant further relies on the defects set out in the report of Messrs Swampthing and Co, dated January 14, 2001 which is annexed hereto at Sch.1.

10. At all materal times, the Claimant has had notice of the said defects.

PARTICULARS OF NOTICE

a) the Defendant informed the Claimant of the defects by letters dated August 26, 1998, September 22, 1998, October 17, 1998;

b) the Defendant has telephoned the Claimant to report the defects on occasions too numerous to particularise;

c) the Defendant's solicitors have reported the defects to the Claimants by letters dated July 21, 1999, September 23, 1999, November 1, 1999, February 15, 2000, June 24, 2000 and January 21, 2001, under cover of the last of which the said report of Messrs Swampthing & Co was sent to the Claimant.

11. By reason of the matter complained of the Defendant has suffered distress, inconvenience, loss and damage.

PARTICULARS OF DISTRESS AND INCONVENIENCE

a) The property is and has been dangerous and unpleasant to live in. The Defendant spends as little time there as she can and is too embarrassed to invite guests home with her.

b) The Defendant has suffered stress in the result of the matters particularised hereinabove.

PARTICULARS OF SPECIAL DAMAGE

a) The Defendant's carpets, curtains, furniture and clothing have been damaged by water. A full schedule of all such losses will be provided on disclosure herein.

b) The value of the tenancy to the Defendant has been diminished.

c) Because of the ingress of water from the roof and dampness, the dwelling has been damp and unsightly.

12. Further, the Defendant claims interest on any sums found to be due to her, pursuant to s.69 of the County Courts Act 1984, at such rate and for such periods as the Court deems just.

AND the Defendant counterclaims

1) an order for specific performance of the Claimant's obligations pursuant to s.17 of the Landlord and Tenant Act 1985;

2) further, or alternatively, an injunction compelling the Claimant to comply with his obligations;

3) damages in excess of £5000;

4) interest.

[CONCLUDE AS IN FORM 46]

PART III: CHECKLIST   **3.43**

1. Landlords should make sure that they have given notice under s.48 of the Landlord and Tenant Act 1987 before they commence proceedings based upon a failure by the tenant to pay rent.

2. Landlords must also ensure that, where works are to be carried out to premises, the cost of which they will seek to recoup by way of service charge, and where such works will cost in excess of the prescribed amount (see above) that the provisions of s.20 of the 1987 Act have been complied with.

3. Where it is sought to recover service charge, landlords must also ascertain that provision has been made in the lease for recovery of the items in question, particularly items such as management fees.

Chapter 4

Legal Remedies for Anti-Social Behaviour

PART I: INTRODUCTION

This chapter considers the remedies available to local authorities and registered social **4.01** landlords ("RSL"s) in respect of anti-social behaviour, whether by their tenants or by anyone else. These remedies are additional to that of possession proceedings (which, in the context of nuisance and introductory tenancy proceedings, are considered in Chapter 6) and may generally be sought either instead of or in combination with a possession action.

Injunctions at common law

Landlords may seek to control anti-social behaviour by tenants, members of their households **4.02** and their visitors by way of injunction, so long as they have a cause of action. Generally, in relation to tenants at least, this will not be a problem as most tenancy agreements contain covenants against nuisance on the part of both the tenant and of members of his or her household and visitors. Accordingly, such behaviour will normally amount to a breach of the tenancy agreement and the cause of action will be in contract.

If the landlord's property is being damaged, moreover, as a result of such behaviour, the landlord may have a cause of action in nuisance or trespass.

In practical terms, most injunction proceedings brought by social landlords will not rely on common law alone (or at all), but will be brought under one or more of the different statutory causes of action which now exist, and which are summarised below.

Housing Act 1996

Statutory Remedies

The Housing Act 1996, s.152, introduced a power available to local authorities to seek **4.03** injunctions in order to combat anti-social behaviour, where there has been violence or the threat of violence.

The section itself provides a statutory cause of action: there is no need to rely on other rights/powers such as the common law or s.222 of the Local Government Act 1972 (see below). Only a local authority, however, can apply for an injunction using s.152, though it will not be liable in nuisance or negligence for failing/refusing to bring proceedings under this section[1] (*Hussein v Lancaster City Council* (1999) 31 H.L.R. 164, CA; *Mowan Wandsworth LBC* [2001] 33 H.L.R. 56).

---

[1] Or for failing to bring possession proceedings.

Certain statutory criteria must be fulfilled for the court to have power to grant a s.152 injunction, namely that:

> the perpetrator has used or threatened violence against a person residing in, visiting or otherwise engaging in lawful activity in any local authority dwelling house held under a secure or introductory tenancy, or other accommodation provided by the authority in discharging its duty towards the homeless, or in the locality of such premises (s.152(3)(a)); and

> there is a significant risk of harm to that or any other such person if the injunction is not granted (s.152(3)(b)).

Accordingly, there must be cogent evidence of violence, or threats of violence, in order to obtain a s.152 injunction. Less serious nuisance, which does not involve such behaviour (*e.g.* noise nuisance, rubbish, pets) will not be sufficient.

There must be a link between the person(s) whom the injunction is intended to protect and the residential premises (*Enfield LBC v B (a minor)*, [2000] 1 W.L.R. 2259, CA; *Nottingham City Council v Thames* [2002] EWCA Civ 1098; [2003] H.L.R. 14; *Manchester CC v Lee* [2003] EWCA Civ 1256). There need not, however, be a geographical nexus between the area where the conduct occurred and the relevant residential premises: see *Manchester City Council v Ali* [2003] H.L.R. 11).

"Harm", for the purposes of s.152(3)(b), means ill-treatment, or the impairment of the physical or mental health of a person of 18 or above, or the ill-treatment (including sexual abuse and non physical forms of ill-treatment), or impairment of the physical or mental health or development of a child (s.158).

Section 152(1) sets out the terms of the injunction that may be granted. The person against whom it has been sought may be prohibited from:

> engaging or threatening to engage in conduct causing or likely to cause a nuisance (including causing damage to property) and annoyance to a person residing in, visiting or otherwise engaging in lawful activity in any dwelling houses held under secure or introductory tenancies from the authority (or other accommodation provided by the authority in discharging their duty towards the homeless or in the locality of such premises);

> using or threatening to use a dwelling house let under a secure or introductory tenancy from the authority, or any other accommodation provided by the authority under the homelessness provisions, for immoral or illegal purposes. Here the injunction may relate to particular acts or conduct or may be in more general terms;

> entering such premises or being found in the locality of such premises. The injunction may relate to particular premises or to a particular locality. In other words, this provision is sufficiently broad to encompass an "exclusion zone". But see *Manchester CC v Lee* (above) as to the permissable terms of an injunction.

An exclusion zone may be delineated in a number of ways – by prohibiting the person from entering an area the boundaries of which have been marked on a map or plan appended to the order, by prohibiting the person from coming within a specific distance of particular premises, or by any other means, so long as it is clear to the person against whom it is made precisely what is prohibited. The use of a marked map, however, is probably the clearest way of communicating the extent of the zone to the defendant.

It is permissible for an order simply to prohibit specified conduct within the "locality" of particular premises. The use of such a term does not render the injunction unenforceable for uncertainty. It is a matter for the judge to decide whether the location in which the conduct complained of took place is within the *locality* for the purposes of the order (see *Manchester City Council v Lawler* (1999) 31 H.L.R. 119, CA).

The injunction may be granted for a specific period or on the basis that it will continue to run unless and until it is varied or discharged (s.152(4)). Either the local authority or the defendant may apply to the court to discharge it (s.152(5)).

Applications

Applications for s.152 injunctions are governed by CPR Sch.2, CCR Ord. 49.6(B) and should **4.04** be made to the county court for the district where the defendant resides, or where the behaviour which led to the seeking of the injunction occurred. The application should be made in the appropriate prescribed form (Form N16A[2]), and must state the terms of the injunction applied for and be supported by a witness statement or affidavit in which the grounds of the application are set out. Witness statements are the usual means of providing the appropriate evidence. Use of affidavits is rare and generally unnecessary. It is also likely to carry costs penalties (see above, General Introduction, para.K).

The application, together with a copy of the witness statement, must be served personally on the Defendant not less than two days before the date on which the application will be heard. If an application is made without notice (see below), the witness statement must state why notice has not been given to the Defendant, and, if the court grants an injunction, the application and witness statement, together with a copy of the injunction, must be served on the Defendant personally and without delay.

Applications without notice

In particularly serious cases it will be usual for the Authority to seek the injunction by **4.05** making an application without giving notice to the perpetrator. There is provision for this form of application under s.152(7) of the Housing Act 1996. The court has to decide whether it is "just and convenient" to grant an order without notice having been given. If the order is made the respondent must be given the opportunity to make representations "as soon as just and convenient".

A Local Authority will not be required to give an undertaking in damages where it is acting in a law enforcement capacity, however it may do so if there are special circumstances to justify such an order (*Coventry CC v Finney*, [1996] T.L.R. 267).

Undertakings

Instead of making an injunction, the court may accept an undertaking from the respondent **4.06** as to his future behaviour. A breach of undertaking can be enforced in the same way as a breach of an injunction, by way of proceedings for contempt of court (*Tower Hamlets LBC v Long* (1998) 32 H.L.R. 219, CA and *Nottingham CC v Cutts* (2000) JHL D57, CA). It must be borne in mind, however, that a power of arrest cannot be attached to an undertaking.

[2] See below para.4.30.

Power of arrest

4.07 A power of arrest can only be granted by the court where there is statutory authority to do so. By s.152(6), a power of arrest may be attached to one or more of the prohibitions contained in a s.152 injunction.

Section 153 of the Housing Act 1996 makes provision for the attachment of a power of arrest to an injunction which the court proposes to grant to restrain a breach of the terms of a tenancy agreement, where the conduct constituting the breach is the tenant's own anti-social behaviour (as defined) and/or illegal or immoral user of the premises, or his allowing a member of his household, a visitor or a sub-tenant or lodger to behave anti-socially or to perpetrate illegal or immoral user (s.153(1) and (5)). The conduct in question is defined (s.153(5)) in similar terms to that set out in s.152(1) (see above, para.4.03).

It is important to remember that s.153 provides authority only for the attachment of a power of arrest to an injunction, it does not provide the statutory authority for the grant of an injunction. The power to grant the injunction arises from the covenants in the tenancy agreement itself. This has the effect that where a possession order is made, terminating the tenancy, the court has no power to grant an injunction to enforce the former covenants, nor to attach a power of arrest under s.153 (see *Medina Housing Association v Case* [2002] EWCA Civ 2001; [2003] 1 All E.R. 1084).

The s.153 power is available to a wider range of claimants than those under s.152, namely, a local housing authority; a housing action trust; a registered social landlord or a charitable housing trust (s.153(2)) acting in its capacity as landlord of the premises subject to the tenancy in question. The tenancy itself must be secure, introductory or assured (including assured shorthold), or relate to other accommodation provided to the statutorily homeless (s.153(4)).

The court must be satisfied, before a power of arrest may be attached to an order, that violence or threats of violence have been used and that there is a significant risk of harm if the power of arrest is not attached to one or more provisions of the injunction immediately (s.153(6)).

In earlier cases, not related to the Housing Act 1996 powers, the courts have held that a power of arrest should not routinely be attached to an injunction (*Lewis v Lewis* [1978] Fam 60, CA), and that it would be unlikely that a court would grant a power of arrest if the violence or threats of violence occurred some time before the application (*Horner v Horner* [1982] Fam 90, CA). It is suggested that the nature of the statutory preconditions under these sections, however, is such that if they are made out, a power of arrest is likely to be granted, although the staleness of the allegations is still liable to be an important influence on the court's decision.

If a power of arrest is attached to an injunction, the provisions of the injunction to which the power is attached must be set out in a separate clause of the injunction and the conduct described in the provision must be conduct of the type referred to in ss.152(1) or 153(5) (set out above: see CPR Sch.2, CCR Ord. 49.6B(6)(a)).

Power of arrest – without notice applications

4.08 A power of arrest may be sought in an application where notice has not been given. If the court is inclined to make such an order, however, it must have regard to all the circumstances and in particular whether the applicant will be deterred or prevented from seeking the order if the power is not exercised immediately (for example as a result of witness intimidation).

Other factors include whether the perpetrator is aware of the proceedings but is evading service, and whether any delay will seriously prejudice residents and visitors in the locality of the premises in question (s.154(1)). If a power of arrest is attached without notice the respondent must be given the opportunity to make representations as soon as is just and convenient (s.154(2)).

Effect of power of arrest

The applicant is required to notify the police of any provisions of an injunction to which a power of arrest has been attached (CPR Sch.2, CCR Ord. 49.6B(6)(b)). The existence of such a power entitles a police officer to arrest without warrant any person whom he has reasonable cause to suspect is in breach of the injunction or otherwise in contempt of court (s.155(1)). If an arrest is effected, the applicant for the injunction must be informed and the perpetrator must be brought before the court within 24 hours of his arrest (s.155(1) and (2)(a)). **4.09**

Sections 155 and 156 contain powers enabling the court to remand the defendant in custody pending a hearing (and for reports). In addition, CPR Sch.2, CCR Ord. 49.6B(8) permits the Judge to adjourn the proceedings to a date within 14 days of the day of the arrest.

Breach of the injunction

A breach of injunction is punishable as a contempt of court, enabling the court to commit the defendant to prison for up to two years and/or impose a fine and/or sequester his assets. Defendants who are aged between 18 and 21 will be committed to a young offenders institute rather than prison (s.9 of the Criminal Justice Act 1982 as amended). Those under 18 years old cannot be committed to custody. For more information about remedies in the event of a breach of an injunction and committal proceedings, see Chapter 5 (paras 5.16–5.18). **4.10**

Injunction/power of arrest against minors

It has been doubted since *Wookey v Wookey* [1991] Fam 121, CA, whether it would generally be appropriate to make an injunction against a minor. The issue arose in the *Enfield* case (above). In that case, the Court of Appeal, while declining to decide the point, doubted that minors were excluded from the jurisdiction of the court under s.152 of the 1996 Act. **4.11**

In *Re H* [2002] 1 FLR 641, CA, which concerned an injunction granted under the Family Law Act 1996, the Court of Appeal confirmed that there was no jurisdictional impediment to the court attaching a power of arrest to an injunction it granted (under that Act) on account of the minority of the person against whom the injunction was made. The reasoning of the Court of Appeal in that case would tend to suggest a similar result in relation to injunctions granted under s.152 (or indeed s.153, if the tenant is a minor).

Anti-Social Behaviour Bill

Clause 13 of this Bill, which is still before Parliament at the time of writing but is expected to receive royal assent in mid-November 2003 and come into force in February 2004, will repeal ss.152 and 153 of the Housing Act 1996, and replace them with a s.153A–153E, by virtue of which a "relevant landlord" (a local authority, registered social landlord or housing action trust) nay apply for an injunction in relation to conduct which is capable of causing nuisance **4.12** or annoyance to any person and which directly or indirectly relates to or affects the housing management functions of a relevant landlord.

4.13 As the Bill is currently drafted, for an injunction to be granted, the conduct must be capable of causing nuisance or annoyance to a person: with a right to occupy housing accommodation owned by the relevant landlord or in the locality of such accommodation; engaged in a lawful activity in the locality of such accommodation; or employed by the relevant landlord wholly or partly in connection with the landlord's housing management functions.

4.14 Injunctions may also be available against the immoral or illegal use of premises owned or managed by a relevant landlord.

4.15 An exclusion zone may be included in an injunction where the conduct in question consisted of or included violence or threats of violence and there is a significant risk of harm to a person mentioned above, in para.4.13. In such a case, a power of arrest may be attached to any provision of the injunction.

Local Government Act 1972

Section 222

4.16 Section 222 confers a general power on local authorities to institute legal proceedings in their own name where they "consider it expedient for the promotion or protection of the interests of the inhabitants of their area". Given that proceedings may be brought in the name of the authority; it is not necessary to join individual local residents as plaintiffs.

The "inhabitants of their area" means all the inhabitants and not simply a section of them: *Stoke-on-Trent CC v B & Q (Retail) Ltd* [1984] Ch.1. *per* Lawton L.J. It is, however, in everybody's interest particularly in urban areas that an authority should do what it can to maintain an ambience of a law abiding community, and what should be done to that end is for the authority to decide. Section 222 is not merely applicable to the restraining of public nuisances: *Stoke-on-Trent* (above).

In using the power to restrain anti-social behaviour, it is necessary to establish a cause of action, usually private nuisance, trespass to land and/or goods etc. The conduct complained of need not be criminal, nor must criminal proceedings have been brought before recourse to the civil courts is permissible: *City of London Corporation v Bovis Construction Ltd* (1988) 86 L.G.R. 660. Accordingly, an injunction may be sought to restrain such conduct, whether without or on notice, whether or not the criminal courts are also involved.

This power, while now less frequently used than the Housing Act powers considered above, will still be useful, particularly where, for example, the anti-social behaviour does not take place in the locality of an authority's housing stock or there is no nexus between the victim of that behaviour and that stock (see *Nottingham CC v Zain (a minor)* [2001] EWCA Civ 1248; [2003] H.L.R. 16; and the *Enfield, Nottingham* and *Manchester* cases above, para.4.03).

Section 111

4.17 Under s.111 of the Local Government Act 1972 a local authority has the power to do "anything. ... which is calculated to facilitate, or is conducive or incidental to the discharge of their functions". It is arguable that this power can be used by an authority to assist victims of nuisance by taking nuisance proceedings on their behalf and that this would facilitate the general power to manage housing properties under s.21 of the Housing Act 1985.

Crime and Disorder Act 1998

Anti-Social Behaviour Orders

Section 1 of the Crime and Disorder Act 1998 introduces the Anti-Social Behaviour Order **4.18** (ASBO), a community-based order akin to an injunction. The provisions relating to ABSOs have now been extensively revised and amended by the Police Reform Act 2002 (ss.61–66). At the time of writing, further amendments have been proposed in the current Anti-Social Behaviour Bill, Clauses 36–38.

ASBOs are available against anyone aged ten or over (1998 Act s.1(1)), in relation to anti-social acts committed on or after the commencement date (April 1, 1999), although evidence of previous anti-social behaviour is permissible in support of an application (Anti-Social Behaviour Orders – Home Office Guidance).

The application for an order should be made within six months of the most recent conduct complained of (s.127 of the Magistrates' Court Act 1980). The court can make an order if the following conditions are satisfied:

The perpetrator has acted in an anti social manner, *i.e.* a manner that caused or was likely to cause harassment alarm or distress

The alarm or distress must be caused to one or more persons who are not members of the same household as the person against the order is made

The order is necessary to "relevant persons" from further anti social acts or conduct. The definition of "relevant persons" depends on the identity of the body seeking the ASBO (see further below).

The court must disregard any act of the defendant which he shows was reasonable in the circumstances (s.1(5)).

Relevant authorities

The ASBO can be applied for by any "relevant authority", namely: **4.19**

(a) the council for a local government area,

(b) the chief officer of police of any police force maintained for a police area,

(c) the chief constable of the British Transport Police Force or

(d) any person registered under s.1 of the Housing Act 1996 as a social landlord who provides or manages any houses or hostel in a local government area ((1998 Act s.1(1A)). Under the 1998 Act as originally enacted, the only relevant authorities were local authorities and chief officers of police. The 2002 Act has extended the potential range of applicants so as now to include the British Transport Police and registered social landlords.

The Secretary of State can add to the list of relevant authorities, by order (1998 Act s.1A, inserted by 2002 Act s.62).

Relevant Persons

4.20 The nature of the "relevant authority" determines the extent of its powers to seek an ASBO by differentiating between the classes of person each type of authority is entitled to seek to protect by means of an order: the "relevant persons". In order to apply for an order, the relevant authority must consider that such an order is necessary to protect relevant persons from further anti-social acts by the perpetrator (see above). Who will be relevant persons depends on the nature of the authority applying for the order. The term means:

> if the authority seeking the order is a local authority, persons within the local government area of that authority;

> if the authority is a chief officer of police, persons within the police area;

> if the authority is the chief constable of British Transport Police, persons who are on or likely to be on policed premises in a local government area, or persons in the vicinity or likely to be in the vicinity of such premises;

> if the authority is a registered social landlord, persons who are residing in or otherwise on or likely to be on premises provided or managed by the registered social landlord, or persons in the vicinity of or likely to be in the vicinity of such premises (1998 Act s.1(1B), inserted by 2002 Act s.61(4)).

Consultation

4.21 Before an order may be applied for, the statutory consultation requirements must be complied with (1998 Act s.1E (inserted by 2002 Act s.66)). Here too, the requirements are different depending on the type of authority seeking the order. Local authorities and chief officers of police must consult with each other (s.1E(2), (3)). The Chief Constable of British Transport Police or a registered social landlord must consult both the local authority for the area in which the perpetrator resides or appears to reside and the chief officer of police for that area (1998 Act s.1E(4)).

Terms of the Order

4.22 The prohibitions that are imposed by the order are those necessary for the purpose of protecting persons (whether or not relevant persons or persons elsewhere in England or Wales) from further anti-social acts by the defendant (1998 Act s.1(6) as amended by 2002 Act s.61(7)) The prohibitions may include the exclusion of the perpetrator from particular places. It is to be noted that while an ASBO application cannot be made unless the relevant authority considers it necessary for the protection of relevant persons, the court, in imposing the terms of an order is not limited by this concept, but may impose any prohibition necessary to protect anyone in England and Wales. The only qualifications on this very broad power appear to be (a) that only prohibitions – *i.e.* negative obligations – may be imposed; and (b) each such prohibition must be "necessary".

An ASBO may now also be made by a Magistrates' Court of its own motion as an additional sentencing option where a person has been convicted of a "relevant offence" *i.e.* an offence committed after the coming into force of s.64 of the 2002 Act (December 2, 2002, see 2002 Act s.64(1), (10)).

In the case of children, the court, when making an ASBO, has power to impose a parenting order in certain cases (1998 Act s.8).

The order must last for a minimum of two years unless it is varied or discharged (1998 Act ss.1(7) and 1(8)). Subject to this minimum requirement, it may last for the period of time specified in the order or until further order (*i.e.* for a fixed or potentially unlimited time: s.1(7)). Either party may apply to vary or discharge the order at any time (1998 Act s.1(8)). Within the first two years of the order's operation, however, discharge requires the consent of both parties (1998 Act s.1(9)).

An order comes into effect on the date it is made, although, by s.1(9), the two-year period (during which discharge requires the consent of both parties, see above) runs from the date of service of the order.

It is recommended that the order should be served personally on the Defendant.

The Application

The application is, generally, made to the Magistrates' Court by way of complaint (1998 Act **4.23** s.1(3)). One of the more important amendments to the 1998 Act by the 2002 Act, however, concerns the ability to apply for one in the county court in certain circumstances (1998 Act s.1B, inserted by 2002 Act s.63).

Where a relevant authority is party to proceedings in the county court in which another party is a person against whom the authority considers it would be reasonable to apply for an ASBO, it may apply for such an order in the county court (s.1B(2)). More controversially, even if a relevant authority is not a party to county court proceedings, it may make an application to be joined to proceedings involving other parties in order to seek an ASBO against one of those other parties, if it considers it reasonable to seek an ASBO against that party (1998 Act s.1B(3)). The procedures, if the court is willing to permit the application to be made, are thereafter identical with those in the Magistrates' Court, described below. See Practice Direction – Anti-Social Behaviour (Orders under s.1B(4) of the Crime and Disorder Act 1998) (2003).

The Magistrates' Courts (Anti-Social Behaviour Orders) Rules 2002, SI 2002/2784 (replacing SI 1998/2682 in relation to all applications made after December 2, 2002), prescribes forms to be used in the making of applications for ASBOs in the Magistrates' Court. A separate application must be made against each single named individual, even though that person may be one of a larger group, each of whom is to be summonsed. The summons must be given to the defendant in person or sent by first class post to his last known address. Where a child or young person is concerned, a person with parental responsibility should also receive a copy of the summons.

The application for an ASBO is a civil matter (*R (McCann) v Manchester Crown Court* [2002] UKHL 39; [2002] 3 W.L.R. 1313) and proof will be to the civil standard (balance of probabilities). This does not mean a bare balance of probabilities, however. The civil standard is flexible, to be applied more or less rigorously depending on the seriousness of the allegations and consequences of the proceedings. Accordingly, it has been held that a civil standard of proof equivalent to the criminal standard (*i.e.* beyond reasonable doubt) is to be required in relation to the allegations of anti-social behaviour sought to be proved in an ASBO application (see *McCann* (above)).

The order is aimed at deterring and preventing an escalation of anti-social behaviour, without recourse to criminal sanctions. The process is not suitable for private disputes between neighbours where there may be harassment (see references to the Protection from Harassment Act 1997 in Chapter 5) or for domestic violence (*cp* the requirement that the conduct relied on must not have been carried out in relation to a person in the same household as the Defendant (1998 Act s.1(1)).

According to Home Office guidance, the ASBO procedure is intended to deal with criminal or sub-criminal activity in relation to which criminal proceedings are not appropriate. The Guidance suggests a number of situations where an application for an ASBO may be appropriate, though this is not an exhaustive list:

a) where individuals intimidate neighbours and others through threats or violence or a mixture of unpleasant actions;

b) where there is persistent unruly behaviour by a small group of individuals on a housing estate or other local area, who may dominate others and use minor damage to property and fear of retaliation, possibly at unsocial hours as a means of intimidating other people;

c) where there are families whose anti-social behaviour, when challenged, leads to verbal abuse, vandalism, threats and graffiti, sometimes using children as the vehicle for action against neighbouring families;

d) where there is persistent abusive behaviour towards elderly people or towards mentally ill or disabled people causing them fear and distress;

e) where there is serious and persistent bullying of children on an organised basis in public recreation grounds or on the way to school or within the school grounds if normal school disciplinary procedures do not stop the behaviour;

f) where there is persistent racial harassment or homophobic behaviour;

g) where there is persistent anti social behaviour as a result of drugs or alcohol misuse.

Evidence

4.24 Professional witnesses may be used to give evidence of conduct, whether or not they were harassed alarmed or distressed by it, and whether or not any other person was present who was harassed alarmed or distressed. Professional witnesses may be police officers or housing officers or enquiry agents. This is permissible because the behaviour to be proved need only be "likely to cause" harassment, alarm or distress (see s.1(1)(a) of the Crime and Disorder Act 1998).

In addition, hearsay evidence may be relied upon. Provisions for the service of hearsay notices 21 days before the hearing are contained in the Magistrates' Courts (Hearsay Evidence in Civil Proceedings) Rules 1999, SI 1999/681. (See also *McCann* (above)).

Applications to vary/discharge

4.25 An application to vary or discharge an order must be made in writing to the court which made the order, setting out the reasons why it is said that the court should vary or discharge the order (Magistrates' Court (Anti-Social Behaviour Order) Rules 2002, r.6(2)).

On an application to vary/discharge an interim ASBO, made without motice to the defendant, the court may not dismiss the application without giving the defendant the right to make oral representations (r.5(8)). In all other circumstances, the court may determine the application without hearing oral representations where it considers there to be no grounds on which it might conclude that it ought to grant the application. Otherwise, a hearing must take place (r.6(3), (4)).

As stated above, an order cannot be discharged within the first two years of its operation unless all parties consent (1998 Act s.1(9)).

Appeals

There is a right of appeal against the making of the order, which lies to the Crown Court. The appeal itself is by way of rehearing (1998 Act s.4). **4.26**

Breach of the ASBO

If a person breaches the terms of an ASBO without reasonable excuse, he commits a criminal **4.27** offence, which is an arrestable offence. The offence is triable either way (1998 Act s.1(10)). At this stage, therefore, the proceedings become criminal in nature and are generally brought by the normal prosecuting authorities (although the Anti Social Behaviour Bill contains a clause that explicitly proposes to permit the breach of proceedings to be brought by the authority which obtained the ASBO, cl 37(4), inserting a new s.1(10A) and 10(B) into the 1998 Act).

Magistrates have the power to impose a sentence of imprisonment for up to six months or a fine up to the statutory maximum (s.1(10)(a)). The Crown Court may impose a sentence of up to five years' imprisonment and/or a fine (s.1(10)(b)). The courts have no power to discharge conditionally, but may impose an absolute discharge or any other sentencing disposal (1998 Act s.1(11)).

Protection from Harassment Act 1997

This is considered elsewhere, see Chapter 5. **4.28**

Other Measures

Race Relations Act 1976, s.71

This provision only applies to local authorities and is a general, rather than a specific duty. It **4.29** obliges:

> "every local authority to make appropriate arrangements with a view to securing that their various functions are carried out with due regard to the need:
>
> (1) to eliminate unlawful racial discrimination; and
> (2) to promote equality of opportunity, and good relations, between persons of different racial groups."

Public Order Act 1986, ss.4A and 5

4.30 This Act creates, *inter alia*, criminal offences of using threatening, abusive or insulting words or behaviour, or disorderly behaviour; or displaying any writing, sign or other visible representation which is threatening, abusive or insulting within the hearing or sight of a person likely to be caused harassment, alarm or distress thereby (s.5), and of causing another person harassment, alarm or distress, in any of the above ways, with intent to do so (s.4A, inserted by the Criminal Justice and Public Order Act 1994).

The usual prosecution authority is the CPS. However, local authorities are entitled to institute criminal proceedings, and frequently do so in related matters, (*e.g.* unlawful eviction). Private prosecutions by other landlords are likely to be rare.

Criminal Justice and Public Order Act 1994

4.31 Part V of this Act introduced new police powers to remove trespassers on land (s.61) and to seize vehicles (s.62). It also created the power to remove persons attending or preparing for raves (ss.63–64), and to prevent them from proceeding towards a rave (s.65). The offence of "aggravated trespass" was provided, where a person does anything on land "in the open air" intended to intimidate, obstruct or disrupt persons engaging in lawful activity on the land or adjoining land (s.68). The Anti-Social Behaviour Bill proposes amendments to these provisions (clauses 60 to 65).

Criminal Justice and Police Act 2001

4.32 Sections 39–41 create new criminal offences relating to intimidation (s.39) and harming (s.40) of witnesses in "relevant proceedings". A witness includes a person who is not proposing to give oral evidence in proceedings but who:

> "provides, or is able to provide, any information or any document or other thing which might be used as evidence in those proceedings or which (whether or not admissible as evidence in those proceedings) (a) might tend to confirm evidence which will be or might be admitted in those proceedings; (b) might be referred to in evidence given in those proceedings by another witness; or (c) might be used as the basis for any cross-examination in the course of those proceedings": s.39(5) see also s.40(7) in similar terms.

Proceedings are "relevant proceedings" if they are in the Court of Appeal, High Court, Crown Court, County Court or Magistrates' Court which are not proceedings for an offence *i.e.* civil proceedings. The proceedings must have been commenced after the coming into force of ss.39–40 (June 19, 2001).

See also 2001 Act s.42 – police directions stopping the harassment of a person in his home. A constable (or if a more senior officer is present, that officer (s.42(6)) may give a direction – including an oral direction (s.42(3)) – requiring a person to do "all such things" (including leaving the vicinity) as the constable considers necessary to prevent the harassment of, or the causing of alarm or distress to, a resident in his home.

The power arises if a person is present outside the dwelling of a person (the "resident") and the constable believes on reasonable grounds that:

(a) the person is present there for the purpose of representing to, or persuading, the resident or anyone else at all that he should not do something he is entitled or required to do, or do something he is not obliged to do; and

(b) his presence amounts to or is likely to result in harassment of, or cause alarm or distress to, the resident.

PART II: PRECEDENTS

4.33   **Form 48**

Claim for final injunction pursuant to s.222 Local Government Act 1972 and s.152 Housing Act 1996

Claim No. BM721285

IN THE BOLMONDELEY COUNTY COURT

B E T W E E N

MAREBROUGH BOROUGH COUNCIL   **Claimant**

and

BARNEY OUTBÚILDING   **Defendant**

PARTICULARS OF CLAIM

---

1.   The Claimant is a local authority within the meaning of the Local Government Act 1972, and a local housing authority for the purposes of the Housing Act 1996.

2.   In pursuance of its duties as housing authority for the district of Marebrough, the Claimant owns and manages properties on an estate within its local authority area, known as the Nottoo Close Estate (the "Close").

3.   By s.222 of the Local Government Act 1972, the Claimant may institute legal proceedings in its own name where it considers it expedient to do so for the promotion or protection of the interests of the inhabitants of its area.

4.   By s.152 of the Housing Act 1996, the Claimant may apply to the court for an injunction to prohibit a person, *inter alia*, from engaging in or threatening to engage in conduct causing or likely to cause a nuisance or annoyance to a person residing in, visiting or otherwise engaging in a lawful activity in residential premises or in the locality of such premises, or from entering or being found in the locality of residential premises to which that section applies.

5.   As part of its management of its said housing stock, the Claimant owns and operates a neighbourhood housing office (the "housing office") at 55 Grady St, Bolmondeley. Tenants and other people may enter the said housing office during its opening hours by virtue of an implied licence from the Claimant to do so. It is an implied term of the said implied licence that those people entering the said office

will not act in such a way as to cause, or be likely to cause, nuisance or annoyance to any person lawfully on the premises.

6. The Defendant is a single man born on December 18, 1932. At all material times, he has lived alone in a third floor flat situated at and known as Flat C, 233 Nottoo Close, Bolmondeley, Marebrough, under a tenancy granted by the Claimant on June 26, 1992.

7. The Defendant has been guilty of conduct in the Close and its locality amounting to nuisance and/or annoyance to persons residing in, visiting or otherwise engaged in lawful activity in or in the locality of the Close.

8. Further, the Defendant has used and/or threatened to use violence against persons residing in, visiting or otherwise engaged in lawful activity in or in the locality of the Close; and there is a significant risk of harm to that person or a person of similar description if an injunction is not granted.

9. Further, the Defendant has been guilty of conduct amounting to a nuisance and annoyance to the Claimant's staff and other tenants, and has damaged property belonging to the Claimant, when inside the housing office.

PARTICULARS

a) On or about the November 13, 2001, the Defendant broke several windows at the housing office, stating that this was because a tradesman had not repaired a minor leak to his hot water tank on the day he reported it;

b) On November 25, 2001, the Defendant became extremely aggressive and abusive in the housing office when he was informed that the replacement of a broken sink plug and chain was the responsibility of the tenant, calling the member of staff who informed him of this a "fucking wanker";

c) On January 8, 2002, the Defendant again attended the housing office and made threats against one Mrs Petal, the Claimant's estate manager for the Close, telling her, "I want your blood" and "I can do what I like and the Police won't touch me." He then smashed a window with his walking stick as he left the building;

d) On February 15, 2002, the Claimant received a complaint from the resident at Flat B, 233 Nottoo Close, that the Defendant had thrown a bag filled with urine out of his window, which had narrowly missed her as she left the main entrance to the building. When she looked up to see what had happened, she saw the Defendant hanging out of his window. The Defendant shouted, "Get you next time, you fucking witch. You're the fucking piss bag";

e) On April 2, 2002, the Defendant, outside 233 Nottoo Close, pinned Mrs Petal, who had been visiting the resident of Flat B, up against her car with his wheelchair, preventing her from climbing into the car or from leaving Nottoo Close. The Defendant verbally abused and threatened her;

f) On July 11, 2002, the Defendant ripped the entry-phone telephone off the wall in his flat and brought it into the housing office. He requested the receptionist to open the security window. She refused, whereupon he threw the telephone at the window, cracking the glass. He then threw the telephone at the window three further times, while calling the receptionist a "whore" and a "bitch" and a "fucking slag".

g) On October 29, 2002, the Defendant came into the housing office at lunchtime to report an item of disrepair on the freephone provided in the reception area. On finding the line to be engaged, the Defendant ripped the telephone off the wall, came into the reception area and was racially abusive to the receptionist.

h) Because of the matters pleaded above, on November 4, 2002, the Claimant wrote to the Defendant withdrawing his implied licence to attend the housing office and informing him that he may only enter the housing office for the purpose of attending an appointment which had been previously arranged in writing. Notwithstanding the above, the Defendant entered the housing office without an appointment and abused staff and other tenants on November 17, and 22, and December 3, 13 and 20, 2002.

i) On January 15, 2003, the Defendant attacked the resident of Flat B, 233 Nottoo Close, with his walking stick, hitting her repeatedly on the head and upper body. He then entered the housing office and shouted "you're all fucking arseholes" and threw his walking stick at another tenant.

10. In the premises, the Defendant has, by continuing the enter the housing office as described above, exceeded the terms of any licence which he may have enjoyed to enter the housing office, and/or has committed a trespass to land.

11. Further, the Defendant has committed assaults upon the Claimant's staff and/or has been guilty of harassment of such staff.

12. Unless restrained by the court, the Defendant threatens and intends to continue in his said conduct referred to above.

13. The Claimant considers it to be expedient to bring these proceedings for the promotion or protection of the interests of the inhabitants of its area.

AND the Claimant claims

1. An order forbidding the Defendant:

   (a) from assaulting, threatening or otherwise interfering with, any of the Claimant's officers or any other tenant or visitor of the Nottoo Close Estate, Bolmondeley, Marebrough;

   (b) from entering, or attempting to enter or coming within ten metres of the housing office at 55 Grady Street, Bolmondeley, Marebrough, save in accordance with the terms of a written appointment to attend the said office, made in advance.

2.   A power of arrest to be attached to the terms of para.1(a) above.

3.   Costs.

STATEMENT OF TRUTH

The Claimant believes that the facts stated in these Particulars of Claim are true.

Signed ....

[CONTINUE AS IN FORM 19]

4.34　**Form 49**

Application for an injunction pursuant to s.152 Housing Act 1996 CPR Rule 4, PD 4

IN THE SPROXTEN COUNTY COURT

Notes on completion

Tick whichever box applies and specify legislation where appropriate

☐ By application in pending proceedings
☑ **Under statutory provisions Section 152 Housing Act 1996**

(1) Enter the full name of the person making the application

The Claimant (Applicant/Petitioner)[1] THE MAYOR AND BURGESSES OF THE LONDON BOROUGH OF SPROXTEN

Applies to the court for an injunction order in the following terms:

(2) Enter the full name of the person the injunction is to be directed to

The Defendant (Respondent)[2] FREDDIE SETGOT be forbidden (whether by himself or by instructing or encouraging any other person)[3]

 (1) from engaging in or threatening to engage in conduct causing or likely to cause a nuisance or annoyance to any person residing in, visiting or otherwise engaging in a lawful activity in the locality of 92 Foggy Hill Sproxten London E22.

 (2) from threatening, assaulting, molesting or otherwise interfering with Mr Andy Manns of 90 Foggy Hill Sproxten London E22.

(3) Set out here the proposed restraining orders (if the defendant is a limited company delete the wording in brackets and insert whether by its servants, agents, officers or otherwise)

(4) Set out here any proposed mandatory orders requiring acts to be done

And that the Defendant (Respondent)[4]

(5) Set out here any further terms asked for including provision for costs

And that[5]

 (1) **A POWER OF ARREST BE ATTACHED TO PARAGRAPHS 1 AND 2 OF THE INJUNCTION**

 (2) **THE RESPONDENT PAY THE CLAIMANT'S COSTS**

(6) Enter the names of all persons who have made witness statements or sworn affidavits n support of this application

The grounds of this application are set out in the witness statement(s) of **MR ANDY MANNS**　　dated

This (these) statement(s) is (are) served with this application.

(7) Enter the names and addresses of all persons

The application is to be served upon[7]
FREDDIE SETGOT
92 Foggy Hill Sproxten London E22

upon whom it is intended to serve this application (8) Enter the full name and address for service and delete as required	**This application is filed by**[8] (the solicitors for) the Claimant (Applicant/Petitioner) whose address for service is: **THE MAYOR AND BURGESSES OF THE LONDON BOROUGH OF SPROXTEN** **TOWN HALL** **MELVINNE** **SPROXTEN** **LONDON** **E22 ARF** **Signed** **Dated**
*Name and address of the person this application is directed to	*This section to be completed by the Court* **To*** **Of** **This application will be heard by the (District) Judge** **At** **On** **the** **day of** **2003 at** **o'clock** **If you do not attend at the time shown the court may make and injunction order in your absence.** *If you do not fully understand this application you should go to a Solicitor, Legal Advice Centre or a Citizens' Advice Bureau.*

The Court Office at is open 10am to 4pm Mon-Fri. Where corresponding with the court, please address all forms and letters to the Court Manager and quote the case number.

4.35 **Form 50**

Witness Statement in support of application for s.152 injunction

Applicants
A. Manns
First Statement
Dated: 13/1/03
Filed: 14/1/03
No Exhibits

Claim No. SP2014002

IN THE SPROXTEN COUNTY COURT

B E T W E E N

THE MAYOR AND BURGESSES OF
THE LONDON BOROUGH OF SPROXTEN **Applicants**

and

FREDDIE SETGOT   **Respondent**

WITNESS STATEMENT OF ANDY MANNS

I ANDY MANNS of 90 Foggy Hill Sproxten London E22, Interior Designer, will say as follows:

1 I am a tenant of 90 Foggy Hill Sproxten. My Landlord is the London Borough of Sproxten the Applicants in this action. I make this statement in support of this claim for an injunction. Insofar as the matters set out below are within my own knowledge, they are true; insofar as they are not within my knowledge, their source is indicated and I sincerely believe them to be true.

2 My next-door neighbour at 92 Foggy Hill, Mr Setgot (the Respondent) is also a tenant of the London Borough of Sproxten.

3 On Friday April 20, 2001 I was in my garden watering my marigolds when Freddie, the Respondent, came into his garden with a large portable stereo player. Freddie proceeded to turn the machine on at full volume. The pop music he was playing was deafeningly loud.

4 I gestured to Freddie to come and speak to me at the fence. I intended to ask him politely if he would turn the music down. Freddie responded with a gesture, which

my army friends and I used to call a "reverse Churchill". In other words, he stuck two fingers up at me. I was deeply shocked by Freddie's reaction and had to go inside for a quiet lie down.

5   The music continued in the garden and soon another stereo was being played in the house. This was at full volume as well. I decided that diplomacy must work in the end and went round to knock at Freddie's door. It took me a while to attract any attention but after a while a woman who I recognise as Freddie's girlfriend, Bunny, came to the door. She said "yeh what do you want". I asked politely if they could turn the music down. I was met with a torrent of abuse. In fact, she called me a number of names I did not even understand, but they sounded very rude indeed. Then she said "Why don't you just fuck off you miserable old bastard" and the door was slammed in my face. The music continued off and on for the rest of the day and all night. I could not sleep a wink.

6   The next day I was walking down Foggy Hill with my dog, Cedric. I had got as far as the junction with Rainy Lane. To my shock Freddie and his pet Rottweiler, Nobby jumped out in front of me. Freddie was waving his arms around aggressively and shouting at me. He shouted, "Don't you ever come round knocking on my door again, with your whinging and your whining, Mr Neighbourhood Fucking Watch, or else I'll fucking stick one on you. All right?" Nobby growled at Cedric and then just stood there, looking at him funny.

7   I was petrified by Freddie and Nobby's behaviour, and so was Cedric (though it's hardly Nobby's fault). We couldn't understand what we had done to upset Freddie. I rang my housing officer, Bob Catt, and complained to him. Bob said he would "drop Freddie a line telling him that his behaviour was unacceptable and was a breach of his tenancy agreement".

8   I thought that would be the end of the matter but I was sadly wrong. Two days later when I was sat in my lounge listening to the Archers, Freddie came up to the window and started shouting at me. He was standing in my back garden. I don't know how he got into my garden. I can only assume that he had scaled the fence. Freddie was calling me all the names under the sun including a "grass" and a "grave dodger" and a "snoop" and a "miserable old git". He then shouted "I am going to fucking kill you for complaining about me to the council. You'll see. Well you won't cause you'll be fucking dead. I'll snap your fucking neck like a stick of celery. All right?"

9   I am petrified that Freddie is going to carry out his threat and I am too afraid to go out even to take poor Cedric for a walk. The music has continued day and night at a ridiculously high level. It's always the same song – "I will always love you" from the soundtrack of that Whitney Houston film. It is all getting too much for me. I am an active person who hates being "confined to barracks", and there's a limit to how much Whitney anyone can take. I don't know how Freddie and Bunny can stand it in their house – it's quite unbearable in mine.

10 Unless the court grants the injunction the Applicants are seeking I am certain Freddie will go through with his threat. I don't want to die. I haven't had a wink of sleep for days now – I am too afraid to nod off even for a little while in case Freddie

breaks into my house and I never wake up. Cedric hasn't slept either and has started spraying round the boundaries of his territory, which is also quite unpleasant, although I think he's trying to help.

11 I understand that the Council has not warned Freddie that they are making this application because they are concerned about repercussions for me if he is warned in advance of the application. If just talking to Mr Catt about the problem has caused Freddie to get quite so unstable, what would he do if he knew about these proceedings? It doesn't bear thinking about.

STATEMENT OF TRUTH

I believe that the facts stated in this Witness Statement are true.

Full Name: Andy Manns
Signed:

Form 51   **4.36**

Injunction Order

Injunction Order

Between

In the Sproxten County Court	
Case Number SP2014002 *Always quote this*	
Applicant's Ref	
Respondent's Ref	

THE MAYOR AND BURGESSES OF THE LONDON BOROUGH OF SPROXTEN

                                                            Applicant

And

FREDDIE SETGO
                                    Respondent

For completion by the court
Issued on   2003

To *[The name of the person the order is directed to]*   **Freddie Setgot**

(Seal)

Of *[The address of the person the order is directed to]*   **92 Foggy Lane Sproxten London E22**

If you do not obey this order you will be guilty of contempt of court and you may be sent to prison

On the   23rd day of   April 2003 the court considered an application for an injunction.

The Court ordered that *[The name of the person the order is directed to]* **Freddie Setgot is forbidden** (whether by himself or by instructing or encouraging any other person) *[The terms of the restraining order. If the defendant is a limited company, delete the words in brackets and insert "whether by its servants, agents, officers or otherwise"]*

   (1) **from engaging in or threatening to engage in conduct causing or likely to cause a nuisance or annoyance to any person residing in, visiting or otherwise engaging in a lawful activity in the locality of 92 Foggy Hill Sproxten London E22.**
   (2) **from threatening, assaulting, molesting or otherwise interfering with Mr Andy Manns of 90 Foggy Hill Sproxten London E22.**

This order shall remain in force until (the   27th day of   April 2003 at 10 o'clock unless before then it is revoked by a further order of the court.
And it is ordered that *[The name of the person the order is directed to]*
shall *[The terms of any orders requiring acts to be done]*

It is further ordered that *[The terms of any other orders costs etc]*

A power of arrest is attached to paragraphs 1 and 2 above.

The Defendant shall pay the costs of this application in any event.

Notice of further hearing *[Use when the order is temporary or ex parte otherwise delete]*

The court will reconsider the application and whether the order should continue at a further hearing at Sproxten County Court

On the   26th day of April 2003 at   10 o'clock.

If you do not attend at the time shown the court may make an injunction order in your absence.

You are entitled to apply to the court to reconsider the order before the day.
[Delete if order made on notice]

If you do not understand anything in this order you should go to a Solicitor, Legal Advice Centre or a Citizens' Advice Bureau.

The Court Office at is open from 10am to 4pm Mon-Fri. When corresponding with the court, address all forms and letters to the Chief Clerk and quote the case number.

Form 52   **4.37**

Application for an Order for Committal

Claim No. SP2014002

IN THE SPROXTEN COUNTY COURT

The MAYOR AND BURGESSES OF
THE LONDON BOROUGH OF SPROXTEN   **Claimant**

FREDDIE SETGOT   **Defendant**

Part A

I, Dawn Breeze, solicitor on behalf of the Claimants, intend to apply for an order that

The Defendant be committed to prison for disobeying the order of the court made by HH Judge Fudge on April 26, 2003. Under the said order the Defendant was forbidden:

from engaging in or threatening to engage in conduct causing or likely to cause a nuisance or annoyance to any person residing in, visiting or otherwise engaging in a lawful activity in the locality of 92 Foggy Hill Sproxten London E22.

from threatening, assaulting, molesting or otherwise interfering with Mr Andy Manns of 90 Foggy Hill Sproxten London E22.

The Defendant has disobeyed the order in the following ways:

1. On April 26, 2003, immediately after HH Judge Fudge had extended the injunction order against the Defendant until April 25, 2004, the Defendant approached Mr Andy Manns of 90 Foggy Hill, Sproxten, London E22 and shouted obscenities at him. He threatened Mr Manns saying "watch your step Pop. I am going to make you wish you never grassed me up". He then knocked Mr Manns's beret off and walked away. When he walked away he was saying something about an axe and "hitting you on the head and you won't know it happens".

2. On May 4, 2003, in Foggy Hill, the Defendant approached Mr Manns and said "It's not over, git face. You might think I've fucking forgotten but I haven't fucking forgotten. I'm just biding my time, watching and waiting. I could snap your spine like a floret of broccoli any time I choose. You're a dead man walking. You're fish food. And your dog's fucking Nobby food."

The Claimant further relies on the affidavit of Andy Manns, which is filed and served with this application notice.

   Unless the Defendant is punished for his actions he will continue to disobey the orders of this court.

Part B

I wish to rely on my statement of case and on the attached affidavit.

Signed   D. Breeze   Position or office held   Solicitor

IMPORTANT NOTICE

The Court has power to send you to prison and to fine you if it finds that any of the allegations made against you are true and amount to a contempt of court.

You must attend court **on the date shown on the front of this form. It is in your own interest to do so. You should bring with you any witnesses and documents, which you think, will help you put your side of the case.**

If you consider the allegations are not true you must tell the court why. If it is established that they are true, you must tell the court of any good reason why they do not amount to a contempt of court, or, if they do, why you should not be punished.

If you need advice you should show this document at once to your solicitor or go to the Citizens' Advice Bureau.

Address to which documents about the case should be sent

London Borough of Sproxten
Legal Department
The Old Hut
Fagworthy Lane
Sproxten
E22 7JJ

STATEMENT OF TRUTH

The Claimant believes that the facts stated in this application are true.
Signed   D. Breeze   **Position or office held**   Solicitor
Date

Form 53   **4.38**

Affidavit in support of Application to Commit

Claimants
A. Manns
First affidavit
Dated: 5/5/03
Filed 5/5/03
No Exhibits

Claim No. SP2014002

IN THE SPROXTEN COUNTY COURT

B E T W E E N

THE MAYOR AND BURGESSES OF
THE LONDON BOROUGH OF SPROXTEN   **Claimants**

and

FREDDIE SETGOT   **Defendant**

AFFIDAVIT OF ANDY MANNS

I ANDY MANNS, of 90 Foggy Hill Sproxten E22, Interior Designer, MAKE OATH and say as follows:

1   I make this affidavit in support of the Claimant's application to commit Mr Setgot to prison for contempt of court for breaching the terms of the injunction made by HH Judge Fudge on April 26, 2003. The matters set out in this affidavit are within my knowledge and are true.

2   On Thursday April 26, 2003 I attended at Sproxten County Court for a hearing in this action. I was in court when HH Judge Fudge made an injunction against Mr Setgot until April 25, 2004. The Defendant was also in court when the injunction was made.

3   The Judge carefully explained the terms and effect of the injunction to the Defendant. I came out of court quite relieved that the injunction had been extended and that I would be protected from Freddie.

4   After the hearing, I was walking towards my car, which was parked across the road from the court entrance. I saw Freddie and his girlfriend Bunny standing on the

corner. They were obviously having a big row. I had to pass them in order to get to my car. Freddie started following me shouting obscenities. He threatened me again saying "Watch your step Pop. I am going to make you wish you never grassed me up". He then knocked my beret off and sauntered off. When he walked away he was saying something about coming back with an axe and 'hitting you on the head and you won't know it happens'.

5   Freddie sounded very aggressive and I was petrified at his behaviour. I was very shaken because I didn't know what he might do next.

6   Still, I had the protection of the injunction and I decided that I couldn't let Freddie intimidate me for the rest of my life but that I had to make a stand against him. So, on May 5, 2003, I decided that Cedric and I should take a walk down the road for a bit of air. As I walked past Freddie's house, down Foggy Hill, I noticed him and Bunny at the window, but I ignored them. Cedric whimpered.

7   I thought we had got away with it, but about thirty seconds later, as we walked on down the hill, I heard footsteps of a man running. I turned round to see Freddie chasing us. I would have run away but Cedric has a heart condition and a verruca, so I turned round to face Freddie. He came up to us, and put his face very close to mine and sort of snarled at me. He said, "It's not over, git face. You might think I've fucking forgotten but I haven't fucking forgotten. I'm just biding my time, watching and waiting. I could snap your spine like a floret of broccoli any time I choose. You're a dead man walking. You're fish food. And your dog's fucking Nobby food." Then he walked away, back up the hill towards his house.

8   I shouted after him that only a damn coward would threaten another man's dog but he just kept walking. We were very frightened and went straight home to call the police. But in Sproxten you can never get through to the police, so I went to see Mr Catt instead and he told me not to worry and that he would sort it out for me.

9   Next thing I knew, he asked me to be a witness again. I bear Freddie no ill will, and I certainly have nothing against Bunny or Nobby, but this man is insane and he must be stopped. I fear for my life and that of my dog. I therefore respectfully ask the court to grant the Claimants' application.

10 I believe that the facts stated in this Affidavit are true.

Sworn by
At
This   day of   2003

Before me

A Solicitor/Commissioner for oaths

Form 54   **4.39**

Application for Anti-Social Behaviour Order

**APPLICATION FOR ANTI SOCIAL BEHAVIOUR ORDER
(CRIME AND DISORDER ACT 1998, s.1)**

POXLEY GREEN MAGISTRATES' COURT

Date:	June 1, 2003
Defendant:	David Dodger (also known as Gary Smith) d.o.b. August 12, 1990.
Address:	9 Box Road, Poxley Green, Echinashire EX2 7AK
Applicant authority:	Poxley District Council
Relevant authorities consulted:	Chief Constable of the Echinashire Constabulary

And it is alleged:

a) that the Defendant has acted on dates between January 1, 2003 and May 25, 2003 at various locations in Poxley Green in an anti-social manner, that is to say in a manner that caused or was likely to cause harassment, alarm or distress to one or more persons not of the same household as herself; and

b) that an Anti-Social Behaviour Order is necessary to protect relevant persons from further anti-social acts by him

And accordingly application is made for an Anti-Social Behaviour Order containing the following prohibitions:

that the Defendant:

1) must not cause harassment, alarm or distress to any person in the local government area of Poxley Green District Council, the boundaries of which are shown on the plan attached to this application at "Appendix 1", delineated in red;

2) must not enter the Grimeley Estate, the boundaries of which are shown on the said attached plan, delineated in blue;

3) must not take without consent any motor vehicle belonging to another person;

4) must not drive a motor vehicle unless he holds a valid and current driving licence and a valid certificate of insurance for that vehicle and unless that vehicle is taxed and, if required by law, has a valid and current MOT certificate;

5) must not travel in a motor vehicle if he knows or ought to know that the driver does not hold a valid and current driving licence or a valid certificate of

insurance for that vehicle or that the vehicle is untaxed or that it does not have a current and valid MOT certificate (if such is required by law);

Short description of acts:

The Defendant has caused harassment, alarm and distress to persons in Poxley Green by subjecting them to violence, threats of violence, theft, verbal abuse and harassment. The following specific matters are relied upon:

1. On January 1, 2003, at about 9am, the Defendant stole a vehicle, a blue Nissan Micra motor car, registration E228 UWR and drove it into a shop "Open All Hours" on the Grimeley Estate. The Defendant then stole a packet of "Chocolate Hob Nobs" from the said shop, shouted "Catch me later" to the shopkeeper and ran away. On April 24, 2003, at Poxley Green Youth Court, the Defendant was convicted, in respect of this incident, of taking a conveyance without authority contrary to s.12 of the Theft Act 1968 and of criminal damage contrary of s.1 of the Criminal Damage Act 1971, and was sentenced to a six month referral order. The Applicant will rely on these convictions, pursuant to s.11 of the Criminal Evidence Act 1967, as evidence of the Defendant's conduct set out above.

2. On January 3, 2003, at about 2pm, the Defendant and three other youths were witnessed stealing a red Honda Civic motor car, registration R223 RUT from outside 23 Blossom Road, Grimeley Estate, Poxley Green. They drove for a short distance then jumped out of the car and kicked the windows in. The Defendant was then seen to jump on top of the bonnet and bounce up and down shouting, "who wants a boot wrapped around their head?" and making obscene gestures.

3. On February 15, 2003, at about 1.45am, the Defendant and two other youths threw stones at the windows of the property at 14 Sunset Close, Grimeley Estate, which is occupied by Reginald Sprot and his family. Several windows were broken. The Defendant then shouted for Mr Sprot to come out of his premises. He shouted, "get out here Sprotty you fucking weirdo, I am going to burn your house down and you and all the little fucking Sprotties'll burn alive, you bastard".

4. On March 3, 2003, at about 11am, the Defendant stole Mr Sprot's purple Reliant Robin motor car, registration SPR 10T from the driveway of 14 Sunset Close and drove it into Brown Lake, on the Grimeley Estate.

5. On April 24, 2003, at about 11pm, the Defendant and another youth broke into the Grimeley Estate Tenant's Association office on Toffee Walk, Grimeley Estate, and ransacked the office causing £3000 worth of damage.

6. On May 1, 3 and 5, 2003, the Defendant and three other youths stood outside Grimeley School and made threats against children as they left the school. They demanded money and biscuits from several of the children and assaulted the caretaker, Sid Stubbins with a chair leg.

7. On May 15, 2003, the Defendant and a number of other youths congregated in Admiral Square at the centre of the Grimeley Estate. They played music at an exceptionally high volume and drank a whisky based cream liqueur, smashing the

used bottles on the floor. When the Community Police Officer, PC Larssen asked them to disperse they threw broken glass and stones at him.

8. On May 25, 2003, the Defendant was seen in Mr Sprot's back garden interfering with Mr Sprot's ferrets. Later that day the Defendant was seen carrying one of the ferrets "Stanley" out of the garden. Stanley was later found dead in a nearby cabbage patch by Mr Sprot.

The complaint of: Bob Bobbins, Head of Legal Services

**Name of Applicant
Authority:**   Poxley Green District Council

**Address of Applicant
Authority:**   Town Hall
                            Itchie Square
                            Poxley Green
                            Echinashire EX2 1GG

Who (upon oath) states that the Defendant was responsible for the acts of which particulars are given above, in respect of which the complaint is made.

Taken (and sworn) before me:

Justice of the Peace

[By order of the clerk of the court]

4.40   <u>Form 55</u>

<u>Statement of Consultation</u>

APPLICATION FOR ANTI-SOCIAL BEHAVIOUR ORDER

David Dodger (also known as Gary Smith).
9 Box Road,
Poxley Green
Echinashire
EX2 7AK

STATEMENT OF CONSULTATION

Poxley Green District Council has undertaken full consultation with the Echinashire Constabulary prior to the application for an Anti-Social Behaviour Order against David Dodger (also known as Gary Smith, d.o.b. August 12, 1990).

The consultation was in accordance with s.1(2) of the Crime and Disorder Act, 1998.

The particulars of consultation are that on May 27, 2003, duly authorised officers of Poxley Green District Council and Echinashire Constabulary met and considered the application in detail.

Both Poxley Green District Council and Echinashire Constabulary agree that this application for an Anti-Social Behaviour Order is required to protect relevant persons in the Poxley Green local government area and, in particular, on the Grimeley Estate.

Dated: May 27, 2003.

....
Bob Bobbins   Superintendent Bill Billings
Poxley Green District Council   Echinashire Constabulary

Form 56   **4.41**

Application for Interim Order

APPLICATION FOR AN INTERIM ORDER (CRIME AND DISORDER ACT 1998, s.1D)

POXLEY GREEN MAGISTRATES' COURT

(Code)

Date	June 1, 2003
Defendant	David Dodger
Address	9 Box Road, Poxley Green, Echinashire EX2 7AK
Applicant Authority	Poxley Green District Council
Relevant Authorities Consulted	Echinashire Constabulary
Reasons for applying for interim order	To protect the witnesses who have come forward and agreed to make statements and attend court to give evidence for the Applicant in this matter. The Applicant believes and fears that the Defendant would be likely to intimidate the witnesses if no order is in place to protect the witnesses prior to the final hearing of this application.
Do you wish this application to be heard	**X Without notice being given to the Defendant**
	~~With notice being given to the defendant~~

If you wish the application to be heard without notice, state the reasons:
The Applicant repeats the matters set out as reasons for seeking an interim order. In addition, the Applicant believes that if the Defendant is given notice of this application, he would be likely to seek to intimidate the witnesses referred to in the main application for an anti-social behaviour order.

Given the seriousness of the conduct alleged (some of which has already been proved in criminal proceedings), the harassment of the witnesses which has already occurred and their vulnerability to further attack, and the terms of the order sought, the Applicant respectfully requests that the hearing of this application be listed without notice to the Defendant.

The complaint of:	Bob Bobbins, Head of Legal Services
Applicant Authority:	Poxley Green District Council

Address of Applicant Authority: Town Hall, Itchie Square, Poxley Green
                                        Echinashire, EX2 1GG

Who (upon oath) states that the information given above is correct.

Taken (and sworn) before me:

Justice of the Peace

[By order of the clerk of the court]

NOTE: This application must be accompanied by an application for an anti-social behaviour order (Crime and Disorder Act 1998, s.1).

Form 57   **4.42**

Statement in support of Anti-Social Behaviour Order

Applicant
F.A. Cheese
First statement
dated 1/6/03
Exhibits "FA-1"-"FA-3"

POXLEY GREEN MAGISTRATES' COURT

B E T W E E N

POXLEY GREEN DISTRICT COUNCIL   **Applicant**

and

DAVID DODGER (a minor)   **Defendant**

WITNESS STATEMENT OF FRED CHEESE

I FREDERICK AGAMMEMNON CHEESE, of Grimeley Neighbourhood Office, The Dark Building, Grimeley Estate, Poxley Green, Echinashire EX2 3BF, local government officer, will say as follows:

BACKGROUND

1. I am a Neighbourhood Housing Manager employed by Poxley Green District Council, by whom I am authorised to make this statement in support of their application for an anti-social behaviour order against the Defendant, David Dodger. Where the facts and matters set out below are within my own knowledge, they are true; where they are not within my own knowledge, their source is indicated and I sincerely believe them to be true.

2. The neighbourhood I manage includes the Grimeley Estate. During the last six months or so the Defendant, who does not live on the estate, and a number of other youths have caused considerable problems on the estate. The residents are living in fear because the Defendant and his gang are basically running amok committing crimes and threatening – and committing – acts of violence.

3. During this time, the estate, which had previously been a very friendly community and a pleasant place to live and work has been turned into what resembles a battle zone, due to the activities of the Defendant and his gang. In the last three months

alone, nine tenants have terminated their tenancies, saying that they could not face living on the estate any longer, and rather than wait for a transfer they would prefer to take their chances with finding accommodation for themselves. In addition, for the first time I can remember in my six years as housing manager of this estate, prospective tenants are refusing offers on the Grimeley Estate, the most common reason for refusal being that they do not want to bring up their children on a sink estate with such serious violence and gang problems.

4. An additional problem is that people on the estate are too afraid the Defendant's gang to speak out against them. Whenever incidents occur, residents will tell me off the record that it was the Defendant who did it but refuse to let me use the information in case they suffer reprisals from the Defendant and his friends. Although I can quite understand why they are afraid to come forward, the effect has been that neither I nor the police have been able to take any effective steps against the gang, because evidence is so hard to come by.

INCIDENTS

5. I can probably best explain and illustrate the severity of the problem by setting out a list of incidents which have occurred this year.

6. On January 1, 2003, at about 9.15am, I received a telephone call from the police to inform me that an incident had taken place at the "Open All Hours" mini-mart, situated at Slurrie Arcade on the Estate, and to ask me to attend. When I arrived, about 15 minutes later, I saw that a blue Nissan Micra car, registration E228 UWR, appeared to have been driven through the plate glass display window of the shop. There were glass fragments spread out over a large area and a group of people standing outside the shop, including two police officers.

7. I recognised one of the people in the group as Mr Hours, the shopkeeper and he told me that he had been standing behind the counter at about 9am, when he heard a loud squeal of brakes and the Micra drove in through his window. He saw the Defendant, whom he recognised, in the driving seat. The Defendant climbed out of the car, picked up a packet of chocolate Hob Nob biscuits, shouted "Catch me later" and ran out of the shop. Mr Hours was still visibly shaken and distressed. I was later informed by the police that the Defendant had been seen stealing the car earlier that morning from the Poxley Green car park in Itchie Square.

8. In this case, unusually, Mr Hours was prepared to come forward and give evidence against the Defendant, but he has since sold his shop and moved out of the area. I was later informed, by the police that on April 24, 2003, at Poxley Green Youth Court, the Defendant was convicted, in respect of this incident, of taking a conveyance without authority contrary to s.12 of the Theft Act 1968 and of criminal damage contrary to s.1 of the Criminal Damage Act 1971, and was sentenced to a six month referral order. A true copy of the charge sheet and the memorandum of conviction are exhibited to this statement at "FAC-1".

9. On January 3, 2003 at about 4pm, an elderly resident came into the neighbourhood office to report an incident she had witnesses earlier that afternoon. I conducted an

interview with her and she told me that at about 2pm she had seen the Defendant and three other youths breaking into a red Honda Civic, registration R223 RUT outside 23 Blossom Road on the estate. Apparently they drove about 50 yards down the road and then jumped out of the car and broke the windows of the car. The Defendant was then seen to jump on top of the bonnet and bounce up and down shouting, "who wants a boot wrapped around their head?" The tenant concerned was extremely shocked and scared as a result of this incident. She has refused to come forward to give evidence because of her fear of reprisals, but I now produce, at "FAC-2", a true copy of the notes I took during the interview that afternoon. I have blanked out the name of the resident as it appeared at the top of the original notes so as to protect the identity of the resident.

10. The Defendant and his gang have been victimising one particular tenant of the estate, Reginald Sprot, who is the head of the local Neighbourhood Watch. On February 15, 2003 at about 1.45am the Defendant and two other youths threw stones at Mr Sprot's windows. Several windows were broken. The Defendant then shouted for Mr Sprot to come out of his premises. He shouted, "get out here Sprotty you fucking weirdo, I am going to burn your house down and you and all the little Sprottiess'll burn alive, you bastard". Not surprisingly the Sprot family were extremely shaken by this incident.

11. The victimisation of Mr Sprot continued on March 3, 2003 at 11am when the Defendant stole Mr Sprot's Reliant Robin car, registration SPR 1OT and drove it into the big lake in the middle of the Grimeley Estate.

12. On April 24, 2003 at 11pm the Defendant and another youth were seen breaking into the Grimeley Estate Tenant's Association office and ransacking the office. I was one of the first people on the scene. The office was in a terrible state and the estimated cost of repair is £3,000. One of the local residents told me that he had seen and videotaped the whole incident. He gave me a copy of the videotape although he has refused to come forward, for fear of being targeted for reprisals by the Defendant. I produce that videotape, marked "FAC-3". The Defendant can be seen clearly as one of the two youths breaking into the office. The quality of the tape is not good enough, however, for me to identify the second youth.

13. In early May, 2003, I was informed by the Head Teacher at Grimeley School that the Defendant and his gang had been robbing and threatening school children as they left the school for home. Apparently this happened on several occasions notably on the following dates May 1, 3 and 5, 2003. On May 5, the gang were approached by the school caretaker, Sid Stubbins, who they assaulted with a chair leg.

14. On May 15, 2003, at about 6.30pm, just as I was locking up the office, I received a call on my mobile phone that the Defendant and a number of other youths had congregated in Admiral Square at the centre of the Grimeley Estate. I walked over to the square. When I was still about two minutes walk away, I heard loud pop music playing. The music was so loud that it sounded distorted. The music was plainly coming from the Square.

15. Sure enough, when I arrived there, I saw the Defendant and about six other young men and women standing in the Square with a large portable stereo player which was on at what sounded like full blast. They were also drinking from bottles what I assumed to be alcohol. Whenever any of them had finished a bottle he or she would smash it on the floor. After about five minutes, a very strong smell of whiskey-based cream liqueur began to emerge and I assume that that is what they were drinking.

16. I ascertained that the Police had already been called and decided it would be safer for me to wait for the police to arrive and discuss with them what action to take. I felt very intimidated and frightened by the actions of these youths. The Defendant appeared to be the ringleader, telling the others what to do.

17. When the Community Police Officer, PC Larssen arrived, I told him what had been going on and he asked the youths to disperse. The Defendant shouted something at him, though the music was so loud that I did not hear what, and the youths, including the Defendant himself started to throw broken glass and stones at him. PC Larssen had to retreat, and after a few more minutes, before the police reinforcements arrived, the group just picked up the stereo and ran away.

18. Most recently, Mr Sprot was again a target for the Defendant's criminality. On May 25, 2003 the Defendant was seen in Mr Sprot's back garden interfering with his ferrets. Later that day the Defendant was seen carrying one of the ferrets, "Stanley" out of the garden. Stanley was later found dead by Mr Sprot in a nearby cabbage patch.

19. I can safely say that in my 18 years as a housing manager, I have never seen the residents of an estate so afraid of a gang of youths. You can see the fear in their eyes when you talk to them. Unless something is done to control the Defendant and his gang, the spiral of violence and criminality will continue. It is only a matter of time before someone is seriously injured by the Defendant's activities and the Estate will gain a reputation of vandalism and violence that could take years to undo.

INTERIM ORDER

20. For all of the above reasons, I would respectfully ask the court to grant the antisocial behaviour order sought. In addition, I would ask that an interim order in the same terms be made, without notice to the Defendant. I have spoken above of the fear of the residents of what might happen if he finds out they have spoken out against him. Mr Sprot has bravely agreed to support this application and has made a statement (included in the application bundle at pp.23–34) and has agreed to attend court to give evidence against the Defendant.

21. I am convinced that if an interim order is not made, before the Defendant is served with the proceedings, the Sprot family will be at severe risk of a resumption of the Defendant's campaign of intimidation against them in an attempt to persuade Mr Sprot to withdraw from the proceedings. I would respectfully suggest that Mr Sprot is entitled to the protection of the court and that the only way to ensure this is for an interim order to be made without notice to the Defendant.

STATEMENT OF TRUTH

I believe that the facts stated in this statement are true.

Full Name

Signed.

4.43   <u>Form 58</u>

<u>Summons on application</u>

SUMMONS ON APPLICATION FOR ANTI-SOCIAL BEHAVIOUR ORDER (CRIME AND DISORDER ACT 1998, s.1)

<u>POXLEY GREEN MAGISTRATES' COURT</u>

(Code)

Date: June 3, 2003

To the Defendant: David Dodger (also known as Gary Smith) d.o.b. August 12, 1990).

Address: 9 Box Road, Poxley Green Echinashire EX2 7AK

You are hereby summoned to appear on July 5, 2003 at 10am before the Magistrates' Court at Poxley Green Magistrates' Court, Poxley Green, to answer an application for an Anti-Social Behaviour Order, which application is attached to this summons.

(Justices' Clerk)

NOTE: Where the court is satisfied that this summons was served on you within what appears to the court to be a reasonable time before the Hearing or Adjourned hearing, it may issue a warrant for your arrest or proceed in your absence.

If an anti-social behaviour order is made against you and if, without reasonable excuse you do anything you are prohibited from doing by such an order, you shall be liable on conviction to imprisonment for a term not exceeding five years or to a fine or to both.

---

1. In a without notice application for an injunction always remember to include in the witness statement or affidavit an explanation as to why no notice has been given (CPR Pt 25, PD 3.4).

2. Try to specify clearly in the injunction application and draft order the type of behaviour that is prohibited. The respondent needs to understand exactly what he or she is forbidden from doing. A map or plan is usually the best way of achieving this.

3. If there is a power of arrest attached to the injunction, the police must be informed of the order and given a copy of the order – and the power of arrest – immediately after it is made. This is likely to involve waiting at court until the order is typed up by the court staff. The order should be served personally on the respondent.

4. Careful consideration is required before an injunction is sought against a minor. The courts' powers to enforce the order are limited. While this does not necessarily preclude the making of an injunction, it may be more effective to seek an anti-social behaviour order against a minor.

5. It is necessary to make sure that s.152 and/or 153 is suitable to deal with the type of nuisance involved in the specific matter. Noise nuisance, for example, will not be sufficient – violence or threats of violence and a continuing risk of harm – are required.

6. The injunction must specify to which of its provisions the power of arrest applies.

7. When making an application to commit this must be supported by an affidavit in support. A witness statement will not be sufficient (CPR Sch.1, RSC Ord.52 PD 3.1).

8. If a local authority is seeking an ASBO it is essential that there is consultation with the police in accordance with s.1(2) of the Crime and Disorder Act 1998. If the applicant is a registered social landlord or the British Transport Police, it must consult both the relevant local authority and the relevant police force for the area.

Chapter 5
Unlawful Eviction and Harassment

PART I: INTRODUCTION

The nature and scope of the legal redress available in cases of unlawful eviction and har-   **5.01**
assment of occupiers displays the overlapping of common law principles of tort and contract
with civil remedies and criminal sanctions derived from statute. The adviser will thus need to
have an understanding of these different sources and of the different routes by which action
may be taken: in outline they are as follows.

Sources: common law

Contract

The relationship of landlord and tenant is contractual in nature. In the absence of express   **5.02**
covenants, there will be implied into every tenancy a covenant by the landlord that the tenant
shall have quiet enjoyment of the premises during the tenancy, and that the landlord will not
derogate from the grant of the tenancy. A substantial interference by the landlord with the
tenant's ordinary and lawful enjoyment of the premises during the tenancy will be a breach of
the covenant for quiet enjoyment at common law. Use by the landlord of land retained by
him in such a way as to render the demised part unfit or materially less fit for the purpose of
the letting will be a breach of the obligation not to derogate from the grant. Breach of
contract is actionable *per se* even though no actual damage is proved.

So called "tolerated trespassers" (where the tenant is in breach of a possession order but
has been allowed by the landlord to remain, see *Burrows v Brent LBC* [1996] 1 W.L.R. 1448
HL) will not however enjoy the benefit of the covenant because their tenancy is at an end, as
are the contractual rights and obligations included within that tenancy.

Terms may be implied into licences so as to give business efficacy on general principles of
contract law, so that a licensee may argue that he has some similar entitlement to that of a
tenant.

Tort

Trespass

The relationship of landlord and tenant also gives rise to an estate in land pursuant to which   **5.03**
the tenant will be entitled to exclusive possession of the premises as against the landlord.
Every unwarrantable entry by the landlord onto the tenant's premises will be a trespass to
land at common law. Trespass, and more widely the violation of a common law right, is

actionable *per se* without proof of loss, though without actual loss only nominal damages will be recoverable unless (in the case of a more than trivial or temporary trespass) it can be shown that the defendant has gained a benefit which can be used as the basis of assessment of substantial damages.

Nuisance

5.04 The landlord's behaviour may also fall within the amorphous tort of nuisance which, for instance, extends to the undue interference with the comfortable and convenient enjoyment of land. Some actual loss (*e.g.* of enjoyment) will be required.

Title to sue in trespass and nuisance

5.05 The traditional view was that a licensee could not sue in trespass because he did not have exclusive possession against the licensor. Some licensees do, however, have exclusive possession. It seems certain that the latter would have the right to sue their licensor in trespass (*Hunter v Canary Wharf Ltd* [1997] A.C. 655 at p.903). A mere licensee has been held to have no interest in land sufficient to sue in nuisance (*Malone v Laskey* [1907] A.C. 655), confirmed by the House of Lords in *Hunter*. A licensee with exclusive possession can, it seems, sue in nuisance (*Pemberton v Southwark LBC* (2000) 32 H.L.R.784).

Harassment

5.06 Harassment has been said not to be a tort at common law (*Patel v Patel* [1988] 2 FLR 179) but conduct of that nature may nevertheless involve a trespass to land, a breach of covenant, a nuisance, and/or a criminal offence. Section 3 of the Protection from Harassment Act 1997 creates a statutory tort in respect of a breach or threatened breach of that Act (see further below).

Sources: statute

5.07 Statute has extended the protection of residential occupiers (not just tenants) in respect both of eviction and harassment. "Residential occupier" is defined (Protection from Eviction Act 1977, s.1(1)) and will include, for instance, contractual tenants and licensees, together with those enjoying security of tenure or protection against eviction.

Protection from Eviction Act 1977

5.08 First, the Protection from Eviction Act 1977 provides criminal sanctions and civil remedies. Section 1 defines and proscribes as criminal offences unlawful eviction and harassment, but breach of this section will not establish a civil cause of action. Section 2 proscribes the exercise of a right of re-entry or forfeiture against a person lawfully in residence of a dwelling except by court proceedings. Section 3 (which applies to tenancies not protected under other statutory regimes such as the Rent Act 1977, and also now to certain licences) proscribes eviction from a dwelling except by court proceedings, and breach of this section will ground a civil action.

Housing Act 1988

Secondly, s.27 of the Housing Act 1988 has created a new statutory tort of unlawfully **5.09**
depriving a residential occupier of occupation, with an enhanced measure of damages under
s.28.

Criminal Law Act 1977

Thirdly, the Criminal Law Act 1977, s.6 proscribes as a criminal offence the use of violence to **5.10**
secure entry to residential premises knowing that a person is present who is opposed to the
entry.

Protection from Harassment Act 1997

Fourthly, the Protection from Harassment Act 1997 prohibits harassment and provides **5.11**
remedies in the civil and criminal courts. The Act can be used in the case of campaigns of
harassment by a landlord. It creates four criminal offences: harassment (s.2); putting another
person in fear of violence (s.4); breach of a restraining order (s.5) and breach of an injunction
(s.3(6)). It also provides a civil claim for actual or apprehended harassment. This section is
potentially of use to anyone who is suffering harassment, even those who have no interest in
land (*e.g.* licensees who do not have exclusive possession).

Sub-occupiers

The adviser may frequently be required to consider the status of sub-occupiers as against the **5.12**
holders of superior interests. Depending on the circumstances, aspects of the foregoing
analysis may be relevant. The position of spouses and children may also have to be
considered.

Civil remedies

The remedies for unlawful eviction and harassment are principally of two kinds: injunctive **5.13**
relief to facilitate re-entry and restrain repetition, and damages. Although claims for damages
and injunctions are in essence parallel forms of relief, in one respect they will be exclusive. Re-
admission to occupation of the premises will disentitle the tenant from any claim for the
enhanced measure of damages under the Housing Act 1988, s.28.

Damages

Except where damages are assessed under the Housing Act 1988, s.28, in many if not most **5.14**
cases it will be appropriate to ask for exemplary and/or aggravated damages in addition to
any items of special damage. Exemplary and aggravated damages are available for claims in
tort for trespass to land (also for trespass to goods and the person) and in private nuisance,
but not in contract. It should also be noted that, for claims in contract based upon the
covenant for quiet enjoyment, unless the breach of covenant causes physical inconvenience

and discomfort, no general damages will be recoverable for injured feelings and mental distress. Under s.3 of the Protection from Harassment Act 1997, however, damages may be awarded for the anxiety caused by the harassment (see s.3(2)).

The appropriate forum

5.15 The County Court has extended jurisdiction to hear a claim for damages under the Housing Act 1988, ss.27 and 28: there is a specific costs penalty for bringing such proceedings in the High Court (s.40(1), (3) and (4)). In respect of claims for damages or injunctions at common law for unlawful eviction or harassment, the county court has unlimited jurisdiction under the County Courts Act 1984, s.15 (High Court and County Courts Jurisdiction Order 1991, art.2(1)(1)): any such claim commenced in the High Court will be liable firstly to be transferred to the county court for trial (since it will be unlikely to meet the criteria for allocation to the High Court lists (CPR Pt 7 PD para.2), and therefore secondly to be the subject of a deduction of up to 25 per cent of the costs on taxation (Supreme Court Act 1981, s.51(8),(9)). The power to impose such a sanction is also reflected in provisions in the Civil Procedure Rules (see CPR Pt 44). For these-reasons, the examples which follow describe proceedings in the County Court alone. The County Court will not allocate a claim to the small claims track if it includes a claim for harassment or unlawful eviction, therefore any trial will be heard on the fast track or multi track (CPR 26.7(4)).

Enforcement of injunctions and undertakings

5.16 Injunctions and undertakings in the county court are enforceable principally by proceedings for committal to prison for contempt of court. The procedure is governed by CPR Sch.2 and CCR Ord. 29. Injunctions and undertakings are also enforceable by proceedings for the sequestration of assets: but this mode of enforcement is now only available in the High Court (see CPR 70 PD 1.2(2)).

Committal

5.17 When an order in the nature of an injunction is sought and obtained, the adviser will need to have in mind the requirements for personal service and the endorsement of a penal notice so as to render the injunction enforceable by committal.

Penal notice The penal notice should be addressed to the person against whom the injunction was made. In the case of corporations (which obviously cannot be committed to prison), the penal notice can ordinarily be addressed to the corporation and the order served upon such director or other officer against whom enforcement by committal may be considered to be appropriate (*R v Wandsworth CC Ex p. Munn* (1994) 26 H.L.R. 697. It is not inappropriate to address the penal notice to a named director or other officer, but this will be subject to the approval of the court (*Munn*). The county court prescribed Form N77 is inapposite in respect of corporations, and may be adapted (*Munn*).

Breach of injunction In the event of a breach of an order or undertaking enforceable by committal, a claimant wishing to enforce the order can issue a claim form (CPR Pt 7) or an application notice (CPR Pt 23) seeking committal for contempt pursuant to CPR Sch.2 and CCR Ord. 29, r.1(4). An affidavit in support is required. The claim form or application notice must, by r.1(4A), identify the provisions in the order alleged to have been breached, and list the ways in which these provisions have been breached. The claim form or application notice must contain a prominent notice stating the possible consequences of the court making the committal order and of the respondent not attending the hearing (CPR Sch.1; RSC PD 52 paras 2.5 and 2.6).

Effect of defects   Given that the liberty of the subject is at stake, the need to follow the procedure correctly has been stressed in many cases (*e.g. Williams v Fawcett* [1986] QB 604) However the court has discretion to waive an irregularity under CPR 3.10 in exceptional circumstances (*Harmsworth v Harmsworth* [1987] 3 All E.R. 816). Alternatively the court can remedy the error on terms, including terms as to the costs, if no injustice is caused. However, careful drafting is obviously required.

Sequestration

A writ of sequestration may be obtained against the property of the person in contempt, or in the case of a body corporate, against the property of any director or other officer: CPR Sch.1; RSC Ord. 45, r.5(1). Permission from the court is required. The permission application (made in accordance with CPR Pt 23) must be made to a judge. The application notice must state the grounds of the application, and be served personally together with a copy of the witness statement of affidavit in support: CPR Sch.1; RSC Ord. 46, r.5. The judge clearly has discretion whether to give permission. If permission is given, the form of the writ which is then issued, is prescribed in the CPR Queens Bench Prescribed Forms.   **5.18**

Criminal proceedings

Protection from Eviction Act 1977

Criminal proceedings under the Protection from Eviction Act 1977 may be instituted by local authorities or by private individuals. The police do not as a matter of general policy initiate proceedings. The offences are triable either summarily or on indictment.   **5.19**

Criminal Law Act 1977

The offence under the Criminal Law Act 1977, s.6 is summary only. There is no specific power for local authorities to initiate a prosecution: private individuals or the police may do so.   **5.20**

Protection from Harassment Act 1997

There is no specific power for local authorities to initiate a prosecution under any of the protection from harassment offences. The s.2 offence of harassment is triable summarily only, although there is a racially aggravated form of the offence which is triable either way. The s.4 offence of putting another person in fear of violence is considered to be more serious, and is triable either way, as is the breach of an injunction under s.3 and breach of a restraining order under s.5.   **5.21**

Method of commencing proceedings

5.22 Criminal proceedings in Magistrates' Courts are started either by charge following arrest and production to the court, or by the laying of an information followed by summons or warrant. The information, summons or warrant is sufficient if it describes the specific offence with which the accused is charged in ordinary language avoiding so far as possible the use of technical terms and without necessarily stating all the elements of the offence, and gives such particulars as may be necessary for giving reasonable information of the nature of the charge (Magistrates' Courts Rules 1981, r.100(1)). If the offence is one created by or under any Act, the description of the offence shall contain a reference to the section of the Act (MCR, r.100(2)). Despite the apparent width of MCR, r.100(1), defects in the drafting of the information or summons may be fatal and invalidate a conviction (*Waring v Wheatley* (1951) 115 JP 630; *Hunter v Coombs* [1962] 1 All E.R. 904), and, although amendment will often be possible at or prior to trial, it will not be possible for instance on appeal to the Crown Court. Consequently, careful drafting is necessary.

Form of information

5.23 The information need not be in writing or on oath unless so required by statute (MCR, r.4). The Magistrates' Courts (Forms) Rules 1981 provide specimen forms of information and summons (Sch.2, Forms 1 and 2).

Indictments

5.24 In the case of trial on indictment, the Indictments Act 1915 and the Indictment Rules 1971 should be considered. Ultimate responsibility for the indictment rests with counsel for the prosecution. A bill of indictment should be preferred within 28 days of the date on which the accused is committed for trial, though this period may be extended (Indictments (Procedure) Rules 1971 r.5(1)–(3)). The indictment may contain counts for any indictable offence disclosed by the evidence from the committal proceedings (Administration of Justice (Miscellaneous Provisions) Act 1933, s.2(2)). Charges for any offences may be joined in the same indictment if those charges are founded on the same facts, or form or are a part of a series of offences of the same or a similar character (IR, r.9). Two or more defendants may be joined in one indictment. The layout of an indictment should substantially follow the form set out in the Indictment Rules, Sch.1 (r.4(1)). The indictment must be signed by a proper officer of the Crown Court (Administration of Justice (Miscellaneous Provisions) Act 1933, s.2(1)).

Duplicity

5.25 It is particularly important to be aware of the rule against duplicity, ie that an information or charge (*not* the summons or other document) or a single count on an indictment must each contain only one offence (MCR, r.12; IR, r.4(2)). It can be a matter of some art to determine whether a single information or count alleges two offences (and is therefore bad for duplicity) or whether it alleges what are collectively the components of a single activity or different methods of committing the same offence (in which case it will be valid). There is a wealth of legal authority: however, common sense and pragmatism appear to be the ultimate considerations (*DPP v Merriman* [1973] A.C. 584).

PART II: PRECEDENTS

Form 59   **5.26**

Letter of Claim[1]

Dear Sir,

LETTER OF CLAIM

RE: YOUR TENANT, FELICITY FIRKIN

We are instructed on behalf of Felicity Firkin, the tenant of 2 Bleak Road, Hazard, Doomshire, and of which you are the landlord.

We are instructed that on December 24, 2000 you unlawfully and intentionally evicted our client when you caused her to leave the premises with her three children by forcing the front door, using and threatening violence, and throwing her clothing and other belongings out of the window into the street.

On December 26, 2002, when our client had recovered sufficiently to return to the premises she found that the lock to the front door of the premises had been changed. Through the ground floor windows she could see that most of her belongings, and those of her children, together with presents and other preparations for Christmas, were still inside. However, by the time she later returned with a policeman, she could see that all these belongings had been removed. The total value of the property is approximately £3000. Our client requires the immediate return of it or compensation for its value.

A description of our client's injuries is as follows: Our client suffered bruising and swelling to both eyes, arms and legs, which were painful for two weeks, and two cracked ribs which were painful for two months. Our client requires compensation for her injuries.

Our client also requires from you exemplary and aggravated damages in respect of the trespass to her belongings and to her person by reason of your motivation for inflicting them and the aggravating manner in which they were caused.

In view of all the circumstances, our client has no desire to return to live at the premises, and requires you to compensate her for depriving her of occupation pursuant to ss.27 and 28 of the Housing Act 1988.

By reason of the evident seriousness of these matters, you may well consider it prudent to seek legal advice before responding. However, unless we receive your sufficient proposals for settlement of this matter within 21 days of posting, we have instructions to issue legal proceedings without further notice to you.

DISCLOSURE

If you decide that you are unwilling to settle this matter, please provide within 21 days of posting, the following:

(i) Copy of the tenancy agreement including tenancy conditions.

We look forward to hearing from you.

Yours faithfully,

---

[1] In the case of a tenant who seeks emergency remedies for unlawful eviction by way of without notice injunctions, no letter of claim will be required. It may occasionally be appropriate though to put the landlord on notice of the application, in particular where the presence of the landlord at court may assist to re-admit the tenant to possession more quickly. In the case of a tenant who has been evicted but who seeks no emergency relief and merely wishes to claim damages, a letter of claim will be appropriate.

Form 60   5.27

Particulars of Claim: unlawful eviction: no claim for re-instatement

---

Claim No. HA0100001

IN THE HAZARD COUNTY COURT

BETWEEN

FELICITY FIRKIN   **Claimant**

and

SIDNEY WIDGET   **Defendant**

PARTICULARS OF CLAIM

---

1. By an agreement made orally on or about April 1, 1997, and evidenced in writing by a rent book, the Defendant granted to the Claimant a weekly tenancy of residential premises at 2 Bleak Road, Hazard, Doomshire (referred to in this pleading as 'the tenancy' and 'the premises' accordingly).

2. By para.3 of the rent book it was an express term of the tenancy that the Defendant covenanted for the Claimant to have quiet enjoyment of the premises during the tenancy; alternatively, the term was to be implied.

3. On December 24, 2000 the Defendant unlawfully entered the premises by forcing open the front door; then assaulted and beat the Claimant threatened to use violence against the Claimant's children unless the Claimant and her children ceased occupation of the premises, interfered with her personal property by throwing her clothing and other belongings out of the window into the street, and thereby intended to and did cause the Claimant to leave the premises with her three children.

4. On a date between 24 and December 26, 2000 the Defendant by himself or by instructing or encouraging others changed the lock to the front door of the premises with the effect that when the Claimant attempted to regain entry to the premises on December 26, 2000 she was unable to do so.

5. By the Defendant's conduct the Claimant was unlawfully and in breach of covenant deprived of occupation of the premises and of the use and enjoyment of personal property which remained inside the premises.

6. On December 26, 2000 the Defendant by himself or by instructing or encouraging others converted to his own use the Claimant belongings and removed them from the premises. Particulars of the Claimant belongings, totalling £3000 in value, are given in the accompanying schedule [not here pleaded].

7. The conduct of the Defendant was calculated to profit himself by obtaining vacant possession of the premises and with a cynical disregard for the Claimant's rights, for which exemplary damages should be awarded.[2]

8. By the Defendant's conduct, the Claimant has sustained pain and suffering, loss and damage.

PARTICULARS

a) Bruising and swelling to both eyes, arms and legs, which were painful for two weeks.[3]

b) Two cracked ribs which were painful for two months.

c) The conduct of the Defendant was violent, and insulting; the manner in which the Claimant and her children were forced to vacate the premises (leaving behind many belongings including all their presents and other preparations for Christmas which the Defendant subsequently converted) was offensive and malicious; and in these circumstances aggravated damages should be awarded.[4]

d) The amount the Claimant expects to recover as Personal Damages for pain, suffering and loss of amenity is more than £1000.

9. The Claimant claims and is entitled to interest pursuant to s.69 of the County Courts Act 1984 at such rate and for such period as the court may consider just.

AND the Claimant claims:

1) Damages in excess of £15,000.[5]

2) An order for the delivery up of her belongings, or £3000 their value.

3) Aggravated and/or exemplary damages.

4) Interest[6].

5) Costs.

DATED this 23rd day of January 2001

STATEMENT OF TRUTH[7]

• (I believe) (The Claimant believes) that the facts stated in these Particulars of Claim are true.

• I am duly authorised by the Claimant to sign this statement.

Full name ....

Name of Claimant's solicitor's firm ....

Signed... Position or office held ....

- (Claimant) (if signing on behalf of firm or company)
  (Claimant's solicitor)

- delete as appropriate

....
Messrs Rue Theday
Sooham Road
Flogborough
DO5 5ER

Claimant's solicitors

who will accept service at the above address

TO the District Judge
AND TO the Defendant

---

[2] CPR 16.4(1)(e).

[3] If a claim has a personal injury element before issuing, the Claimant will have to consider the pre-action protocol on personal injury. Also where the action is for personal injuries and the Claimant is seeking to rely on the evidence of a medical practitioner, he must attach to, or serve with, the particulars of claim on the medical report. He must also attach a schedule giving details of any past and future expenses and losses which he claims (CPR Pt 16 PD para.4).

[4] CPR 16.4(1)(b).

[5] CPR 16.3(2) and (3). In a claim for personal injuries, the Claimant must state whether the amount he expects to recover as general damages for pain suffering and loss of amenity is not more than £1000, or more than £1000.

[6] CPR 16.4(2).

[7] CPR 22.1.

5.28   Form 61

Particulars of Claim: unlawful eviction: claim for re-instatement

---

Claim No. UR0000001

IN THE URBANE COUNTY COURT

B E T W E E N

HARRY SLOPE   **Claimant**

and

MARC SHIMAN   **Defendant**

PARTICULARS OF CLAIM

---

1. By an oral agreement made in about February 1995 the Defendant granted the Claimant a weekly tenancy of residential premises at 13b Rockingham Towers, Urbane (in this pleading referred to as 'the tenancy' and 'the premises' accordingly).

2. It was an implied term of the tenancy that the Defendant covenanted for the Claimant to have quiet enjoyment of the premises during the tenancy.

3. On a date between 9 April and May 6, 2000 the Defendant by himself or by instructing or encouraging others unlawfully entered upon the premises and obstructed the doorway by fitting a locked metal screen over the front door, the conduct complained of being also in breach of covenant.

4. By reason of the Defendant's conduct, the Claimant was unable to enter the premises on May 6, 2000 or thereafter, and was caused to spend the weekend of May 7, 2000 sleeping rough.

5. The conduct of the Defendant was a serious infringement of the Claimant's rights for which aggravated damages should be awarded.

6. [AS IN FORM 60 PARAGRAPH 7]

7. [AS IN FORM 60 PARAGRAPH 9]

AND the Claimant claims:

   1) An order requiring the Defendant forthwith to remove the locked metal screen from the front door to the premises.

2) An order requiring the Defendant forthwith to re-admit the Claimant to occupation of the premises.

3) An order forbidding the Defendant, by himself or by instructing or encouraging any other person, from in any way interfering with the Claimant's entry to or quiet enjoyment of the premises.

4) Damages in excess of £15,000.

5) Aggravated and/or exemplary damages.

6) Interest.

7) Costs.

STATEMENT OF TRUTH

- (I believe) (The Claimant believes) that the facts stated in these Particulars of Claim are true.

- I am duly authorised by the Claimant to sign this statement.

Full name ....

Name of Claimant's solicitor's firm ....

Signed.. Position or office held ....

- (Claimant) (if signing on behalf of firm or company) (Claimant's solicitor)

- delete as appropriate

ALEC SMART

DATED this 9th day of May 2000

....
Charden Ambers & Co
Charden House
Enterprise Road
Urbane
Northshire
NO8 8LE
Claimant's solicitors

who will accept service at the above address

TO the District Judge
AND TO the Defendant

5.29 Form 62

Particulars of Claim: harassment

Claim No. **UR 0000002**

IN THE URBANE COUNTY COURT

B E T W E E N

<table>
<tr><td>HARRY SLOPE</td><td>**Claimant**</td></tr>
<tr><td>and</td><td></td></tr>
<tr><td>MARC SHIMAN</td><td>**Defendant**</td></tr>
</table>

PARTICULARS OF CLAIM

---

1. [AS IN FORM 61 PARAGRAPH 1]

2. [AS IN FORM 61 PARAGRAPH 2]

3. It was an implied term of the tenancy that the Defendant would not derogate from his grant of the tenancy to the Claimant.

4. On dates between July 15, 2000 and September 1, 2000, in breach of covenant the Defendant interrupted the electricity supply to the premises for periods varying between 30 minutes and 12 hours by removing the main fuses.

5. Between 2 and September 6, 2000, the Defendant introduced into adjoining premises within the Defendant's possession and control, namely 13a Rockingham Towers, his brother-in-law, Fortissimo Sottovoce, who from about midnight each night sang 'Nessun dorma' with the aid of a karaoke machine for periods of approximately three hours continuously at loud volume.

6. Between 7 and September 9, 2000, the Defendant deposited and left a quantity of foul-smelling dung on premises retained within his possession and control, namely the landing outside 13a Rockingham Towers, the odour from which percolated into and pervaded the premises.

7. The matters in paras 5 and 6 above were a nuisance and/or in breach of covenant.

8. The matters complained of were committed by the Defendant with the intention of causing the Claimant to cease occupation of the premises as his residence and thereby calculated to profit the Defendant with a cynical disregard for the Claimant's rights, for which exemplary damages should be awarded.

9. By reason of the matters complained of the Claimant has suffered loss and damage.

PARTICULARS

a) When the supply of electricity was interrupted the Claimant was unable to run any electrical appliances so that he could not cook, heat water or heat or light the premises. On September 1, 2000 when the lights went out, the Claimant tripped and fell over his cat breaking his glasses and landing on an antique chamber-pot thereby causing it to break irreparably.

Cost of: repairing glasses   £150
replacing chamber-pot   £300

b) Between 2 and September 6, 2000 the Claimant was prevented from sleeping by reason of the noise.

c) From 7 to September 9, 2000 the Claimant was made physically sick by the smell, and could not eat or sleep. The smell pervaded and lingered on the Claimant's clothes and bedding necessitating cleaning.

Cost of cleaning: £200

d) By reason of the manner in which the Defendant inflicted the loss upon the Claimant and the particular effect upon the Claimant, aggravated damages should be awarded.

10. [AS IN FORM 60 PARAGRAPH 9]

AND the Claimant claims:

1) An order forbidding the Defendant whether by himself or by instructing or encouraging any other person from in any way interfering with the Claimant's quiet enjoyment of the premises; or from making or causing or permitting any noise or odour upon the Defendant's premises which is or may become a nuisance toward the Claimant.

2) An order forbidding the Defendant from interfering in any way with the electricity supply to the premises.

3) Damages in excess of £5000 but less than £15,000.

4) Exemplary and/or aggravated damages.

5) Costs.

[CONCLUDE AS IN FORM 61]

5.30   **Form 63**

Notice of application for interlocutory injunction

THE URBANE COUNTY COURT

General form of application for an injunction[1]
CPR 4, PD 4

Notes on completion	
Tick whichever box applies and specify legislation where appropriate	☑ By application in pending proceedings ☐ Under statutory provisions
(1) Enter the full name of the person making the application	**The Claimant[1] Harry Slope applies to the court for an injunction order in the following terms:**
(2) Enter the full name of the person the injunction is to be directed to	**The Defendant[2] Marc Shipman be forbidden (whether by himself, or by instructing or encouraging any other person)[3]** from in any way interfering with the Claimant's entry to or quiet enjoyment of the premises at 13b Rockingham Towers, Urbane ("the premises").
(3) Set out here the proposed restraining orders (if the defendant is a limited company, delete the wording in brackets and insert "Whether by its servants, agents, officers or otherwise"	
(4) Set out here any proposed mandatory orders requiring acts to be done	And that the Defendant[4] be required forthwith upon service upon him of this order to remove the locked metal screen from the front door to, and readmit the Claimant to occupation of, the premises.
(5) Set out here any further terms asked for including provision for costs	And that[5] the Defendant pays the costs of this application.
(6) Enter the names of all persons who have made witness statements or sworn affidavits in support of this application	**The grounds of this application** are set out in the witness statement(s) of the Claimant dated May 9, 2000. This (these) sworn statement(s) is (are) served with this application.
(7) Enter the names and addresses of all persons upon whom it is intended to serve this application	**The application is to be served upon[7]** Marc Shipman of Dunromin Arcacia Avenue Hazard Doomshire

(8) Enter the full name and address for service and delete as required	**This application is filed by**[8] **Charden Ambers and Co** **(the Solicitors for) the Claimant whose address for service is Charden, Enterprise Road, Urbane, Northshire NO8 8LE.** **Signed** **Dated**
*Name and address of the person this application is directed to	*This section to be completed by the Court* **To*** **Of** **This application will be heard by the (District) Judge** **At** **on the day of 1999 at o'clock** **If you do not attend at the time shown the court may make and injunction order in your absence.** *If you do not fully understand this application you should go to a Solicitor, Legal Advice Centre or a Citizens' Advice Bureau.*

The Court Office at is open 10am to 4pm Mon–Fri. Where corresponding with the court, please address all forms and letters to the Court Manager and quote the case number.

[1] County Court Prescribed Form N16A which has been retained under the Civil Procedure Rules.

5.31   Form 64

Witness Statement in support of application for interlocutory injunction[9]

Claimant
H Slope
First
Exhibits: none
Date: May 9, 2000

Claim No. UR 0000001

IN THE URBANE COUNTY COURT

B E T W E E N

HARRY SLOPE   **Claimant**

and

MARC SHIMAN   **Defendant**

I, Harry Slope, unemployed, of 13b Rockingham Towers, Urbane, will say:

1.   I make this statement in support of my application for interim relief against the Defendant. The matters contained in this witness statement are within my own knowledge and are true.

2.   By an oral agreement made in about February 1995 the Defendant granted me a weekly tenancy of a one-bedroom flat at 13b Rockingham Towers, Urbane.

3.   Until the end of March 2000, I was working as a grommet-groover at Grimbles Grommets in Urbane. However, I was made redundant on April 1, 2000, and have been unemployed since. After I lost my job, I had no money to pay the rent which was due the following week on Friday April 8, 2000, and when the Defendant's father-in-law, Ken Krush, came round to collect my rent that evening he said I would have to get out if I did not pay. I explained that I had already made a claim for income support and housing benefit so that the rent would be paid, but he said this was no good. He said the Defendant did not allow "parasites" to live in his properties, and that in any case the benefit office was so inefficient it would take months before they would pay the rent. I said I had nowhere else to go, to which he retorted that if I did not go he would throw me out. By this point he was shouting loudly at me when a friend of mine arrived, and Mr Krush suddenly left.

4.   By reason of this unpleasantness, on April 9, 2000 I went to stay with my parents in Boring-on-Sea. I had intended to stay there only a short while, but that same evening my mother had an accident when her hair curlers overheated and she was

rushed to hospital with severe burns. In the result, I stayed for four weeks to care for my invalid father until she had recovered.

5. When I returned to the premises on May 6, 2000 I found that a solid metal screen had been fixed over the outside of my front door so that I could not get in. I went round to the Defendant's address but there was no-one there.

6. I was forced to spend Saturday and Sunday night sleeping rough. I had no money left on me by the time that I returned from my parents, and none of my friends would accommodate me because they will not even acknowledge me now I am unemployed.

7. I have been unlawfully evicted. I want to resume occupation of the premises. I have nowhere else to live. All my belongings except for the contents of one rucksack which I have with me were left inside the premises.

8. I therefore ask the court to grant me interim relief in the terms of my application herein.

STATEMENT OF TRUTH

- I believe that the contents of my Witness Statement are true.

Full name ....

Signed ....

Date

---

[9] Evidence will normally be given by witness statement (CPR 32.6(1)) unless the court, practice direction or other enactment requires otherwise. Statements of case and application notices may also be used as evidence, provided they are supported with a statement of truth (CPR 32.6(2)). A party can decide to give evidence by affidavit, but the extra cost of doing so cannot be recovered (CPR 32.15).

5.32   **Form 65**

Draft form of order upon without notice interim application

[HEADING AS FORM 64]

Upon hearing [counsel/the solicitor] for the Claimant

AND upon the Claimant by his [counsel/solicitor] undertaking to abide by any order which the court may make as to damages in case the court shall hereafter consider that the Defendant shall have sustained any by reason of this order which the Claimant ought to pay[10]

IT IS ORDERED that until after May 16, 2000 or further order in the meantime the Defendant be

1)   required forthwith upon service upon him of this order to remove the locked metal screen from the front door to, and re-admit the Claimant to occupation of, the premises at 13b Rockingham Towers, Urbane ("the premises");

2)   forbidden, whether by himself or by instructing or encouraging any other person, from in any way interfering with the Claimant's entry to or quiet enjoyment of the premises.

AND IT IS FURTHER ORDERED that this application be further considered by the court on May 16, 2000
Costs reserved

---

[10] This is the standard undertaking in damages required by the court from applicants when granting interim injunctions.

Form 66   **5.33**

Penal notice: (Prescribed Form N77)

PENAL NOTICE

To Marc Shiman of Dunromin, Acacia Avenue, Hazard, Doomshire
You must obey the directions contained in this order. If you do not, you will be guilty
of contempt of court, and you may be sent to prison.

5.34   Form 67 (In the form of a Part 23 application on Form N244)

Application for an Order for Committal

Claim No. UR0000001

IN THE URBANE COUNTY COURT

HARRY SLOPE   **Claimant**

MARC SHIPMAN   **Defendant**

PART A

I, Stanley Squib, solicitor, on behalf of the Claimant intend to apply for an order that:

(1) the Defendant be committed to prison for disobeying the order of the court made on May 9, 2000 and that

(2) the Defendant be ordered to pay the costs of this application, assessed at £320 in accordance with the bill annexed.

Because:

1.   On May 9, 2000 the court made an order in the following terms:

That until May 16, 2000 or further order in the mean time, the Defendant be:

2)   required forthwith upon service upon him of this order to remove the locked metal screen from the front door to, and to readmit the Claimant to occupation of, the premises at 13b Rockingham Towers, Urbane ("the premises");

3)   forbidden whether by himself, or by instructing, or encouraging any other person, from in any way interfering with the Claimant's entry to, or quiet enjoyment of, the premises.

2.   On May 16, 2000 the court continued the above orders until trial or further order in the meantime.

3.   The Defendant was in court when the order was made and heard the Judge warn him that he would go to prison if he disobeyed it.

4.   The order included a penal notice and was served on the Defendant by a process server whose witness statement is filed and served with this application notice.

5. The Defendant has broken the order by:

   1) Refusing or failing to remove the metal screen forthwith upon service upon him of the orders of May 9, 2000 and May 16, 2000 or at all.

   2) Refusing or failing to re-admit the Claimant to occupation of the premises.

   3) By reason of the matters aforesaid, interfering with the Claimant's entry or quiet enjoyment of the premises.

6. The Claimant further relies on his affidavit, which is filed and served with this application notice.

7. Unless the Defendant is punished for his actions he will continue to disobey the orders.

PART B

I wish to rely on my statement of case and on the attached affidavit

Signed S. Squib   **Position or office held** Solicitor

IMPORTANT NOTICE

The court has power to send you to prison and to fine you if it finds that any of the allegations made against you are true and amount to a contempt of court.

You must attend court on the date shown on the front of this form. It is in your own interest to do so. You should bring with you any witnesses and documents which you think will help you put your side of the case.

If you consider the allegations are not true you must tell the court why. If it is established that they are true, you must tell the court of any good reason why they do not amount to a contempt of court, or, if they do, why you should not be punished.

If you need advice you should show this document at once to your solicitor or go to the Citizens' Advice Bureau.

Address to which documents about the case should be sent

Charden Ambers & Co
Charden House, Enterprise Road, Urbane, Northshire
NO8 8LE

STATEMENT OF TRUTH

The applicant believes that the facts stated in this application are true

Signed S. Squib   **Position or office held** Solicitor
Date

5.35   Form 68

Affidavit/affirmation in support of Application to Commit

Claimant
H Slope
Second
Exhibits: none
Date: May 17 2000

Claim No. UR0000001

IN THE URBANE COUNTY COURT

B E T W E E N

HARRY SLOPE   **Claimant**

and

MARC SHIMAN   **Defendant**

I, Harry Slope, unemployed, of 13b Rockingham Towers, Urbane, STATE ON OATH as follows[11]:

1. I make this affirmation in support of my application for the Defendant to be committed to prison for contempt of this court. The matters contained in this affirmation which are within my own knowledge are true; where they are not within my own knowledge their source is indicated and I believe them to be true.

2. On the 9th day of May 2000, the court made an order as follows: that until after May 16, 2000 or further order in the meantime the Defendant be:

    1) required forthwith upon service upon him of this order to remove the locked metal screen from the front door to, and re-admit the Claimant to occupation of, the premises at 13b Rockingham Towers, Urbane ('the premises');

    2) forbidden, whether by himself or by instructing or encouraging any other person, from in any way interfering with the Claimant's entry to or quiet enjoyment of the premises.

2. On the 16th day of May 2000, the court continued the above orders until trial or further order in the meantime.

3. I am informed by my solicitor that the order dated May 9, 2000 was duly served personally on the Defendant on that same day, and that the order dated May 16, 2000 was also served personally on that same day. Despite this, the Defendant has not removed the metal screen nor re-admitted me to occupation of the premises at all.

[CONCLUDE AS IN FORM 64]

[11] Under CPR Sch.1 PD 52, para.3.1, written evidence in support of a committal application must be given by affidavit.

Form 69 (In the form of a Part 23 application on Form PF244) **5.36**

Application for permission to issue a writ of sequestration

Claim No. 0000001

HIGH COURT OF JUSTICE
QUEENS BENCH DIVISION

B E T W E E N

HARRY SLOPE   **Claimant**

MARC SHIPMAN   **Defendant**

APPLICATION NOTICE

Part A   I, Stanley Squib, solicitor on behalf of the Claimant apply for an order, a draft of which is attached for:

(1) permission may be granted to issue a writ of sequestration against the Defendant for disobeying the order of this court made on May 9, 2000 and that:

(2) the Defendant be ordered to pay the costs of this application, assessed at £320 in accordance with the bill annexed.

Because

1. On May 9, 2000 the court made an order in the following terms:

That until May 16, 2000 or further order in the mean time the Defendant be:

2) required forthwith upon service upon him of this order to remove the locked metal screen from the front door to, and to readmit the Claimant to occupation, of the premises at 13b Rockingham Towers, Urbance ("the premises");

3) forbidden whether by himself, or by instructing, or encouraging any other person, from in any way interfering with the Claimant's entry to, or quiet enjoyment of, the premises.

2. On May 16, 2000 the court continued the above orders until trial or further order in the meantime.

3. The Defendant was in court when the order was made and heard the Judge warn him that he would go to prison if he disobeyed it.

4. The order included a penal notice and was served on the Defendant by a process server whose witness statement is filed and served with this application notice.

5. The Defendant has broken the order by:

    1) Refusing or failing to remove the metal screen forthwith upon service upon him of the May 9, 2000 and May 16, 2000 orders or at all.

    2) Refusing or failing to re-admit the Claimant to occupation of the premises.

    3) By reason of the matters aforesaid, interfering with the Claimant's entry or quiet enjoyment of the premises.

6. The Claimant further relies on his affidavit, which is filed and served with this application notice.

7. Unless the writ of sequestration is issued the Defendant will continue to disobey court orders.

Part B
I wish to rely on my statement of case and on the attached affidavit

Signed   S. Squib   **Position or office held**   Solicitor

Address to which documents about the case should be sent
Charden Ambers & Co
Charden House,
Enterprise Road,
Urbane,
Northshire
NO8 8LE

STATEMENT OF TRUTH

The applicant believes that the facts stated in this application are true

Signed   S. Squib   **Position or office held**   Solicitor
Date

Form 70 5.37

Defence and Part 20 Claim to Form 61

Claim No. UR0000001

IN THE URBANE COUNTY COURT

B E T W E E N

HARRY SLOPE **Claimant**

and

MARC SHIMAN **Defendant/Part 20 Claimant**

DEFENCE AND PART 20 CLAIM

DEFENCE

---

1. References to paragraph numbers in this pleading are references to the Particulars of Claim save where indicated otherwise.

2. Paragraphs 1 and 2 are admitted. It is averred that the tenancy was an assured tenancy within the meaning of the Housing Act 1988.

3. It is admitted that on April 29, 2000 the Defendant himself fitted a locked metal screen over the front door to the premises.

4. It is denied[12] that the matters aforesaid were either unlawful or in breach of covenant as follows in paras 5 to 8.

5. By reason of notice to quit given orally by the Claimant on April 8, 2000 to the Defendant's father-in-law, Ken Krush, and expiring on May 6, 2000 the Defendant waiving the requirement to give proper notice in writing, the tenancy duly determined on May 6, 2000.[13]

6. Further or alternatively, if which is denied the Claimant was still the tenant of the premises at the material time, the Defendant's entry on to the premises was justified[14] by the necessity to preserve the premises from the acts of vandals who had broken the door down, and further permitted by an implied term[15] that the tenant should afford to the Defendant access to the premises for executing repairs to the door.

7. In the further alternative, at the material time the Defendant believed and had reasonable cause to believe that the Claimant had ceased to reside in the premises.[16]

8. It is accordingly denied that the Defendant is liable to the Claimant as alleged or at all.

9. If which is denied, the Defendant is liable to the Claimant in any sum, the Defendant will set off in diminution or extinction thereof any sum awarded to him pursuant to the Counterclaim below.

10. Save as is expressly admitted or denied herein, the Defendant is unable to admit, or deny, the allegations contained in the particulars of claim and requires the Claimant to prove them.

PART 20 CLAIM

11. Paragraphs 2 and 5 above are repeated.

12. The Defendant is the freehold owner and entitled to possession of the premises.

13. The weekly rent pursuant to the tenancy was £70 per week. Up to May 6, 2000 the Claimant was and is £700 in arrear with the rent.

14. On May 20, 2000 the Claimant was permitted by the Defendant to enter into occupation of the premises pursuant to the order of this court made on May 16, 2000. The Claimant has made no payment since that date in respect of his occupation.

15. The Defendant is entitled to and claims interest pursuant to s.69 of the County Courts Act 1984 at such rate and for such period as the court may consider just.

AND the Defendant counterclaims:

1) £500 arrears of rent.

2) Mesne profits or alternatively rent at the rate of £10 per day from May 20, 2000.

3) Possession of the premises.[17]

4) Interest.

5) Costs.

DATED this   day of   20

STATEMENT OF TRUTH

- (I believe) (the Defendant believes) that the facts stated in this Defence are true.

- I am duly authorised by the Defendant to sign this statement.

Full name ....

Name of Defendant's solicitor's firm ....

Signed.....................................Position or office held...

- (Defendant)   (if signing on behalf of firm or company)
  (Defendant's solicitor)

- delete as appropriate

....

TO the District Judge
AND TO the Claimant

---

[12] Where the defendant denies an allegation he must state his reason for doing so and if he intends to put forward a different version of events from that given by the Claimant, he must state that version. A defendant who fails to deal with an allegation will be taken to admit that allegation (CPR 16.5(2)).

[13] Since the tenancy is an assured tenancy within the provisions of the Housing Act 1988, although the service of a notice to quit by the landlord is of no effect (s.5(1)), the tenancy may yet be brought to an end by the tenant giving notice to quit. Although such notice to quit must be in writing so as to comply with s.8(1) of the Protection from Eviction Act 1977 and be valid, nevertheless the landlord can waive the defect and accept the notice as valid (*Elsden v Pick* [1980] 1 W.L.R. 898; *Snowden v Hackney LBC*, [2000] J.H.L. D9). The termination of the tenancy would prevent liability of the landlord in trespass or in contract from arising, because thereafter the Claimant would be a trespasser; the Protection from Eviction Act 1977, s.3 would not apply because the tenancy was statutorily protected.

[14] Justification is a defence to trespass and may occur in a number of ways, *e.g.* by reason of necessity.

[15] Housing Act 1988, s.16.

[16] This is the statutory defence to a claim for damages under the Housing Act 1988, ss.27–28 (s.28(8)).

[17] Possession is counterclaimed here because if the tenancy was brought to an end by the Claimant he will be a trespasser.

5.38　Form 71

Particulars of Claim for harassment and for an injunction against harassment pursuant to the Protection from Harassment Act 1997

Claim No. UR0166613

IN THE URBANE COUNTY COURT

B E T W E E N

DEIDRE SPRATT　　　　　　　　　　**Claimant**

and

REGGIE FISH　　　　　　　　　　　**Defendant**

PARTICULARS OF CLAIM

1.　The Claimant is a football manager and is a tenant at 19 Eel Mansions by reason of an assured shorthold tenancy agreement dated January 1, 2000. The Defendant is her landlord.

2.　It was an implied term of the said tenancy that the Defendant covenanted for the Claimant to have quiet enjoyment of the premises during the tenancy.

3.　Since July 14, 2000 the Defendant has maintained a campaign of unwanted letters and telephone calls to the Claimant which has caused considerable distress to the Claimant.

PARTICULARS

(i)　On July 14, 2000 the Defendant rang the Claimant at work on four separate occasions suggesting that she could pay her rent "in kind" and made lewd and improper remarks. The Defendant persisted in making these calls despite a request from the Claimant that he should stop.

(ii)　On July 15, 2000 when the Claimant arrived home from work the Defendant was waiting for her in his car. He gave her a large bunch of roses and said that he would be round the next day "to collect the rent". The Claimant again told the Defendant that she was not interested and that she wanted to pay the rent in a proper way.

(iii)　On July 16, 2000 at approximately 7pm the Defendant rang the Claimant and said that he was on his way round and asked the Claimant "to put something nice on". The Claimant became extremely concerned that the Defendant was persisting with his advances despite her protestations. She telephoned her boyfriend and asked him to come round. The Defendant arrived at the same time as the Claimant's boyfriend and immediately left leaving a letter which said only "Darling either you pay your rent in the way we agreed or you will have to go".

(iv) On July 23, 2000 the Defendant again rang the Claimant at work and made lewd suggestions as well as stating that he would "collect the rent tonight" and that "if you want to ensure that you keep the flat make sure your boyfriend is away tonight".

4. As a result of the Defendant's conduct the Claimant has suffered considerable anxiety and stress. She has missed two days at work as a result of the anxiety and as a result has been asked to leave her job.[18]

5. The Defendant's conduct amounts to harassment of the Claimant contrary to ss.1 and 3 of the Protection from Harassment Act 1997, as the Defendant has at all times known or ought to have known, and he has thereby alarmed the Claimant and caused her distress and anxiety.

6. Further or alternatively the Defendant's conduct amounts to a breach of the implied covenant of quiet enjoyment.

7. The Defendant intends to continue his harassment unless restrained by order of the court.

8. The Claimant claims interest[19] on the damages under s.69 of the County Courts Act 1984 at such rates and over such periods as may be just.

AND the Claimant claims:

(1) an injunction restraining the Defendant from pursuing any conduct which amounts to harassment of her;

(2) damages in excess of £5000 but less than £15,000

(3) interest on damages under s.69 of the County Courts Act 1984 at such rates and for such periods as may be just

[CONCLUDE AS PER FORM 62 WITH STATEMENT OF TRUTH]

---

[18] Under s.3(2) of the PHA 1997 damages can be awarded for any anxiety caused by harassment and financial loss resulting from the harassment.
[19] CPR 16.4 (1)(b) and (2) – if the Claimant is seeking interest the particulars must claim a statement to that effect and details as to the basis on which the right to interest is said to arise.

5.39   **Form 72**

Information: unlawful eviction

Unlawful eviction contrary to s.1(2) of the Protection from Eviction Act 1977

MARC SHIMAN on April 29, 2000 unlawfully deprived Harry Slope, the residential occupier, of his occupation of premises, namely 13b Rockingham Towers, Urbane, by changing the locks of the said premises during the absence of the residential occupier.

5.40   **Form 73**

Information: using violence to secure entry

Using violence for the purpose of securing entry contrary to s.6 of the Criminal Law Act 1977

SIDNEY WIDGET on December 24, 2000 at 2 Bleak House, Hazard, Doomshire (hereafter referred to as 'the premises'), without lawful authority used violence by forcing open a door for the purpose of securing entry to the premises for himself at a time when to his knowledge there was a person, namely Felicity Firkin, on the premises who was opposed to the entry which the violence was intended to secure.

5.41   **Form 74**

Information: harassment contrary to sections 1 and 2 of the Protection from Harassment Act 1997

REGGIE FISH on July 14, 2000, July 15, 2000, July 16, 2000 and July 23, 2000 pursued a course of conduct amounting to harrassment of Deidre Spratt by making malicious and lewd telephone calls and delivering malicious and lewd correspondence on the said dates when he knew, or ought to have known, that his conduct amounted to harrassment of Ms Spratt.

Form 75 5.42

Indictment

Indictment No.

IN THE CROWN COURT AT HAZARD

THE QUEEN v MARC SHIMAN and FORTISSIMO SOTTOVOCE
who are charged as follows:

COUNT 1

STATEMENT OF OFFENCE

Unlawful harassment contrary to s.1(3) of the Protection from Eviction Act 1977

PARTICULARS OF OFFENCE

MARC SHIMAN between July 15, 2000 and September 1, 2000 persistently withdrew services reasonably required for occupation, namely the supply of electricity, from Harry Slope, the residential occupier of premises at 13b Rockingham Towers, Urbane, with intent to cause the residential occupier to give up his occupation of the said premises.

COUNT 2

STATEMENT OF OFFENCE

Unlawful harassment contrary to s.1(3) of the Protection from Eviction Act 1977

PARTICULARS OF OFFENCE

MARC SHIMAN between 7 and September 9, 2000 did acts likely to interfere with the peace or comfort of Harry Slope, the residential occupier of premises at 13b Rockingham Towers, Urbane, namely deposited and left a large quantity of guano on the landing outside 13a Rockingham Towers, with intent to cause the residential occupier to give up his occupation of the said premises.

COUNT 3

STATEMENT OF OFFENCE

Unlawful harassment contrary to s.1(3A) of the Protection from Eviction Act 1977

PARTICULARS OF OFFENCE

MARC SHIMAN and FORTISSIMO SOTTOVOCE[20] between September 2 and September 6, 2000 did acts likely to interfere with the peace or comfort of Harry Slope, the residential occupier of premises at 13b Rockingham Towers, Urbane, namely caused noise by singing and electronic amplification to emanate from 13a Rockingham Towers, knowing or having reasonable cause to believe that that conduct was likely to cause the residential occupier to give up occupation of the premises, without reasonable grounds for doing those acts.

[signed]

An officer of the court

---

[20] The two defendants have been joined in this count on the premise that there is evidence of a joint enterprise and that Fortissimo Sottovoce can be shown to have acted as the landlord's agent.

PART III: CHECKLIST

Civil

---

1. If you are bringing proceedings, consider whether interim relief is required.

2. If interim relief is not required or appropriate, prepare letter of claim.

3. If interim relief is required, prepare notice of application, witness statement, draft order, and draft particulars of claim (if time).

4. Particularly if you are applying without notice for interim relief, make sure that you have made full and proper disclosure in the witness statement of all relevant facts and matters, including any unfavourable ones.

5. Upon obtaining any injunction, make sure that the order contains a penal notice in proper form.

6. If an undertaking is given, in the county court use Form N117.

7. Make sure that the pleadings are in the proper form. Do they contain all the necessary particulars? If not, consider what may be done to amend them.

8. Where the action includes a claim for personal injury, check that you have complied with the pre-action protocol, and remember the obligation to file a medical report.

9. If you are seeking to enforce an injunction/undertaking, consider which method of enforcement is appropriate and prepare documents as necessary.

10. If you are applying to commit the contemnor to prison, make sure in particular that the application notice is in proper form and gives full particulars of the alleged breaches. Make sure also that the affidavit in support gives adequate detail.

11. When pursuing a claim for damages to trial, consider whether you need to prepare a schedule of special and general damages. If the claimant is not reinstated in the premises, damages are recoverable under the Housing Act 1988, ss.27 and 28: this will require expert valuation evidence.

5.44 *Criminal*

1. Prepare and lay the information.

2. Check the wording of the summons.

3. If the proceedings are triable either way, and if requested to provide advance information, consider whether to provide a summary of the evidence or copies of written statements.

4. If the proceedings are committed for trial on indictment, make sure the indictment is drafted correctly.

Chapter 6
Possession Proceedings

PART I: INTRODUCTION

Proceedings for the recovery of possession form a very substantial and crucial part of housing **6.01** law practice. In addition, they are technically complex, so that the correct choice and drafting of documents is particularly important. These factors are reflected in the comparative length of this chapter, and the introduction in particular. The opportunity will be taken in the introduction to address the impact of the more important substantive and procedural questions upon the use of the forms and pleadings. This chapter also includes the various notices which are likely to be required as a preliminary to the commencement of proceedings.

Various legislative schemes have significantly affected the existence or enforceability of an owner's right to possession at common law. Moreover, the law leans heavily against the recovery of possession of residential premises by self-help. Consequently, in the vast majority of cases it will be necessary to bring proceedings, and where not necessary often still desirable to do so. An understanding of the common law, the statutory schemes, and the way in which the two interact, is necessary in order both to prepare for, and then conduct (or defend), proceedings for possession.

The Civil Procedure Rules (CPR) have introduced a new set of procedures for bringing and defending possession proceedings in the County Court and High Court. Part 55 of the CPR came into force on October 15, 2001. The procedures in Pt 55 are described in some detail later in this chapter. The procedure for mortgage possession cases is described in Chapter 7.

Termination of tenancy/licence at common law

Generally

At common law, the right to recover possession will depend upon the termination of any **6.02** permission or contract for the occupation of the premises. Termination may occur in a variety of ways. At one extreme, a bare licence or tenancy at will may be terminated immediately, simply by a demand for possession. Contractual licences may be terminated by notice which, in the absence of other contractual provision, revokes the licence immediately but is operative only from the expiration of a reasonable time. A periodic tenancy may be terminated by the giving of notice to quit. A fixed term tenancy will terminate upon expiry of the term. A tenancy may be terminated prematurely by the landlord if the agreement contains an express entitlement to re-enter for breach of convenant (forfeiture), or where a limiting condition of the agreement operates. If an agreement so provides, it may also be terminated prematurely by the giving of notice (usually referred to as a "break clause"), or by the satisfaction of a condition. A tenancy may also terminate in other ways including by surrender, merger, or disclaimer. The termination of a superior interest will furthermore bring to an end at common law any lesser interest, except in the case of a surrender, merger, or disclaimer, and subject to a sub-tenant's right to claim relief from forfeiture.

Deserted premises

6.03   Although probably little used, there is a special procedure in the County Court under the Landlord and Tenant Act 1954, s.54 in relation to deserted premises for a landlord who has power to serve a notice to quit, to apply and have the court terminate the tenancy. The procedure, by application under Pt 55 CPR[1] is designed for situations where the landlord cannot locate or communicate with the tenant (and thus may be in difficulty as to proper service of documents). There is similar provision under the Distress for Rent Act 1737, s.16, by the making of a complaint to a Magistrates' Court.

Notices to quit: formalities

6.04   The adviser will frequently have to prepare or consider the form and content of notices to terminate, in particular, periodic tenancies and licences. Termination of a residential agreement by notice, at common law, is subject to such formality and conditions as are imposed first by the agreement itself, second by common law rules, and third by statutory provision. The statutory rules are contained in the Protection from Eviction Act 1977, s.5: they do not reduce any other requirement of the notice (*e.g.* the period of notice), but they do establish general and minimum conditions of validity which cannot be excluded by agreement.

The statutory provisions apply to any notice to quit in respect of a dwelling (cf a demand for possession terminating a tenancy at will), with the one exception of an "excluded tenancy" entered into after January 14, 1989 (unless such a tenancy was itself entered into pursuant to an agreement made before that date). The provisions also apply to any notice to determine a periodic licence in respect of a dwelling (cf an employment licence), with the one exception of an "excluded licence". Excluded tenancies and licences are defined in the PEA 1977, s.3A.

Where the statutory provisions apply, the notice must be in writing, must contain certain prescribed information (See the Notice to Quit (Prescribed Information) Regulations 1988 (SI 1988/2201)), and must be given not less than four weeks before the date on which it is to take effect. Failure to comply with these requirements renders the notice invalid. Although the statutory provisions apply to a notice given by either the occupier or the owner, to date no regulations have been made in respect of any prescribed information to be given in an occupier's notice.

Longer periods of notice than the four weeks provided statutorily will be required where the period of the tenancy is a month or longer. At common law, monthly, quarterly and half-yearly tenancies require notice respectively of one month, one quarter, or six months' duration; a yearly tenancy requires six months' notice.

At common law, the notice must also be expressed to expire either on the last day of the appropriate period of the tenancy, or on the first day of the next: a notice expiring at another time will be invalid.

Forfeiture: formalities

6.05   Common law termination of a tenancy by forfeiture also requires the service of a formal notice in many cases. Except in cases of non-payment of rent and limited excluded situations (See the Law of Property Act 1925, s.146(9), exempting forfeitures on bankruptcy or in

---

[1] The procedure was formally by way of originating application. This procedure no longer exists under Pt 55 CPR.

execution in the case of certain tenancies), it is a prerequisite to a valid forfeiture to serve a notice under the LPA 1925, s.146. The notice must:

(a) specify the breach complained of;

(b) if the breach is capable of remedy, require the tenant to remedy the breach; and

(c) in any case, require the tenant to pay compensation for the breach.

In relation to forfeiture for non-payment of service charges there is now statutory intervention under Housing Act 1996, s.81. Under this section, the landlord cannot exercise a right of re-entry or forfeiture for failure to pay a service charge generally (see s.81(1)). A s.146 notice served for breaches which include non-payment of service charges must state that s.81 applies and set out the effect of subs.(1) (s.81(3)). Further s.82(4) imposes requirements as to the form of this statement.

Statutory schemes for security of tenure

Generally

Most, though not all, residential tenancies are affected by statutory regulation. Where statute **6.06** does not intervene, the common law will apply. The statutory schemes affording security of tenure to residential occupiers are principally contained in the Landlord and Tenant Act 1954, Pt I (long tenancies at low rents), the Rent (Agriculture) Act 1976 (agricultural protected occupancies and statutory tenancies), the Rent Act 1977 (private sector regulated tenancies and restricted contracts), the Housing Act 1985 (public sector secure tenancies), the Housing Act 1988 (private sector assured tenancies and agricultural occupancies), the Local Government and Housing Act 1989, Sch.10 (long tenancies at low rents and the Housing Act 1996 (introductory tenancies). For agreements arising after January 14, 1989, in general the provisions of the HA 1988 replace those of the R(A)A 1976 and RA 1977. For long tenancies ending after January 14, 1999, the provisions of Pt I of the 1954 LTA will be replaced by those of the 1989 LGHA, Sch.10. Reference should be also be made to: the Caravan Sites Act 1968 and the Mobile Homes Act 1983 (in respect of mobile homes); the Agricultural Holdings Act 1986 (for agricultural holdings, which may include dwellings) and the Agricultural Tenancies Act 1995 (farm business tenancies).

The method by which security of tenure is afforded differs, and in any particular case the adviser will need to understand whether any statutory scheme is superimposed upon, or supplants, the common law, and if so how. Statutory protection for the occupier is dependent upon continued occupation of the premises, so that if occupation ceases the owner may exercise contractual rights of termination and recover possession.

Statutory notices

In the case of the HA 1985, HA 1988 and the HA 1996, the ability of the court to entertain **6.07** proceedings for possession is made subject to the provision of an appropriate statutory notice prior to the commencement of proceedings (unless, under the HA 1985 and HA 1988 the court agrees to dispense with this where permissible). Except in the cases of an assured shorthold tenancy under the HA 1988 and an introductory tenancy under the HA 1996, an order for possession can only be made on one or more of the statutory grounds, and only on a ground specified in the statutory notice (although the court has discretion to grant leave to alter or add to the grounds in the notice).

In the case of periodic secure and assured tenancies, common law notices to quit are rendered ineffective. Where occupation has ceased, however, as noted above (para.6.06) the statutory provisions will not apply; and so in a case where it is unclear whether or not a statutory notice is required, such a notice could be served – in addition to eg a notice to quit – on a "without prejudice" basis.

Long tenancies at low rents

6.08 A landlord's notice under s.4 of the LTA 1954 must be in the prescribed form (see the Landlord and Tenant (Notices) Regulations 1957 (SI 1957/1157)) and specify the date at which the tenancy is to come to an end, being either the term date of the tenancy or a later date. Such a notice is ineffective unless it is given between six to twelve months inclusive before the specified date of termination. The notice will also be ineffective unless it specifies the premises which the landlord believes to be, or to be likely to be, the premises qualifying for protection and either (a) contains proposals for a statutory tenancy, or (b) contains notice that if the tenant is not willing to vacate at the termination date, the landlord proposes to apply to the court for possession and stating the ground(s) so proposed. The notice must also invite the tenant, within two months, to notify the landlord in writing whether he is willing to give up possession. Similar requirements are made in respect of a notice given under the LGHA 1989, Sch.10, para.4(1).

Secure tenancies

6.09 A notice under the HA 1985, s.83 must be in the prescribed form (1985 Act, s.83(2)(a) and the Secure Tenancies (Notices) Regulations 1987 (SI 1987/755)) as amended, or at least in a form which is substantially to the same effect (*City of London v Devlin* (1995) 29 H.L.R. 58, CA). Two different forms exist depending upon whether the tenancy is periodic or for a fixed term (but subject to a right of termination by the landlord). The notice must also specify the statutory ground relied on, and must give particulars of that ground. In the case of a secure periodic tenancy, the notice must also specify a date after which proceedings for possession may be begun, and that date must not be earlier than the date on which a notice to quit given on the same date could take effect. Where the ground in the notice or one of the grounds is ground 2 in Sch.2 (nuisance or other anti social behaviour), the notice should state that the possession proceedings can be commenced immediately and the date when the landlord is seeking that the tenant is to give up possession (which must not be earlier than the date on which a notice to quit given on the same date could take effect). The court may then not make an order for possession until the date given in the notice. In the case of a secure periodic tenancy, the notice remains valid only for a period of twelve months after the specified date. Although the court cannot make a possession order on any of the statutory grounds unless that ground is specified in the notice, the grounds so specified may be altered or added to with the leave of the court.

If ground 2A (domestic violence ground against remaining partner) is the ground or one of the grounds in the notice of seeking possession, and the departed partner was not a tenant, the court is not to entertain the proceedings for possession unless satisfied that the landlord has served a copy of the notice on her, or has taken reasonable steps to do so. The court can however dispense with this requirement if it is just and equitable to do so and where ground 2 (nuisance and anti-social behaviour) is also pleaded (s.83A(5)).

Assured tenancies

There are two varieties of notice under the HA 1988. Where there are joint landlords, either **6.10** type of notice may be provided by at least one of them.

Section 8 notice

First, a notice under s.8 of the HA 1988 must be in the prescribed form (1988 Act, s.8(3) and **6.11** the Assured Tenancies etc (Forms) Regulations 1997 (SI 1997/94)). It must inform the tenant that:

(a) the landlord intends to begin proceedings for possession on one or more of the grounds specified in the notice;

(b) those proceedings will not begin earlier than a date specified in the notice, calculated as appears below; and

(c) those proceedings will not begin later than twelve months from the service of the notice.

The period under (b) above is calculated as follows. If ground 14 of Sch.2 (nuisance or other anti-social behaviour) is included in the notice (either as the sole ground or alongside other grounds) the date specified in the notice shall not be earlier than the date of service of the notice. If grounds 1, 2, 5, 6, 7, 9 or 16 of Sch.2 are included in the notice, the notice period is either two months from service of the notice or, if the tenancy is periodic, the earliest date on which a notice to quit served on the same date could have terminated the tenancy, whichever is the later. Otherwise, the period must be at least two weeks from service of the notice.

The court cannot entertain possession proceedings unless a proper notice has been served, and the proceedings are started within the proper time limits stated in the notice, unless the court considers it just and equitable to dispense with the requirement of such a notice. The court cannot dispense with the requirement of a proper notice if the landlord seeks to recover possession on ground 8 in Sch.2 (the mandatory ground for non-payment of rent).

Section 21 notice

The second variety of notice under the HA 1988 is that required by s.21(1) or (4) as a pre- **6.12** requisite to the special right of possession arising upon the expiry or termination of an assured shorthold tenancy. Although there is no prescribed form for such a notice, the notice must be in writing (ss.21(1)(b) and 21(4)(a)).

Section 21(1) notice

A notice under s.21(1) merely has to state that the landlord requires possession. It must give **6.13** at least two months' notice. It may be given before or on the day on which the tenancy comes to an end.

Section 21(4) notice

6.14 A notice under s.21(4) (for assured shorthold periodic tenancies) has to state that possession is required by virtue of s.21. It must also specify a date after which possession is required. That date must be the last day of a period of the tenancy. The date must not be earlier than two months after the giving of the notice, and no earlier than the earliest day when a notice to quit given on the same day would have validly expired. Sufficient notice is given if the s.21(4) notice states that it will expire at the end of the period of the tenancy ending after the expiry of two months from the date of service of the notice (*Lower Street Properties v Jones* (1996) 28 H.L.R. 877, CA)

Introductory Tenancies

6.15 In order to bring proceedings for possession (usually for nuisance or arrears) the landlord has to serve on the tenant a notice of proceedings. This notice is not prescribed but it must state that the court will be asked to make an order for possession, set out the reasons for the landlord's decision to apply for such an order, and specify a date after which proceedings may be begun. The latter date must not be earlier than the date on which the tenancy could be brought to an end by notice to quit given by the landlord on the same day as the notice of proceedings. Finally the notice shall inform the tenant of his right to request a review of the landlord's decision to seek an order for possession; the time within which such a request should be made and inform the tenant that if he needs help or advice about the notice, and what to do about it, he should take it immediately to the CAB, a housing aid centre, a law centre or a solicitor (HA 1996, s.128).

It is important that these notice requirements are all complied with. If they are, the court must order possession (s.127(2)). The court has no discretion, and there is no requirement on the landlord to show reasonableness nor the provision of alternative accommodation (*Manchester City Council v Cochrane* (1999) 31 H.L.R. 810, CA)

The introductory tenant must seek a review if s/he wants one within 14 days of the notice of proceedings being served (s.129(1)). The Introductory Tenants (Review) Regulations 1997 (SI 1997/72), provide for the procedure to be followed in a review conducted pursuant to s.129. If the review decision is to uphold the original decision to seek possession, the landlord must notify the introductory tenant of the reasons for the review decision (s.129(5)). The review must be carried out and the tenant notified of the outcome before the date specified in the notice of proceedings as the date after which proceedings for possession of the dwelling house may be begun (s.129(6)). The only challenge open to the tenant if the review upholds the landlord's decision is an application to the High Court for judicial review, for which purpose the county court has the power to grant an adjournment but not a stay (*Manchester City Council v Cochrane* (1999) 31 H.L.R. 810, CA and *R v Bracknell Forest BC, Ex p. McLlellan; Reigate and Banstead BC v Benfield and Forest and others*, [2001] EWCA Civ 1510; 33 H.L.R. 86, CA and *Merton LBC v Williams* [2002] EWCA Civ 980).

Other restrictions on the recovery of possession

6.16 In cases where the landlord's entitlement to recover possession is not restricted by the operation of one of the above schemes of security of tenure, the exercise of self-help in the recovery of possession (assuming a contractual entitlement to do so) may yet be restrained by the provisions of the PEA 1977 and the Criminal Law Act 1977.

Possession procedure under the Civil Procedure Rules Part 55

Introduction

The general rules in CPR Pt 55 which came into force on October 15, 2001 now dictate the procedure to be used in all possession proceedings brought by a landlord (or former landlord), mortgagee or licensor (or former licensor).[2] The general rules also cover a possession claim against trespassers[3] or a claim by a tenant seeking relief from forfeiture.[4] The provisions in Pt 55 are, however, subject to any enactment or practice direction which sets out special provisions with regard to any particular category of claim (CPR 55.2(2)(a)).[5]

6.17

Claims

Venue

The claim must be started in the county court for the district in which the land is situated, unless the claim is brought in the High Court or an enactment provides otherwise.[6] The claim may be started in the High Court if the claimant files a certificate stating the reasons for bringing the claim in that court, verified by a statement of truth in accordance with CPR 22.1(1).[7] The practice direction to Pt 55 states that, except where the county court does not have jurisdiction, claims should normally be brought in the county court. Only exceptional circumstances justify starting a claim in the High Court.[8] If the claim is brought in the High Court when it should have been started in the county court, the court will normally either strike out the claim or transfer it to the county court. This will result in delay and the court will normally disallow the costs of starting the claim in the High Court and of the transfer.[9]

6.18

Circumstances where a claim may in an appropriate case, be brought in the High Court are where[10]

a) there are complicated disputes of fact

b) there are points of law of general importance; or

---

[2] CPR 55.2(1)(a).
[3] "A possession claim against trespassers" means a claim for the recovery of land which the Claimant alleges is occupied only by a person or persons who entered or remained on the land without the consent of a person entitled to possession of that land. It does not include a claim against a tenant or subtenant whether his tenancy has been terminated or not.
[4] CPR 55.2(1)(b) and (c).
[5] It does not apply to accelerated possession for assured shorthold tenancies for which there is a separate procedure (section II).
[6] CPR 55.3(1).
[7] CPR 55.3(2).
[8] CPR 55 PD 1.1.
[9] CPR 55 PD 1.2.
[10] CPR 55 PD 1.3.

c) the claim is against trespassers and there is a substantial risk of public disturbance or of serious harm to persons or property which properly require immediate determination.

The value of the property and the amount of the financial claim may also be relevant circumstances, but these factors alone will not normally justify starting the claim in the High Court.

Claim form

6.19 Where a claimant does not know the name of a person in occupation or possession of the land the claim must be brought against "persons unknown" in addition to any named defendants.[11] The claim for possession form, and the form of defence sent with it, must be in the forms set out in the relevant practice direction.[12]

Particulars of claim

6.20 The particulars of claim must be filed and served with the claim form.[13] The particulars must:[14]

a) identify the land to which the claim relates, and state whether the claim relates to residential property;

b) state the ground on which possession is claimed;

c) give full details about any mortgage or tenancy agreement; and

d) give details of every person who, to the best of the claimant's knowledge, is in possession of the property.

Claims for non-payment of rent

6.21 If the claim relates to residential property let on a tenancy, and the claim includes a claim for non-payment of rent, the particulars of claim must also set out:[15]

a) the amount due at the start of the proceedings;

b) in schedule form, the dates when the arrears of rent arose, all amounts of rent due, the dates and amounts of all payments made and a running total of the arrears;

c) the daily rate of any rent and interest;

d) any previous steps taken to recover the arrears of rent with full details of any court proceedings; and

e) any relevant information about the defendant's circumstances, in particular:

[11] CPR 55.3(4).
[12] CPR 55.3(5).
[13] CPR 55.4.
[14] CPR 55 PD 2.1.
[15] CPR 55 PD 2.2 and 2.3.

    i)   whether the defendant is in receipt of social security benefits; and

    ii) whether any payments are made on his behalf directly to the claimant under the Social Security Contributions and Benefits Act 1992.

If the claim relates to residential property let on a tenancy and the claimant knows of any person (including a mortgagee) entitled to claim relief against forfeiture as underlessee under s.146(4) of the Law of Property Act 1925 (or in accordance with s.38 of the Supreme Court Act 1981, or s.138(9C) of the County Courts Act 1984) then the particulars of claim must state the name and address of that person and the claimant must file a copy of the particulars of claim for service on that person.[16]

Trespassers

If the claim is a possession claim against trespassers, the particulars of claim must state the   **6.22** claimant's interest in the land, or the basis of his right to claim possession, and the circumstances in which it has been occupied without license or consent.[17]

Hearing date

The court will fix a hearing date when it issues the claim form.[18]   **6.23**
    In a possession claim against trespassers the defendant must be served with the claim form, particulars of claim, and any witness statements:

(a) in the case of residential property, not less than five days; and

(b) in the case of other land, not less than two days, before the hearing date.[19]

In all other types of possession claim the hearing date will be not less than 28 days from the date of issue of the claim form.[20] The standard period in such cases between the issue of the claim form and the hearing will be no more than eight weeks,[21] and the defendant must be served with the claim form and particulars of claim not less than 21 days before the hearing date.[22]

    The court may exercise its powers under CPR 3.1(2)(a) and (b) to shorten the time periods for hearing dates.[23] The practice direction to Pt 55 states that the court should consider exercising its power in this regard, particularly if the defendant has assaulted or threatened to assault the claimant or a member of the claimant's staff or another resident in the locality, or there are reasonable grounds for fearing such an assault, or the defendant or a person for whom the defendant is responsible has caused serious damage or threatened to cause serious damage to property or to the home or property of another resident in the locality.[24] Further

[16] CPR 55 PD 2.4.
[17] CPR 55 PD 2.6.
[18] CPR 55.5(1).
[19] CPR 55.5(2).
[20] CPR 55.5(3)(a).
[21] CPR 55.5(3)(b).
[22] CPR 55.5(3)(c).
[23] CPR 55 PD 3.1.
[24] CPR 55 PD 3.2.

in such cases if the matter cannot be dealt with at the first hearing, the court will consider what steps are needed finally to determine the case as quickly as reasonably practicable.[25]

Service on trespassers

6.24   If the possession claim against trespassers has been issued against "persons unknown", the claim form, particulars and witness statements must be served on those persons by either:

(a)   attaching copies of these documents to the main door or some other part of the land so that they are clearly visible; and (ii) if practicable, inserting copies of these documents in a sealed transparent envelope addressed to "the occupiers" through the letter box; or

(b)   by placing stakes in the land in places where they are clearly visible, and attaching to each stake copies of the documents in a sealed transparent envelope addressed to "the occupiers".[26]

If the claim form is to be served by the court and in accordance with CPR 55.6(b) the claimant must provide sufficient stakes and transparent envelopes.[27] Once an order has been obtained against the trespasser in the county court, it may be enforced in either the county court or the High Court.[28]

Defendant's response

6.25   The defendant to possession proceedings is not required to file an acknowledgement of service, and CPR Pt 10 does not apply. In a possession claim against trespassers, the occupier is not required to file a defence, and CPR 15.2 does not apply.[29] In other possession claims, if the defendant does not file a defence within the time prescribed in CPR 15.4,[30] he can take part in the hearing but the court is entitled to take his failure into account when deciding on what costs order to make. It is not possible to get judgment in default in a possession claim to which Pt 55 applies.[31]

Forms to be used under the Pt 55 procedure

6.26   **N5** – A single claim form to be used for starting a claim in all possession claims
N5A – Claim for relief against forfeiture
N5B – Claim for possession – (accelerated procedure)
N11 – Defence
N11B – Defence (accelerated procedure)
N11R – Defence (rented residential premises)

---

[25] CPR 55 PD 3.3.
[26] CPR 55.6.
[27] CPR 55 PD 4.1.
[28] The High Court and County Courts Jurisdiction (Amendment No.2) Order 2001.
[29] CPR 55.7(2). The normal requirement is that a defendant who wishes to defend a claim must file a defence.
[30] 14 days after service of particulars, or 28 days when an acknowledgement of service is filed. These rules are subject to certain exceptions, for which see CPR 15.4(2).
[31] CPR 55.7(4).

N11M – Defence (mortgaged residential premises)
N119 – Particulars of claim (rented residential premises)
N120 – Particulars of claim (mortgaged residential premises)
N121 – Particulars of claim (trespassers)

Hearing

At the hearing of the claim the court can decide the claim or give case management direc-   **6.27**
tions.[32] Where there is a genuine dispute on grounds, which appear to be substantial, case
management directions will include the allocation of the claim to a track or directions to
enable it to be allocated.[33] Except where the claim is allocated to the fast track or multi-
track, or the court orders otherwise, any fact that needs to be proved by evidence at the
hearing can be proved by evidence in writing. Each party should wherever possible include all
evidence he wishes to present in his statement of case, verified by a statement of truth.[34] If
relevant, the claimant's evidence should include the amount of any rent or mortgage arrears
and interest on those arrears. These amounts should if possible be up to date at the date of
the hearing, however if this is not possible the evidence can be brought up to date orally or in
writing on the day of the hearing.[35] If relevant, the defendant should give evidence of the
amount of any outstanding social security or housing benefit payments that are relevant to
the rent or mortgage arrears, and the status of any outstanding claims for benefit or appeals/
reviews.[36]

   All witness statements must be filed and served at least two days before the hearing except
in the case of a possession claim against trespassers when the witness statements must be filed
and served with the claim form.[37] Where the claimant serves the claim form and particulars
of claim, he must produce at the hearing a certificate of service of those documents.[38] If the
maker of a witness statement does not attend at the hearing and the material evidence is
disputed by the other party, the court will normally adjourn the hearing so that oral evidence
can be given.[39]

Allocation

When the court decides the track for a possession claim, the matters to which it shall have   **6.28**
regard include:

a)   the matters set out in CPR 26.8[40] as modified by the practice direction;

b)   the amount of any arrears of rent or mortgage instalments;

c)   the importance to the defendant of retaining possession of the land; and

---

[32] CPR 55.8(1).
[33] CPR 55.8(2).
[34] CPR 55 PD 5.1.
[35] CPR 55 PD 5.2.
[36] CPR 55 PD 5.3.
[37] CPR 55.8(4) and (5).
[38] There is no requirement to comply with CPR 6.14(2)(a) which states that the certificate of service must be filed
within seven days of service of the claim form – see CPR 55.8(6).
[39] CPR 55 PD 5.4.
[40] These are the general matters that should be taken into account in allocation decisions, including the financial
value of the claim, complexity, nature of the remedy sought etc.

d)   the importance of vacant possession to the claimant.[41]

The financial value of the claim will not necessarily be the most important factor in deciding the appropriate track. The court may direct a possession claim to be allocated to the fast track even though the value of the property is in excess of £15,000.[42] The court will only allocate possession claims to the small claims track if all the parties agree; and if the claim is allocated to this track the claim shall be treated for the purposes of costs as if it were proceeding on the fast track, except that the trial costs shall be in the discretion of the court and shall not exceed the amount that would be recoverable under CPR 46.2 (amount of fast track costs) if the value of the claim were up to £3000 (currently £350).[43]

Where all the parties agree the court may, when it allocates the claim, order that CPR 27.14 (costs on the small claims track) applies, and where it does so the provisions in CPR 55.9(3) (above) do not apply.

Accelerated possession claims under CPR 55 (property let on assured shorthold tenancies)

Preliminary note on assured shorthold tenancies

6.29   The Housing Act 1996 altered the procedural requirements for the creation of assured shorthold tenancies granted after February 28, 1997, by removing the need for the service of a preliminary notice under s.20 of the Housing Act 1988. The Act also removed the requirement that all assured shorthold tenancies should be of a fixed duration of at least six months (Housing Act 1988, s.19A). As a result of these changes, provision is made in the Act to prevent the court ordering possession until at least six months have elapsed from the grant of the tenancy. The six month period runs from the grant of the first tenancy, and not from the start of any replacement tenancy (Housing Act 1988, s.21(5)–(7)).

Accelerated possession claims

6.30   Section II of CPR 55 deals specifically with the accelerated possession procedure in the case of assured shorthold tenancies. In order to use the procedure, the claim for possession must be brought under s.21 of the HA 1988 and all the conditions in CPR 55.12 must be satisfied. The claim must be started in the county court for the district in which the property is located.[44]

The conditions in CPR 55.12 are the following:

a)   the tenancy and any agreement for the tenancy were entered into on or after January 15, 1989;

b)   the only purpose of the claim is to recover possession of the property and no other claim is made;

---

[41] CPR 55.9(1).
[42] CPR 55 PD 6.1.
[43] CPR 55.9(2) and (3).
[44] CPR 55.11.

c)   the tenancy did not immediately follow an assured tenancy which was not an assured shorthold tenancy;

d)   the tenancy fulfilled the conditions provided by s.19A or 20(1)(a) to (c) of the HA 1988;[45]

e)   the tenancy:

  i)   was the subject of a written agreement;
  ii)   arises by virtue of s.5 of the HA 1988 but follows a tenancy that was the subject of a written agreement; or
  iii) relates to the same or substantially the same property let to the same tenant and on the same terms (though not necessarily as to rent and duration) as a tenancy which was the subject of a written agreement;

f)   a notice in accordance with ss.21(1) or 21(4) of the 1998 Act was given to the tenant in writing.[46]

Claim Form

The claim form must be in the prescribed form (Form N5B) and must contain such infor-   **6.31**
mation and be accompanied by such documents as are required by that form. All relevant sections of the form must be completed and the court will serve the form by first class post.[47]

Defence

A Defendant who wishes to oppose the claim, or seek a postponement in accordance with   **6.32**
CPR 55.18 (see below), must file his defence within 14 days after the service of the claim form. The defence should be in the prescribed form (Form N11B).[48]

Claim referred to the Judge

On receipt of the defence the court will send a copy to the Claimant and refer the claim and   **6.33**
defence to a judge.[49] If the 14 day period has expired without the Defendant filing a defence, the Claimant can file a written request for an order for possession and the court will refer that request to a judge.[50] If a defence is filed after the 14 day period but before the request for an order is filed, the court will still refer the claim and defence to a judge.[51] If the Claimant fails to make a request for an order within three months after the expiry of the 14 day period, the claim will be stayed.

---

[45] Briefly, these provisions contain the substantive requirements for the two different sorts of assured shorthold tenancy. Section 19A of the HA 1988 governs post HA 1996 tenancies (after February 28, 1997), and s.20(1) of the HA 1988 governs pre-HA 1996 tenancies.
[46] There is no prescribed form for the s.21 notice but it must be in writing.
[47] CPR 55.13.
[48] CPR 55.14.
[49] CPR 55.15(1).
[50] CPR 55.15(2).
[51] CPR 55.15(3).

Judge's consideration of the claim[52]

6.34 Having considered the claim and any defence, the judge will:

    a) make an order for possession under CPR 55.17,[53] or

    b) where he is not satisfied that the claim form was served or that the Claimant is not entitled to recover possession under s.21 of the HA 1988 against the Defendant he will:

        i) direct that a date be fixed for a hearing; and

        ii) give any appropriate case management directions; or

        iii) strike out the claim if the claim form discloses no reasonable grounds for bringing the claim. When this happens the court will serve its reasons for striking out the claim with the order and the claimant may apply to restore the claim within 28 days after the date that the order was served on him.

The court will give all parties not less than 14 days notice of a hearing fixed by the judge.

Postponement of possession[54]

6.35 Where the Defendant seeks postponement of possession on the grounds of exceptional hardship under s.89 of the Housing Act 1980,[55] the judge may direct a hearing of that issue. The judge will only postpone possession without having a hearing if he considers that possession should be given up six weeks after the date of the order or, if the Defendant has requested postponement to an earlier date, on that date; and if the Claimant indicated on his claim form that he would be content for the court to make such an order without a hearing.[56] The hearing must be held before the date on which possession is to be given up, and the judge will direct how many days notice the parties must be given of that hearing.

At the hearing, if the judge is satisfied that exceptional hardship would be caused by requiring possession to be given at the date of the order for possession, he may vary the date on which possession must be given up. The varied date must be no later than six weeks after the making of the order for possession, in accordance with HA 1980, s.89.[57]

Application to set aside or vary

6.36 The court may on application by a party within 14 days of service of the order or, of it's own initiative, set aside or vary any order made under CPR 55.17.[58]

---

[52] CPR 55.16.
[53] Without the attendance of the parties.
[54] CPR 55.18.
[55] Under which possession can be postponed for up to six weeks after the date of the order.
[56] CPR 55 PD 8.2.
[57] CPR 55 PD 8.4.
[58] CPR 55.19.

Interim Possession Orders

Section III of CPR 55[59] applies where the Claimant seeks an Interim Possession Order. The **6.37** conditions[60] that must be satisfied for an Interim Possession Order to be made are: first, that the only claim is against trespassers for the recovery of possession; secondly that the Claimant has an immediate right to possession of the premises and has had such a right throughout the period of alleged unlawful occupation; and thirdly, that the application for an IPO is not made against a Defendant who entered or remained on the premises with the consent of a person who, at the time consent was given, had an immediate right to possession of the premises.

The claim form for an IPO must be in form N5, the application notice is in Form N130 and the defendant's form of witness statement must use N133.[61] When the Claimant files the claim form he is also required to file the application notice and, where the Claimant is a body corporate, it must be signed by a duly authorised officer.[62] The Claimant must give the written evidence personally.[63] The court will then issue the claim form and the application for the IPO and set a date for the hearing of the application. The hearing of the application will be as soon as practicable but not less than three days after the date of issue.[64]

Service

Within 24 hours of the issue of the application the Claimant must serve on the Defendant: the **6.38** claim form, the application notice together with the written evidence in support and a blank form for the Defendant's witness statement which must be attached to the application notice.[65] The Claimant is required to serve these documents in accordance with CPR 55.6(a).[66] At or before the hearing, the Claimant must file a certificate of service in relation to the documents mentioned above. CPR r.6.14(2)(a) does not apply.[67]

Defendant's response

At any time before the hearing the Defendant may file a witness statement in response to the **6.39** application.[68]

Hearing of the application

In deciding whether to grant an IPO, the court will have regard to whether the Claimant has **6.40** given, or is prepared to give undertakings: firstly, to reinstate the Defendant if ordered to do so and pay damages that the court may order (if the court decides after the IPO is granted that the Claimant was not in fact entitled to the order); and. Secondly, not to damage the

---

[59] Introduced by Civil Procedure (Amendment) Rules 2002 (SI 2002/2058) revoking Sch.2 CCR O 24 Pt II.
[60] See CPR 55.21.
[61] CPR PD 9.1.
[62] CPR 55.22(3).
[63] CPR 55.22(4), or by an authorised officer, where the claimant is a body corporate.
[64] CPR 55.22(5–6).
[65] CPR 55.23(3).
[66] By attaching copies to the main door or some other part of the land so that they are clearly visible; and if practicable, inserting copies of those documents in a sealed transparent envelope addressed to the "the occupiers" through the letterbox.
[67] CPR 55.23(3).
[68] CPR 55.24.

premises, grant a right of occupation to any other person or damage or dispose of the Defendant's property before the claim for possession is finally decided.[69]

The court will make an IPO if the Claimant has filed a certificate of service of the documents referred to in CPR 55.23(1) or proved service of those documents and the court considers that the conditions set out in CPR 55.21(1) are satisfied and any undertakings given by the Claimant as a condition of the order are adequate.[70] The IPO will be in Form N134 and will require the Defendant to vacate the premises within 24 hours of the service of the order.[71] On making the IPO the court will set a date for the hearing of the claim for possession which will be not less than 7 days after the date on which the IPO is made.[72] Where the court does not make the IPO it will set a date for hearing of the claim; it may give directions for the future conduct of the claim and subject to such directions the claim shall proceed in accordance with a possession under s.1 of Pt 55.[73]

Service and enforcement of the IPO

6.41   An IPO must be served within 48 hours after it is sealed.[74] The Claimant is required to serve the IPO on the Defendant together with copies of the claim form and the written evidence in support in accordance with CPR 55.6(a).[75] CCR Order 26, r.17[76] does not apply to the enforcement of an IPO. If an IPO is not served within the 48 hour time limit, the Claimant may apply for directions to continue the claim as a possession claim under s.1 of Pt 55.[77]

After IPO is made

6.42   Before the date of the hearing of the claim, the Claimant must file a certificate of service in relation to the documents specified in CPR 55.26(2).[78] The IPO will expire on the date of the hearing of the claim.[79] At the hearing, the court may make any order it considers appropriate and may, in particular: make a final order for possession; dismiss the claim for possession; give directions for the claim for possession to continue under s.1 of Pt 55; or enforce any of the Claimant's undertakings.[80]

Unless the court directs otherwise, the Claimant must serve any order or directions in accordance with CPR 55.6(a).[81] CCR Order, r.6 applies to the enforcement of a final order for possession.[82]

Application to set aside an IPO

6.43   If the Defendant has left the premises, he may apply on grounds of urgency for the IPO to be

---

[69] CPR 55.25(1).
[70] CPR 55.25(2).
[71] CPR 55.25(3).
[72] CPR 55.25(4).
[73] CPR 55.25(5).
[74] CPR 55.26(1).
[75] CPR 55.25(2).
[76] Warrant of possession.
[77] CPR 55.26(4).
[78] CPR 55.27(1).
[79] CPR 55.27(2).
[80] CPR 55.27(3).
[81] CPR 55.27(4).
[82] CPR 55.27(5).

set aside before the date of the hearing of the claim.[83] An application must be supported by a witness statement.[84] On receipt of the application, the court will give directions as to the date for the hearing and the period of notice, if any, to be given to the Claimant and the method of service of any such notice.[85] Where no notice is required, the only matters to be dealt with at the hearing of the application to set aside are: whether the IPO should be set aside; and whether any undertaking to re-instate the Defendant should be enforced. All other matters will be dealt with at the hearing of the claim.[86] The court will serve on all the parties a copy of the order made and, where no notice was required, a copy of the Defendant's application to set aside and the witness statement in support.[87] Where notice is required, the court can treat the hearing of the application to set aside as the hearing of the claim.[88] No application to set aside an IPO can be made under CPR 39.3.[89]

Extended discretion in certain possession proceedings

The statutory schemes for Rent Act, secure and assured tenancies all provide the court with extended discretion in certain possession proceedings.[90] Among the court's options is the power to stay or suspend the execution of the possession order. The exercise of these powers will be considered when a possession order is made, but a party's right to apply for the court to exercise its discretion continues until the order is actually executed. Successive applications can be made. If conditions are complied with, the possession order can eventually be discharged altogether.   **6.44**

One of the areas in which the extended discretion is important is in the case of the so-called tolerated trespasser.[91] These are former tenants whose tenancies have come to an end when they breached the conditions on which the court stayed or suspended the possession order, but who have been allowed to remain in possession by the landlord. These occupiers can apply to the court for a new order to be made, the effect of which will be to revive the tenancy retrospectively, and with it all the contractual obligations of both parties, including the repairing obligations.[92] The court has no power to make such an order where a former tenant makes an application to postpone after having voluntarily given up occupation without enforcement of the order (*Dunn v Bradford MDC* [2002] EWCA Civ 1137). The landlord can make an application to bring the date of possession forward or replace the suspended order with an outright offer or to seek additional Conditions of suspension (*Manchester City Council v Finn* [2002] EWCA Civ 1998; [2003] H.L.R. 41, CA).

Execution

In addition to the availability of committal proceedings, a judgement or order for the recovery of land is enforceable (and usually enforced) in the county court by a warrant of possession, for which a request has to be filed (CPR Sch.2; CCR Ord. 26, r.17(2); Practice   **6.45**

---

[83] CPR 55.28(1).
[84] CPR 55.28(2).
[85] CPR 55.28(3).
[86] CPR 55.28(5).
[87] CPR 55.28(6).
[88] CPR 55.28(7).
[89] Provision for set aside where there is a failure to attend trial.
[90] RA 1977, s.100; HA 1985, s.85; HA 1988, s.9.
[91] See *Burrows v Brent LBC* (1996) 29 H.L.R. 167, HL.
[92] *Lambeth LBC v Rogers* (1999) 32 H.L.R. 361, CA.

Form N325). The warrant is in prescribed Form N49 generally, and in prescribed Form N52 in respect of an order made against trespassers. A warrant of restitution may be issued in prescribed Form N51, with the permission of the court, in aid of any warrant of possession.

In the High Court, except where the possession claim is made against trespassers, a judgment or order for possession of land may be enforced by (a) writ of possession, and (b) in some cases, by order of committal or writ of sequestration, though a writ of possession cannot be issued without the permission of the court. The preconditions to the grant of permission are set out in CPR Sch.1; RSC Ord. 45, r.3(3). The writ of possession should be in prescribed Form 66. The two other modes of enforcement will not usually be available in the recovery of land, since they depend upon the order specifying a time within which the giving of possession must be done, which in practice does not happen. However, it would be possible to apply under CPR Sch.1; RSC Ord. 45, r.6 for an order fixing a time, and thus make use of these procedures.

In High Court proceedings against trespassers the writ of possession should be in Form 66A.

Setting aside Possession Warrants

6.46   Once a possession order has been enforced by warrant of possession, the court no longer has the extended discretion to stay or suspend the execution of the order. The court retains, though, the power to set the warrant aside, and thus restore the tenant's rights on any of the following grounds:

- where the possession order has been or is liable to be set aside under CPR 39.3[93];

- where the warrant has been obtained by fraud; or

- where there has been an abuse of process or oppression in its execution.[94]

---

[93] *Governors of the Peabody Donation Fund v Hay* (1996) 19 H.L.R. 145, CA.
[94] *Leicester v Aldwinkle* (1991) 24 H.L.R. 40, CA and *L.B. Hammersmith and Fulham v Hill* (1994) 27 H.L.R. 368, CA.

PART II: NOTICES

Form 76   **6.47**

Demand for possession/notice to quit/notice of termination in respect of tenancy at will/service occupancy/excluded tenancy or licence

---

Dear [name],

RE: [premises]

We are instructed on behalf of [name], through whom you have occupied the above premises as [tenant at will/service occupant/tenant/licensee].

Our client requires you to leave the premises, and will give you until [date] to do so. Your [tenancy/licence] is hereby terminated.

In the event that you do not leave by the required date, we are instructed to issue legal proceedings without further reference to you, and to seek an order that you pay the costs of those proceedings, though we trust it will not be necessary to do so.

Yours faithfully,

6.48   Form 77

Landlord's/licensor's notice to quit/notice to determine in accordance with s.5 of the Protection from Eviction Act 1977

TO: [name]
OF: [address]

[I/we], [on behalf of] your [landlord/licensor] [name], of [address], hereby give you [notice to quit/notice to determine] and deliver up to [me/him/us/them] possession of the premises known as [address], on [date] or the day on which the next complete period of your [tenancy/licence] expires after the end of four weeks from the date of service of this notice.

SIGNED
DATED
[Name and address of agent, if agent serves notice]
This notice was served by [name] by [method] on [date].[1]

PRESCRIBED INFORMATION

[Notices to Quit etc (Prescribed Information) Regulations 1988 (SI 1988/2201)]

1.   If the tenant or licensee does not leave the dwelling, the landlord or licensor must get an order for possession from the court before the tenant or licensee can lawfully be evicted. The landlord or licensor cannot apply for such an order before the notice to quit or notice to determine has run out.

2.   A tenant or licensee who does not know if he has any right to remain in possession after a notice to quit or a notice to determine runs out can obtain advice from a solicitor. Help with all or part of the cost of legal advice and assistance may be available under the Legal Aid Scheme. He should also be able to obtain information from a Citizens' Advice Bureau, a Housing Aid Centre or a rent officer.

---

[1] Although not required, it is often helpful to have an indorsement of this sort, for the purposes subsequently of establishing service.

Form 78   **6.49**

Section 146 notice

TO: [name]
OF: [address]

[I/we] [name] hereby give you notice pursuant to s.146(1) of the Law of Property Act 1925 that:

(1) By a lease dated ... [I/we] let the above premises to you for a term of ... years from [date].

(2) By clause ... of the lease you covenanted [set out terms of covenant].

(3) In breach of the above covenant you [set out particulars of the breach].

(4) [I/we] require you to remedy the breach (if it is capable of remedy) on or before [date].[2]

[(5) [I/we] require you to make compensation in money for the breach on or before [date].[3]]

---

[2] A reasonable time should be given.
[3] The landlord does not need to require compensation in the notice, but cannot claim it otherwise.

6.50   Form 79

Landlord's notice to resume possession under s.4 of the Landlord and Tenant Act 1954

(Landlord and Tenant (Notices) Regulations 1957 (SI 1957/1157) – Form 2

Form 2

As substituted by the Landlord and Tenant (Notices) Regulations 1967 (SI 1967/1831).

LANDLORD AND TENANT ACT, 1954

Landlord's Notice to resume Possession

To   , tenant of premises known as

1. I,   of   , landlord of the above-mentioned premises, hereby give you notice terminating your tenancy of the said premises on the   day of   20   . [See Notes 4 and 10.]

2. You are requested within two months after the giving of this Notice to notify me in writing whether you are willing to give up possession of the premises on the said date. [See Notes 5 and 6.]

Consequences of this Notice if tenant claims the freehold or an extended lease

3. If you have a right under Pt I of the Leasehold Reform Act, 1967, to acquire the freehold or an extended lease of property comprised in the tenancy, you must give me notice of your desire to have the freehold or an extended lease not later than two months after the service of this Notice; in that event, this Notice will not operate, and I will [*or* will not, *as the case may be*] be entitled to apply to the county court for possession of the premises under s.17 [*or* 18, *as the case may be*] of that Act and propose [*or* do not propose, *as the case may be*] to do so. [See Note 3.]

4. The following are the names and addresses of other persons known or believed by me to have an interest superior to your tenancy or to be the agent concerned with the premises on behalf of a person having such an interest – [*The names and addresses of any such persons should be stated here*]

Consequences of this Notice if tenant does not claim the freehold or an extended lease

5. I believe that you are entitled to the protection of Pt I of the Landlord and Tenant Act 1954, in respect of the whole of the premises [*or, if part only of the premises qualifies for protection*, in respect of the following part of the premises, namely   ]. [See Note 2.]

6. If you are not willing to give up possession of the premises on the day of , 20 , I propose to apply to the county court for possession of the premises on the ground that [*here state ground or grounds*]. [See Notes 7 and 8.]

7. This Notice is given under the provisions of s.4 of the Landlord and Tenant Act 1954.

Your attention is called to the Notes below.

Dated this day of , 20 .

Signed............................(Landlord)

....(Address)

NOTES

1. Part I of the Landlord and Tenant Act 1954, as amended by the Leasehold Reform Act 1967, provides that a tenant of residential premises under a tenancy granted for more than 21 years at a rent which is less than two-thirds of the rateable value of the premises shall, at the end of the period of the original tenancy, be entitled to continue as a tenant on the same terms as before unless he terminates the tenancy himself or it is terminated by the landlord in accordance with the provisions of the Act. For the purposes of the Act the rateable value is normally that shown in the valuation list on March 23, 1965: the rateable value of the premises must not, however, have exceeded £400 in Greater London or £200 elsewhere.

2. The tenant's right to remain in occupation in confined to parts of the premises which he occupies at the end of the original tenancy.

3. Your rights under Pt I of the Landlord and Tenant Act 1954, are in addition to, and distinct from, any right you may have under the Leasehold Reform Act 1967, to acquire the freehold or an extended lease of the premises. Any such right must, however, be exercised by service of the appropriate notice (in the form prescribed by the Leasehold Reform (Notices) Regulations 1967) within two months of the giving of this Notice. As a general rule, a person has such a right if:

    (*a*) he has his only or main residence in a house which he occupies under a tenancy granted for more than 21 years at a rent which is less than two-thirds of its rateable value;

    (*b*) he has so occupied the house for at least the previous five years or a total of five out of the previous 10 years; and

    (*c*) the house has a rateable value not exceeding £400 in Greater London, or £200 elsewhere.

4. The Landlord may terminate the tenancy by notice given not more than 12 nor less than six months before the date of termination specified in the notice. That date must not normally be earlier than the date on which the original tenancy expires.

5. If you are willing to give up possession of the premises comprised in the tenancy, you should notify the landlord to that effect within two months of the giving of this Notice and vacate the premises on the date of termination specified in it. Failure to notify the landlord may lead to an unnecessary application to the county court and consequent expense, which you may have to bear.

6. If you are not willing to give up possession of the premises comprised in the tenancy you should within two months after the giving of this Notice notify the landlord to that effect. This will ensure that you do not lose the right conferred by the Landlord and Tenant Act 1954, to remain in possession unless the landlord obtains an order for possession of the premises from the county court. If you fail to notify the landlord and are not in occupation of the premises two months after the giving of this notice, you may lose the protection of the Act. If you fail to notify the landlord, but are in occupation two months after the giving of this notice, you will not lose that protection.

7. The grounds on which a landlord may apply for possession are—

(i)   that suitable alternative accommodation will be available for the tenant at the date of termination of the tenancy;

(ii) that the tenant has failed to comply with any term of the tenancy as to payment of rent or rates or as to insuring or keeping insured any premises:

(iii) that the tenant or a person residing or lodging with him or being his sub-tenant has been guilty of conduct which is a nuisance or annoyance to adjoining occupiers, or has been convicted of using any premises comprised in the tenancy or allowing such premises to be used for an immoral or illegal purpose and, where the person in question is a lodger or sub-tenant, that the tenant has not taken such steps as he ought reasonably to have taken for the removal of the lodger or sub-tenant;

(iv) that the premises, or any part of them which is entitled to protection under the Act, are reasonably required by the landlord for occupation as a residence for himself or any son or daughter of his over 18 years of age or his father, mother, father-in-law or mother-in-law. But the court is precluded from making an order for possession on this ground where the landlord's interest was purchased or created after February 18, 1966, or where it is satisfied that having regard to all the circumstances of the case, including the question whether other accommodation is available for the landlord or the tenant, greater hardship would be caused by making the order than by refusing to make it;

(v)   in certain cases where the landlord is a public body, that for the purposes of redevelopment relevant to its functions the landlord proposes after the termination of the tenancy to demolish or reconstruct the whole or a substantial part of the premises.

The landlord must state in this Notice on which of these grounds he proposes to apply for possession.

8. The landlord may apply to the county court for an order for possession on any of the grounds listed above which he has stated in this Notice. In order to succeed in his application he must establish that ground and also, except where he is applying on the ground of (v) above, satisfy the court that it is reasonable that he should be granted possession. You will be given the opportunity to state your case before the court if you wish to resist the landlord's application.

9. Should the landlord fail in his application for possession this Notice will lapse, but he will be at liberty to serve a fresh notice on you proposing the new terms on which your tenancy is to continue, and it will be open to you and the landlord either to agree the terms or to have them determined by the court or the rent officer, as appropriate.

10. The term "landlord" for the purposes of this Notice does not necessarily mean the landlord to whom you pay the rent; it means the person who is your landlord for the purposes of Pt I of the Act.

6.51   <u>Form 80</u>

<u>Notice under Case 19 of Sch.15 to the Rent Act 1977</u>

TO: [name]
OF: [address]

[I/we], [on behalf of] your [landlord] [name], of [address], hereby give you notice expiring on [date[4]] that proceedings for possession under Case 19 of Sch. 15 to the Rent Act 1977 may be brought in respect of the premises known as [address] after the expiry of this notice.

SIGNED

DATED

[Name and address of agent, if agent serves notice]

This notice was served by [name] by [method] on [date].[5]

---

[4] The date of expiry must be no earlier than three months after *service* nor, if the tenancy is periodic at the date of service, before the periodic tenancy could be brought to an end by a notice to quit served by the landlord on the same day.

[5] The date of service is vital: the notice must be served (a) either in the period of three months immediately preceding the date on which the protected shorthold tenancy comes to an end, or (if that date has passed) in the period of three months immediately preceding any anniversary of that date; and (b) where the landlord has served a previous valid notice on the tenant, not earlier than three months after the expiry of the previous notice.

Form 81 6.52

Notice seeking possession under s.83 of the Housing Act 1985 (periodic tenancy)

NOTICE OF SEEKING POSSESSION

Housing Act 1985, section 83

[Secure Tenancies (Notices) Regulation 1987, SI 1987/755. As amended by Secure Tenancies (Notices) (Amendment) Regulations SI 1997/71]

This Notice is the first step towards requiring you to give up possession of your dwelling. You should read it very carefully.

1. To .... **(name(s) of secure tenant(s))**

   • *If you need advice about this Notice, and what you should do about it, take it as quickly as possible to a Citizens' Advice Bureau, a Housing Aid Centre, or a Law Centre, or to a Solicitor. You may be able to receive Legal Aid but this will depend on your personal circumstances.*

---

2. **The [name of landlord] intends to apply to the court for an order requiring you to give up possession of:**

   .... **(address of property)**
   ....
   ....

   • *If you are a secure tenant under the Housing Act 1985, you can only be required to leave your dwelling if your landlord obtains an order for possession from the court. The order must be based on one of the Grounds which are set out in the 1985 Act (see paras 3 and 4 below).*

   • *If you are willing to give up possession without a court order, you should notify the person who signed this Notice as soon as possible and say when you would leave.*

---

3. **Possession will be sought on Ground(s)...........of Sch.2 to the Housing Act 1985, which reads:**

   [give the text in full of each ground which is being relied on]

   • *Whatever grounds for possession are set out in para.3 of this Notice, the court may allow any of the other grounds to be added at a later stage. If this is done, you will be told about it so you can argue at the hearing in court about the new ground, as well as the grounds set out in para.3, if you want to.*

4. **Particulars of each Ground are as follows:**

[give a full explanation of why each ground is being relied upon]

- *Before the court will grant an order on any of the grounds 1 to 8 or 12 to 16, it must be satisfied that it is reasonable to require you to leave. This means that, if one of these grounds is set out in para.3 of this Notice, you will be able to argue at the hearing in court that it is not reasonable that you should have to leave, even if you accept that the ground applies.*

- *Before the court grants an order on any of the grounds 9 to 16, it must be satisfied that there will be suitable alternative accommodation for you when you have to leave. This means that the court will have to decide that, in its opinion, there will be other accommodation which is reasonably suitable for the needs of you and your family, taking into particular account various factors such as the nearness of your place of work, and the sort of housing that other people with similar needs are offered. Your new home will have to be let to you on another secure tenancy or a private tenancy under the Rent Act of a kind that will give you similar security. **There is no requirement for suitable alternative accommodation where grounds 1 to 8 apply.***

- *If your landlord is not a local authority, and the local authority gives a certificate that it will provide you with suitable accommodation, the court has to accept the certificate.*

- *One of the requirements of ground 10A is that the landlord must have approval for the redevelopment scheme from the Secretary of State (or, in the case of a housing association landlord, the Housing Corporation). The landlord must have consulted all secure tenants affected by the proposed redevelopment scheme.*

"Cross out this paragraph if possession *is* being sought on ground 2 of Sch.2 to the Housing Act 1985 (whether or not possession is also sought on another ground)

5. **The court proceedings for possession will not be begun until after** ....

[give the date after which court proceedings can be brought]

- *Court proceedings cannot be began until after this date, which cannot be earlier than the date when your tenancy or licence could have been brought to an end. This means that if you have a weekly or fortnightly tenancy, there should be at least four weeks between the date this Notice is given and the date in this paragraph.*

- *After this date, court proceedings may be begun at once or at any time during the following 12 months. Once the 12 months are up this Notice will lapse and a new Notice must be served before possession can be sought.*

Cross out this paragraph if possession *not* being sought on ground 2 of Sch.2 to the Housing Act 1985

5. Court proceedings for possession of the dwelling-house can be begun immediately. The date by which the tenant is to give up possession of the dwelling-house is

....

[give the date by which the tenant is to give up possession of the dwelling-house]

- *Court proceedings may be begun at once or at any time during the following 12 months. Once the 12 months are up this Notice will lapse and a new notice must be served before possession can be sought.*

- *Possession of your dwelling-house cannot be obtained until after this date, which cannot be earlier than the date when your tenancy or licence could have been brought to an end. This means that if you have a weekly or fortnightly tenancy, there should be at least four weeks between the date inserted above and the date possession is ordered.*

Signed ....

On behalf of ....

Address ....

....

....

Tel. No. ....

Date ....

6.53   Form 82

<u>Notice of seeking termination of a fixed term secure tenancy and recovery of possession under s.83 of the Housing Act 1985</u>

<u>NOTICE OF SEEKING POSSESSION</u>

<u>Housing Act 1985, s.83</u>

This Notice may lead to your being required to leave your dwelling. You should read it very carefully.

1.   **To** .... **(name(s) of secure tenant(s))**

- *If you need advice about this Notice, and what you should do about it, take it as quickly as possible to a Citizens' Advice Bureau, a Housing Aid Centre, or a Law Centre, or to a Solicitor. You may be able to receive Legal Aid but this will depend on your personal circumstances.*

---

2.   **The** [name of landlord] **intends to apply to the Court for an order terminating your tenancy and requiring you to give up possession of:**

.... **(address of property)**
....
....

- *This Notice applies to you if you are a secure tenant under the Housing Act 1985 and if your tenancy is for a fixed term, containing a provision which allows your landlord to bring it to an end before the fixed term expires. This may be because you have got into arrears with your rent or have broken some other condition of the tenancy. This is known as a provision for re-entry or forfeiture. The Act does not remove the need for your landlord to bring an action under such a provision, nor does it affect your right to seek relief against re-entry or forfeiture, in other words to ask the court not to bring the tenancy to an end. The Act gives **additional** rights to tenants, as described below.*

- *If you are a secure tenant and have a fixed term tenancy, it can only be terminated and you can only be evicted if your landlord obtains an order for possession from the court. The order must be based on one of the grounds which are set out in the 1985 Act (see paras 3 and 4 below).*

- *If you are willing to give up possession without a court order, you should notify the person who signed this Notice as soon as possible and say when you would leave.*

---

3.   Termination of your tenancy and possession will be sought on Ground(s)..........of Sch.2 to the Housing Act 1985, which reads:

[give the text in full of each ground which is being relied on]

- *Whatever grounds for possession are set out in para.3 of this Notice, the Court may allow any of the other grounds to be added at a later stage. If this is done, you will be told about it so you can argue at the hearing in court about the new ground, as well as the grounds set out in para.3, if you want to.*

4.   Particulars of each ground are as follows:

[give a full explanation of why each ground is being relied upon]

- *Before the court will grant an order on any of the grounds 1 to 8 or 12 to 16, it must be satisfied that it is reasonable to require you to leave. This means that, if one of these grounds is set out in para.3 of this Notice, you will be able to argue at the hearing in court that it is not reasonable that you should have to leave, even if you accept that the ground applies.*

- *Before the court grants an order on any of the grounds 9 to 10, is must be satisfied that there will be suitable alternative accommodation for you when you have to leave. This means that the court will have to decide that, in its opinion, there will be other accommodation which is reasonably suitable for the needs of you and your family, taking into particular account various factors such as the nearness of your place of work, and the sort of housing that other people with similar needs are offered. Your new home will have to be let to you on another secure tenancy or a private tenancy under the Rent Act of a kind that will give you similar security. **There is no requirement for suitable alternative accommodation where grounds 1 to 8 apply.***

- *If your landlord is not a local authority, and the local authority gives a certificate that it will provide you with suitable accommodation, the court has to accept the certificate.*

- *One of the requirements of ground 10A is that the landlord must have approval for the redevelopment scheme from the Secretary of State (or, in the case of a housing association landlord, the Housing Corporation). The landlord must have consulted all secure tenants affected by the proposed redevelopment scheme.*

Signed ....

On behalf of ....

Address ....

....

....

Tel. No. ....

Date ....

6.54   **Form 83**

<u>Notice seeking possession of premises let on an assured tenancy, under s.8 of the Housing Act 1988</u>

[Form No 3 Assured Tenancies and Agricultural Occupancies (Forms) Regulations 1997]

Housing Act 1988 s.8 as amended by s.151 of the Housing Act 1996

Notice seeking possession of a property let on an Assured Tenancy or an Assured Agricultural Occupancy

- Please write clearly in black ink.

- Please tick boxes where appropriate and cross out text marked with an asterisk (*) that does not apply.

- This form should be used where possession of accommodation let under an assured tenancy, an assured agricultural occupancy or an assured shorthold tenancy is sought on one of the grounds in Sch.2 to the Housing Act 1988.

- Do not use this form if possession is sought on the "shorthold" ground under s.21 of the Housing Act 1988 from an assured shorthold tenant where the fixed term has come to an end or, for assured shorthold tenancies with no fixed term which started on or after February 28, 1997, after six months has elapsed. There is no prescribed form for these cases, but you must give notice in writing.

1. To: [_____]   *Name(s) of tenant(s)/licensee(s)**

2. Your landlord/licensor* intends to apply to the court for an order requiring you to give up possession of:

   [_____]   *Address of premises*
   [_____]
   [_____]

3. Your landlord/licensor* intends to seek possession on ground (s) [_____] in Sch.2 to the Housing Act 1988, as amended by the Housing Act 1996, which read(s):

   Give the full text (as set out in the Housing Act 1988 as amended by the Housing Act 1996) of each ground which is being relied on. Continue on a separate sheet if necessary.

   [_____]

4.   Give a full explanation of why each ground is being relied on:

```
┌─────────────────────────────────────────────────────────────────────┐
│                                                                       │
│                                                                       │
└─────────────────────────────────────────────────────────────────────┘
```

Continue on a separate sheet if necessary.

Notes on the grounds for possession

- If the court is satisfied that any of grounds 1 to 8 is established, it must make an order (but see below in respect of fixed term tenancies).

- Before the court will grant an order on any of grounds 9 to 17, it must be satisfied that it is reasonable to require you to leave. This means that, if one of these grounds is set out in s.3, you will be able to suggest to the court that it is not reasonable that you should have to leave, even if you accept that the ground applies.

- The court will not make an order under grounds 1, 3 to 7, 9 or 16, to take effect during the fixed term of the tenancy (if there is one) and it will only make an order during the fixed term on grounds 2, 8, 10 to 15 or 17 if the terms of the tenancy make provision for it to be brought to an end on any of these grounds.

- Where the court makes an order for possession solely on ground 6 or 9, the landlord must pay your reasonable removal expenses.

5.   The court proceedings will not begin until after:

```
┌─────────────────────────────────────────────────────────────────────┐
│                                                                    19 │
└─────────────────────────────────────────────────────────────────────┘
```

Give the earliest date on which court proceedings can be brought

- Where the landlord is seeking possession on grounds 1, 2, 5 to 7, 9 or 16, court proceedings cannot begin earlier than two months from the date this notice is served on you (even where one of grounds 3, 4, 8, 10 to 13, 14A, 15 or 17 is specified) and not before the date on which the tenancy (had it not been assured) could have been brought to an end by a notice to quit served at the same time as this notice.

- Where the landlord is seeking possession on grounds 3, 4, 8, 10 to 13, 14A, 15 or 17, court proceedings cannot begin earlier than two weeks from the date this notice is served (unless one of 1, 2, 5 to 7, 9 or 16 grounds is also specified in which case they cannot begin earlier than two months from the date this notice is served).

- Where the landlord is seeking possession on ground 14 (with or without other grounds), court proceedings cannot begin before the date this notice is served.

- Where the landlord is seeking possession on ground 14A, court proceedings cannot begin unless the landlord has served, or has taken all reasonable steps to serve, a copy of this notice on the partner who has left the property.

- After the date shown in s.5, court proceedings may be begun at once but not later than 12 months from the date on which this notice is served. After this time the notice will lapse and a new notice must be served before possession can be sought.

6. Name and address of landlord/licensor*.

To be signed and dated by the landlord or licensor or his agent (someone acting for him). If there are joint landlords each landlord or the agent must sign unless one signs on behalf of the rest with their agreement.

Signed   *Date*

....

....

Please specify whether: landlord ☐ licensor ☐ joint landlords ☐ landlord's agent ☐

Name(s) (Block Capitals)

....

....

Address

....

....

....

Telephone – Daytime   Evening

....

What to do if this notice is served on you

- This notice is the first step requiring you to give up possession of your home. You should read it very carefully.

- Your landlord cannot make you leave your home without an order for possession issued by a court. By issuing this notice your landlord is informing you that he intends to seek such an order. If you are willing to give up possession without a court order, you should tell the person who signed this notice as soon as possible and say when you are prepared to leave.

- Whichever grounds are set out in s.3 of this form, the court may allow any of the other grounds to be added at a later date. If this is done, you will be told about it so you can discuss the additional grounds at the court hearing as well as the grounds set out in s.3.

- If you need advice about this notice, and what you should do about it, take it immediately to a Citizens' Advice Bureau, a housing advice centre, a law centre or a solicitor.

Form 84   **6.55**

Notice requiring possession of premises let on a fixed term assured shorthold tenancy, under s.21(1) of the Housing Act 1988

NOTICE REQUIRING POSSESSION

[Section 21 of the Housing Act 1988]

TO: [name]
OF: [address]

[I/we], [on behalf of] your landlord, [name], of [address], require you to deliver up to [me/him/us/them] possession of premises known as [address] on [date].[6]

SIGNED
DATED
[Name and address of agent, if agent serves notice.]

This notice was served by [name] on [date] by [method].

---

[6] Not less than two months notice must be given under s.21(1).

6.56 Form 85

Notice requiring possession of premises let on a periodic assured shorthold tenancy, under s.21(4) of the Housing Act 1988

NOTICE REQUIRING POSSESSION

[Section 21 of the Housing Act 1988]

TO: [name]
OF: [address]

[I/we], [on behalf of] your landlord, [name], of [address], require you by virtue of s.21(4) of the Housing Act 1988 to deliver up to [me/him/us/them] possession of premises known as [address] on [date][7] or on the next date on which a complete period of your tenancy expires not earlier that two months after the giving of this notice.

SIGNED
DATED
[Name and address of agent, if agent serves notice.]

This notice was served by [name] on [date] by [method].

---

[7] In the case of a statutory periodic tenancy, the notice must be at least two months, and not less than would have been required by notice to quit, *i.e.* four weeks under the Protection From Eviction Act 1977, or one period of the tenancy whichever is greater. If the notice specifies a date on which possession is required, that date must be the last day of a period of the tenancy, but sufficient notice is given if the notice states that it will expire at the end of the period of the tenancy ending after the expiry of two months from the date of service of the notice: *Lower Street Properties v Jones* (1996) 28 H.L.R. 877, CA.

Form 86   6.57

Notice of Possession Proceedings – Introductory Tenancy (HA 1996, s.128)[8]

INTRODUCTORY TENANCY

NOTICE OF POSSESSION PROCEEDINGS

[(Housing Act 1996, s.128)]

To: Reginald Hedge

Your landlords The Mayor and Burgesses of the London Borough of Downtown intend to apply for an order for the possession of the dwelling house at 9a Big Tower, Cutglass Road, Downtown ("the premises").

The reasons for your landlords seeking such an order can be summarised as follows:[9]

a) You currently have rent arrears of £900, which have arisen because you have paid no rent since the commencement of your tenancy.

b) You have caused nuisance and annoyance to neighbours and visitors at Big Tower by playing excessively loud music until the early hours of the morning and by allowing your visitors to drive their cars noisily and dangerously around the communal car park:

(i) On March 4, 2003, you played loud music from 10pm until 4am. When a neighbour asked you to turn the music down you replied, "drop dead grandad".

(ii) On March 5, 2003, you played loud music from 9pm until 5am. When an Environmental Health Officer came to warn you that you were at risk of being served with an abatement notice, you turned the music down, but as soon as the officer left you again turned the music up.

(iii) On March 6–20, 2003, there were repeated incidents of loud music from your flat. On March 21, you were visited by your landlord's housing officer, Mr Sprott. You told Mr Sprott that you did not play loud music and that all your neighbours who were complaining had a grudge against you.

(iv) On March 21, 2003, you played loud music and had a party at the premises which lasted all night. In the early hours of the morning two of your visitors had a car race in the communal car park causing considerable noise disturbance and danger to other occupiers of Big Tower.

(v) Throughout the remainder of March, April and May 2003, there were further incidents of noise nuisance from your flat.

The court proceedings will not be begun until July 30, 2003.

You have the right to request a review of your landlord's decision to seek an order for possession. If you wish to seek such a review you must request it within 14 days of the service of this notice.

If you need help or advice about this notice and what to do about it you should take it immediately to a Citizens Advice Bureau, a housing aid centre, a Law Centre or a Solicitor.

Signed

---

[8] There is no prescribed form but s.128 sets out what must be included.

[9] D.o.E. Circular 2/97 advises (at para.16) that the statement of reasons should contain as much information as possible to enable the tenant to meet the allegations. It should not, however, contain names and addresses of witnesses, or other information, which could lead to witness intimidation.

PART III: PRECEDENTS

Form 87: Claim Form for Possession of Property   6.58

Claim form for possession of property

In the
Claim No.

Claimant
(name(s) and address(es))

SEAL

Defendant(s)
(name(s) and address(es))

The claimant is claiming possession of :

which (includes) (does not include) residential property. Full particulars of the claim are attached.
(The claimant is also making a claim for money).

This claim will be heard on: 20   at   am/pm

at

At the hearing
• The court will consider whether or not you must leave the property and, if so, when.
• It will take into account information the claimant provides and any you provide.

What you should do
• Get help and advice immediately from a solicitor or an advice agency.
• Help yourself and the court by **filling in the defence form** and **coming to the hearing** to make sure the court knows all the facts.

Defendant's name and address for service

Court fee	£
Solicitor's costs	£
Total amount	£

Issue date	

N5 Claim form for possession of property (10.01)   Printed on behalf of The Court Service

Claim No.	

Grounds for possession

The claim for possession is made on the following ground(s):

☐ rent arrears

☐ other breach of tenancy

☐ forfeiture of the lease

☐ mortgage arrears

☐ other breach of the mortgage

☐ trespass

☐ other *(please specify)* _____

See full details in the attached particulars of claim

Does, or will, the claim include any issues under the Human Rights Act 1998?   ☐ Yes ☐ No

Anti-social behaviour

The claimant is alleging:

☐ actual or threatened assault

☐ actual or threatened serious damage to the property

Statement of Truth

*(I believe)(The claimant believes) that the facts stated in this claim form are true.
* I am duly authorised by the claimant to sign this statement.

signed _____ date _____

*(Claimant)(Litigation friend *(where the claimant is a child or a patient)*)(Claimant's solicitor)
delete as appropriate

Full name _____

Name of claimant's solicitor's firm _____

position or office held _____
                        (if signing on behalf of firm or company)

Claimant's or claimant's solicitor's address to which documents or payments should be sent if different from overleaf.

	if applicable
Ref. no.	
fax no.	
DX no.	
e-mail	
Postcode Tel. no.	

Form 88   **6.59**

Particulars of Claim: service licence

Claim No. BU 03

IN THE BUSY COUNTY COURT

B E T W E E N

RUPERT RULE   **Claimant**

and

BRIAN BARREL   **Defendant**

PARTICULARS OF CLAIM

---

1. The Claimant is the freehold owner and entitled to possession of residential property at 47a The Parade, Busy (referred to below as "the premises").

2. By an oral agreement (referred to below as "the agreement") made on April 1, 2000 the Claimant granted to the Defendant a licence (hereafter referred to below as "the licence") to occupy the premises for the better performance of his duties as a security officer in the employment of the Claimant from April 1, 2000 in consideration of a payment of £35 per week payable weekly in arrear.

3. It was an express term of the agreement that the licence should terminate immediately upon the termination of the Defendant's employment.

4. On February 23, 2003 the Claimant orally gave the Defendant notice terminating the employment on February 23, 2003, since which time the Defendant has wrongfully remained in possession of the premises. To the best of the Claimant's knowledge, the Defendant's wife, Betty Barrel, is also in possession of the premises.

5. The Claimant is entitled to and claims interest pursuant to s.69 of the County Courts Act 1984 at such rate and for such period as the court may consider just.[10]

AND the Claimant claims:

(1) Possession of the premises.

(2) Mesne profits at the rate of £5 per day from February 24, 2003 until possession be delivered up.

(3) Interest on such mesne profits as pleaded.

(4) Costs.

STATEMENT OF TRUTH

- (I believe) (The Claimant believes) that the facts stated in these Particulars of Claim are true.

- I am duly authorised by the Claimant to sign this statement.

Full name ....

Name of Claimant's solicitor's firm ....

Signed..Position or office held ....

- (Claimant) (if signing on behalf of firm or company) (Claimant's solicitor)

- delete as appropriate

DATED this   day of   20

....
Uppe & Attem
59 High Street
Busy
Claimant's solicitors
who will accept service at the above address

TO the District Judge
AND TO the Defendant

---

[10] In practice, it is quite rare for the court to order interest on mesne profits unless they have been due over a substantial period. Consequently, this pleading, together with the prayer for interest, is often omitted.

Particulars of Claim: non-secure tenancy – (Part VII Housing Act 1996)

Claim No. ME0305009

IN THE METROPOLITAN COUNTY COURT

B E T W E E N

THE MAYOR AND BURGESSES
OF THE LONDON BOROUGH OF DOWNTOWN   **Claimants**

and

SIDNEY TENNANT   **Defendant**

PARTICULARS OF CLAIM

---

1. The Claimants are entitled to possession of residential property at 59 Warden House, Drane Avenue, London, NE 1 ("the premises").

2. Pursuant to their duties under Pt VII of the Housing Act 1996, on February 2, 2003 the Claimants granted to the Defendant a weekly periodic tenancy ("the tenancy") of the premises at a rent of £58 per week. A copy of the tenancy agreement is attached.[11]

3. The tenancy was a non-secure tenancy by virtue of para.4 of Sch.1 Housing Act 1985 and the Claimants had not notified the Defendant that the tenancy was to be secure.

4. It was a condition of the tenancy that the Defendant pays the weekly rent of £58 each week in advance.

5. By a notice to quit in writing dated May 31, 2003 served on the Defendant the Claimants terminated the tenancy on July 3, 2003.

6. The Defendant wrongfully remains in possession of the premises. To the best of the Claimants' knowledge the Defendant's wife and four children are also in possession of the premises.

7. Further in breach of the tenancy the Defendant failed to pay his weekly rent of £58 per week and at the date of the expiry of the notice to quit the arrears were £1026.

8.   Further pursuant to s.69 of the County Courts Act 1984, the Claimant is entitled to and claims to recover interest upon the sums due, at a rate of 8% per annum from February 2, 2003 to November 25, 2003 namely £23.

AND the Claimants claim:

(1) Possession of the premises

(2) Judgement for the sum of £1026 – the rent arrears.

(3) Damages for use and occupation since the expiry of the notice to quit – £400.

(4) Mesne profits at the rate of £8.28 per day from today's date until possession be delivered up.

(5) Interest as pleaded under para.8.

(6) Costs.

STATEMENT OF TRUTH

- (I believe) (The Claimants believe) that the facts stated in these Particulars of Claim are true.

- I am duly authorised by the Claimants to sign this statement.

Full name ....

Name of Claimants' solicitor's firm ....

Signed... Position or office held ....

- (Claimants)   (if signing on behalf of firm or company) (Claimants' solicitor)

- delete as appropriate

Dated etc

---

[11] See CPR 16 PD para.8.3(1).

Form 90   **6.61**

<u>**Particulars of Claim: secure tenancy: security ended**</u>

Claim No. ME0306092

IN THE METROPOLITAN COUNTY COURT

B E T W E E N

THE MAYOR AND BURGESSES OF
THE LONDON BOROUGH OF DOWNTOWN   **Claimant**

and

SIDNEY TENNANT   **First Defendant**

PARTICULARS OF CLAIM

---

1. The Claimants are the freehold owners and entitled to possession of residential property at 59 Warden House, Drane Avenue, London NE1 ("the premises").

2. By an agreement in writing dated June 24, 1996 the Claimant granted the First Defendant a weekly tenancy ("the tenancy") of the premises from June 24, 1996 at a rent of £70 per week. A copy of the tenancy agreement is attached.

3. On a date unknown to the Claimants but on or between December 1, 2002 and February 1, 2003 the Defendant ceased to occupy the premises as his residence, and thereupon the tenancy ceased to be a secure tenancy for the purposes of Pt IV of the Housing Act 1985.

4. Further or alternatively, on or between the dates above the Defendant parted with possession of the premises or sub-let the whole of it to Stephanie Stranger, and thereupon the tenancy ceased to be a secure tenancy.[12] To the best of the Claimant's knowledge, Stephanie Stranger is in possession of the premises.

5. By a notice to quit in writing dated February 2, 2003 and served on the Defendant, the Claimants terminated the tenancy on March 6, 2003.

6. In breach of the implied covenant to deliver up possession at the end of the tenancy, the Defendant has failed to yield up vacant possession of the premises to the Claimants.

7. [AS IN FORM 88 PARAGRAPH 5]

[CONCLUDE AS IN FORM 88]

---

[12] See Housing Act 1985, s.93(2).

6.62   Form 91

Particulars of Claim for possession under the Landlord and Tenant Act 1954, Pt I

Claim No. BU 03

IN THE BUSY COUNTY COURT

In the matter of Pt I of the Landlord and Tenant Act 1954

B E T W E E N

MARBLEPROP COMPANY LIMITED   **Claimant**

and

ANNA LUNGHI-SELESE   **Defendant**

PARTICULARS OF CLAIM

---

1. The Claimant is the freehold owner of a residential property at 54 Marble Mansions, Busy ("the premises").

2. By a lease in writing dated July 2, 1900 the Quarry Prop Company Limited demised the premises to Edward Selese upon a tenancy (hereafter referred to as "the lease" and "the tenancy") for the term of 99 years from June 24, 1900 at an annual rent then of £1 per year rising to £5 per year.

3. The reversion immediately expectant upon the determination of the tenancy is now vested in the Claimant.

4. The tenancy is now vested in the Defendant.

5. The tenancy is a long tenancy within the meaning of Pt I of the Landlord and Tenant Act 1954 referred to below as "the Act"), and the Claimant is the landlord for the purpose of proceedings under Pt I of the Act.

6. By a notice in writing to resume possession dated June 24, 2000 and given to the Defendant on the same date under s.4(1) of the Act, the Claimant terminated the tenancy on December 25, 2000 and notified the Defendant that the Claimant proposed to apply to the court for possession of the premises upon the ground set out in s.12(1)(a) of the Act.

7. The Claimant applies for possession of the premises on the ground that for purposes of redevelopment after the termination of the tenancy the Claimant proposes to demolish the whole of the premises.

8. To the best of the Claimant's knowledge only the Defendant is in possession of the premises

AND the Claimant claims:

(1) Possession of the premises.

(2) Costs.

[CONCLUDE AS IN FORM 88]

6.63   **Form 92**

Particulars of Claim for possession on grounds of non-payment of rent (for use on prescribed Form N119)[13]

Claim No.

IN THE METROPOLITAN

THE LONDON BOROUGH OF DOWNTOWN   **Claimant**

PENNY LESS   **Defendant**

[1]   The claimant has a right to possession of:

> 5 VERNON GROVE, LONDON N2

[2]   To the best of the claimant's knowledge the following persons are in possession of the property:

> PENNY LESSON

About the tenancy

[3]   (a)   The premises are let to the defendant(s) under a(n) | SECURE | tenancy which began on November 16, 1999

     (b)   The current rent is £60 and is payable each week.

     (c)   Any unpaid rent or charge for use and occupation should be calculated at £8.55 per day.

[4]   The reason the claimant is asking for possession is:

     (a)   because the defendant has not paid the rent due under the terms of the tenancy agreement.

        (*Details are set out below*) (*Details are shown on the attached rent statement*)

> £1080 rent is outstanding up to the date of this notice. No payments have been made in the period of 18 weeks prior to todays date. A statement is attached showing how the arrears have arisen.

(b) because the defendant has failed to comply with other terms of the tenancy. *Details are set out below.*

> Not applicable

(c) because: (including any (other) statutory grounds)

> Ground 1 Sch. 1 of the Housing Act 1985 – Rent lawfully due from the tenant
> has not been paid or an obligation of the tenancy has been broken or not performed.

5 The following steps have already been taken to recover any arrears

> Letters dated November 15, 2002 and December 13, 2002 were sent by the Claimants to the Defendant requiring payment of the arrears. In response to the latter the Defendant agreed by letter to pay the current rent plus £10 per week in respect of the arrears.

6 The appropriate notice seeking possession was served on the defendant

on | January 24, 2003.

About the Defendant

7 The following information is known about the defendant's circumstances:

> So far as the Claimants are aware the Defendant is employed as a motorcycle courier. She failed to respond to requests to attend meetings to discuss her financial circumstances with the Claimants.
>
> No payments are made directly under the Social Security Contributions and Benefits Act 1992.

About the Claimant

8 The Claimant is asking the court to take the following financial or other information into account when making its decision whether or not to grant an order for possession:

> The Claimant is required to make provision for all bad debts within its housing revenue account. Any bad debt provision is effectively met by other tenants in the form of rent increases.

Forfeiture

9 (a) There is no underlessee or mortgagee entitled to claim relief against forfeiture.

or (b)

          is entitled to claim relief against forfeiture as underlessee or mortgagee.

What the court is being asked to do:

10 The Claimant asks the court to order that the Defendant(s)

   (a) give the Claimant possession of the premises.

   (b) pay the unpaid rent and any charge for use and occupation up to the date an order is made.

   (c) pay rent and any charge for use and occupation from the date of the order until the Claimant recovers possession of the property;

   (d) pay the Claimant's costs of making this claim.

STATEMENT OF TRUTH

*(I believe)(The claimant believes) that the facts stated in these particulars of claim are true.

*I am duly authorised by the claimant to sign this statement.

signed...date...

*(Claimant)(Litigation friend (*where claimant is a child or a patient*) (Claimant's solicitor)
delete as appropriate

Full name..

Name of defendant's solicitor's firm ....

position or office held ....
(if signing on behalf of firm or company)

---

[13] Proceedings relating to the recovery of rent are more fully considered in Chapter 3.

Form 93   **6.64**

Particulars of Claim: Rent Act 1977: overcrowding/unlawful sub-occupiers

---

Claim No. ME 03

IN THE METROPOLITAN COUNTY COURT

B E T W E E N

PAULA SCARLETT   **Claimant**

and

ANDREW BLACK   **Defendant**

PARTICULARS OF CLAIM

---

1. The Claimant is the leasehold owner and entitled to possession of residential property at 23 Ivory Towers, Paradise Lane, London NE9 ("the premises").

2. By an agreement in writing dated January 14, 1989 the Claimant granted to the Defendant a weekly tenancy ("the tenancy") of the premises from January 16, 1989[14] at a rent of £70 per week. A copy of the agreement is attached.

3. It was an express term of the tenancy that the Defendant would not assign, sub-let, or part with possession of the whole or any part of the premises, or cause or permit the premises to be occupied by any person other than the Defendant.

4. The premises are overcrowded within the meaning of Pt X of the Housing Act 1985, by reason that six adults including the Defendant occupy two rooms available as sleeping accommodation, and so as to render the Defendant guilty of an offence under s.327 of the Housing Act 1985. The Claimant does not know the identities of the persons other than the Defendants who are in possession of the property.

5. By reason of the matters in para.4 above, the Defendant is and, since about January 2003, has been in breach of the term set out in para.3 above.

6. By a notice to quit in writing dated February 24, 2003 and served on the Defendant, the Claimant terminated the tenancy on March 27, 2003.

7. The tenancy is one to which the provisions of the Rent Act 1977 apply.

AND the Claimant claims:

(1) Possession of the premises pursuant to s.101 of, or alternatively Case 1 of Sch.15 to, the Rent Act 1977.

[CONTINUE AS IN FORM 89]

[CONCLUDE AS IN FORM 88]

[14] Although the tenancy began after the commencement of the Housing Act 1988 on January 15, 1989, it is still a protected tenancy since it was entered into prior to that date.

Form 94   **6.65**

Particulars of Claim: Rent Act 1977 and Housing Act 1988: lawful sub-letting: claim against tenant and sub-tenant[15]

                                        Claim No. ME03060082

IN THE METROPOLITAN COUNTY COURT

B E T W E E N

PAULA SCARLETT   **Claimant**

and

ANDREW BLACK   **First Defendant**

NICOLA WHITE   **Second Defendant**

PARTICULARS OF CLAIM

---

1. [AS IN FORM 93 PARAGRAPH 1]

2. [AS IN FORM 93 PARAGRAPH 2]

3. By or before October 1, 1998[16] the First Defendant sub-let the whole of the premises to the Second Defendant without the consent of the Claimant.[17] The Claimant is unsure whether the First Defendant and or the Second Defendant is in possession of the premises.

4. [AS IN FORM 93 PARAGRAPH 6]

5. The Rent Act 1977 applies to the tenancy, but only insofar as the First Defendant occupies the premises as his residence.[18]

6. Insofar as may be necessary, the Claimant claims possession of the premises against the First Defendant upon Case 6 of Sch.15 to the Rent Act 1977.

7. Further or alternatively, the condition of the premises has deteriorated owing to acts of waste by, or the neglect or default of, the First and/or Second Defendant(s).

PARTICULARS

(a) All the fitted kitchen units have been removed, damaged and dumped in the rear garden.

(b) The front and rear gardens have not been maintained and are seriously neglected.[19]

(c) Water has been permitted to overflow from the bath and seriously damage the bathroom floor and living room ceiling by causing the boards and joists to warp and crack.

8. The sub-tenancy of the Second Defendant is an assured shorthold tenancy within the meaning of the Housing Act 1988, and the Claimant served a notice dated February 24, 2002 upon the Second Defendant pursuant to s.21 of that Act informing the Second Defendant that the Claimant intended to seek possession of the premises.

9. The Claimant claims possession against the Second Defendant upon the Housing Act 1998, s.21 and, insofar as may be necessary, against the First Defendant upon Case 3 of Sch.15 to the Rent Act 1977.

AND the Claimants claim:

(1) Possession of the premises.

(2) Mesne profits at a rate of £5.23 per day from January 27, 2003 until possession is delivered up.

(3) Costs.

[CONCLUDE AS IN FORM 88]

---

[15] As in *Leith Properties Ltd v Byrne* [1983] QB 433.

[16] *i.e.* after commencement of the Housing Act 1988, s.19A. If the sub-tenancy may have been entered into prior to this date the subtenancy could be an assured tenancy requiring an additional notice under s.8 and proof of statutory grounds.

[17] *i.e.* not unlawfully, merely without consent.

[18] See Rent Act 1977, s.2. The Claimant commonly does not know precisely what the nature or effect of sub-arrangements may be.

[19] See *e.g. Holloway v Povey* (1984) 271 EG 195.

Form 95   **6.66**

Particulars of Claim: Rent Act 1977: owner/occupier

[HEADING AS IN FORM 93]

1. [AS IN FORM 93 PARAGRAPH 1]

2. [AS IN FORM 93 PARAGRAPH 2]

3. The Claimant herself occupied the premises as her residence between May 16, 1965 and December 3, 1988, and having given the Defendant notice orally[20] on January 14, 1989 that possession might be recovered under Case 11 of Sch.15 to the Rent Act 1977, requires the premises as a residence for her daughter, Michaela Scarlett, who resided with the Claimant when she last occupied the premises.

4. It is just and equitable to make an order for possession, and the requirement of a notice in writing pursuant to sub-paragraph (a) of Case 11 should be dispensed with, by reason of such notice having been given orally as set out in para.3 above.

5. Further or alternatively, the premises are reasonably required by the Claimant for occupation as a residence by her daughter, Michaela.

6. [AS IN FORM 93 PARAGRAPH 6]

7. The tenancy is subject to the provisions of the Rent Act 1977.

AND the Claimant claims;

(1) Possession of the premises pursuant to Case 11 or alternatively Case 9 of Sch.15 to the Rent Act 1977.

[CONCLUDE AS IN FORM 93]

---

[20] Having failed to give notice in writing, the Claimant will need to ask the court to dispense with the requirement of para.(a) of Case 11.

6.67   Form 96

Particulars of Claim: secure periodic tenancy: nuisance (with claim for injunction)

Claim No. ME0305009

IN THE METROPOLITAN COUNTY COURT

B E T W E E N:

THE MAYOR AND BURGESSES OF
THE LONDON BOROUGH OF DOWNTOWN   **Claimants**

and

(1) STANLEY SOAP
(2) SANDY SOAP
(3) SHANE SOAP   **Defendants**

PARTICULARS OF CLAIM

---

1.   The Claimant are the freehold owners and claim possession of residential property at 33 Friendly Fields, London NE5 (hereafter referred to as "the premises").

2.   By an agreement in writing dated December 3, 2000 the Claimant granted to the First Defendant a weekly tenancy of the premises from December 6, 2000 at a rent of £50 per week payable weekly in advance.

3.   The Second and Third Defendants are the First Defendant's wife and son respectively, and also reside at the premises.

4.   On dates between December 2002 and March 2003 the Defendants have been guilty of conduct which is a nuisance or annoyance to neighbours.

PARTICULARS

(1) (a) On about December 7, 2002 the First Defendant verbally abused Ranjit Singh, the occupier of neighbouring premises at 31 Friendly Fields, by shouting for a period of about 10 minutes from the rear garden of the premises words such as "Go home, Paki".

(b) About 12 occasions since December 7, 2002 involving the Defendants singly and collectively shouting abuse of a similar nature either from or in the vicinity of the premises.

(2) (a) On about December 15, 2002 all three Defendants verbally abused Mohammed and Zuleika Smith, the children of John and Farouka Smith, the occupiers of neighbouring premises at 35 Friendly Fields, by shouting for a period of about five minutes from the front garden of the premises words such as "We're going to have your mother deported, half breed wogs".

(b) About seven occasions since December 15, 2002 involving the Defendants singly and collectively shouting abuse of a similar nature either from or in the vicinity of the premises.

4. Unless restrained, the Defendants threaten to continue with the conduct set out above.

5. The tenancy is subject to the provisions of Pt IV of the Housing Act 1985 (referred to below as "the Act"), and on January 31, 2003 the Claimants served a notice dated January 31, 2003 on the First Defendant complying with s.83 of the Act.

AND the Claimants claim:

(1) Possession of the premises pursuant to Ground 2 of Sch.2 to the Act.

(2) An order that the Defendants and each of them be forbidden whether by themselves or by instructing or encouraging any other person from in any way interfering with the quiet enjoyment of 31 and 35 Friendly Fields, London NE5 by the occupiers thereof, or from using or uttering any language towards or for the attention of those occupiers which is calculated or likely to cause those occupiers harassment or distress.

(3) Costs.

[CONCLUDE AS IN FORM 88]

6.68   **Form 97**

Particulars of Claim – secure periodic tenancy – Ground 15

IN THE METROPOLITAN COUNTY COURT   **Claim No. ME0311111**

B E T W E E N

THE MAYOR AND BURGESSES
OF THE LONDON BOROUGH OF DOWNTOWN   **Claimants**

and

DALE YORKSHIRE   **Defendant**

PARTICULARS OF CLAIM

---

1.   The Claimants are the freehold owners of the residential property known as The Firs, Downtown ("the premises").

2.   The premises were let to the Defendant under a secure tenancy at a rent of £55 per week on February 4, 1997. A copy of the tenancy agreement is attached

3.   The premises have special features namely adaptations for a wheelchair user which are designed to make the premises suitable for a disabled person.

4.   The Defendant is not physically disabled. His daughter, Delia was disabled but she no longer resides at the premises.

5.   The Claimants require the premises for occupation by a disabled person.

6.   The Defendant was offered suitable alternative accommodation at 9 Frog House, Clapper Street, Downtown on April 23, 2003, but refused the offer without viewing the alternative premises.

7.   By notice in writing dated April 25, 2003 the Defendant was informed that proceedings might be commenced against him after June 27, 2003 on Ground 15 of Sch.2 to the Housing Act 1985, and was given particulars of this.

8.   The tenancy is a secure tenancy and possession is claimed pursuant to Ground 15 of Sch.2 to the Housing Act 1985.

AND the Claimants claim:

(1)   possession of the premises;

(2)   rent, alternatively mesne profits, at the rate of £55 per week from the date hereof until possession be given up.

STATEMENT OF TRUTH

- (I believe) (The Claimants believe) that the facts stated in these Particulars of Claim are true.

- I am duly authorised by the Claimants to sign this statement.

Full name ....

Name of Claimant's solicitor's firm ....

Signed... Position or office held ....

- (Claimants)   (if signing on behalf of firm or company)
(Claimant's solicitor)

- delete as appropriate

Dated etc

6.69   <u>Form 98</u>

<u>Particulars of Claim: secure fixed term tenancy</u>

[HEADING AS IN FORM 89]

1. The Claimants are the freehold owners and claim possession of residential property at 59 Warden House, Drane Avenue, London NE1 ("the premises").

2. By an agreement in writing dated October 15, 1993 "the Claimants" granted to the Defendant a tenancy ("the tenancy") for a term of 10 years from September 29, 1995 at an annual rent of £12,000 payable quarterly in advance. A copy of the tenancy agreement is attached.

3. It was an express term of the tenancy agreement that the Defendant covenanted *inter alia* not to make any alteration to the structure of the internal walls within the premises without the prior consent of the Claimants in writing.

4. The tenancy was subject to a proviso for forfeiture should any of the Defendant's covenants be broken or not performed.

5. In breach of the term set out in para.3 above, on or about February 28, 2003 the Defendant, without the prior consent of the Claimants, cut into and removed sections of the internal wall dividing the kitchen from the living room, and causing the floor and wall above to collapse into the premises, thereby in turn also causing the collapse of the floor in the premises into the flat below.

6. On March 4, 2003 the Claimants served a notice in writing dated March 4, 2003 on the Defendant specifying the breach of covenant in para.5 above, in accordance with s.146 of the Law of Property Act 1925.

7. Further, on March 4, 2003 the Claimants served a notice dated March 4, 2003 on the Defendant in accordance with s.83 of the Housing Act 1985.

8. By reason of the breach of covenant in para.5 above, the building in which the premises are situated, and the Claimants' interest therein, has been damaged, particulars of which are set out in the schedule herewith [not here set out].

9. The tenancy is subject to the provisions of Pt IV of the Housing Act 1985. To the best of the Claimants' knowledge, the Defendant alone is in possession of the premises.

10. [AS IN FORM 88 PARAGRAPH 5]

AND the Claimants claim:

    (1) An order terminating the tenancy.

    (2) An order for possession of the premises pursuant to ground 1 of Sch.2 to the Housing Act 1985.

(3) Damages exceeding £5000 but less than £15,000.

(4) Interest as pleaded.

(5) Costs.

[CONCLUDE AS IN FORM 88]

6.70   **Form 99**

Particulars of Claim: assured periodic tenancy: suitable alternative accommodation

---

[HEADING AS IN FORM 88]

1. The Claimant is the freehold owner and claims possession of residential property at 47a The Parade, Busy ("the premises").

2. By an oral agreement made on January 15, 1989 the Claimant granted to the Defendant a monthly tenancy (hereafter referred to as "the tenancy") of the premises from February 1, 1989 at a rent of £400 per month payable monthly in advance.

3. The premises comprise two bedrooms, living room, kitchen and bathroom.

4. Suitable alternative accommodation is available for the Defendant at 56 Belgrave Road, Newtown, consisting of two bedrooms, living room, kitchen and bathroom which will be let to the Defendant pursuant to an assured tenancy at a rent of £500 per month.

5. The tenancy is subject to the provisions of Pt I of the Housing Act 1988 ("the Act"), and on January 25, 2003 the Claimant served a notice dated January 25, 2003 on the Defendant in accordance with s.8 of the Act informing the Defendant that the Claimant intended to begin proceedings for possession of the premises on ground 9 of Sch.2 to the Act and that such proceedings would not begin earlier than two months from the date of service of the notice.

AND the Claimant claims:

(1) Possession of the premises pursuant to ground 9 of Sch.2 to the Act.

[CONTINUE AS IN FORM 89]

[CONCLUDE AS IN FORM 88]

Form 100   **6.64**

Particulars of Claim: assured periodic tenancy: unlawful sub-occupier/nuisance

---

Claim No. ME0306092

IN THE METROPOLITAN COUNTY COURT

B E T W E E N:

PAULA SCARLETT   **Claimant**

and

ANDREW BLACK   **First Defendant**

STEPHANIE STRANGER   **Second Defendant**[21]

PARTICULARS OF CLAIM

---

1. [AS IN FORM 93 PARAGRAPH 1]

2. By an agreement in writing dated June 24, 1996 the Claimant granted to the First Defendant a weekly tenancy (hereafter referred to as "the tenancy") of the premises from June 24, 1996 at a rent of £70 per week. A copy of the tenancy agreement is attached.

3. It was an express term of the tenancy that the First Defendant would not assign, sub-let, or part with possession of the whole or any part of the premises, or cause or permit the premises to be occupied by any person other than the First Defendant.[22]

4. Between about June and November 2002 the First Defendant sublet or parted with possession of the whole or part of the premises to, or caused or permitted the premises to be occupied by, the Second Defendant.

5. Further or alternatively, the Second Defendant has been guilty of conduct causing, or likely to cause a nuisance or annoyance to persons residing or otherwise engaging in a lawful activity in the locality, and has been convicted of using the premises for immoral or illegal purposes.

PARTICULARS

(a) The Second Defendant was convicted at Busy Crown Court on February 25, 2003 of four offences of supplying controlled drugs, namely MDMA and LSD, from the premises, contrary to s.4(3)(a) of the Misuse of Drugs Act 1971, and asked for 14 other similar offences to be taken into consideration.

(b) On very numerous occasions the Second Defendant and the persons to whom drugs were supplied over the period from June to November 2002 caused noise and disturbance when in the vicinity of the premises, particularly in the early hours of the morning, by shouting, threatening neighbouring occupiers and damaging parked vehicles.

6. By a notice to quit dated February 24, 2003, the Claimant terminated the tenancy on March 28, 2003.

7. Alternatively, and without prejudice to the Claimant's contention that the First Defendant ceased to occupy the premises as his only or principal home, the tenancy is subject to the provisions of Pt I of the Housing Act 1988 ("the Act"), and the Claimant served a notice dated February 24, 2003 on the First Defendant in accordance with s.8 of the Act informing the First Defendant that the Claimant intended to begin proceedings for possession of the premises on grounds 12 and/or 14 of Sch.2 to the Act.

AND the Claimant claims:

(1) Possession of the premises.

[CONCLUDE AS IN FORM 93]

[21] Although the Second Defendant would not have any security of tenure as against the Claimant since any sub-letting was unlawful and so not within the protection afforded by the Housing Act 1988, s.18, nonetheless the Second Defendant has been joined in order to resolve all issues of occupation and make her bound by the judgment.
[22] This express term supplants the qualified term which otherwise would be implied by reason of the Housing Act 1988, s.15.

Form 101   **6.72**

Particulars of Claim: periodic assured tenancy: Ground 1

Claim No. ME0366666

IN THE METROPOLITAN COUNTY COURT

B E T W E E N

BILL OBONDEYS   **Claimant**

and

SIDNEY KIDNEY   **Defendant**

PARTICULARS OF CLAIM

---

1. The Claimant is the leasehold owner and entitled to possession of a residential property at 13 Out House, Codkipper Estate, London NE9 ("the premises").

2. By an agreement in writing dated December 14, 1998 the Claimant granted to the Defendant a weekly assured tenancy of the premises at a rent of £55 per week. A copy of the tenancy agreement is attached.

3. The Claimant himself occupied the premises between December 3, 1989 and December 13, 1998, prior to the commencement of the tenancy.

4. The Claimant orally gave the Defendant notice that possession might be recovered under ground 1 of Sch.2, Housing Act 1988, on December 13, 1998.

5. The Claimant requires the premises as his only or principal home.

6. It is just and equitable to dispense with the requirement of notice in writing pursuant to ground 1 Sch.2, Housing Act 1988,[23] by reason of such notice having been given orally as set out in para.4 above.

7. To the best of the Claimant's knowledge the Defendant and his wife, Deidre are in possession of the premises.

AND the Claimant claims:

(1) Possession

(2) Costs

STATEMENT OF TRUTH

- (I believe) (The Claimant believes) that the facts stated in these Particulars of Claim are true.

- I am duly authorised by the Claimant to sign this statement.

Full name ....

Name of Claimant's solicitor's firm ....

Signed..................................Position or office held ....

- (Claimant) (if signing on behalf of firm or company) (Claimant's solicitor)

- delete as appropriate

Dated etc

[23] *Boyle v Verrall* (1996) 29 H.L.R. 436, CA.

Form 102   **6.73**

Particulars of Claim: periodic assured tenancy: Ground 6

Claim No. ME0399229

IN THE METROPOLITAN COUNTY COURT

B E T W E E N

TOUCHEN FEELEN HOUSING ASSOCIATION LTD   **Claimant**

and

MAUREEN MORRIS   **Defendant**

PARTICULARS OF CLAIM

---

1. The Claimant is the freehold owner of the residential property at 9 Stibley Terrace, Lowerdown ("the premises").

2. The premises were let to the Defendant on an assured tenancy at a rent of £55 per week on August 9, 1999. A copy of the tenancy agreement is attached.

3. The Claimant intends to carry out substantial works of construction to the premises and the work cannot be carried out without the Defendant giving up possession.

PARTICULARS

The proposed works consist of removing all internal floors which are riddled with dry rot, and replacing them. No variation to the tenancy which would permit the Defendant to retain possession of the demised premises is practicable.

4. By a notice in the prescribed form dated April 4, 2003, the Claimant informed the Defendant of its intention to commence proceedings against the Defendant not earlier than June 6, 2003 and not later than twelve months from the date of service of the notice, on the ground that the Claimant intends to carry out the above-mentioned works and the Claimant gave particulars of that ground.

5. The Claimant claims possession of the premises pursuant to ground 6 of Sch.2 to the Housing Act 1988.

AND the Claimant claims:

(1) possession of the premises;

(2) rent or alternatively mesne profits at the rate of £55 per week from the date of these proceedings until possession be delivered up.

STATEMENT OF TRUTH

- (I believe) (The Claimant believes) that the facts stated in these Particulars of Claim are true.

- I am duly authorised by the Claimant to sign this statement.

Full name ....

Name of Claimant's solicitor's firm ....

Signed..Position or office held ....

- (Claimant) (if signing on behalf of firm or company) (Claimant's solicitor)

- delete as appropriate

Dated etc

Form 103   **6.74**

Particulars of Claim: fixed term assured tenancy: early termination: Ground 2

[HEADING AS IN FORM 88]

1. [AS IN FORM 99 PARAGRAPH 1]

2. By an agreement in writing made on December 28, 2001 the Claimant granted to the Defendant an assured tenancy ("the tenancy") of the premises for a term of three years from January 1, 2002 at a rent of £400 per month payable monthly in advance. A copy of the tenancy agreement is attached.

3. The premises are subject to a mortgage granted on April 15, 1997 by the Claimant to MM Mortgages Limited ("the mortgagee").

4. The mortgagee requires possession of the premises for the purpose of disposing of them with vacant possession in the exercise of a power of sale conferred by the mortgage.

5. The power of sale became exercisable when on September 15, 2002 the Defendant defaulted in repayment under the mortgage.

6. The tenancy is subject to the provisions of Pt I of the Housing Act 1988 ("the Act"), and on December 28, 2001 the Claimant gave the Defendant notice in writing that possession of the premises might be recovered on ground 2 in Sch.2 to the Act.

7. It was an express term of the tenancy that it would be terminable upon ground 2 and by the service of a notice in writing to that effect upon the Defendant, which notice was served upon the Defendant on January 21, 2003.

To the best of the Claimant's knowledge the Defendant alone is in possession of the premises.

AND the Claimant claims:

(1) Possession of the premises pursuant to ground 2.

[CONCLUDE AS IN FORM 93]

6.75   Form 104

Particulars of Claim: assured shorthold tenancy pre-Housing Act 1996

[HEADING AS IN FORM 88]

1. [AS IN FORM 88 PARAGRAPH 1]

2. By an agreement in writing dated December 24, 1996 the Claimant let the premises to the Defendant for a term of 6 months from December 24, 1996 at a rent of £500 per month. A copy of the tenancy agreement is attached.

3. Before the grant of the tenancy the Claimant served upon the Defendant notice stating that the tenancy was to be an assured shorthold tenancy within the meaning of the Housing Act 1988.

4. By reason of the above matters, the tenancy was an assured shorthold tenancy.

5. The tenancy came to an end on June 23, 1997 and thereafter a statutory periodic monthly tenancy arose upon the same terms.

6. By a notice in writing dated March 1, 2003 the Claimant gave the Defendant two months' notice pursuant to s.21 of the Housing Act 1988 stating that he required possession of the premises.

To the best of the Claimant's knowledge the Defendant alone is in possession of the premises.

AND the Claimant claims:

(1) Possession of the premises.

(2) Rent or alternatively mesne profits at the rate of £500 per month from the date of the order for possession until possession be delivered up.

(3) Costs.

[CONCLUDE AS IN FORM 88]

Form 105   **6.76**

Claim Form for Possession of Property (Accelerated Procedure – Assured Shorthold Tenancy)

**Claim form for
possession of property**
(accelerated procedure)
(assured shorthold tenancy)

In the
Claim No.

Claimant
(name(s) and address(es))

SEAL

Defendant(s)
(name(s) and address(es))

The claimant is claiming possession of:

for the reasons given in the following pages.
[The claimant is also asking for an order that you pay the costs of the claim.]

IMPORTANT - TO THE DEFENDANT(S)

This claim means that the court will decide whether or not you have to leave the premises and, if so, when. There will not normally be a court hearing. You must act immediately.

Get help and advice from an advice agency or a solicitor.
Read all the pages of this form and the papers delivered with it.
Fill in the defence form and return it **within 14 days** of receiving this form.

The notes on the last page of this form tell you more about what you can do.

Defendant's
name and
address for
service

Court fee	£
Solicitor's costs	£
Total amount	£

Issue date	

N5B Claim form for property (accelerated procedure) assured shorthold tenancy) (10.01)

Claim No.	

1. The claimant seeks an order that the defendant(s) give possession of

    ("the premises") which is a dwelling house [part of a dwellinghouse].

2. On   , the claimant entered into a written tenancy agreement with the defendant(s).
   A copy of it, marked "A" is attached to this claim form. The tenancy did not immediately follow an assured
   tenancy which was not an assured shorthold tenancy.
   [One or more subsequent written tenancy agreements have been entered into. A copy of the most recent
   one, made on   , marked "A1", is also attached to this claim form.]

3. Both the [first] tenancy and the agreement for it were made on or after 28th February 1997.

    a) No notice was served on the defendant stating that the tenancy would not be, or continue to
       be, an assured shorthold tenancy.

    b) There is no provision in the tenancy agreement which states that it is not an assured shorthold tenancy.

    c) The "agricultural worker condition" defined in Schedule 3 to the Housing Act 1988 is not fulfilled
       with respect to the property.

(or)

4. Both the [first] tenancy and the agreement for it were made on or after 15 January 1989.

    a) The [first] tenancy agreement was for a fixed term of not less than six months.

    b) There was no power for the landlord to end the tenancy earlier than six months after it began.

    c) On the   19   (before the tenancy began) a notice in writing, stating that the tenancy
       was to be an assured shorthold tenancy, was served on the defendant(s). It was served by:

    d) Attached to this claim form is a copy of that notice marked "B" [and proof of service marked "B1"].

5. Whenever a new tenancy agreement has replaced the first tenancy agreement or has replaced a replacement
   tenancy agreement,

    a) it has been of the same, or substantially the same, premises, and

    b) the landlord and tenant were the same people at the start of the replacement tenancy as the landlord
       and tenant at the end of the tenancy which it replaced.

6. On the   20   , a notice in writing, saying that possession of the premises was
   required, was served upon the defendant(s). It was served by:

   The notice expired on the   20   .

   Attached to this claim form is a copy of that notice marked "C" [and proof of service marked "C1"].

Claim No.	

7. *(any further information, continue on separate sheet if necessary)*

8. If the defendant(s) seek(s) postponement of possession on the grounds of exceptional hardship, the claimant is content that the request be considered without a hearing.

9. The claimant asks the court

to order that the defendant(s) deliver up possession of the property.

[to order the defendant(s) to pay the costs of this claim.]

Statement of Truth

*(I believe)(The claimant believes) that the facts stated in this claim form (and any attached sheets) are true.
* I am duly authorised by the claimant to sign this statement.

signed_____ date _____

(Claimant)(Litigation friend(where claimant is a child or a patient)*)(Claimant's solicitor)
*delete as appropriate

Full name _____

Name of claimant's solicitor's firm _____

position or office held _____
(if signing on behalf of firm or company)

Claimant's or claimant's solicitor's address to which documents should be sent if different from that on the front page		*if applicable*	
		Ref. no.	
		fax no.	
		DX no.	
		e-mail	
	Postcode	Tel. no.	

Notes for the defendant

The claimant has used the accelerated procedure because it is said you have an assured shorthold tenancy. If so, the court is not allowed to consider whether it is reasonable or fair to make the order for possession. Therefore, if what is written in the claim form and in the defence form make it clear that the claimant is entitled to possession, the court will make the order without fixing a hearing.

If you think there are reasons why the court should not make a possession order, you should consider getting advice from a solicitor or an advice agency immediately. If you dispute the claim, fill in the defence form and return it to the court office within 14 days of receiving the claim form. If you cannot give exact dates in your defence form, give them as nearly as you can. Make it clear that the dates you give are approximate. The judge can only take account of legally valid reasons.

You may qualify for assistance from Community Legal Service Fund (CLSF) to meet some or all of your legal costs. Ask about the CLSF at any county court office or any information or help point which displays this logo.

Court staff can only help you complete the defence form and tell you about court procedures. **They cannot give legal advice.**

If the court makes a possession order without a hearing, you will be entitled to apply, within 14 days of receiving the order, for it to be reconsidered. The application would have to show some good legal reason for varying or revoking the order.

Normally, if the court makes a possession order, it will tell you to leave the premises within 14 days. The judge can allow up to 42 days but only if satisfied that leaving within 14 days would cause you hardship which is exceptional (that is, worse than would usually be suffered by someone having to leave within 14 days). If you believe there are exceptional circumstances in your case, fill in section 9 of the defence form and return it to the court office. Usually, an order for possession in 14 days will still be made but a hearing will be fixed within the 14 day period. The judge will decide at the hearing whether or not to extend the period.

If the court orders you to pay the claimant's costs, normally the order requires payment within 14 days. If you would be unable to pay in that time, fill in section 10 of the defence form and give details of your means.

If you use the defence form, you **must** sign the Statement of Truth. Proceedings for contempt of court may be brought against a person who signs a Statement of Truth without an honest belief in its truth.

CERTIFICATE OF SERVICE
(completed on court copy only)
I certify that the claim form of which this is a true copy was served by me on

_____

by posting it to the defendant(s) on

_____

at the address stated on the first page of the claim form.

OR

The claim form has not been served for the following reasons:

Officer of the Court

Send documents for the court to the court office at

Telephone:
Fax:

Please address all correspondence to "The Court Manager".

Application for Possession – Introductory Tenancy

Claim No. ME0322222

IN THE METROPOLITAN COUNTY COURT

B E T W E E N

THE MAYOR AND BURGESSES
OF THE LONDON BOROUGH OF DOWNTOWN   **Claimants**

and

REGINALD HEDGE   **Defendant**

PARTICULARS OF CLAIM

---

1. The Claimants are the freehold owners of residential property at 9a Big Tower, Cutglass Road, Downtown ("the premises"), and are entitled to possession.

2. The Claimants are a local housing authority within the meaning of s.230 of the Housing Act 1996.

3. On November 3, 1999, the Claimants elected to operate an introductory tenancy regime.

4. On March 3, 2003, the Claimants granted to the Defendant a weekly periodic tenancy of the premises. A copy of the tenancy agreement is attached. The tenancy is an introductory tenancy within the meaning of s.124 of the Housing Act 1996.

5. On June 13, 2003, the Claimants served upon the Defendant notice, in accordance with the provisions of s.128 of the Housing Act 1996, informing the Defendant that the Claimants would be asking the court to make an order for possession of the premises. The reason given in the notice was rent arrears of £500 at that date.

6. The Defendant has not requested the Claimants to review their decision to seek an order for possession.[24]

7. The Claimant claims possession of the premises pursuant to s.127 of the Housing Act 1996.

8. To the best of the Claimant's knowledge the Defendant and her boyfriend, Stanley Ferret are the only people in possession of the premises.

AND the Claimant claims:

(a) Possession of the said premises;

(b) Rent alternatively mesne profits at the rate of £55 per week from the date of the order for possession until possession be delivered up.

STATEMENT OF TRUTH

- (I believe) (The Claimants' believe) that the facts stated in these Particulars of Claim are true.

- I am duly authorised by the Claimants to sign this statement.

Full name ....

Name of Claimant's solicitor's firm ....

Signed.................................. Position or office held ....

- (Claimant) (if signing on behalf of firm or company) (Claimant's solicitor)

- delete as appropriate

Dated etc

---

[24] Or, if a review was requested, the particulars ought to state that the decision to seek possession was confirmed, giving the reason. The provision of this information, and that at para.5, in the particulars of claim is helpful in case a claim for judicial review should be initiated.

Form 107   **6.78**

Particulars of Claim for possession claim against trespassers

---

Form N121 – Particulars of Claim (trespassers)

Claim No. HA0313091

IN THE HAMMERSMITH COUNTY COURT

SARAH SMITH   **Claimant**

and

TERI GREEN (1)
PERSONS UNKNOWN (2)   **Defendant(s)**

1. The Claimant has a right to possession of: 31 South Street, London W6 which is occupied by the defendants who entered or have remained on the land without the Claimant's consent or license.

2. The Defendants have never been tenants or sub tenants of the land.

3. The land mentioned at para.1 does include residential property.

4. The Claimant's interest in the land (or the basis of the claimant's right to claim possession) is: The Claimant is the freehold owner of the land

5. The circumstances in which the land has been occupied are: Please refer to the witness statement of Denzil Weeks attached hereto.

6. The Claimant does not know the names of all the defendants.

7. The Claimant asks the court to order that the Defendants:

   (a) give the Claimant possession of the land;

   (b) pay the Claimant's costs of making this claim.

STATEMENT OF TRUTH

- (I believe) (The Claimant believes) that the facts stated in these Particulars of Claim are true.

- I am duly authorised by the Claimant to sign this statement.

Full name ....

Name of Claimant's solicitor's firm ....

Signed................................Position or office held ....

- (Claimant) (if signing on behalf of firm or company) (Claimant's solicitor)
- delete as appropriate

Dated etc.

Witness Statement in support of possession claim against trespassers

---

D Weeks
Claimant
First
DWI-3
Date: 9 July 2003

Claim No. HA0313091

IN THE HAMMERSMITH COUNTY COURT
IN THE MATTER OF 31 SOUTH STREET, LONDON W6

B E T W E E N

SARAH SMITH   **Claimant**

and

TERI GREEN
PERSONS UNKNOWN   **Defendants**

WITNESS STATEMENT OF DENZIL WEEKS

I, DENZIL WEEKS, lettings manager employed by Properties Unlimited, of 48 Woodfield Avenue, London W6, WILL SAY

1. I am employed as lettings manager by Properties Unlimited, who act as agents for the Claimant in respect of residential premises at 31 South Road, London W6 ("the premises"). I am duly authorised to make this statement on behalf of the Claimant in support of her application for possession of the premises. The matters herein are within my own knowledge and are true.

2. The Claimant is the freehold owner of the premises, title to which is registered, as shown in the office copy entry, a true copy of which is now produced and shown to me marked "DW/1".

3. By an agreement in writing dated June 1, 1996, the Claimant let the premises to Gordon Green, the First Defendant's former husband, on a weekly tenancy, pursuant to which Mr Green and the First Defendant then resided at the premises.

4. By a notice to quit in writing dated April 5, 2003, and served on the Claimant, Mr Green terminated the tenancy on May 9, 2003. A true copy of the notice to quit is now produced and shown to me marked "DW/2".

5. Upon receipt of the notice to quit, by letter dated April 6, 2003 I wrote to the First Defendant to inform her that she should vacate the premises on May 9, 2003, and that if she did not do so she would be trespassing, proceedings might be commenced for her eviction from the premises, and any money paid in respect of continued occupation of the premises would be accepted on account of damages for use and occupation. A true copy of the letter is now produced and shown to me marked "DW/3".

6. The First Defendant has remained in occupation without the licence or consent of the Claimant.

7. When I visited the premises on May 9, 2003, I discovered that there were apparently three other persons in occupation of the premises without the licence or consent of the Claimant. All four persons refused to leave, and the three whose identities are unknown to me refused to give me their names.

8. I therefore ask that the court order that possession of the premises be delivered up to the Claimant forthwith.

STATEMENT OF TRUTH

- I believe that the facts stated in this Witness Statement are true.

Full name ....

Dated:

Form 109 6.80

Particulars of Claim for possession claim against trespassers – suitable for High Court

---

Form N121 – Particulars of Claim (trespassers)

Claim No. HQ424

IN THE HIGH COURT QUEENS BENCH DIVISION

SID SIMMONS **Claimant**

and

PERSONS UNKNOWN **Defendant(s)**

1. The Claimant has a right to possession of: The Cut, Scissor Street, Marsham which is occupied by the Defendants who entered or have remained on the land without the Claimant's consent or licence.

2. The Defendants have never been tenants or sub tenants of the land.

3. The land mentioned at para.1 does include residential property.

4. The Claimant's interest in the land (or the basis of the claimant's right to claim possession) is:

   The Claimant is the freehold owner of the land

5. The circumstances in which the land has been occupied are:

   Please refer to the Witness Statement of Charlie Coroley, Director of The Copper Residential Agents

6. The Claimant does not know the names of all the Defendants.

7. The Claimant asks the court to order that the Defendants:

   (a) give the Claimant possession of the land;

   (b) pay the Claimant's costs of making this claim.

8. The Claimant hereby certifies[25] that the reason for bringing this claim in the High Court is that there is a substantial risk of serious harm to persons or property which properly require immediate determination. The Defendants are using the Claimant's property as a "crack house". Threats of violence have been made against people living in the vicinity and several of the visitors to the property have been witnessed carrying firearms.

STATEMENT OF TRUTH

- (I believe) (The Claimant believes) that the facts stated in these Particulars of Claim are true.

- I am duly authorised by the Claimant to sign this statement.

Full name ....

Name of Claimant's solicitor's firm ....

Signed............................... Position or office held..

- (Claimant) (if signing on behalf of firm or company) (Claimant's solicitor)

- delete as appropriate

[25] CPR 55.3(2).

Form 110

Application for an Interim Possession Order

Application for an interim possession order

In the	
Claim No.	

Claimant's full name and address

Address for service (if different from above) Ref / Tel No.

Defendant's name (if known including title e.g. Mr, Mrs or Miss) and address

Seal

The claimant is claiming possession of

on the grounds that the claimant has an immediate right to possession and that the person(s) in occupation of the premises is (are) in occupation without consent.

Application issued on

The court will consider whether an interim possession order should be made on

at   am/pm

at

Service

Insert time, day and date 24 hours after time of issue

For this notice to be valid it **must** be served before   am/pm on   the   day of 20   . It must be **affixed** to the main door or another conspicuous part of the premises and, if practicable, inserted through the letterbox in a sealed transparent envelope addressed to 'the occupiers'. In addition it may be attached to stakes in the ground in conspicuous parts of the adjoining land if this is appropriate.

What you should do

- if you have no right to occupy the premises you must leave.

- if you think you have a right to occupy the premises or you believe that the applicant is not entitled to an interim possession order you may file a witness statement at the court before the date and time shown on this notice. The form you must use is attached to this notice.

- if you need advice you should go to a Solicitor, Legal Advice Centre or Citizens Advice Bureau. Court staff are unable to give legal advice.

If you give a false or misleading information in your witness statement you will be guilty of a criminal offence and on conviction you may be sent to prison and/or fined.

What can happen next

- if the court makes an interim possession order you will have 24 hours from the time it is served on you to leave the premises. It will be served on you in the same way that this notice was - it does not have to be served on you personally. The interim possession order must be served within 48 hours of its being approved by the court.

- after you have left the premises you may apply to the court for the interim possession order to be set aside. If you wish to do so, you should go to a Solicitor, Legal Advice Centre or Citizens Advice Bureau.

- if you do not obey an interim possession order (by leaving the premises within 24 hours) you may be arrested and on conviction sent to prison and/or fined.

- a date for hearing (when the claim for possession will be considered) will be shown on the interim possession order. You have a right to attend that hearing.

- if the court does not make an interim possession order you will be told in writing.

Further Information

- a leaflet is available free of charge from any county court office.

Statement to support an application
for possession and
for an interim possession order

Paragraph 1
Insert your full name, address
and occupation of person
making this statement.

1   I

make this statement in to support of the claim for possession and
for an interim possession order

Paragraph 2
Give the address of the
premises

2   I

have an immediate right to possession of ´

Give a description of the
premises (house, flat, shop etc)

which is a

and have had this right since

Paragraph 3
Give details of proof of interest
(deeds, lease etc)

3   Proof of my interest in the premises is in the form
of

Paragraph 4
Give the date when you found
out that the premises were
being occupied illegally. Explain
how you found out and why you
could not have been expected
to find out sooner

4   I

first knew of the occupation of the premises on
the   day of   20   by
and could not reasonably have been aware of this earlier because

5 The defendant(s) entered the premises without my consent and without the consent of anyone who on the date of entry had an immediate right to possession of the premises. Since that date I have not granted the defendant(s) any such consent.

Paragraph 6
Delete if you do not know the names of any of the occupier(s)

6 As well as the defendant(s) named in this application there are (no) other occupiers who names I do not know.

Paragraph 7
Give the names of those people and which part of the building they occupy. Delete the words in brackets as appropriate.

7 There are (no) other people who are entitled to possession of other parts of the building in which the premises are situated (and they are:)

Paragraph 8
The court must take into account whether or not you have given undertakings when deciding whether to make an interim possession order.
Delete any undertakings you are not prepared to give.

8 I hereby give the following undertakings:

(a) to re-instate the defendant, if so ordered by the court

(b) to pay such damages as the court may order

AND

(c) before the claim for possession is finally decided, not to damage the premises

(d) not to grant a right of occupation to any other person

(e) not to damage or dispose of any of the defendant's property

9   I ask the court to grant me an interim possession order in relation to the premises described at paragraph 2.
I also ask the court to grant me possession of the premises.

10   I understand the undertaking(s) I have given, and that if I break any
of my promises to the court I may be sent to prison for contempt of court and/or
fined.

11   I understand that if I make a false or misleading statement without an honest belie
in its truth proceedings for contempt of court may be brought against me.

Statement of truth

I believe that the facts stated in this statement are true.

Signed   Date

6.82 **Form 111**

Defence to Form 88 (denial of service occupancy) and counterclaim for declaration as to status

---

IN THE BUSY COUNTY COURT　　　　　　　　**Claim No. BU 03**

B E T W E E N

RUPERT RULE　　　**Claimant/Part 20 Defendant**

and

BRIAN BARREL　　　**Defendant/Part 20 Claimant**

DEFENCE AND COUNTERCLAIM

DEFENCE

1.　It is admitted that the Claimant is the freehold owner of the residential property at 47a The Parade, Busy ("the premises"), but denied that the Claimant is entitled to possession thereof.

2.　Save that it is denied that the arrangement described in para.2 of the Particulars of Claim was a licence whereby the Defendant was to occupy the premises for the better performance of the Defendant's duties as a security officer, para.2 of the Particulars of Claim is admitted.

3.　It is averred that the Claimant granted the Defendant a weekly tenancy of the premises, and the Defendant claims the protection of the Housing Act 1988.

4.　Save that it is admitted that the Claimant purported to terminate the Defendant's employment on February 23, 2003 and that the Defendant and his wife, Betty remain in occupation of the premises, paras 3 and 4 of the Particulars of Claim are denied.

COUNTERCLAIM

5.　Paragraphs 2 and 3 of the Defence are repeated.

AND the Defendant counterclaims:

(1) A declaration that the Defendant holds a weekly assured shorthold tenancy of 47a The Parade, Busy, pursuant to the provisions of Chapter 1 of the Housing Act 1988.

(2) Costs.

STATEMENT OF TRUTH

- (I believe) (The Defendant believes) that the facts stated in this Defence and Counterclaim are true.

- I am duly authorised by the Defendant to sign this statement.

Full name ....

Name of Defendant's solicitor's firm ....

Signed............................... Position or office held ....

- (Defendant)   (if signing on behalf of firm or company) (Defendant's solicitor)

- delete as appropriate

Defendant's solicitors
who will accept service at the above address

TO the District Judge
AND to the Claimant

6.83   Form 112

Defence to Form 90 (denial that security ended, challenge to validity of notice of quit) and counterclaim for completion of the right to buy

Claim No. ME0305009

IN THE METROPOLITAN COUNTY COURT

B E T W E E N

THE MAYOR AND BURGESSES OF
THE LONDON BOROUGH OF DOWNTOWN

Claimants/Part 20 Defendants

and

SIDNEY TENNANT

Defendant/Part 20 Claimant

DEFENCE AND COUNTERCLAIM

1. Save that it is denied that the Claimants are entitled to possession of a residential property at 59 Warden House, Drane Avenue, London NE1 ("the premises"), paragraph 1 of the Particulars of Claim is admitted and averred.

2. Paragraph 2 of the Particulars of Claim is admitted and averred.

3. It is denied that the Defendant ceased to occupy the premises as his residence as alleged or at all, or that the tenancy ceased to be a secure tenancy for the purposes of Pt IV of the Housing Act 1985.

4. It is admitted that the Defendant permitted Stephanie Stranger to reside at the premises between the dates alleged, but averred that she did so only as the Defendant's lodger, and it is accordingly denied that thereby the tenancy ceased to be a secure tenancy.

5. Save that service upon the premises of a notice to quit in writing dated February 2, 2003 ("the notice to quit") is admitted, para.5 of the Particulars of Claim is denied.

6. Further or alternatively the notice to quit was void and of no effect by reason that service thereof was occasioned by the intention of Angela Stedside, council leader of the Claimants, to secure vacant possession of the premises in pursuance of an unlawful policy known as "Flats for our Friends" whereby the premises (*inter alia*) were to be relet to political supporters of the Jam Tomorrow Party.

7. Further or alternatively, the notice to quit was void and of no effect by reason that the Claimant, through their neighbourhood housing officer, Archy Bold, at all times well knew from conversations with the Defendant in November 2002 that Stephanie Stranger was merely a lodger at the premises during a temporary absence of the Defendant between December 2002 and May 2003 so that service of the notice to quit was effected in bad faith.

8. It is admitted and averred that the Defendant has not delivered up possession of the premises to the Claimants and denied that he is or has ever been obliged to do so.

9. Further, the Defendant relies upon the Counterclaim below.

COUNTERCLAIM

10. Paragraphs 1 and 2 of the Defence are repeated.

11. By letter dated December 1, 2002 the Claimants admitted the Defendant's right to buy the premises pursuant to Pt V of the Housing Act 1985.

12. On or before February 14, 2003 all matters relating to the grant of the leasehold estate in the premises had been agreed between the Claimants and the Defendant.

13. The Defendant is ready, able and willing to complete the purchase of the premises.

AND the Defendant counterclaims:

(1) An order that the Claimants do within such time as the court may allow make a grant to the Defendant of the leasehold estate in the premises.[26]

(2) Costs.

[CONCLUDE AS IN FORM 111]

---

[26] See Housing Act 1985, s.138.

6.84   **Form 113**

Defence form (rented residential premises) on Form NIIR

In the   **Claim No.**

                                                               Claimant

                                                               Defendant(s)

                             Date of hearing
Personal details

1.   Please give your:

     Forename(s)

     Surname

     Address (*if different from the address on the claim form*)

     post code

Disputing the claim

2.   Do you agree with what is said about the   ☐Yes   ☐No
     premises and the tenancy agreement?

     If No, set out your reasons below:

3.   Did you receive the notice from the claimant   ☐Yes   ☐No
     referred to at paragraph 5 of the particulars of
     claim?

     If Yes, when: _____

4.   Do you agree that there are arrears of tent as   ☐Yes   ☐No
     stated in the particulars of claim?

     If No, state how much the arrears are: £_____   ☐None

5. If the particulars of claim give any reasons for   ☐Yes   ☐No
    possession other than rent arrears, do you agree
    with what is said?

    If No, give details below:

6. Do you have a money or other claim (a   ☐Yes   ☐No
    counterclaim) against your landlord?

    If Yes, give details:

Arrears

7. Have you paid any money to your landlord since   ☐Yes   ☐No
    the claim was issued?

    If Yes, state how much you have paid and when: £_____   date_____

8. Have you come to any agreement with your   ☐Yes   ☐No
    landlord about repaying the arrears since the
    claim was issued?

    I have agreed to pay £_____each
    (week)(month)

9. If you have not reached an agreement with your   ☐Yes   ☐No
    landlord, do you want the court to consider
    allowing you to pay the arrears by instalments?

10. How much can you afford to pay in addition to   £_____per (week)(month)
    the current rent?

About yourself

State benefits

11. Are you receiving Income Support?   ☐Yes   ☐No

12. Have you applied for Income Support?   ☐Yes   ☐No

    If Yes, when did you apply?   _____

13. Are you receiving housing benefit?   ☐Yes   ☐No

    If Yes, how much are you receiving   £_____per (week)(month)

14. Have you applied for housing benefit?   ☐Yes   ☐No

    If Yes, when did you apply?   _____

15. Is the housing benefit paid   ☐to you   ☐to your landlord

Dependants (*people you look after financially*)

16. Have you any dependant children?   ☐Yes   ☐No

If Yes, give the number in each age group below:

☐ under 11   ☐11–15   ☐16–17   ☐18 and over

Other dependants

17. Give details of any other dependants for whom you are financially responsible:

Other residents

18. Give details of any other people living at the premises for whom you are not financially responsible:

Money you receive		Weekly	Monthly
19. Usual take- home pay or income if self-employed *including overtime, commission, bonuses*	£_____	☐	☐
Job Seekers allowance	£_____	☐	☐
Pension	£_____	☐	☐
Child benefit	£_____	☐	☐
Other benefits and allowances	£_____	☐	☐
Others living in my home give me	£_____	☐	☐
I am paid maintenance for myself (or children) of	£_____	☐	☐
Other income	£_____	☐	☐
Total income	£_____	☐	☐

Bank accounts and savings

20. Do you have a current bank or building society account?   ☐Yes   ☐No

If Yes, is it

☐in credit? If so, by how much?   £_____

☐overdrawn? If so, by how much? £_____

21. Do you have a savings or deposit account?   ☐Yes   ☐No

    If Yes, what is the balance? £_____

Money you pay out

22. Do you have to pay any court orders or fines?

Court	Claim/Case number	Balance owing	Instalments paid
		Total Instalments paid £	per month

23. Give details if you are in arrears with any of the court
     payments or fines:

24. Do you have any loan or credit debts?   ☐Yes   ☐No

Loan/credit from	Balance owing	Instalments paid
Total Instalments paid £	per month	

25. Give details if you are in arrears with any loan/credit
    repayments:

Regular expenses

(*Do not include any payments made by other*
members of the household out of their own income)

26. What regular expenses do you have?

(*List below*)		Weekly	Monthly
Council tax	£_____	☐	☐
Gas	£_____	☐	☐
Electricity	£_____	☐	☐
Water charges	£_____	☐	☐
TV rental & licence	£_____	☐	☐
Telephone	£_____	☐	☐
Credit repayments	£_____	☐	☐
Mail order	£_____	☐	☐
Housekeeping, food, school meals	£_____	☐	☐
Travelling expenses	£_____	☐	☐
Clothing	£_____	☐	☐
Maintenance payments	£_____	☐	☐
Other	£_____	☐	☐
Total expenses	£_____	☐	☐

Priority debts

27. This section is for **arrears** only. **Do not** include regular expenses listed at Question
    26.

		Weekly	Monthly
Council tax arrears	£_____	☐	☐
Water charges arrears	£_____	☐	☐
Gas account	£_____	☐	☐
Electricity account	£_____	☐	☐
Maintenance arrears	£_____	☐	☐
Others (*give details below*)			
	£_____	☐	☐
	£_____	☐	☐

£_____   ☐   ☐

28. If an order for possession were to be made, would
    you have somewhere else to live?   ☐ Yes   ☐ No

    If Yes, say when you would be able to move in: _____

29. Give details of any events or circumstances which have led to your being in arrears
    of rent (*for example divorce, separation, redundancy, bereavement, illness, bank-
    ruptcy*) or any other particular circumstances affecting your case. If there are any
    reasons why the date any possession order takes effect should be delayed, give them
    here. If you believe you would suffer exceptional hardship by being ordered to leave
    the property immediately, say why.

STATEMENT OF TRUTH

*(I believe)(The defendant(s) believe(s)) that the facts stated in this defence form are
true.

*I am duly authorised by the defendant(s) to sign this statement.

signed .... date ....

*(Defendant(s))(Litigation friend (*where the claimant is a child or a patient*)
(Defendant's solicitor)

delete as appropriate

Full name ....

Name of defendant's solicitor's firm ....

position or office held ....
                    (*if signing on behalf of firm or company*)

6.85   <u>Form 114</u>

<u>Defence to Form 95 (denial of satisfaction of cases 9 and 11, allegations as to reasonableness)</u>

[HEADING AS IN FORM 93]

1. Paragraphs 1, 2 and 7 of the Particulars of Claim are admitted.

2. It is denied that the Claimant gave the Defendant notice whether as alleged or at all that possession might be recovered under Case 11 of Sch.15 to the Rent Act 1977.

3. It is denied that the Claimant occupied the premises as his residence at all times between the dates alleged in para.3 of the Particulars of Claim. The Claimant let the premises on protected tenancies with respect to which no notice in writing was given as required pursuant to sub-paragraph (a) of Case 11 as follows: (a) in about 1970 to Jacob Jacobs; (b) in about 1980 to Michael Michaels; and (c) in about 1985 to Richard Richard.[27]

4. It is denied that it would be just and equitable to dispense with the requirements of sub-paragraph (a) and/or (b) of Case 11.

5. Further or alternatively, as to para.5 of the Particulars of Claim, in about 1991 the Claimant transferred the reversion immediately expectant upon the determination of the tenancy to Steely Prop Limited, and in about 1992 the Claimant re-purchased the reversion from Steely Prop Limited.[28]

6. It is denied that the Claimant either requires or reasonably requires the premises as a residence for his daughter.

7. Further or alternatively, it is denied that, for the purposes of Case 9, it would be reasonable to make an order for possession of the premises. Without prejudice to the generality of the foregoing: (a) on January 2, 2003 the Claimant erected a sign at the front of the premises saying "Health hazard! Occupiers have AIDS"; (b) on January 26, 2003 the Claimant procured the withdrawal by Downtown Borough Council of the Defendant's disabled parking bay outside the premises by representing that the Defendant had died; and (c) on February 12, 2003 the Claimant caused the Child Protection Agency to demand from the Defendant maintenance for the Claimant's daughter's child, Maisie, well-knowing that the Defendant was not Maisie's father.

STATEMENT OF TRUTH

- (I believe) (The Defendant believes) that the facts stated in this Defence are true.

- I am duly authorised by the Defendant to sign this statement.

Full name ....

Name of Defendant's solicitor's firm ....

Signed......................... Position or office held ....

- (Defendant   (if signing on behalf of firm or company)
  (Defendant's solicitor)

- delete as appropriate

Dated etc

---

[27] *i.e.* a denial that the requirement of sub-para.(b) of Case 11 is satisfied.
[28] *i.e.* the Claimant has become landlord by purchase, thus not satisfying Case 9.

6.86   Form 115

Defence to Form 96 including Human Rights Defence

Claim No. ME0305009

IN THE METROPOLITAN COUNTY COURT

B E T W E E N

THE MAYOR AND BURGESSES OF
THE LONDON BOROUGH OF DOWNTOWN   **Claimants**

and

(1) STANLEY SOAP
(2) SANDY SOAP
(3) SHANE SOAP   **Defendants**

DEFENCE

---

1. It is admitted that the Claimants are the freehold owners of the premises but denied that the Claimants are entitled to possession.

2. Paragraphs 2 and 3 of the Particulars of Claim are admitted.

3. Paragraph 4 is denied.

    (a) The First Defendant did not verbally abuse Ranjit Singh in the manner alleged or at all on December 7, 2002. The First Defendant had a conversation with Mr Singh about the way he parked his car outside the front door of 33 Friendly Fields. Both parties began arguing but the First Defendant denies that he abused Mr Singh.

    (b) The Defendants have not shouted abuse in the manner alleged or at all on 12 occasions since December 7, 2002. There have been arguments between the families, usually about the way the Singhs park their cars, but there has been no abuse by the Defendants.

    (c) The Defendants did not abuse the Singh children or the Smith children on December 15, 2002 either in the way alleged or at all. There were rows between children of all three families on the date alleged but the abuse by the Defendants is denied.

    (d) The Defendants have not shouted abuse as alleged in para.2(b) or at all.

4. The Defendants are unable to admit or deny that the Claimants served the notice as alleged in para.5 of the Particulars of Claim and the Claimants are required to prove service.

5. If, which is denied, grounds to make a possession order do exist, it is denied that it is reasonable to make a possession order against the Defendants.

PARTICULARS

(a) Stanley Soap, the First Defendant has a severe heart condition. This will be exacerbated if the family is made homeless.

(b) The Defendants further rely on their Convention rights under the Human Rights Act 1998.[29]

    i) The making of a possession order in this case is not proportionate under Article 8(2).

    ii) Neither is the making of a possession order in this case in the public interest or proportionate under Article 1 Protocol 1.

4. Accordingly it is denied that the Claimants are entitled to the relief that they claim or any relief.

STATEMENT OF TRUTH

- (I believe) (The Defendant believes) that the facts stated in this Defence are true.

- I am duly authorised by the Defendant to sign this statement.

Full name ....

Name of Defendant's solicitor's firm ....

Signed................................. Position or office held ....

- (Defendant)   (if signing on behalf of firm or company)
(Defendant's solicitor)

- delete as appropriate

Dated etc

---

[29] The convention rights are unlikely in this case to add any substance in addition to the ordinary statutory provisions, but could still be pleaded for emphasis.

6.87   Form 116

Defence to Form 98 (waiver of forfeiture) and counterclaim for relief from forfeiture

---

Claim No. ME0305009

IN THE METROPOLITAN COUNTY COURT

B E T W E E N

THE MAYOR AND BURGESSES OF
THE LONDON BOROUGH OF DOWNTOWN

Claimants/Part 20 Defendants

and

SIDNEY TENNANT

Defendant/Part 20 Claimant

DEFENCE AND COUNTERCLAIM

DEFENCE

1. Paragraphs 1 to 7, and 9, of the Particulars of Claim are admitted.

2. By the acceptance of £3000 rent on March 25, 2003, with full knowledge of the alleged breach, the Claimant waived the alleged forfeiture before the commencement of this action.

3. No admission is made as to the quantum of any loss suffered by the Claimant as alleged in para.8 of the Particulars of Claim.

COUNTERCLAIM

4. Paragraphs 1 and 2 above are repeated.

5. If, contrary to the matters above, the lease is liable to be forfeit, the Defendant seeks relief from the forfeiture on such terms as the court may consider just.

[CONCLUDE AS IN FORM 111]

Form 117 6.88

Defence to Form 99 (denial that alternative accommodation suitable)

[HEADING AS IN FORM 88]

DEFENCE

1. Paragraphs 2 and 3 of the Particulars of Claim are admitted.

2. It is further admitted and averred that the provisions of the Housing Act 1988 apply to the tenancy.

3. The Defendant denies that suitable alternative accommodation is available for him.

4. The accommodation referred to in para.4 of the Particulars of Claim is not reasonably suitable to the needs of the Defendant as regards extent and character, in that hitherto the Defendant has had the exclusive use of a garden, tended and cultivated extensively by him, by which the Defendant enjoyed particular relief from symptoms of chronic depression.[30]

STATEMENT OF TRUTH

- (I believe) (The Defendant believes) that the facts stated in this Defence are true.

- I am duly authorised by the Defendant to sign this statement.

Full name ....

Name of Defendant's solicitor's firm

Signed....................................Position or office held ....

- (Defendant)   (if signing on behalf of firm or company) (Defendant's solicitor)

- delete as appropriate

Dated etc

---

[30] The need for a garden may be a need for these purposes, though the accommodation may still be suitable even though that need cannot be met: *Enfield Borough Council v French* (1984) 49 P & CR 223.

6.89   Form 118

Defence to Form 101

Claim No. ME0366666

IN THE METROPOLITAN COUNTY COURT

B E T W E E N

BILL OBONDEYS   **Claimant**

and

SIDNEY KIDNEY   **Defendant**

DEFENCE

---

1. It is admitted that Claimant is the leasehold owner of the premises, but denied that the Claimant is entitled to possession either on the grounds alleged or at all.

2. Paragraph 2 is admitted.

3. It is denied that the Claimant occupied the premises as his only or principal home between the dates alleged or at all. The Claimant only purchased the premises on November 30, 1998 from Mr R.M. Type, and did not occupy prior to letting the premises to the Defendant.

4. It is denied that the Claimant gave any notice as alleged in paragraph 4. The Defendant had no conversations with the Claimant prior to signing the tenancy agreement. All communication with the Claimant was via his agent "Big Les". Accordingly it is denied that it is just and equitable to dispense with the requirement of notice.

5. It is further denied that the Claimant requires the premises as his only or principal home. The Claimant owns six other premises in London, four of which are currently vacant.

STATEMENT OF TRUTH

- (I believe) (The Defendant believes) that the facts stated in this Defence are true.

- I am duly authorised by the Defendant to sign this statement.

Full name ....

Name of Defendant's solicitor's firm ....

Signed............................Position or office held ....

- (Defendant)   (if signing on behalf of firm or company)
  (Defendant's solicitor)

- delete as appropriate

Dated etc

6.90   Form 119

Defence to Form 104 (denial that tenancy is assured shorthold tenancy)

[HEADING AS IN FORM 88]

DEFENCE

---

1.   It is admitted that the Claimant is the freehold owner and, but for the Defendant's tenancy, entitled to possession of the premises.

2.   Paragraphs 2 and 5 of the Particulars of Claim are admitted.

3.   It is denied that any notice was given as required by s.20 of the Housing Act 1988 and as alleged in para.3 of the Particulars of Claim.

4.   It is accordingly denied that the tenancy was an assured shorthold tenancy, and averred that it was an assured tenancy.

5.   It is admitted that the notice alleged in para.6 of the Particulars of Claim was served, but denied that it was in the circumstances valid or of any effect.

6.   The Defendant claims the protection of the Housing Act 1988.

[CONCLUDE AS IN FORM 111]

Form 120   **6.91**

Defence form (accelerated possession procedure) (assured shorthold tenancy) Form N11B

Claim No.

IN THE COUNTY COURT

Claimant

Defendant(s)

To the Defendant

Please read the notes on the back page of the claim form before completing this form. Some of the questions in this form refer to numbered sections in the claim form. You will find it helpful to have that open as you answer them.

You **must** complete and sign the statement of truth.

[1] Please write clearly and in black ink. If there is not enough room for an answer, continue on the last page.

Are you the tenant(s) named in the tenancy agreement, marked 'A' (or 'A1'), attached to the claim form? ☐Yes ☐No

Does that tenancy agreement (or do both) set out the present terms of your tenancy (except for any changes in the rent or the length of the tenancy)? If not, say what terms have changed and what the changes are: ☐Yes ☐No

[2] Do you agree the date, in section 2 of the claim form, when the claimant says the tenancy began? ☐Yes ☐No
If not, on what date did it begin? on_____

[3] If the claimant has completed section 3 of the claim form, do: agree with what is said there? ☐Yes ☐No
If not, what do you disagree with and why?

[4] If the claimant has completed section 4 of the claim form, did you receive the notice (a copy of which is attached to the claim form and marked 'B') and, if so, when? ☐Yes ☐No

If Yes, give date _____

Do you agree with the rest of what is said in section 4
If not, what do you disagree with and why?

☐Yes   ☐No

⑤ If the claimant has not deleted section 5 of the claim form, do you agree that what is said there is correct?
If not, what do you disagree with and why?

☐Yes   ☐No

⑥ Did you receive the notice referred to in section 6 of the claim form, (a copy of which is attached to the claim form and marked 'C') and, if so, when?

☐Yes   ☐No

If Yes, give date_____

⑦ If the claimant has put any additional information in section 7 of the claim form, do you agree that what is said there is correct?
If not, what do you disagree with and why?

☐Yes   ☐No

⑧ If there is some other reason, not covered above, why you say the claimant is not entitled to recover possession of the property, please explain it here.

Postponement of possession

⑨ Are you asking the court, if it makes a possession order, to allow you longer than 14 days to leave the premises because you would suffer exceptional hardship?
If so, explain why the hardship you would suffer would be exceptional.

☐Yes   ☐No

Say how long you wish to be allowed to remain in the premises. (The court cannot allow more than 42 days after the order is made.)

up to_____20_____

Payment of costs

[10] If the court orders you to pay the claimant's costs, do you ask it to allow you more than 14 days to pay?   ☐Yes   ☐No

If so, give details of your means
(*continue onto last page if necessary*)

STATEMENT OF TRUTH

*(I believe)(The defendant(s) believe(s)) that the facts stated in this defence form (and any attached sheets) are true.
*I am duly authorised by the defendant(s) to sign this statement.

signed.....................................date ....
*(Defendant)(Litigation friend (*where defendant is a child or a patient*) (Defendant's solicitor)
delete as appropriate

Full name...

Name of defendant's solicitor's firm ....

position or office held
            (*if signing on behalf of firm or company*)

Defendant's or defendant's solicitor's address to which documents should be sent.			*if applicable*
		Ref. no.	
		fax no.	
		Dx no.	
		e-mail	
		Tel. no.	
	Postcode	Claim no.	

Claim No.

Additional Information

(Include the number of the section which is being continued or to which the information relates)

Signed...   Date ....

(Continue on a separate sheet if necessary, remembering to sign and date it and heading it with the Claim Number)

Form 121   **6.92**

Defence to Claim for Possession against trespassers (Form 108–pleading adverse possession)

Claim No. HA0313091

IN THE HAMMERSMITH COUNTY COURT

B E T W E E N

SARAH SMITH   **Claimant**

and

TERI GREEN (1)
JACK PITT (2)   **Defendant(s)**

DEFENCE OF THE SECOND DEFENDANT

---

1. Paragraphs 1–3 of the Particulars of Claim are admitted save that it is denied that the Claimant has a right to possession of the premises at 31 South Street, London W6 ("the premises").

2. As to para.4 it is denied that the Claimant has any title to or is the owner of the premises, by reason of the matters set out below.

3. In or before the month of April 1990 the Claimant discontinued possession of the premises or alternatively was dispossessed by the Second Defendant. Since April 1990 the Second Defendant has been continuously and still is in exclusive possession of the premises.

4. By reason of the above matters the Claimant's claim for possession is time barred and the Claimant's title was prior to the bringing of this action extinguished by virtue of the provisions of the Limitation Act 1980.

5. Paragraph 5 of the Particulars of Claim is accordingly denied.

6. No admissions are made as to para.6.

7. In the circumstances it is denied that the Claimant is entitled to the relief claimed in the Particulars of Claim or any relief.

STATEMENT OF TRUTH

- (I believe) (The Second Defendant believes) that the facts stated in this Defence are true.

- I am duly authorised by the Second Defendant to sign this statement.

Full name ....

Name of Second Defendant's solicitor's firm ....

Signed........................... Position or office held ....

- (Second Defendant)   (if signing on behalf of firm or company)
  (Second Defendant's solicitor)

- delete as appropriate

Dated etc

Reply and Defence to Counterclaim (Form 112) (allegation that tenant not entitled to exercise right to buy)

Claim No. ME0305009

IN THE METROPOLITAN COUNTY COURT

B E T W E E N

THE MAYOR AND BURGESSES OF
THE LONDON BOROUGH OF DOWNTOWN

Claimants/Part 20 Defendants

and

SIDNEY TENNANT

Defendant/Part 20 Claimant

REPLY AND DEFENCE TO COUNTERCLAIM

REPLY

1. It is admitted that at all material times Angela Stedside was council leader and that there was a policy known as "Flats for our Friends".

2. The Claimants join issue with the Defendant upon the Defence save in so far as it consists of admissions.

DEFENCE TO COUNTERCLAIM

3. Paragraphs 1 and 2 above, and paras 1 to 5 of the Particulars of Claim, are repeated.

4. Paragraph 12 of the Counterclaim is admitted.

5. Paragraph 13 of the Counterclaim is not admitted.

6. The Defendant has a bankruptcy petition pending against him issued by the Claimants in the Metropolitan County Court under number 9406971 in respect of £2065 due to the Claimants by reason of a liability order made by the Central Magistrates' Court on account of Council tax.

7. If, which is denied, the Defendant has any right to buy the premises, that right cannot be exercised by reason of the matters in para.6 above.

8. It is accordingly denied that the Defendant is entitled to the relief sought, or any relief.

STATEMENT OF TRUTH

- (I believe) (The Claimant believes) that the facts stated in this Reply and Defence to Counterclaim are true.

- I am duly authorised by the Claimant to sign this statement.

Full name ....

Name of Claimant's solicitor's firm ....

Signed.................................... Position or office held ....

- (Claimant) (if signing on behalf of firm or company) (Claimant's solicitor)

- delete as appropriate

Dated etc

Form 123 6.94

Witness statement of the Defendant to oppose the making of an Interim Possession Order

Witness statement of the
defendant to oppose the making of
an interim possession order

Witness statement of ....
(defendant)

made on

completed by defendant

Between   Claimant   Claim No.

and   Defendant

the occupier(s) of ....   **In the**
....   **County Court**
....

For completion by the court

Appointment on   **20**

at   **am/pm**

(1) Insert full name, address and occupation of witness

I, (1)

make oath and say as follows:

(2) Insert address of premises

1. I consider that I have a right to occupy the premises at (2)

2. I have been in occupation since

    Give date

3. The claimant (name)

    was aware of my occupation of the premises. I know this because

3 Witness statement of the respondent to oppose the making of an interim possession order   Crown Copyright. Reproduced by Sweet & Maxwell

⁽³⁾ Give name, address and date

4.   I was told by [2]

     of

     on   that I could occupy the premises named in paragraph 1.

⁽⁴⁾ Say who this person is and describe any documents they showed you

I believe that he/she had the right to allow me to occupy the premises because [2]

5.   I have written evidence to show my right of occupation. It is in the form of

                               (eg rent book, tenancy agreement) and a copy is

⁽⁵⁾ Delete if you have no written evidence

attached and marked 'A' [5]

6.   The claimant is **not** entitled to an interim possession order because

7.   **I understand that if I have made a false or misleading statement in this affidavit I will be guilty of a criminal offence and on conviction may be sent to prison or fined or both.**

Statement of Truth

*(I believe)(The defendant(s) believe(s)) that the facts stated in this witness statement (and any continuation sheets) are true.

* I am duly authorised by the defendant(s) to sign this form.

signed _____ date _____

*(Defendant(s))(Litigation friend *(where the defendant is a child or a patient)*) (Defendant's solicitor)
* *delete as appropriate*

Full Name _____

Name of defendant's solicitor's firm _____

position or office held _____
               (if signing on behalf of firm or company)

Defendant's or defendant's solicitor's address to which documents should be send.		if applicable	
		Ref. no.	
		Tel no.	
		fax no.	
		e-mail	
	Postcode	DX no.	

Form 124 6.95

Order for possession (Form N26)

Order for possession in the   Claim No

Claimant

Defendant(s)

On   20 ,

sitting at

heard

SEAL

and the court orders that

1. The defendant give the claimant possession of

    on or before   20 ,

2. The defendant pay the claimant £   for
    [and £   per day from   20 , until possession of the property is given to
    the claimant.]

3. The defendant pay the claimant's costs of £
    [The defendant pay the claimant's costs, within 14 days after they are assessed [and in the
    meantime pay the claimant £   on account of those costs].]
    [The claimant's costs will be added to the amount owing under the mortgage.]

4. The defendant pay the total amount of £   to the claimant [on or before 20][by
    instalments of £   per   , the first instalment to be paid to the claimant on or
    before   20]

To the defendant

The court has **ordered you to leave** the
property by the date stated in paragraph 1
above.
If you do not do so, the claimant can ask the
court, without a further hearing, to authorise
a bailiff or Sheriff to evict you. (In that case,
you can apply to the court to stay the
eviction; a judge will decide if there are
grounds for doing so.)

Ref

(if detailed assessment of costs is ordered)
The claimant will send you a copy of the bill
of costs with a notice telling you what to do if
you object to the amount. If you do object,
the claimant will ask the court to fix a hearing
to assess the amount.

*(If there is an order to pay money – paragraph
2.3 or 4)* Payments should be made to the
claimant, not to the court. If you need more
information about making payments, you
should contact the claimant.

*(If there is an order to pay money: made in a
county court)*
If you do not pay the money owed when it is
due and the claimant has to take steps to
enforce payment, the order will be registered
in the Register of County Court Judgments.
This may make it difficult for you to get
credit. Further information about
registration is available in a leaflet which you
can get from any county court office.

6.96   Form 125

Order for possession (accelerated procedure) (assured shorthold tenancy) Form N26A

**Order for possession
(accelerated procedure)
(assured shorthold tenancy)**

In the   Claim No

County Court

Claimant

Defendant(s)

SEAL

On the   20 ,

sitting at

read the written evidence of the claimant (and the defendant)

and the court orders that

1.   The defendant give the claimant possession of

   on or before   20 ,

2.   The defendant pay the claimant's costs of £   [on or before   20]
   [by instalments of £   per   the first payment to be made on or before   20].

[3.   The date for possession may be varied when the judge considers the defendant's request to postpone it.]

Note: This order was made without a hearing. Within 14 days of its being served, either party may apply for it to be set aside or varied.

To the defendant
The court has **ordered you to leave** the premises by the date stated in paragraph 1 above. (If notice is attached of a hearing to consider your request to remain longer, the date you must leave may be varied at that hearing.)
If you do not leave by the date fixed by the court, the claimant can ask the court, without a further hearing, to authorise a bailiff to evict you.

(*If there is an order to pay costs*)Payments should be made to the claimant, not to the court. If you need more information about making payments, you should contact the claimant.
If you do not pay the money owed when it is due and the claimant takes steps to enforce payment, the order will be registered in the Register of County Court Judgments.
This may make it difficult for you to get credit. Further information about registration is available in a leaflet which you can get from any county court office.

Ref

Form 126   6.97

County Court: order for possession (possession suspended): Prescribed Form N28

Order for possession in the   Claim No
(rented premises)
(suspended)

                                                                    Claimant

                                                                    Defendant(s)

On   20 ,

sitting at   (SEAL)

heard

and the court orders that

1. The defendant give the claimant possession of
    on or before   20 ,

2. The defendant pay the claimant £   for

3. The defendant pay the claimant's costs of the claim £

4. The defendant pay the total of £   to the claimant on or before   20 ,

5. This order is not to be enforced so long as the defendant pays the claimant the rent arrears
    and the amount for use and occupation [and costs, totalling] £   by the payments set
    out below **in addition to the current rent.**

    Payments required

    [£   on or before   20 and]
    £   per   , the first payment being made on or before   20 ,

To the defendant

The court has ordered that **unless you pay the arrears** and costs at the rate set out above in **addition to** your **current rent,** you must leave the premises.

Payments should be made to the claimant, not to the court. If you need more information about making payments, you should contact the claimant.

If you do not make the payments or leave the premises, the claimant can ask the court, without a further hearing, to authorise a bailiff or Sheriff to evict you. (In that case, you can apply to the court to stay the eviction; a judge will decide if there are grounds for doing so.)

(If there is an order to pay money made in a county court)

If you do not pay the money owed when it is due and the claimant takes steps to enforce payment, the order will be registered in the Register of County Court Judgments. This may make it difficult for you to get credit. Further information about registration is available in a leaflet which you can get from any county court office.

Ref

6.98   Form 127

Interim Possession Order

Interim possession order

<table>
<tr><td colspan="2">In the</td></tr>
<tr><td></td><td>County Court</td></tr>
<tr><td>Claim No.</td><td></td></tr>
<tr><td>Applicant's Ref.</td><td></td></tr>
<tr><td>Respondent's Ref.</td><td></td></tr>
</table>

Between .... Applicant

and .... Respondent

To the Respondent

of

For completion by the applicant
Served on   [19   ][20   ]
at   am/pm

Seal

If you do not obey this order within 24 hours of the time of service you may be arrested and on conviction sent to prison and/or fined

As a result of this order any person(s) entering the premises as trespassers while this order is in force may also be arrested and on conviction sent to prison and/or fined. In addition, if those in occupation at the time of service of this order. return as trespassers within a year of service of this order they may be arrested and on conviction sent to prison and/or fined

On the   of   [19   ][20   ] the court considered an application for an interim possession order

The court ordered that all person(s) in occupation of

must vacate the premises within 24 hours of service of this order.

The court further ordered

Insert the terms of any other orders eg costs

Notice of return date

The court will consider making a final possession order

at

on   the   day of   [19   ][20   ] at   o'clock

If you do not attend at the time shown the Court may make a final possession order in your absence.

You are entitled to apply to the Court to set aside this interim possession order before the date given above provided that you have left the premises.

To the Applicant – What you must do

Insert time and date 48 hours after approval by the court

- You **must** serve this order before   am/pm on the   day of   [19   ][20   ].
- It **must** be affixed to the main door or another conspicuous part of the premises and. if practicable, inserted through the letter box in a sealed transparent envelope addressed to 'the occupiers'. In addition it may be attached to stakes in the ground in conspicuous parts of the adjoining land if that is appropriate.
- Immediately before you serve this order you **must** write in the date and time in the box in the top right-hand corner of this form.

To the Respondent – What you must do

- You **must** leave the premises within 24 hours of the time this interim possession order is served
- **If you do not leave the police may arrest you and on conviction you may be sent to prison and/or fined**
- If you think you have a right to occupy the premises or any of the information given is incorrect you should go to a Solicitor, Legal Advice Centre or Citizens Advice Bureau after you have left the premises. Take any evidence with you (e.g. rent book, tenancy agreement)

The court office at

is open between 10am and 4pm. Monday to Friday. When writing to the court. please address forms or letters to the Court Manager and quote the claim number.

N134 Interim posession order (April 1999)   Crown Copyright. Reproduced by Sweet & Maxwell Ltd.

Interim possession order
record of appointment

Claim no. . . . .

On . . . . the . . . . day of . . . . [19   ][20   ]

Before (H   Honour) (District) Judge. . . . .

The court was sitting at . . . .

The Applicant

☐ was represented by Counsel

☐ was represented by a Solicitor

☐ attended in person

☐ did not attend

The Respondent

☐ was represented by Counsel

☐ was represented by a Solicitor

☐ attended in person

☐ did not attend

The court read the affidavit(s) of

☐ the Applicant   sworn on . . . .

☐ the Respondent   sworn on . . . .

And of . . . .   sworn on . . . .

Delete
as
appropriate

The Applicant gave undertaking(s) (through his counsel or solicitor) (in his affidavit) promising:

(a) to re-instate the respondent if, after an interim possession order has been made, the court holds that
the applicant was not entitled to the order

(b) to pay damages if, after an interim possession order has been made, the court holds that the applicant
was not entitled to the order

(c) not to damage the premises pending final determination of the possession proceedings

(d) not to grant a right of occupation to any other person pending final determination of the possession proceedings

(e) not to damage or dispose of any of the respondent's possessions pending final determination of the
possession proceedings

The court made this interim possession order on the grounds that

Signed   Dated
(H   Honour) (District) Judge

6.99   Form 128

Application for an adjournment of possession proceedings on public law grounds (By CPR Part 23 application)[31]

Claim No. ME0305009

IN THE METROPOLITAN COUNTY COURT

B E T W E E N

THE MAYOR AND BURGESSES OF THE
LONDON BOROUGH OF DOWNTOWN   **Claimant**

SIDNEY TENNANT   **Defendant**

PART A

I, Bob Stopper, solicitor on behalf of the Defendant, intend to apply for an order that: (1) the possession proceedings in this matter be adjourned pending the outcome of Judicial Review proceedings.

Because:

(1) The Claimants are a local housing authority having the functions imposed by Pt VII Housing Act 1996 ("Pt VII").

(2) In February 2003, the Defendant made an application to the Claimants pursuant to Pt VII.

(3) In pursuance of the duty arising pursuant to s.188 Housing Act 1996, the Claimants temporarily accommodated the Defendant at the premises pending a decision as to the Defendant's homelessness.

(4) In May 2003, the Claimant decided that the Defendant was homeless, in priority need, but intentionally homeless.

(5) The Defendant has sought a review of this decision pursuant to the Housing Act 1996, s.202. The Claimants allege that the Defendant made himself intentionally homeless by voluntarily leaving private rented accommodation at 4 Rachman Villas, NE9. The Defendant was however forced to leave these premises because he was suffering serious harassment from the landlord, and the Claimant erred in law by failing to take this into account.

(6) The Defendant requires accommodation pending the review because he suffers from Parkinson's disease. The Claimants have refused to continue to provide such accommodation pursuant to their power under s.188, which decision is either (a) unlawful, because it failed to take into account the seriousness of the

Defendant's medical condition; or (b) unlawful because it is an unjustified and disproportionate interference with the Defendant's convention rights under Article 8. The Defendant wishes to seek a Judicial Review of this decision.[32]

PART B

I wish to rely on my statement of case.

Signed   B. Stopper   **Position or office held**   Solicitor

Address to which documents about the case should be sent
Fred Fudge and Co.
Downtown Annexe
Cheesy House
Stoat Street
Downtown

STATEMENT OF TRUTH

The applicant believes that the facts stated in this application are true

Signed   B. Stopper   **Position or office held**   Solicitor

Date

---

[31] For use with Form N244, though often it will be the case that an application such as this will be made at the possession hearing without, perhaps, time for preparing a formal notice of application in advance. The procedure of applying for an adjournment pending judicial review proceedings, where no defence can be made out in private law proceedings but where arguable grounds for judicial review exist, was endorsed in *London Borough of Hackney v Lambourne* (1992) 25 H.L.R. 172; see also *Manchester City Council v Cochrane* (1999) 31 H.L.R. 810, CA; *R v Bracknell Forest BC, Ex p. McLlellan*; *Reigate and Banstead BC v Benfield and Forest and Others* [2001] EWCA Civ 1510; 33 H.L.R. 86, CA.
[32] see *R v Camden LBC Ex p. Mohammed* (1997) 30 H.L.R. 315, QBD.

6.100 Form 129

County Court: request for warrant for possession of land: Form N325

Request for Warrant of Possession of Land
To be completed and signed by the claimant or his solicitor and sent to the court with the appropriate fee

1 Claimant's name and address

In the County Court

Claim Number

2 Name and address for service and payment (if different from above) Ref/Tel No.

For court use only
Warrant No.
Issue date:
Warrant applied for at ___ o'clock
Foreign court code/name (execution only):

3 Defendant's name and address

I certify that the defendant has not vacated the land as ordered (* and that the whole or part of any instalments due under the judgment or order have not been paid) (†and the balance now due is as shown)

4 Warrant details
(A) Balance due at the date of this request
(B) Amount for which warrant to issue
Issue fee
Solicitor's costs
Land Registry fee
TOTAL
If the amount of the warrant at (B) is less than the balance at (A), the sum due after the warrant is paid will be

Signed
Claimant (Claimant's solicitor)
Dated
* delete unless defendant is in arrears with the suspended possession order or judgment
† delete unless warrant is to issue for execution also

IMPORTANT
You must inform the court immediately of any payments you receive after you have sent this request to the court

5 Property/land details
Date of judgment/order
Date of possession
Describe the land (as set out in the particulars of claim)

If there is more than one defendant and you are not proceeding against all of them, enter here the name(s) of the defendant(s) you wish to proceed against

You should provide a contact number so that the bailiff can speak to you if he/she needs to:
Daytime phone number: Evening phone number (if possible):
Contact name (where appropriate):
Defendant's phone number (if known):
If you have any other information which may help the bailiff or if you have reason to believe that the bailiff may encounter any difficulties you should write it below.

N325 -w3- Request for warrant for possession of land (4.99)

Form 130 6.101

High Court: Writ of Possession: Prescribed Form 66A

No. 66A
Writ of possession (Schedule 1–RSC O 113 r.7)

Claim No.

IN THE HIGH COURT OF JUSTICE QUEEN'S BENCH DIVISION
[   ] District Registry

Claimant

Defendant

ELIZABETH THE SECOND, by the Grace of God, of the United Kingdom of Great Britain and Northern Ireland and of Our other realms and territories Queen, Head of the Commonwealth, Defender of the Faith.

TO THE SHERIFF of (*county*) greeting:

IN THIS CLAIM a Judgment or Order was made that the claimant (*name*) recover possession of the land detailed in Schedule 1 below [and pay the sums set out in Schedule 2 below].

YOU ARE NOW COMMANDED:
(1) to enter the land detailed in Schedule 1 and cause the claimant (*name*) to have possession of it,
[(2) (*where there is an order for costs against a named defendant*) to seize in execution the goods, chattels and other property of the defendant (*name*) authorised by law and raise therefrom the sums detailed in Schedule 2 [together with sheriff's poundage, officers' fees, costs of levying and all other legal, incidental expenses], and immediately after execution to pay the claimant (*name*), the said sums and interest].

YOU ARE ALSO COMMANDED to indorse on this writ immediately after execution a statement of the manner in which you have executed it and send a copy of the statement to the claimant[defendant] (*name*).

THIS WRIT WAS ISSUED by the Central Office [the   District Registry] of the High Court on (*date*) on the application of (*name*) of (*address*) [agent for (*name*) of (*address*)] solicitor for [the claimant] [*or* the claimant (*name*) in person] who resides at (*address*).

WITNESS (*name*) Lord High Chancellor of Great Britain, the (*date*)

The address[es] for enforcement are (*give address[es] including county and postcode*).

SCHEDULE 1

Date of Judgment or Order:-

Details of land:-
        (*describe the land the subject of the judgment or order*)

SCHEDULE 2

[1.   Fixed costs on Judgment or Order   £

2.   Assessed costs (if any) [by costs certificate
dated (*date*)]   £

3.   <u>LESS</u> credits or payments received since Judgment
or Order   £

                    Sub Total   **£**

4.   Costs of execution   £   [71.75]

                    Total   **£**   ]

together with:-

A.   Judgment interest[1] at [8]% from date of Judgment on sub-total above until payment,

B.   Sheriff's poundage, Officer's fees, costs of levying and other legal, incidental expenses.

---

[1] s.17 Judgments Act 1838.

Form 131   **6.102**

Application to set aside a possession order and/or warrant for possession (on Form N244)

Claim No. ME0305009

IN THE METROPOLITAN COUNTY COURT

B E T W E E N

THE MAYOR AND BURGESSES OF THE LONDON BOROUGH OF DOWNTOWN   **Claimant**

and

TED CHEDDAR   **Defendant**

PART A

I, Bob Stopper, solicitor on behalf of the Defendant intend to apply for an order that:

(1) The possession order made on April 2, 2003 be set aside and the case be adjourned for trial; and or

(2) The warrant for possession be set aside or suspended.

Because:

1. The Defendant was not served with notice of these proceedings until May 25, 2003, when he was served with notice of a bailiff's appointment scheduled for June 3, 2003.

2. Accordingly, the possession order made on April 2, 2001 was made in the absence of the Defendant.

3. The Defendant has a right to defend and a counterclaim, in that there is disrepair at the premises for which the Claimant is liable in damages.

4. Further or alternatively, the Claimants acted oppressively in the execution of the warrant for possession on June 3, 2003, by reason that on May 25, 2003 the Defendant contacted the Claimants Legal Officer, who promised that the warrant would not be executed provided that within 14 days the Defendant filed an application to have the order set aside and a defence and counterclaim in draft.

PART B

I wish to rely on the attached witness statement.

Signed B. Stopper   **Position or office held** Solicitor

Address to which documents about the case should be sent
Fred Fudge and Co
Downtown Annexe
Cheesy House
Stoat Street
Downtown

STATEMENT OF TRUTH

The applicant believes that the facts stated in this application are true

Signed B. Stopper   **Position or office held** Solicitor

Date

1. Check what the status of the occupier is before you commence proceedings – is he or she a tenant with statutory protection? or has this protection been lost? (For example by failure to occupy the premises as the only or principal home in the case of a secure and assured tenants).

2. Check whether there have been any previous proceedings against the particular occupier. If a previous suspended possession order has not been complied with the occupier may only have the status of a tolerated trespasser.

3. Has the contractual agreement expired, or been brought to an end (so far as possible): *e.g.* has any necessary notice to quit been validly served? If not, and you are intending to commence proceedings, consider whether (and if so how) the agreement can now be terminated.

4. Has any necessary statutory notice been validly served: *e.g.* notice of seeking possession? If not, and you are intending to commence proceedings, serve one immediately.

5. Is the leave of the court required before commencement of proceedings, *i.e.* by reason of the Leasehold Property (Repairs) Act 1938?

6. Check that any notice previously served is or was still effective at the commencement of proceedings: *e.g.* has any notice of seeking possession expired?

7. Which is the appropriate court for the proceedings? If you are intending to bring proceedings in the High Court, have you considered any consequences as to costs?

8. Prepare applications statements of case as may be required in the particular case.

9. Make sure that the witness statements etc are in the proper form. Do they contain all the necessary particulars? If not, consider what may be done to amend them.

10. Keep the tenant fully informed of all impending proceedings and hearings. Do not advise the tenant that they do not need to attend any hearings.

11. At the conclusion of proceedings, has the order been drawn up correctly? If not, consider what may be done to have it corrected.

Chapter 7
Mortgage Possession Proceedings

PART I: INTRODUCTION

The position of owner-occupiers, particularly in relation to claims for possession by a **7.01** mortgagee, has come to be recognised as an important part of housing law in its wider sense. This chapter accordingly deals with mortgage possession proceedings, as well as proceedings relating to consumer credit agreements. Issues can range from straightforward debt claims to complicated tri-partite claims involving a lender, a borrower, and a co-owner.[1]

Mortgages generally

Mortgages may be both legal and equitable. A legal mortgage of land must be created either **7.02** by a demise of the land for a term of years, or by a charge by way of legal mortgage.[2] Most domestic mortgages are now created by a charge and, although this does not grant any legal estate to the mortgagee (or lender), it gives the same powers and remedies as if it did so.[3] In contrast to this statutory method of creating a mortgage, at common law a mortgage involves a conveyance or assignment of the mortgagor's (or borrower's) estate. The origins and nature of mortgages are significant in understanding how the right to possession of the mortgaged property operates (see below).

An equitable mortgage is a contract, falling short of creating a legal mortgage, but which nonetheless operates as security for the mortgagee and which is enforceable under the equitable jurisdiction of the court. In the domestic context, the significance of an equitable mortgage is likely to be that, even though the mortgagee may have no right to possession, there is an interest in the property sufficient to enable the mortgagee to apply for an order for the sale of the property in order to recover a debt.

Right to possession at common law

At common law, because a mortgage operates as a demise of the property, the mortgagee is **7.03** entitled to possession as soon as the mortgage has been executed.[4] The fact that the mortgagor may have a counterclaim will not defeat the mortgagee's claim for possession.[5] In

---

[1] See, for example, the succession of husband and wife cases involving undue influence and misrepresentation, particularly *Barclays Bank v O'Brien* [1994] 1 A.C. 180, HL, and *Royal Bank of Scotland v Etridge* (No2) [2001] 4 All E.R. 449, HL.
[2] Law of Property Act 1925, ss.85–86.
[3] *ibid.*, s.87(1).
[4] *Four-Maids Ltd v Dudley Marshall (Properties) Ltd* [1957] Ch. 317, Ch D.
[5] *National Westminster Bank plc v Skelton* [1993] 1 All E.R. 242, CA.

practice, however, most domestic mortgages defer the exercise of this right, providing the mortgagor complies with the terms of the mortgage, including as to payment.

Generally, at common law, the court can only adjourn an order for possession in a mortgage case for a short period to allow the mortgagor to pay off the loan and redeem the mortgage.[6] But this limited protection for the mortgagor has been substantially enlarged by statute (see below).

Right to possession under statute

7.04 In deciding whether or not to make a possession order of mortgaged residential premises, the court must consider the Administration of Justice Act 1970, s.36(1)–(4).[7] Under these provisions the court may:

  i)   adjourn the proceedings

  ii) stay or suspend the execution of the judgement or order

  iii) postpone the date for delivery of possession for such periods as the court thinks reasonable[8]

if it appears to the court that in the event of its exercising the power the mortgagor is likely to be able within a *reasonable period* to pay any sums due under the mortgage or to remedy a default under the mortgage.[9]

What is a reasonable period?

7.05 The key question which arises in practice, is the length of the period. The court can take into account the whole of the remaining part of the original term in assessing what is a reasonable period for repayment.[10] The court should look at the following matters in deciding whether to exercise its discretion:[11]

  i)   How much the mortgagee can reasonably afford to pay both now and in the future.

  ii) If the mortgagee has a temporary difficulty in making payments, how long is this likely to last?

  iii) Why did the arrears accrue in the first place?

  iv) How long is left on the original term?

  v)   What are the terms of the original mortgage contract?

  vi) Is it a case where the court should exercise its power to disregard accelerated payment provisions?[12]

[6] *Birmingham Citizens Permanent Building Society v Caunt* [1962] 1 All E.R. 163.
[7] Regulated agreements under the Consumer Credit Act 1974 have separate rules, which are dealt with below.
[8] s.36(2). The adjournment, stay etc., can be made subject to conditions as to payment or as to remedying the default (s.36(3)). These conditions, if imposed, can subsequently be varied or revoked (s.36(3)).
[9] s.36(1).
[10] *Cheltenham and Gloucester B.S. v Norgan* [1996] 1 All E.R. 449, CA.
[11] See *Norgan*, above.
[12] See Administration of Justice Act 1973, s.8, below.

vii) Is it reasonable to expect a mortgagee to recoup the arrears of interest over the whole of the original term or within a shorter period or longer repayment period?

viii) Are there any reasons affecting the security which could influence the length of the period for payment?

A mortgagor may seek to adjourn or suspend the granting of possession pending a sale of the property. There is no rule that the sale must take place within a short period of time but the court should be satisfied that the sale proceeds will be enough to discharge the whole of the mortgage debt.[13] In *Bristol & West B.S. v Ellis* (1996) 29 H.L.R. 282, CA, however, the court held that if there was likely to be considerable delay in effecting the sale, and/or if the value of the property was close to the outstanding mortgage debt and the arrears, immediate possession or only a short suspension might be appropriate.

Administration of Justice Act 1973, s.8

Where the mortgagor is entitled to pay the principal sum by instalments, or otherwise to defer **7.06** the payment of it in whole or in part, the court may treat as sums due only those instalments which are actually in arrear, even if the mortgage makes the whole of the balance outstanding in the event of any default.[14] The court is, however, only able to exercise its discretion if the mortgagor is likely to be able within a reasonable period also to pay any further instalments which are then due.[15] These provisions do not apply to an *all monies charge* connected with a bank loan.[16]

Order for sale

The remedies open to a mortgagee include the power of sale, the exercise of which normally **7.07** follows after a possession order has been obtained. There is usually an express power of sale in the mortgage, but there is also a general statutory power.[17] Sometimes, the mortgagee may need to seek an order for sale, and the court has a broad statutory power under the Law of Property Act 1925, s.91, to order sale. It may order sale even when the proceeds will not be sufficient to discharge the mortgage debt.[18]

Consumer credit agreements

Consumer credit agreements are subject to a separate statutory regime. The Consumer Credit **7.08** Act 1974 governs *regulated* agreements. An agreement can only be regulated if the loan is for £25,000[19] or less and the agreement is not exempt.[20]

---

[13] *National and Provincial B.S. v Lloyd* [1996] 1 All E.R. 630, CA.
[14] s.8(1).
[15] s.8(2).
[16] *Habib Bank Ltd v Tailor* [1982] 1 W.L.R. 1218, CA.
[17] Law of Property Act 1925, s.101
[18] *Palk v Mortgage Services Funding plc* [1993] 2 All E.R. 481, CA.
[19] Or £15,000 if the agreement was entered into before May 1, 1998.
[20] See s.16.

In the case of a regulated agreement, s.87 requires the lender to serve a default notice in the prescribed form.[21] The default notice must specify:[22]

a) the nature of the alleged breach,

b) if the breach is capable of remedy,

    a. what action is required to remedy it, and
    b. the date before which that action is to be taken, being at least seven days after the notice;[23]

c) if the breach is not capable of remedy,

    a. the sum (if any) required to be paid as compensation for the breach and,
    b. the date before which it is to be paid;

d) information in the prescribed form about the consequences of failure to comply with the notice.[24]

If no notice is served, the lender cannot enforce the security. If the borrower complies with the default notice, she is treated as though s/he is not in default.[25] If the borrower fails to comply with the default notice, the lender must enforce his security by court proceedings.[26]

Under the Consumer Credit Act 1974, the court is entitled to make a "time order" in relation to any sums owed or any other breaches of agreement. The time order will provide for payment of the arrears by instalments or for the remedying of the breach within a certain time period.[27] The court can also suspend an order for possession, and impose conditions in relation to any such order.[28] Finally, the court also has the power to amend the actual agreement or security in consequence of a term of any order made.[29] This is in relation to both past and future sums due.[30]

The court can make a time order or suspend a possession order if it appears just to do so. If there is no prospect of the debtor being able to pay any part of the principal sum owed (*e.g.* if only payments of interest can be afforded) the court is unlikely to exercise its discretion in the debtor's favour.[31]

Matrimonial cases

7.09   There are particular provisions of both substantive and procedural law which affect matrimonial property, using this term in a very broad sense. The Family Law Act 1996 requires the claimant in a mortgage possession action to carry out a search at the Land Registry or the Land Charges Department to determine if a notice, caution or Class F land charge has been

---

[21] Consumer Credit (Enforcement, Default and Termination Notices) Regulations 1983 (SI 1983/1561, as amended by SI 1984/1109).
[22] s.88(1).
[23] s.88(2).
[24] s.88(4).
[25] s.89.
[26] s.126.
[27] s.129.
[28] s.135.
[29] s.136.
[30] *Southern & District Finance v Barnes* [1996] 1 F.C.R. 679, CA.
[31] *First National Bank plc v Syed* [1991] 2 All E.R. 250, CA.

registered to protect matrimonial home rights (unless the defendants are husband and wife who are joint mortgagors). If the search reveals an interest this must be included in the particulars of claim, and the protected spouse will need to be served.[32] The non-owning spouse can then apply to be made a party.[33]

County Court jurisdiction

The county court has jurisdiction to hear all claims for mortgage possession.[34] It also has **7.10** exclusive jurisdiction to hear mortgage possession claims where the land consists of or includes a dwelling house located outside Greater London,[35] except where the claim for possession is made in an action for foreclosure or sale.[36] All Consumer Credit Act 1974 cases must be brought in the county court.[37]

Procedure

Mortgage possession claims, like other possession claims, must be commenced in the county **7.11** court for the district in which the land is situated.[38] The summons is the same as in other possession cases (N5 summons). There is a prescribed form for the particulars of claim (N120). An additional copy of the proceedings needs to be served in a case where the search has revealed a person with matrimonial home rights (see above). There is a prescribed form for the defence (N11M). An application for a time order under the Consumer Credit Act 1974 can be made either in the defence or by application.[39]

Particulars of Claim

In mortgage possession cases there are additional requirements for the particulars of claim **7.12** over and above the standard requirements for a possession case (for which see Chapter 6, above).

The particulars of claim in a mortgage possession case must set out:[40]

    a) if the claim relates to residential property whether:

        i) a land charge of Class F has been registered under s.2(7) of the Matrimonial Homes Act 1967;

        ii) a notice registered under s.2(8) or 8(3) of the Matrimonial Homes Act 1983 has been entered and on whose behalf; or

        iii) a notice under s.31(10) of the Family Law Act 1996 has been registered and on whose behalf; and

---

[32] s.56(2) Family Law Act 1996; and see CPR 55 PD 2.5(1).
[33] s.55 FLA 1996.
[34] s.21(1) County Courts Act 1984.
[35] s.21(3) CCA 1984.
[36] s.21(4) CCA 1984.
[37] ss.21(9) and 141 of the Consumer Credit Act 1974.
[38] CPR 55.2 and CPR 55.3.
[39] CPR 55 PD para.7.1, see below.
[40] CPR 55 PD para.2.5.

if so, that the claimant will serve notice of the claim on the persons on whose behalf the land charge is registered or the notice or caution entered.

b)   the state of the mortgage account by including:

 i)   the amount of:

 - the advance;
 - any periodic repayment; and
 - any payment of interest required to be made

 ii)   the amount that would have to be paid (after taking into account any adjustment for early settlement) in order to redeem the mortgage at a stated date not more than 14 days after the claim started specifying the amount of solicitors costs and administration charges which would be payable;

 iii) if the loan which is secured by the mortgage is a regulated consumer credit agreement, the total amount outstanding under the terms of the mortgage; and

 iv)   the rate of interest payable:

 - at the commencement of the mortgage;
 - immediately before any arrears referred to in paragraph c accrued;
 - at the commencement of the proceedings

c)   if the claim is brought because of failure to pay the periodic payments when due:

 i)   in schedule form, the dates when the arrears arose, all amounts due, the dates and amounts of all payments made and a running total of the arrears;

 ii)   give details of:

 - any other payments required to be made as a term of the mortgage (such as for insurance premiums, legal costs, default interest, penalties, administrative or other charges);
 - any other sums claimed and stating the nature and amount of each such charge; and
 - whether any of these payments is in arrears and whether or not it is included in the amount of any periodic payment.

d)   whether or not the loan which is secured by the mortgage is a regulated consumer credit agreement and, if so, specify the date on which any notice required by ss.76 or 87 of the Consumer Credit Act 1974 was given;

e)   if appropriate details that show the property is not one to which s.141 of the Consumer Credit Act 1974 applies;

f)   any relevant information about the defendant's circumstances in particular:

 i)   whether the defendant is in receipt of social security benefits; and

 ii)   whether any payments are made on his behalf directly to the Claimant under the Social Security Contributions and Benefits Act 1992

g)   give details of any tenancy entered into between the mortgagor and mortgagee (including any notices served); and

h)   state any previous steps which the Claimant has taken to recover the money secured by the mortgage or the mortgaged property and, in the court proceedings, state:

i)   the date when the claim started and concluded; and

ii) the dates and terms of any orders made.

Service on occupiers

Where a mortgagee seeks possession of land which includes residential property, not less that **7.13** 14 days before the hearing the claimant must send a notice to the property addressed to "the occupiers". The notice must:

a)   state that a possession claim for the property has started:

b)   show the name and address of the claimant, the defendant and the court which issued the claim form; and

c)   give details of the hearing.

Then, at the hearing, the claimant must produce a copy of the notice and provide evidence that it has been served.[41]

Defence

The requirements for the defence, which should be in Form N11M, are those which apply **7.14** generally.[42]

Application for time orders

An application by the defendant for a time order under s.129 of the Consumer Credit Act **7.15** 1974 may be made either in the defence or by application notice.[43]

Hearing

A mortgage possession claim will initially be heard in private.[44] The practice direction to Pt **7.16** 55 draws attention to the fact that, in mortgage possession claims, the Land Registration Act 1925, s.113, provides that office copies of the register and of documents filed in the Land Registry, including original charges, are admissible in evidence to the same extent as the originals.[45]

---

[41] CPR 55.10.
[42] See CPR 16.5 and CPR 16 PD para.11.1 onwards.
[43] CPR 55 PD para.7.1.
[44] CPR PD 2B.
[45] CPR 55 PD para.5.5.

7.17   Form 132

<u>Particulars of Claim for possession (mortgaged residential premises)</u>

Claim No. T02789

IN THE TOP COUNTY COURT

DODGY BARGAIN LOANS

Claimant

SIDNEY WRENCH

Defendants

1.   The Claimant has a right to possession of:
     The Ushy Knoll
     1 Haddock Parade
     Top
     TP25

About the mortgage:

2.   On **July 2, 1998** the Claimant and the Defendant entered into a mortgage of the above premises.

3.   To the best of the Claimant's knowledge the following persons are in possession of the property:

     Sidney Wrench, Mary Wrench and their two children, Jack and Dawn Wrench

[Delete (a) or (b) as appropriate]

4.   (a) ~~The agreement for the loan secured by the mortgage (or at least one of them) is a regulated consumer credit agreement. Notice of default was given to the Defendant(s) on   20 .~~

     (b) The agreement for the loan secured by the mortgage is not (or none of them is) a regulated consumer credit agreement.

5.   The Claimant is asking for possession on the following ground(s):

     (a) the Defendant has not paid the agreed repayments of the loan and interest.

     Give details

     Please see the attached schedule

     (b) because:

     N/A

6. (a) The amount loaned was £ **58,000**

   (b) The current terms of repayment are: (include any current periodic repayment and any current payment of interest)

   Current periodic repayments are £700 per calendar month as at February 13, 2002
   Interest is charged at 22.1%

   (c) The total amount required to pay the mortgage in full as at **February 13**, 2002 (not more than 14 days after the claim was issued) would be **£60,000** taking into account any adjustment for early settlement. This includes **£1200** payable for solicitor's costs and administration charges.

   (d) The following additional payments are also required under the terms of the mortgage:

£ 15 per month	for	**Insurance**	[not] included in 6(c)
£	for		[not] included in 6(c)
£	for		[not] included in 6(c)

   (e) Of the payments in paragraph 6(d), the following are in arrers:

Insurance	arrears of £	**200**
	arrears of £	
	arrears of £	

   [(f) The total amount outstanding under the regulated loan agreement secured by the mortgage is £
   ]

   (g) Interest rates which have been applied to the mortgage:

   (i) at the start of the mortgage **7%** p.a.
   (ii) immediately before any arrears were accrued **10%** p.a.
   (iii) at the start of the claim **21%** p.a.

7. The following steps have already been taken to recover the money secured by the mortgage:

   The Defendant has been written a number of letters and has had a home visit by Norman Big of the Claimants on April 23, 2001

About the Defendant(s)

8. The following information is known about the Defendant's circumstances: (*in particular say whether the Defendant(s) (is) (are) in receipt of social security benefits and whether any payments are made directly to the claimant*)

The Defendant is married with two children. He is working full time as a plug chain salesman

[Delete either (a) or (b) as appropriate]

9. (a) ~~There is no one who should be given notice of these proceedings because of a registered interest in the property under s.31(10) of the Family Law Act 1996 or s.2(8) or 8(3) of the Matrimonial Homes Act 1983 or s.2(7) of the Matrimonial Homes Act 1967.~~

    (b) Notice of these proceedings will be given to **Mary Wrench** who has a registered interest in the property.

Tenancy
[Delete if inappropriate]

10. ~~A tenancy was entered into between the mortgagor and the mortgagee on~~

    ~~A notice was served on~~

What the court is being asked to do

11. The Claimant asks the court to order that the Defendant:

    (a) give the Claimant possession of the premises;

    (b) pay to the Claimant the total amount outstanding under the mortgage.

STATEMENT OF TRUTH

*~~(I believe)~~(The claimant believes) that the facts stated in these particulars of claim are true.
*I am duly authorised by the claimant to sign this statement.

Signed   **Peter Strauss**   date   **February 13, 2002**

*~~(Claimant)~~(Litigation friend ~~(where claimant is a child or a patient)~~ (Claimant's solicitor)

delete as appropriate

Full name **Peter Cosmo Strauss**

Name of defendant's solicitor's firm **Strauss, Barney and Dickinson and Tiff**

position or office held **Partner**

(if signing on behalf of firm or company)

Form 133   **7.18**

Particulars of Claim for possession (mortgaged residential premises)

Claim No. TO2790

IN THE TOP COUNTY COURT

FAIRLOAN AND COMPANY	**Claimant**
(1) BILL STICKER AND (2)ARNOLD CEDRICKSON	**Defendant(s)**

1. The Claimant has a right to possession of:
    23a Artichoke Mansions
    Trout Head
    Top
    TP24

About the mortgage:

2. On **June 27, 1998** the Claimant and the Defendants entered into a mortgage of the above premises.

3. To the best of the Claimant's knowledge the following persons are in possession of the property:

    Bill Sticker and Arnold Cedrickson

[Delete (a) or (b) as appropriate]

4. (a) The agreement for the loan secured by the mortgage (or at least one of them) is a regulated consumer credit agreement. Notice of default was given to the Defendant(s) on **December 24, 2000**

    (b) ~~The agreement for the loan secured by the mortgage is a regulated consumer credit agreement.~~

5. The Claimant is asking for possession on the following ground(s):

    (a) the Defendants have not paid the agreed repayments of the loan and interest.

    Give details:

    See schedule attached

    (b) because:

    N/A

6. (a) The amount loaned was **£10,000**

   (b) The current terms of repayment are: *(include any current periodic repayment and any current payment of interest)*

   £225 per month payable on the 9th of the month. The current rate of interest is 35% a.p.r.

   (c) The total amount required to pay the mortgage in full as at **February 13, 2002** (not more than 14 days after the claim was issued) would be £ **17,000** taking into account any adjustment for early settlement. This includes **£1,200** payable for solicitor's costs and administration charges

   (d) The following additional payments are also required under the terms of the mortgage:

£ **15 per month**	for **Administration**	[not] included in 6(c)
£	for	[not] included in 6(c)
£	for	[not] included in 6(c)

   (e) Of the payments in paragraph 6(d), the following are in arrears:

   arrears of £ **250**
   arrears of £
   arrears of £

   [(f) The total amount outstanding under the regulated loan agreement secured by the mortgage is £ **17,000**]

   (g) Interest rates which have been applied to the mortgage:

   (i) at the start of the mortgage **35%** p.a.
   (ii) immediately before any arrears were accrued **35%** p.a.
   (iii) at the start of the claim **35%** p.a.

7. The following steps have already been taken to recover the money secured by the mortgage:

   Repeated visits to the defendants property and a number of letters written.

About the Defendant(s):

8. The following information is known about the Defendant's circumstances:

   (in particular say whether the Defendant(s) (is)(are) in receipt of social security benefits and whether any payments are made directly to the Claimant)

   The Defendants are partners who both work full time in advertising

   [*Delete either (a) or (b) as appropriate*]

9. (a) There is no one who should be given notice of these proceedings because of a registered interest in the property under s.31(10) of the Family Law Act 1996

or s.2(8) or 8(3) of the Matrimonial Homes Act 1983 or s.2(7) of the Matrimonial Homes Act 1967.

(b) ~~Notice of these proceedings will be given to~~ ~~who has a registered~~ ~~interest in the property.~~

Tenancy

[Delete if inappropriate]

~~10. A tenancy was entered into between the mortgagor and the mortgagee on~~ ~~A notice was served on~~

What the court is being asked to do

11. The claimant asks the court to order that the defendants:

(a) give the claimant possession of the premises;

(b) pay to the claimant the total amount outstanding under the mortgage.

STATEMENT OF TRUTH

~~(I believe)~~(The claimant believes) that the facts stated in these particulars of claim are true.

*I am duly authorised by the claimant to sign this statement.

signed **Peter Strauss**   date **February 13, 2002**

*~~(Claimant)(Litigation friend~~ *~~(where claimant is a child or a patient)~~* (Claimant's solicitor)

**delete as appropriate*

Full name **Peter Cosmo Strauss**

Name of defendant's solicitor's firm **Strauss, Barney, Dickinson and Tiff**

position or office held **Partner**

(if signing on behalf of firm or company)

7.19 Form 134

Defence Form (mortgaged residential premises)

In the   **Claim No**.

                                                          Claimant

                                                          Defendant(s)

                          Date of hearing

Personal details

1. Please give your:

    Forename(s)

    Surname

    Address (*if different from the address on the claim form*)

    post code

Disputing the claim

2. Do you agree with what is said about the   ☐Yes   ☐No
    property and the mortgage agreement in the
    particulars of claim?

    If No, set out your reasons below:

3. Do you agree that there are arrears of mortagage   ☐Yes   ☐No
    repayments as stated in the particulars of claim?

    If No, state how much the arrears are: £_____   ☐None

4. If the particulars of claim give any reasons for   ☐Yes   ☐No
    possession other than arrears of mortgage
    repayments, do you agree with what is said?

    If No, give details below:

(only answer these questions if you loan secured by the mortgage (or part of it) is a regulated consumer credit agreement)

5. Do you want the court to consider whether or not the terms of your original loan agreement are fair? ☐Yes ☐No

6. Do you intend to apply to the court for an order changing the terms of your loan agreement (a time order)? ☐Yes ☐No

Arrears

7. Have you paid any money to your landlord since the claim was issued? ☐Yes ☐No

   If Yes, state how much you have paid and when: £_____ date_____

8. Have you come to any agreement with your mortgage lender about repaying the arrears since the claim was issued? ☐Yes ☐No

   I have agreed to pay £_____each (week)(month)

9. If you have not reached an agreement with your mortgage lender, do you want the court to consider allowing you to pay the arrears by instalments? ☐Yes ☐No

10. How much can you afford to pay in addition to the current instalments? £_____per (week)(month)

About yourself

State benefits

11. Are you receiving Income Support? ☐Yes ☐No

12. Have you applied for Income Support? ☐Yes ☐No

    If Yes, when did you apply? _____

13. Does the Department of Social Security pay your mortgage interest? ☐Yes ☐No

Dependants (*people you look after financially*)

14. Have you any dependant children?   ☐Yes   ☐No

    If Yes, give the number in each age group below:

    ☐ under 11   ☐11–15   ☐16–17   ☐18 and over

Other dependants

15. Give details of any other dependants for whom
    you are financially responsible:

Other residents

16. Give details of any other people living at the
    premises for whom you are not financially
    responsible:

Money you receive		Weekly	Monthly
17. Usual take- home pay or income if self-employed *including overtime, commission, bonuses*	£_____	☐	☐
Job Seekers allowance	£_____	☐	☐
Pension	£_____	☐	☐
Child benefit	£_____	☐	☐
Other benefits and allowances	£_____	☐	☐
Others living in my home give me	£_____	☐	☐
I am paid maintenance for myself (or children) of	£_____	☐	☐
Other income	£_____	☐	☐
Total income	£_____	☐	☐

Bank accounts and savings

18. Do you have a current bank or building society account?   ☐Yes   ☐No

    If Yes, is it

        ☐in credit? If so, by how much?   £_____

        ☐overdrawn? If so, by how much? £_____

19. Do you have a savings or deposit account?   ☐Yes   ☐No

    If Yes, what is the balance?   £_____

Money you pay out

20. Do you have to pay any court orders or fines?

Court	Claim/Case number	Balance owing	Instalments paid

Total Instalments paid £   per month

21. Give details if you are in arrears with any of the court payments or fines:

22. Do you have any loan or credit debts?   ☐Yes   ☐No

Loan/credit from	Balance owing	Instalments paid

Total Instalments paid £   per month

23. Give details if you are in arrears with any loan/credit repayments:

Regular expenses
(*Do not include any payments made by other
members of the household out of their own income*)

24. What regular expenses do you have?
    (*List below*)

		Weekly	Monthly
Council tax	£_____	☐	☐
Gas	£_____	☐	☐
Electricity	£_____	☐	☐
Water charges	£_____	☐	☐
TV rental & licence	£_____	☐	☐
Telephone	£_____	☐	☐
Credit repayments	£_____	☐	☐
Mail order	£_____	☐	☐
Housekeeping, food, school meals	£_____	☐	☐
Travelling expenses	£_____	☐	☐
Clothing	£_____	☐	☐
Maintenance payments	£_____	☐	☐
Other	£_____	☐	☐
Total expenses	£_____	☐	☐

Priority debts

25. This section is for **arrears** only. **Do not** include regular expenses listed at Question 24.

		Weekly	Monthly
Council tax arrears	£_____	☐	☐
Water charges arrears	£_____	☐	☐
Gas account	£_____	☐	☐
Electricity account	£_____	☐	☐
Maintenance arrears	£_____	☐	☐
Others *(give details below)*			
	£_____	☐	☐
	£_____	☐	☐
	£_____	☐	☐

26. If an order for possession were to be made, would
    you have somewhere else to live?   ☐ Yes   ☐ No

If Yes, say when you would be able to move in: _____

27. Give details of any events or circumstances which have led to your being in arrears of with your mortgage *(for example divorce, separation, redundancy, bereavement, illness, bankruptcy)*. If you believe you would suffer exceptional hardship by being ordered to leave the property immediately, say why.

STATEMENT OF TRUTH

*(I believe)(The defendant(s) believe(s)) that the facts stated in this defence form are true.

*I am duly authorised by the defendant(s) to sign this statement.

signed... date ....

*(Defendant(s))(Litigation friend *(where defendant is a child or a patient)* (Defendant's solicitor)

**delete as appropriate*

Full name ....

Name of Defendant's solicitor's firm ....

position or office held ....

(if signing on behalf of firm or company)

7.20   **Form 135**

Defence and Counterclaim to Form 132 alleging overriding interest

---

Claim No. TO2789

IN THE TOP COUNTY COURT

B E T W E E N

DODGY BARGAIN LOANS

Claimant

and

SIDNEY WRENCH

First Defendant

MARY WRENCH

Second Defendant

A N D   B E T W E E N

MARY WRENCH

Part 20 Claimant

and

SIDNEY WRENCH

Part 20 First Defendant

and

DODGY BARGAIN LOANS

Part 20 Second Defendant

**DEFENCE AND COUNTERCLAIM
OF THE SECOND DEFENDANT**

---

1. It is denied that the Claimant has a right to possession of the premises at The Ushy Knoll, 1 Haddock Parade, Top, TP25 ("the premises").

2. Paragraphs 2 and 3 of the Particulars of Claim are admitted save that it is denied that the First Defendant is still in occupation of the premises.

3. Paragraph 4 is admitted.

4. Paragraph 5 is not admitted and the Claimant is put to proof that all of the

payments made by the First and Second Defendants are shown on the attached schedule.

5. Paragraph 6 is admitted.

6. Paragraph 7 is denied. The Defendants have received no letters at all from the Claimant. The Second Defendant did receive a telephone call from Mr Big on April 23, 2001 when he threatened to call unless the debt was paid. Save for this the Second Defendant has had no communication with the Claimant, its servants or agents.

7. Paragraph 8 is admitted save that the First Defendant is now employed in cheese packaging and has left the premises.

8. In or about June 30, 1997, for the sum of £65,000, the First Defendant in his sole name purchased the premises. The First and Second Defendant occupied the premises as their matrimonial home until January 2001.

9. The premises were held on trust for the First and Second Defendants either jointly or alternatively in equal shares. The said trust arose by reason of the following matters.

   i)   Periodically throughout the Defendants' marriage, at times which cannot now be more particularly identified, the First Defendant told the Second Defendant that "everything we have is 50/50" or words to that effect; and/or it was evidenced thereby that there was a common intention between the Defendants to similar effect.

   ii) In the purchase of the premises there were applied the proceeds of sale from the Defendants' previous matrimonial home at Choppers Nook, Shingles, Hodpus, which had similarly been held on trust.

10. The Second Defendant has remained in occupation of the premises at all times since June 30, 1997.

11. Prior to advancing any money to or at the request of the First Defendant, and/or prior to obtaining any charge on the premises, the Claimant knew of the Second Defendant's occupation of the premises by reason of a report on title to it dated June 25, 1998 by Chimp Solicitors, and took no steps to make inquiry of her or to procure any priority over her interests.

12. By reason of these matters, the Second Defendant's interest in the premises is an overriding interest binding upon the Claimant.

13. Accordingly the Claimant is not entitled to possession of the premises from the Second Defendant, and it is denied that the Claimant is entitled to the relief claimed in paragraph 11 of the Particulars of Claim or any relief.

COUNTERCLAIM

14. Paragraphs 8–13 of the Defence are repeated.

AND the Second Defendant counterclaims:

A declaration that she is entitled to a beneficial interest in the premises to the extent of one half of the whole beneficial estate and free from the Claimant's charge over the premises and that, by reason of occupation of the premises from June 30, 1997, such interest is an overriding interest.

Arnold De La Vere Spiggot

Date

STATEMENT OF TRUTH

- (I believe) (The Second Defendant believes) that the facts stated in this Defence and Counterclaim are true.

- I am duly authorised by the Second Defendant to sign this statement.

Full name ....

Name of Second Defendant's solicitor's firm ....

Signed.............................Position or office held ....

- (Second Defendant)   (if signing on behalf of firm or company) (Second Defendant's solicitor)

- delete as appropriate

Form 136 7.21

Defence and Counterclaim to Form 132 alleging undue influence and overriding interest

Claim No. TO2789

IN THE TOP COUNTY COURT

B E T W E E N

DODGY BARGAIN LOANS

Claimant

and

SIDNEY WRENCH

First Defendant

MARY WRENCH

Second Defendant

A N D B E T W E E N

MARY WRENCH

Part 20 Claimant

and

SIDNEY WRENCH

Part 20 First Defendant

and

DODGY BARGAIN LOANS

Part 20 Second Defendant

**DEFENCE AND COUNTERCLAIM
OF THE SECOND DEFENDANT**

---

1. It is denied that the Claimant has a right to possession of the premises at The Ushy Knoll, 1 Haddock Parade, Top, TP25 ("the premises").

2. Paragraphs 2 and 3 of the Particulars of Claim are admitted save that it is denied that the First Defendant is still in occupation of the premises.

3. Paragraph 4 is admitted.

4. Paragraph 5 is not admitted and the Claimant is put to proof that all of the payments made by the First and Second Defendants are shown on the attached schedule.

5. Paragraph 6 is admitted.

6. Paragraph 7 is not admitted.

7. Paragraph 8 is admitted save that the First Defendant is now employed in cheese packaging and has left the premises.

8. In or about June 30, 1997, for the sum of £65,000, the First and Second Defendants in their joint names purchased the premises. The First and Second Defendant occupied the premises as their matrimonial home until January 2001. Legal title to the property is registered in the joint names of the First and Second Defendants.

9. The legal charge on the premises was granted to the Claimant by the First and Second Defendants, to the Claimant's knowledge, solely as security for the First Defendant's business loan of £58,000. The First Defendant told the Second Defendant that he planned to "go it alone" in the plug chain business.

10. The Second Defendant was induced into granting the charge whilst acting under the undue influence of the First Defendant and owing to the trust and confidence she reposed in him.

PARTICULARS

a) The financial arrangements between the parties were carried out at the instigation of and under the direction of the First Defendant to whom the Second Defendant generally deferred in such matters and any documents to be signed by her were signed under the direction of the First Defendant.

b) The First Defendant told the Second Defendant to sign the documents granting the charge to the Claimants without giving her a reasonable opportunity to read them.

c) In requiring the Second Defendant to sign the documents granting the charge the First Defendant exercised undue influence over the Second Defendant arising from (a) the love and affection which the Second Defendant had for the First Defendant, (b) the Second Defendant's general deference to the First Defendant in matters of this sort, (c) a general bullying and threatening manner, which the First Defendant had exercised over the Second Defendant, (d) fear and apprehension which the Second Defendant had if she did not accede to the First Defendant's wishes and demands. The First Defendant required the Second Defendant to sign the form and she consequently did so.

11. Further or alternatively the Second Defendant was induced into granting the charge by reason of and in reliance upon material misrepresentations made to her by the First Defendant.

PARTICULARS

Prior to requiring the Second Defendant to sign the charge documentation the First Defendant told her that the transaction would have no effect on her or her interest in the property at all and her signature was purely a formality.

12. By reason of the matters aforesaid the Claimant knew or ought to have known that the transaction was to the manifest disadvantage of the Second Defendant. Accordingly the Claimant was put on enquiry and on constructive notice of the possibility of undue influence and of its exercise by the First Defendant on the Second Defendant.

13. The Claimant made no inquiries of the Second Defendant and took no steps to ensure that the Second Defendant understood the proposed transaction or that the Second Defendant's consent to the charge was true and informed.

14. Further the Claimant made no effort to meet the Second Defendant, whether separately from the First Defendant or at all, or to advise the Second Defendant as to the nature of the proposed charge, or to recommend the Second Defendant to take independent legal advice.

15. Accordingly the Claimant is bound by the Second Defendant's interest in the premises which by virtue of the Second Defendant's continued occupation of the premises at all times since June 30, 1997 is an overriding interest.

16. In the premises the Claimant is not entitled to the relief claimed in the Particulars of Claim or any relief.

COUNTERCLAIM

17. Paragraphs 8–16 of the Defence are repeated.

AND the Second Defendant counterclaims:

A declaration that the Claimant's charge against the Second Defendant's interest in the premises be set aside.

Arnold De La Vere Spiggot

Date

STATEMENT OF TRUTH

- (I believe) (The Second Defendant believes) that the facts stated in this Defence and Counterclaim are true.

- I am duly authorised by the Second Defendant to sign this statement.

Full name ....

Name of Second Defendant's solicitor's firm ....

Signed.............................. Position or office held..

- (Second Defendant)   (if signing on behalf of firm or company)
  (Second Defendant's solicitor)

- delete as appropriate

7.22   <u>Form 137</u>

<u>Defence to Form 133 alleging money not due and extortionate credit bargain</u>

Claim No. TO 2790

IN THE TOP COUNTY COURT

B E T W E E N

FAIRLOAN AND COMPANY

Claimant

and

(1) BILL STICKER

(2) ARNOLD CEDRICKSON

Defendants

DEFENCE OF THE SECOND DEFENDANT

---

1. It is denied that the Claimant has the right to possession of the premises at 23a Artichoke Mansions ("the premises") for the reasons in this Defence.

2. Paragraph 2 of the Particulars of Claim is admitted.

3. Paragraph 3 is denied. The First Defendant has not been in occupation of the premises since 1999. The Claimant is aware of this fact through letters from the Second Defendant.

4. Paragraph 4(a) of the Particulars of Claim is not admitted and the Claimant is put to strict proof that notice of default was given on the said date.

5. Paragraph 4(b) is admitted and averred.

6. Paragraph 5 is denied. The Second Defendant will maintain that the payment schedule attached to the Particulars of Claim is inaccurate and does not properly reflect the payments made by the Second Defendant, which the Second Defendant is not presently able to particularise further. These payments will be proved at trial.

7. Paragraph 6(a) and (b) are admitted. Paragraph 6(c) is not admitted (see paragraph 6 above).

8. Paragraph 6(d) is denied. The Claimant has never previously mentioned or demanded an administration charge.

9. Paragraph 6(f) is not admitted (see para.6 above).

10. Paragraph 6(g) is admitted.

11. Paragraph 7 is denied. The Claimant has failed to make any visits and has only written one letter, which was said to contain the notice of default, but did not. The Claimant has also made threatening telephone calls.

12. Paragraph 8 is denied. The Claimant is aware that the Defendants' relationship ended in 1999. The Claimant is also aware that the Second Defendant lost his job following the terrorist attacks on America on September 11, 2001.

13. Further or alternatively, if which is not admitted, the alleged sums are due to the Claimant, it is averred that the loan agreement between the parties represents an extortionate credit bargain within the meaning of the Consumer Credit Act 1974.[37] The interest rate of 35% means that the Second Defendant is liable for grossly extortionate repayments.

Slim Jeppard

Date

STATEMENT OF TRUTH

- (I believe) (The Second Defendant believes) that the facts stated in this Defence are true.

- I am duly authorised by the Second Defendant to sign this statement.

Full name ....

Name of Second Defendant's solicitor's firm ....

Signed................................. Position or office held ....

- (Second Defendant)   (if signing on behalf of firm or company) (Second Defendant's solicitor)

- delete as appropriate

---

[37] ss.137–140 of the CCA 1974.

7.23   Form 138

Reply and Defence to Counterclaim to Form 135

Claim No. TO2789

IN THE TOP COUNTY COURT

B E T W E E N

DODGY BARGAIN LOANS

Claimant

and

SIDNEY WRENCH

First Defendant

MARY WRENCH

Second Defendant

A N D   B E T W E E N

MARY WRENCH

Part 20 Claimant

and

SIDNEY WRENCH

Part 20 First Defendant

and

DODGY BARGAIN LOANS

Part 20 Second Defendant

REPLY AND DEFENCE TO COUNTERCLAIM

---

1. Except where the Defence consists of admissions, and except as is admitted below, the Claimant joins issue with the Second Defendant on her Defence.

2. As to paragraph 6 of the Defence and Counterclaim, the Claimant will produce copy letters at trial.

3. As to paragraphs 9–10, it is not admitted that the matters therein gave rise to a trust as alleged. The Second Defendant is put to proof of the actual words that were used by the First Defendant; of the times and dates when the said representations

were made; and that the property at Choppers Nook had been held on trust and the circumstances giving rise to such a trust.

4. As to paragraphs 11–12, the Second Defendant is put to proof that she has been in occupation at all times since June 30, 1997 and in particular she is put to proof that she was in actual occupation at the time of the Claimant's charge on the premises.[38] Further it is denied that the Claimant knew of the Second Defendant's occupation in the manner alleged or at all. The premises were registered in the First Defendant's sole name. The Claimant only became aware of the Second Defendant's existence following Mr Big's telephone call on April 23, 2001.

5. In the premises it is not admitted that the Second Defendant has an interest in the premises or that any interest is an overriding interest binding upon the Claimants.

Charles Coroley

Date

STATEMENT OF TRUTH

- (I believe) (The Claimant believes) that the facts stated in these Reply and Defence to Counterclaim are true.

- I am duly authorised by the Claimant to sign this statement.

Full name ....

Name of Claimant's solicitor's firm ....

Signed...................................... Position or office held...

- (Claimant)   (if signing on behalf of firm or company)
  (Claimant's solicitor)
- delete as appropriate

STATEMENT OF TRUTH

The Claimants believe that the contents of the Reply and Defence to Counterclaim are true.

---

[38] The relevant date for determining if the interest is protected by actual occupation under s.70(1)(g) Land Registration Act 1925 is the date when the mortgage is created and not when it is registered (*Abbey National Building Society v Cann* [1991] AC 56).

7.24   <u>Form 139</u>

<u>Reply and Defence to Counterclaim to Form 136 seeking order for sale.</u>

Claim No. TO2789

<u>IN THE TOP COUNTY COURT</u>

B E T W E E N

DODGY BARGAIN LOANS

Claimant

and

SIDNEY WRENCH

First Defendant

MARY WRENCH

Second Defendant

A N D   B E T W E E N

MARY WRENCH

Part 20 Claimant

and

SIDNEY WRENCH

Part 20 First Defendant

and

DODGY BARGAIN LOANS

Part 20 Second Defendant

REPLY AND DEFENCE TO COUNTERCLAIM

---

1.   Save insofar as it consists of admissions of allegations made in the Particulars of Claim, the Claimant joins issue with the Second Defendant on her Defence and Counterclaim.

2.   Paragraphs 10–12 are not admitted. The Second Defendant is put to proof of the facts and allegations contained in these paragraphs.

3.   Paragraphs 13 and 14 are specifically denied. The Claimant took sufficient steps to ensure that the Second Defendant was aware of the implications of the charge and the need for her to take independent advice.

PARTICULARS

4. a. Prior to the signing of the charge documentation the Claimant saw the Second Defendant on her own and advised her as to the implications of the charge. The Claimant also asked the Second Defendant for the name of the solicitor that she wanted to act for her in the transaction.

   b. The Second Defendant told the Claimant that the solicitors firm she wanted to use was B. Bunter and Co.

   c. Following notification of this the Claimant wrote to Messrs B. Bunter and Co and provided them with all relevant financial information concerning the proposed charge in order to allow them to explain this to the Second Defendant.

   d. Subsequently the Claimant received written confirmation from Messrs B. Bunter and Co that they had met the Second Defendant in the absence of her husband (the First Defendant) and had advised her fully as to the implications of the charge and the nature and effect of their written confirmation to the Claimant.

5. Accordingly it is denied that the Claimant is bound by the Second Defendant's interest in the premises and not admitted that such interest is an overriding interest as alleged in paragraph 15 of the Defence and Counterclaim.

6. In the premises it is denied that the Second Defendant is entitled to the relief claimed in her Counterclaim or any relief.

7. Further or alternatively if which is denied the Claimant is bound by the Second Defendant's interest in the premises the Claimant will maintain that in any event it has a valid charge over the First Defendant's interest in the premises and is thereby entitled to an order for sale of the premises pursuant to s.14(1) of Trusts of the Land and Appointment of Trustees Act 1996; and so far as necessary the Claimant will seek an order for sale of the premises pursuant to s.14(1) of the Trusts of Land and Appointment of Trustees Act 1996 and an order that the proceeds of sale be distributed according to interests.

Billie Morgan

Date

STATEMENT OF TRUTH

- (I believe) (The Claimant believes) that the facts stated in this Reply and Defence to Counterclaim are true.

- I am duly authorised by the Claimant to sign this statement.

Full name ....

Name of Second Claimant's solicitor's firm ....

Signed.................................... Position or office held ....

- (Claimant)   (if signing on behalf of firm or company)
  (Claimant's solicitor)
- delete as appropriate

PART III: CHECKLIST

1. The claimant should expect to show reasonable efforts in seeking to recover or resolve the mortgage arrears by correspondence, before commencing proceedings, in the spirit of the CPR.

2. Check the terms of the mortgage or charge carefully.

3. Check whether the special statutory provisions for regulated consumer credit agreements apply, or whether the general provisions for mortgaged residential premises apply.

4. Check that the Land Registry and land charges searches have been carried out.

5. Make sure the particulars of claim contain all the prescribed information under CPR 55.4 and PD para.2.5.

6. Make sure that the notice under CPR 55.10 has been served at the premises, and that a copy of the notice and evidence of service are available at the hearing.

7. At the hearing, the claimant should be ready to produce office copies of title, and any up to date evidence as to the arrears.

Chapter 8
Rights of Acquisition and Succession

PART I: INTRODUCTION

This chapter is concerned with the statutory rights of a tenant to acquire a freehold or long **8.01**
leasehold interest in the demised premises, and with the right of a person to succeed to a
tenancy on the death of the tenant.

Right to buy/right to acquire

Under the Housing Act 1985, Pt V (right to buy), certain secure tenants have the right to **8.02**
acquire from the landlord the freehold or long leasehold interest in the demised premises. An
analogous right (right to acquire) arises in favour of tenants of registered social landlords,
under the Housing Act 1996, s.16.

These rights are enforced by a claim for an injunction (see Housing Act 1985, ss.138(3) and
150(3)). Where these claims involve substantial disputes of fact, the claim should be brought
under CPR Pt 7; otherwise they may be brought under CPR Pt 8. The county court has
jurisdiction to entertain any proceedings under the 1985 Act, Pt V, and to determine any
question arising (see s.181(1)). Costs are not recoverable for proceedings brought in the High
Court which could have been brought in the county court (s.181(3)).

Compulsory acquisition and enfranchisement

Under this heading, two different categories of tenants' rights can be discerned. First, there is **8.03**
the individual right of long leaseholders to acquire the freehold or an extended lease of the
premises, applicable initially only to "houses", under the Leasehold Reform Act 1967. This
right was extended to flats by the Leasehold Reform, Housing and Urban Development Act
1993, Chap.II, under which the leaseholder can acquire a new lease. The exercise of this right
is triggered by the service of notice by the tenant. In the event of any default in carrying out
the obligations of either party arising from the notice, the other party has the same rights and
remedies as if a contract had been entered into (1967 Act, s.5(3); 1993 Act, s.43(4)).

Second, there is the collective right of long leaseholders in a predominantly residential
building to acquire the freehold, under the 1993 Act, Chap.I. The right is triggered by the
service of notice.

These rights are enforceable by application to the court for an order (s.24 and s.92). The
county court has general jurisdiction (1967 Act, s.20; 1993 Act, s.90). Leasehold valuation
tribunals, however, have exclusive jurisdiction in respect of a number of detailed matters
(1967 Act, s.21; 1993 Act, s.91).

Claims under these provisions are not landlord and tenant claims for the purposes of CPR Pt 56, s.I; but some specific provisions are made under CPR 56.4, by paras 13 and 14 of the practice direction, in relation to claims under the 1967 and 1993 Acts. Where these claims involve substantial disputes of fact, the claim should be brought under CPR Pt 7; otherwise they may be brought under CPR Pt 8.

Right of first refusal

8.04   Under the Landlord and Tenant Act 1987, there are two different rights relating to acquisition. First, under Pt I, there is the right of first refusal for certain tenants of flats, if the landlord wishes to dispose of the reversion. Second, under Pt III, there is the right of certain tenants of flats to apply for compulsory acquisition of the reversion, as a last resort in cases of bad management of the building.

Enforcement of the right of first refusal is achieved in two ways: first by a right of application to the court for an order to make good any default (s.19), and second by the creation of a criminal offence by a landlord in failing to comply with the provisions (s.10A).

Compulsory acquisition under Pt III of the Act is enforced by application to the court for an acquisition order (s.28).

The County Court has general jurisdiction in respect of such claims, subject to certain detailed matters which fall within the jurisdiction of a leasehold valuation tribunal (s.52(1), (2)). Claims brought in the High Court, which could have been brought in the county court, are in general subject to county court costs (s.52(4)).

These claims are landlord and tenant claims for the purposes of CPR Pt 56 (see CPR 56.1), and should generally be brought in the county court for the district in which the land is situated (CPR 56.2(1)). Claims may be brought in the High Court, but a certificate is required with the claim form explaining the reasons for doing so (CPR 56.2(2)). Use of the High Court can be justified if there are complicated disputes of fact or there are points of law of general importance (CPR Pt 56 PD para.2.4). The procedure is a modified version of the Part 8 claim procedure (*ibid.*, para.2.1).

In a claim to enforce the right of first refusal, a copy of the tenants' notice under s.19(2)(a) must accompany the claim form (*ibid.*, para.7.1).

There are specific requirements for the contents of the claim form where an acquisition order is being sought (*ibid.*, para.8.2). A copy of the notice served on the landlord under s.27 must accompany the claim form unless the court has dispensed with the requirement for the notice (*ibid.*, para.8.3). The landlord must be made a defendant, as must the person nominated by the tenants to acquire the landlord's interest, if that person is not a claimant (*ibid.*, para 8.4). A copy of the claim must be served on every person named in the claim form as being a person known to the claimants who is likely to be affected by the application, together with a notice that s/he may apply to be made a party (*ibid.*, para.8.5).

Succession

8.05   All the main schemes for providing statutory of tenure contain provisions entitling certain persons to succeed to the tenancy on the death of the tenant (see Rent Act 1977, s.2(1)(b); Housing Act 1985, s.89; Housing Act 1988, s.17).

The county court has general jurisdiction in respect of claims to determine or enforce the succession provisions (1977 Act, s.141; 1985 Act, s.110; 1988 Act s.40). Where they involve disputes of fact, such claims should be brought by a Pt 7 claim; otherwise the Pt 8 procedure may be used.

8.06 **Form 140**

Particulars of Claim to enforce right to buy[1]

Claim No. MC9999

IN THE METROPOLITAN COUNTY COURT

B E T W E E N

SIDNEY TENNANT   **Claimant**

and

THE MAYOR AND BURGESSES OF THE
LONDON BOROUGH OF DOWNTOWN   **Defendants**

1. The Claimant is the secure tenant of residential premises at 33 North Street, London NE1, (hereafter referred to as "the premises") of which the Defendants are the landlords and freehold owners.

2. The Claimant claimed to exercise the right to buy the premises pursuant to the provisions of Pt V of the Housing Act 1985, and by letter dated December 1, 2001 the Defendants admitted that right.

3. On or before February 14, 2002 all matters relating to the grant of the estate in fee simple absolute in the premises had been agreed between the Claimant and the Defendants.

4. The Claimant is ready, able and willing to complete the purchase of the premises, and has called upon the Defendants to complete but they have failed or refused to do so.

AND the Claimant claims:

  (1) An order that the Defendants do make a grant to the Claimant of the estate in fee simple absolute of the premises at 33 North Street, London, NE1, with liberty to apply as to the implementation of that order.

  (2) Costs.

CAROLINE COUNSEL

STATEMENT OF TRUTH

  *(I believe)(The claimant believes) that the facts stated in these particulars of claim are true.

*I am duly authorised by the claimant to sign this statement.

signed   date

*(Claimant)(Litigation friend) *(where claimant is a child or a patient)* (Claimant's solicitor)

**delete as appropriate*

Full name ....

Name of defendant's solicitor's firm ....

position or office held ....

(if signing on behalf of firm or company)

Claimant's or claimant's solicitors address to which documents or payments should be sent if different from overleaf including (if appropriate) details of DX, fax or e-mail.

---

[1] This Claim has been formulated under CPR Pt 7 rather than Pt 8, on the basis that substantial disputes of facts arise: See Defence Form 146 below.

8.07   Form 141

Particulars of Claim to enforce individual right of enfranchisement

---

Claim No. MC5555

IN THE METROPOLITAN COUNTY COURT

B E T W E E N

IVOR LONGLEASE   **Claimant**

and

MEGA PROPERTIES LTD   **Defendant**

PARTICULARS OF CLAIM

---

1. The Claimant is the tenant of residential premises comprising a house at 2 Jill Street, London WC1, registered under title number NGL999994 ("the house"), of which the Defendant is the landlord and freehold owner.

2. The Claimant's tenancy ("the tenancy") is a long tenancy within the meaning of Pt I of the Leasehold Reform Act 1967 ("the Act"), being granted by a lease made between the Defendant and the Claimant dated September 3, 1975 and for a term of 99 years from June 24, 1975. A true copy of the tenancy is attached at schedule 1.

3. At all material times, the tenancy is and has been a tenancy at a low rent within the meaning of the Act, and within the rateable value limit.

PARTICULARS

(1) Appropriate day: March 23, 1965.

(2) First day of term: June 24, 1975.

(3) Rateable value on appropriate day: £350.

(4) Rateable value on first day of term: £500.

(5) Yearly rent: £50.

4. By a notice dated July 27, 2002,[1] in the prescribed form, the Claimant gave notice to the Defendant of his desire to have the freehold estate of the house, pursuant to the Act. A true copy of the notice is attached at schedule 2.

5. The Claimant has occupied the house as his residence since the grant of the tenancy on September 3, 1975.

6. By notice dated September 1, 2002, the Defendant stated that it did not admit the Claimant's right to have the freehold on the grounds that the Claimant had not occupied the house as his residence for the requisite period of two years. A true copy of the notice is attached at schedule 3.

AND the Claimant claims:

1) A declaration that the Claimant is entitled to acquire the freehold of the house under the Leasehold Reform Act 1967.

2) Costs.

BARRY BARRISTER

[CONCLUDE AS IN FORM 140]

---

[1] *i.e.* after the amendments offered by the Commonhold and Household Reform Act 2002.

8.08   <u>Form 142</u>

<u>Particulars of Claim to enforce collective right of enfranchisement</u>

Claim No. MC6666

IN THE METROPOLITAN COUNTY COURT

B E T W E E N

NORMAN NOMINEE   <u>Claimant</u>

and

MEGA PROPERTIES LTD   <u>Defendant</u>

PARTICULARS OF CLAIM

---

1. The Claimant is the person appointed as the nominee purchaser for the purposes of the Leasehold Reform, Housing and Urban Development Act 1993, Pt I, Chap.I ("the Act").

2. The Claimant is appointed by, and acts on behalf of, the participating tenants named in schedule 1 attached.

3. The claim relates to residential premises, being land and a self-contained, detached block of flats known as Sunny Point, Hill Road, Downtown, registered under title number NGL999995 ("the block").

4. The participating tenants hold the leases ("the leases") of flats in the block as identified in schedule 1 attached.

5. The Defendant is the freehold owner of the block and the reversioner under the leases.

6. The total number of flats contained in the block is 30, and the total number of flats held by qualifying tenants is not less than two-thirds of that number, being 25 in total, as shown in the list of flats, tenants and leases in schedule 2 attached.

7. By an initial notice ("the initial notice") in writing dated January 2, 2002 ("the relevant date") under s.13 of the Act, 23 of the 25 qualifying tenants gave notice of claim by hand to the Defendant to exercise the right to collective enfranchisement. A true copy of the notice is attached at schedule 3.

8. 20 of the qualifying tenants giving the initial notice satisfied the residence condition, as identified in schedule 2 attached.

9.   By a counter-notice in writing dated March 1, 2002 under s.21 of the Act, the Defendant did not admit that the participating tenants were entitled to exercise the right to collective enfranchisement in relation to the block, on the grounds that less than one half of the qualifying tenants giving the initial notice satisfied the residence condition; and stated that an application for an order under s.23(1) of the Act was to be made by the Defendant on the grounds that the Defendant intended to redevelop a substantial part of the block. A true copy of the counter-notice is attached at schedule 4.

10. No application has been made to the court by the Defendant under s.23 of the Act, and the period for making such an application has expired.

AND the Claimant claims:

1)   A declaration that the participating tenants were, on the relevant date, entitled to exercise the right to collective enfranchisement in relation to the block.

2)   A declaration that the Defendant's counter-notice shall be of no effect.

3)   An order requiring the Defendant to give a further counter-notice to the Claimant by such date as is specified in the order.

4)   Further as other relief.

5)   Costs.

BARBARA BARRISTER

[CONCLUDE AS IN FORM 140]

8.09   Form 143

Details of Claim to enforce right of first refusal[1]

Claim No. MC7777

IN THE METROPOLITAN COUNTY COURT

B E T W E E N

LAURA le SEE   **Claimant**

and

MEGA PROPERTIES LTD   **Defendant**

DETAILS OF CLAIM

---

1. CPR Pt 8 applies to the claim.[2]

2. The claim is made under s.19 of the Landlord and Tenant Act 1987 ("the Act").

3. The claim relates to residential premises, being land and a self-contained, detached block of flats known as Sunny Point, Hill Road, Downtown, registered under title number NGL999995 ("the block").

4. The Claimant acts, in relation to the block for the purposes of the Act, as representative on her own behalf and on behalf of the other qualifying tenants, as identified in schedule 1 attached.

5. The Defendant is the freehold owner of the block and the reversioner under the leases of the qualifying tenants.

6. The total number of flats contained in the block is 30, and the total number of flats held by qualifying tenants exceeds 50 per cent of that number, being 25 in total, as shown in the list of flats, tenants and leases in schedule 2 attached; and the Act accordingly applies to the block because none of the exceptions applies.

7. On or about April 3, 2002, the Defendant caused, directly or indirectly, the freehold interest in the block to be advertised for sale by contract in property particulars issued by Ace Properties, property agents. A true copy of the particulars is attached at schedule 3.

8. The Defendant failed to serve on the qualifying tenants an offer notice complying with s.5 of the Act.

9. By a notice in writing dated April 10, 2002 under s.19(2) of the Act, served by hand on the Defendant on the same date, the qualifying tenants required the Defendant to make good the default, and more than 14 days have elapsed since service without the Defendant having done so. A true copy of the notice is attached at schedule 4.[3]

10. Accordingly, the Defendant threatens to make a relevant disposal affecting the block in breach of s.1(1) of the Act.

AND the Claimant claims:

1) An injunction under s.19 of the Act requiring the Defendant to serve on the qualifying tenants a notice complying with s.5 of the Act.

2) An injunction under s.19 of the Act restraining the Defendant until further order from taking any steps in relation to the proposed disposal of the freehold interest in the block to any person or persons otherwise than as nominated by the qualifying tenants, in breach of s.1(1) of the Act.

3) Further or other relief.

4) Costs.

BRIAN BARRISTER

[CONCLUDE AS IN FORM 140]

---

[1] For use with Form N208.
[2] CPR 56 PD para.2.1 requires use of the Pt 8 procedure, as modified. Any further witness evidence must be served with the Claim Form.
[3] CPR 56 PC para.7.1 requires that a copy of the notice must accompany the Claim Form.

8.10   Form 144

Defence and Counterclaim claiming right of succession

Claim No. MC7777

IN THE METROPOLITAN COUNTY COURT

B E T W E E N

LONDON BOROUGH OF DOWNTOWN
Claimants/Part 20 Defendant

and

TERRY TENNANT
Defendant/Part 20 Claimant

DEFENCE AND COUNTERCLAIM

DEFENCE

1. It is admitted and averred that:

    a) the Claimants are the freehold owners of the premises,

    b) the Claimants let the premises to Sidney Tennant on about April 20, 1993 on a weekly secure tenancy,

    c) Sidney Tennant died on March 13, 2002, and

    d) on April 1, 2002 the Claimants served a notice to quit expiring on May 1, 2002 on the premises and on the Public Trustee.

2. It is denied that the notice to quit is of any effect, or that the Claimants are entitled to possession of the premises, by reason of the matters below.

3. The Defendant is a person qualified to succeed Sidney Tennant under the tenancy because:

    a) the Defendant occupied the premises as his only or principal home at the time of Sidney Tennant's death; and

    b) he is the child of Sidney Tennant; and

    c) he resided with Sidney Tennant throughout the period of 12 months ending with the latter's death.

4. Accordingly, the secure tenancy vested in the Defendant by virtue of s.89 of the Housing Act 1985 ("the Act").

5. The Claimants cannot bring the secure tenancy to an end except by obtaining an order of the court in accordance with ss.82–84 of the Act.

COUNTERCLAIM

6. Paragraphs 1 to 5 above inclusive are repeated.

AND the Claimant counterclaims:

1) A declaration that since March 13, 2002 he has been the secure tenant by succession of the premises.

2) Costs.

BARBARA BARRISTER

[CONCLUDE AS IN FORM 135]

8.11   **Form 145**

Details of Claim to enforce compulsory acquisition[1]

Claim No. MC7777

IN THE METROPOLITAN COUNTY COURT

B E T W E E N

(1) LORRAINE LAW
(2) MARTIN MORE
(3) NORRIS NORR
(4) OWEN ORR
(5) PETER POOR
(6) QUENTIN QUORRE
(7) ROGER RAW   **Claimants**

and

MEGA PROPERTIES LTD   **Defendant**

DETAILS OF CLAIM

---

1.   CPR Pt 8 applies to the claim.[2]

2.   The claim is made under s.28 of the Landlord and Tenant Act 1987 ("the Act").

3.   The claim relates to residential premises, being land and a self-contained, detached block of flats known as Lower Point, Hill Road, Downtown, and which is registered under title number NGL999999 ("the block").

4.   The Claimants are qualifying tenants in relation to the block for the purposes of Pt III of the Act, and hold the leases of flats in the block as identified in schedule 1 attached.

5.   The Defendant, whose registered office is at Sunny Point, Hill Road, Downtown, is the freehold owner of the block and the reversioner under the leases of the qualifying tenants.

6.   The total number of flats contained in the block is 10, and the total number of flats held by qualifying tenants is not less than two thirds of that number, being seven in total, as shown in the list of flats, tenants and leases in schedule 2 attached. Section 25 of the Act applies to the block because none of the exceptions in s.25(4) and (5) applies; and the Claimants constitute the requisite majority of qualifying tenants under Pt III of the Act.

7. On October 10, 2001, the Claimants served notice on the Defendant under s.27 of the Act. A true copy of the notice is attached at schedule 3.

8. The person nominated by the Claimants for the purposes of Pt III of the Act is the First Claimant, Lorraine Law.

9. The persons known by the Claimants who are likely to be affected by the application are:

   a) the three tenants of the flats named in schedule 2 other than the Claimants, whose addresses are shown in the schedule;

   b) Loan Arrangers Ltd, mortgagees of the freehold interest, whose address is 20 Bank Street, Downtown.

10. The grounds of the claim are:

   a) The Defendant is in breach of clause 4(5) of the Claimants' leases, namely the obligation "to keep in good repair and condition the structure and exterior of the block", by reason of the very numerous defects detailed in the report of Merryweathers, chartered surveyors, dated September 1, 2001, a true copy of which is attached at schedule 4.

   b) The above-mentioned defects have existed and been known by the Defendant since at least January 2000, as recorded in a letter dated January 15, 2000 from the First Claimant to the Defendant, a true copy of which is attached at schedule 5.

   c) The above-mentioned defects were the subject of an order for specific performance made by this court on February 2, 2001 and requiring remedial works to be completed by August 2, 2001. A true copy of the order is attached at schedule 6.

   d) The notice dated October 10, 2001 served under s.27 of the Act, above, required the Defendant to complete remedial works by March 10, 2002.

   e) The Defendant has carried out no remedial works.

   f) In the circumstances, the Defendant's breach of clause 4(5) of the Claimants' leases is likely to continue.

AND the Claimants claim:

   1) An acquisition order under s.30 of the Act in respect of the block.

   2) Further or other relief.

   3) Costs.

BRIAN BARRISTER

[CONCLUDE AS IN FORM 140]

---

[1] For use with Form N208. See CPR 56 PD para.8 for particular requirements of pleading and service.
[2] CPR 56 PD para.2.1 requires use of the Pt 8 procedure as modified. Any additional witness evidence must be served with the Claim Form.

8.12   **Form 146**

Defence to Particulars of Claim to enforce right to buy

[HEADING AS IN FORM 140]

DEFENCE

1. The Claimant is not and never was the secure tenant of the premises by reason of para.2 of Sch.1 to the Housing Act 1985 (premises occupied in connection with employment).

2. Further or alternatively, the right to buy did not arise by reason of para.5 of Sch.5 to the Housing Act 1985 (dwelling-houses let in connection with employment).

3. At all material times the Claimant was employed by the Defendants as a gardener and required to occupy the premises (which are situated in a cemetery) for the better performance of his duties, and/or the premises were let to the Claimant in consequence of that employment.

4. The Defendants' admission of the right to buy and all other acts in consequence thereof up until March 15, 1994 were procured by fraud in that the Claimant and the Defendants' lettings officer, Rosy Wright, conspired together to deceive the Defendants by removing the original tenancy file and substituting for it a forged and false file which concealed the matters in paragraphs 1 to 3 above.

5. In the circumstances, the Defendants are not bound by their admission of the right to buy, and no such right exists.

[CONCLUDE AS IN FORM 137]

Chapter 9
Appeals

PART I: INTRODUCTION

Although appeals do not present problems of drafting particular to housing law, the need to have appropriate forms to hand will frequently arise it is therefore convenient to include here a selection of the necessary documents for use in practice. For the purposes of this chapter, appeals are given an extended meaning to include applications for re-hearings and to set aside orders previously made, and also judicial review of inferior courts.   **9.01**

There are many different avenues of appeal, review or rehearing which arise across the range of proceedings concerned with housing law practice: no attempt will be made here to describe them even summarily. However, the following table indicates the various types of appeal, the documents required in each case, together with relevant time limits and any requirement for seeking permission or leave to appeal.

Appeal/review/ re-hearing	Legal provisions	Documents	Time[1]	Permission required?
Appeal from local authority to magistrates' court	Various[2] Magistrates' Courts Rules 1981, rr.4 and 34	Complaint	Generally 21 days[3]	No
Appeal from magistrates' court to Crown Court (defendant only)	Magistrates' Courts Act 1980, s.108 Crown Court Rules 1982, r.7(2)	Notice of appeal	21 days	No
Appeal from local authority to Crown Court	Various.[4] Crown Court Rules 1982, r.7(2)	Notice of appeal	21 days	No
Appeal from magistrates' or Crown Court to High Court, by case stated	Magistrates' Courts Act 1980, s.111 Supreme Court Act 1981, s.28. CPR Pt 52	Application to state a case[5] Appellant's notice (Form N161), if application granted	21 days[6]	Yes[7]

[1] Time limits can generally be extended in the discretion of the court, unless otherwise indicated, below.
[2] Appeals lie to the magistrates' court (and sometimes direct to the Crown Court) against administrative decisions by local authorities, particularly under public health legislation.
[3] The applicable time limits are prescribed by the relevant statute, and cannot be extended by the court.
[4] See note 2, above.
[5] Magistrates' Court Rules 1981, r.76(1); Crown Court Rules 1982, r.26.
[6] In relation to the magistrates' court, this period is strict and cannot be extended: *Michael v Gowland* [1977] 1 W.L.R. 296.
[7] No permission is needed to make the application, but the substantive procedure is dependent on the lower court agreeing to state a case.

Judicial review of magistrates' or Crown Court	Supreme Court Act 1981, s.31. CPR Pt 54	Claim form (N461)	Promptly, and within 3 months	Yes
Appeal from Crown Court to Court of Appeal (Criminal Division) (defendant only)[8]	Criminal Appeals Act 1968, ss.1, 9, 12 and 15	Notice of appeal	28 days	Yes
Appeal from local authority to county court	Various.[9] CPR Pt 52	Appellant's notice (Form N161)	Generally 21 days.[10]	No
Appeal from county court district judge to circuit judge[11]	CPR Pt 52	Appellant's notice (Form N161)	14 days	In almost all cases[12]
Appeal from county court to High Court[13]	CPR Pt 52	Appellant's notice (Form N161)	14 days	In almost all cases[14]
Appeal from county court to Court of Appeal[15]	CPR Pt 52	Appellant's notice (Form N161)	14 days	In almost all cases[16,17]
Judicial review of county court	Supreme Court Act 1981, s.31. CPR Pt 54	Claim form (Form N461)	Promptly, and within 3 months	Yes
Revoking or varying order (High Court and county court	CPR 3.1(7)	Application	N/A	No

[8] There is a further right of appeal, for either party, to the House of Lords, but only with leave and only in cases of public importance: Criminal Appeals Act 1968, s.33.
[9] Appeals lie to the county court against administrative decisions by local authorities, particularly under homelessness legislation (see Chapter 1), but also in respect of housing conditions.
[10] The applicable time limits are prescribed by the relevant statute, and cannot be extended by the court.
[11] A decision of a district judge is usually appealable to the circuit judge: Access to Justice Act 1999 (Destination of Appeals) Order 2000, SI 2000/1071, art.3(2). The principal exception to this is where, rarely, a district judge has made a final (not case management) decision in a case allocated to the multi-track (not Pt 8 claims), in which case the appeal lies direct to the Court of Appeal: *ibid.*, art.4(a). An appeal can also, exceptionally, be transferred to the Court of Appeal: CPR 52.14.
[12] A very few appeals do not require permission, such as in respect of committal orders: CPR 52.3(1)(a)(i).
[13] A decision of a circuit judge is usually appealable to the High Court: Access to Justice Act 1999 (Destination of Appeals) Order 2000, SI 2000/1071, art.3(1). The principal exceptions to this are (1) final (not case management) decisions in a case allocated to the multi-track (not Pt 8 claims), and (2) decisions which were appeals to the county court, such as homelessness appeals ("second appeals"). In these cases, the appeal lies direct to the Court of Appeal: *ibid.*, arts 4(a) and 5. An appeal can also, exceptionally, be transferred to the Court of Appeal: CPR 52.14.
[14] See note 12, above.
[15] This will usually only be applicable in respect of (1) final decisions in cases allocated to the multi-track, (2) second appeals: see notes 11 and 13, above. An appeal can also, exceptionally, be transferred to the Court of Appeal: CPR 52.14.
[16] See note 12, above.
[17] If the intended appeal is a second appeal (see note 13, above), permission can only be granted by the Court of Appeal, and will not be granted unless there is an important point of principal or practice, or some other compelling reason: CPR 52.13.

Setting aside or varying order made on court's own initiative (High Court and county court)	CPR 3.3	Application	7 days, or as directed	No
Setting aside after striking out (High Court and county court)	CPR 3.6	Application	14 days after service	No
Setting aside or varying default judgment (High Court and county court)	CPR 13	Application[18]	N/A	No
Setting aside or varying default judgment in certain Pt 20 claims (High Court and county court)	CPR 20.11(5)	Application	N/A	No
Setting aside order made without notice (High Court and county court)	CPR 23.10	Application	7 days	No
Re-listing application where non-attendance (High Court and county court)	CPR 23.11	Application	N/A	No
Setting aside or varying summary judgment[19] (High Court and county court)	CPR 24 PD para.8.1	Application	N/A	No
Setting aside where failure to attend trial (High Court and county court)	CPR 39.5	Application	N/A	No
Setting aside or varying by non-party[20] (High Court and county court)	CPR 40.9	Application	N/A	No

[18] Supporting evidence is also required if under CPR 13.3.
[19] *i.e.* by a respondent who did not appear at the hearing.
[20] The non-party must be directly affected.

Setting aside order under accelerated possession procedure (High Court and county court)	CPR 55.19	Application	14 days	No
Setting aside interim possession order (High Court and county court)	CPR 55.28	Application and witness statement	Before date of hearing of the claim	No
Appeal from Master to High Court Judge[21]	CPR Pt 52	Appellant's notice (Form N161)	14 days	In almost all cases[22]
Appeal from High Court to Court of Appeal	CPR Pt 52	Appellant's notice	14 days	In almost all cases[23]
Appeal from High Court to House of Lords[24]	Administration of Justice Act 1969, s.12	(1) Petition for leave[25] (2) Petition of appeal[26]	(1) 1 month (2) 3 months	Yes[27]
Appeal from Court of Appeal to House of Lords	Appellate Jurisdiction Act 1876, s.3; Administration of Justice (Appeals) Act 1934, s.1	(1) Petition for leave[28] (2) Petition of appeal[29]	(1) 1 month (2) 3 months	Yes[30]

[21] As in note 11, above.
[22] See note 12, above.
[23] In respect of second appeals, see note 17, above. Also, see note 12, above.
[24] These are exceptional "leap-frog" appeals.
[25] See House of Lords: Practice Directions and Standing Orders applicable to Civil Appeals (November 2002).
[26] See note 25, above.
[27] In addition to requiring leave (which can only be granted by the House of Lords), a certificate from the High Court is also required.
[28] i.e. if leave is not granted by the Court of Appeal. See note 25, above.
[29] See note 25, above.
[30] Either from the Court of Appeal, or the House of Lords.

PART II: PRECEDENTS

Form 147   **9.02**

Complaint to Magistrates' Court[1]

Metropolis Magistrates' Court [Code]

Date: January 31, 2002
Defendant: Metropolis Borough Council
Address: Metropolis Centre, Metropolis, MS1 1AA
Matter of complaint: By notice dated January 20, 2002, the defendant served on the
                       complainant a notice pursuant to the Building Act 1984, s.59,
                       requiring works to be carried out to the foul sewer in the
                       vicinity of 1 Station Road, Metropolis, and alleging that the
                       sewer is a private sewer whereas it is a public sewer maintain-
                       able by Crystal Clear Water plc
The complaint of: Daniel Drinkwater
Address: 1 Station Road, Metropolis

who [upon oath] states that the defendant was responsible for the matter of complaint
of which particulars are given above.

[Signature]

Taken [and sworn] before me

[Signature]
Justice of the Peace
[*or* Justices clerk]

---

[1] Unless otherwise provided, the complaint does not need to be in writing or on oath: Magistrates' Courts Rules 1981, r.4(2).

9.03   <u>Form 148</u>

<u>Notice of appeal from Magistrates' Court to Crown Court[1]</u>

TO the Clerk to the Justices of [name] Magistrates' Court

AND TO [prosecutor]

TAKE NOTICE that I, [name], of [address] wish to appeal against (a) my conviction before the [name] Magistrates' Court on [date] on a charge of [specify], and (b) the sentence of [specify].

The grounds of my appeal are that[2]:

(1) The conviction was against the weight of the evidence.

(2) The sentence was excessive.

DATED   SIGNED

---

[1] The only formal requirements are that the notice be in writing and state whether the appeal is against conviction or sentence or both: Crown Court Rules 1982, r.7(2) and (4).
[2] Grounds are not formally required to be stated, and are frequently framed generally as here.

Form 149   9.04

Application to Crown Court for extension of time in which to appeal

---

TO the Chief Clerk of the Crown Court at Hazard

TAKE NOTICE that I, Marc Shiman, of Dunromin, Acacia Avenue, Hazard, Doomshire, wish to apply for an extension of time in which to appeal against (a) my conviction before the Hazard Magistrates' Court on July 4, 2001 on a charge of unlawful eviction contrary to s.1(2) of the Protection from Eviction Act 1977, and (b) the sentence of 240 hours' community service.

The grounds of this application are:

(1) I am four days out of time for appealing.

(2) I had represented myself before the magistrates' court. I did not know at the time of the hearing on July 4, 2001 that I had any right of appeal, and only discovered that I did have a right when my friend, Godfrey Knowall, told me on July 25, 2001

(3) Mr Knowall led me to believe that I had 28 days in which to appeal, and I therefore sent my notice of appeal to the magistrates' court and the prosecutor by first class post on July 26, 2001.

(4) Today, July 29, 2001, I received by post a letter dated July 27, 2001 but postmarked July 28, 2001, from the clerk to the justices informing me that I am out of time for my appeal.

The grounds of my appeal are:[3]

(5) The Magistrates' Court on July 4, 2001 refused my application for an adjournment of the hearing. Neither of my witnesses attended court on July 4, 2001 because, unknown to me, they suffered acute food poisoning on the evening of July 3, 2001 and were in hospital.

(6) There is a substantial conflict of evidence between the alleged victim, Harry Slope, and myself, and the justices' verdict indicates that they must have disbelieved me. The corroborative evidence of my witnesses is therefore vital, and was not heard by the justices. In outline, my witnesses will say that they saw and heard Harry Slope instructing his own brother-in-law to change the locks, an act for which I have wrongly been convicted.

(7) The sentence was excessive, in that I am of good character and the justices imposed the maximum number of hours for community service.

DATED   SIGNED

---

[3] Under r.7(6) of the Crown Court Rules the notice should include the proposed grounds of appeal as well as the reasons for applying out of time. This is so that the court can take into account the merits of the appeal. Consequently, the grounds of the intended appeal should be fully stated here.

Form 150

Application to Magistrates' Court to state a case

TO [name], [name] and [name], three of Her Majesty's Justices of the Peace for [area]

AND TO the clerk of the magistrates' court sitting at [place]

WHEREAS an information wherein I the undersigned [name] of [address] was prose-cutor and [name] of [address] was defendant was heard before and determined by the Magistrates' Court sitting at [place] on [date]

NOW I, the undersigned, being aggrieved and dissatisfied with your determination upon the hearing of the above information as being wrong in law hereby apply, pur-suant to s.111 of the Magistrates' Courts Act 1980, to you to state and sign a case for the opinion of the High Court of Justice on the following questions:

(1) Whether the justices were right, as matter of law, to hold that, for the purposes of s.79(1)(a) and (7) of the Environmental Protection Act 1990, premises were prejudicial to health by being likely to cause injury if it was more likely than not that they would case injury.

(2) Whether there was any evidence upon which a reasonable tribunal properly directing itself could have concluded that the defendant was not either the person responsible for the nuisance and/or the owner of the premises.

DATED   SIGNED

9.06   <u>Form 151</u>

<u>Application to Crown Court to state a case</u>

No.[0]

IN THE CROWN COURT AT [NAME]

To the Chief Clerk of the Crown Court

B E T W E E N

[NAME]   **Appellant**

and

[NAME]   **Respondent**

WHEREAS the above-named Appellant is aggrieved and dissatisfied with the determination of His Honour Judge [name] and justices given on [date] upon the hearing of the above appeal as being wrong in law.

TAKE NOTICE that the Appellant hereby applies pursuant to s.28(1) of the Supreme Court Act 1981 for a case to be stated for the opinion of the High Court of Justice upon the following question:

[CONCLUDE AS IN FORM 150]

Form 152   **9.07**

Appellant's notice for appeal to County Court

Appellant's Notice

In the   Whitelake County Court

Notes for guidance are available which will help
you complete this form. Please read them
carefully before you complete each section.

Seal

For Court use only	
Appeal Court Reference No.	
Date filed	February 1, 2002

Section 1   Details of the claim or case

Name of court	Whitelake Borough Council

Case or claim number	Ref H/DH/HMO/666

Names of claimants/ applicants/ petitioner

Harvey Sherlock

Names of defendants/ respondents

Whitelake Borough Council

In the case or claim, were you the
(tick appropriate box)

☐ claimant   ☑ applicant   ☐ petitioner

☐ defendant   ☐ respondent   ☐ other (please specify) _____

Section 2   Your appellant's name and address

Your (appellant's) name ___Harvey Sherlock_____

Your solicitor's name ___Sharp & Hinds_____ (If your are legally represented)

Your (your solicitor's) address

1 High Street,
Whitelake,
Northshire,
WL1 5HX.

reference or contact name	CC/1001
contact telephone number	022-424 2422
DX number	Whitelake 29

Section 3	Respondent's name and address

Respondent's name   Whitelake Borough Council

Solicitor's name   Not known   *(if the respondent is*
legally represented)

Respondent's (solicitor's) contact address

	reference or contact name	Mr Stock, Director of Housing
Civic Centre, Whitelake, Northshire, WL1 0XO	contact telephone number	022-424 1000
	DX number	Not known

Details of other respondents are attached   ☐ Yes   ☑ No

Section 4	Time estimate for appeal hearing

Do no complete if appealing to the Court of Appeal

	Days	Hours	Minute
How long do you estimate it will take to put your appeal to the appeal court at the hearing?	1		

Who will represent you at the appeal hearing?   ☐ Yourself   ☐ Solicitor   ☑ Counsel

Section 5	Details of the order(s) or part(s) of order(s) you want to appeal

Was the order you are appealing made as the result of a previous appeal?   Yes ☐   No ☑

Name of Judge

Date of order(s)

Housing committee, Whitelake Borough Council	January 15, 2002

If only part of an order is appealed, write out that part (or those parts)

Was the case allocated to a track?   Yes ☐   No ☑

If Yes, which track was the case allocated to?   ☐ small claims track   ☐ fast track   ☐ multi-track

Is the order you are appealing a case management order?   Yes ☐   No ☑

Section 6	Permission to Appeal

Has permission to appeal been granted?

Yes ☐   complete box **A**   No ☑ complete box **B**

if you are asking for permission or it is not required

A

Date of order granting permission _____

Name of judge_____

Name of court _____

B

☑ I do not need permission

☐ I _____
appellant('s solicitor) seek permission to appeal the order(s) at **section 5** above.

Are you making any other applications?   Yes ☐   No ☑
If Yes, complete section 10

Is the appellant in receipt of legal aid certificate or a
community legal service fund (CLSF) certificate?   Yes ☐   No ☑

Does your appeal include any issues arising from the Human Rights Act 1998?   Yes ☐   No ☑

Section 7	Grounds for appeal

I (the appellant) appeal(s) the order(s) at **section 5** because:

1.   The respondents were wrong and/or acted unreasonably in refusing the appellant's application for first registration of the premises at 13 Dark Lane, Whitelake, as a house in multiple occupation, as follows.

2.   The respondents purported to refuse the application, first, by reference to special control provisions in their registration scheme for houses in multiple occupation, on the ground that the existence of the premises or the behaviour of the residents would adversely affect the amenity or character of the area in which they are situated. Because the premises had been in operation as a house in multiple occupation before the introduction of their registration scheme, the respondents could only lawfully refuse the application on this ground if there had been a relevant management failure. The respondents made no finding that there had been such a failure; nor was there any or any sufficient evidence to support such a finding.

3.   The respondents purported to refuse the application, secondly, on the grounds that the appellant was not a fit and proper person. The purported reason for this conclusion was that the appellant had allegedly threatened and shouted abuse at the respondents' director of housing when the latter visited to inspect the premises on December 12, 2001. This conclusion was flawed, contrary to evidence and insufficient to justify the refusal of the application because (1) the incident with the director of housing had not involved the appellant, but rather the appellant's younger brother; (2) the conduct of the appellant's younger brother in shouting at the director of housing had been provoked by the comment from the director of housing that "we're going to close this place down"; and (3) this was a single incident in an otherwise unblemished history of conduct.

Section 8	Arguments in support of grounds

My skeleton argument is:

☐ set out below   ☐ attached   ☑ will follow within 14 days of filing this notice

I (the appellant) will rely on the following arguments at the hearing of the appeal:

Section 9	What decision are you asking the appeal court to make?

I (the appellant) am (is) asking that:

(tick appropriate box)

☑ the order(s) at **section 5** be set aside

☐ the order(s) at **section 5** be varied and the following order(s) substituted:

☐ a new trial be ordered

☑ the appeal court makes the following additional orders :

> 1. That the respondents be directed to grant the application for registration as made by the appellant.
>
> 2. That the respondents pay the appellant's costs of the appeal.

Section 10	Other applications

I wish to make an application for additional orders   ☑ in this section

☐ in the Part 23 application
form (N244) attached

Part A
I apply (the appellant applies) for an order (a draft of which is attached) that:

because:

Part B
I (we) wish to rely one:

☐ evidence in Part C

☐ witness statement (affidavit)

Part C
I (we) wish to rely on the following evidence in support of this application:

Statement of Truth

~~I believe~~ (the appellant believes) that the facts stated in Section 10 are true.

Full name CHARLIE HINDS

Name of appellant's solicitor's firm SHARP & HINDS

signed _____ position or office held SOLICITOR

Appellant ('s solicitor) (if signing on behalf of firm or company)

| Section 11 | Supporting documents |

If you do not yet have a document that you intend to use to support your appeal, identify it, give the date when you expect it to be available and give the reasons why it is not currently available in the box below.

Please tick the papers you are filing with this notice and any you will be filing later.

☐ Your skeleton argument *(if separate)*

☐ A copy of the order being appealed

☐ A copy of any order giving or refusing permission to appeal together with a copy of the reasons for that decision

☐ Any witness statements or affidavits in support of any application included in this appellant's notice

☐ A copy of the legal aid or CLSF certificate *(if legally represented)*

☐ A bundle of documents for the appeal hearing containing copies of your appellant's notice and all the papers listed

above and the following:

    ☐ a suitable record of the reasons for the judgment of the lower court;

    ☐ any statements of case;

    ☐ any other affidavit or witness statement filed in support of your appeal;

    ☐ any relevant transcript or note of evidence;

    ☐ any relevant application notices or case management documents;

    ☐ any skeleton arguments relied on by the lower court;

      relevant affidavits, witness statements, summaries, experts' reports and exhibits;

    ☐ any other documents ordered by the court; (give details)

    _____

    ☐ in a second appeal, the original order appealed, the reasons given for making that order and the appellant's

    notice appealing that original (first) order

    ☐ if the appeal is from a decision of a Tribunal, the Tribunal's reasons for that decision, the original decision

    reviewed by the Tribunal and the reasons for that original decision

Reasons why you have not supplied a document and date when you expect it to be available:

Signed_____ Appellant ('s Solicitor)

Form 153   9.08

Application for re-hearing

Application Notice

You should provide this information for listing the application

1. How do you wish to have your application dealt with

   a) at a hearing?   ✓ } *complete all questions below*

   b) at a telephone conference?   ☐

   c) without a hearing?   ☐   *complete Qs 5 and 6 below*

2. Give a time estimate for the hearing/conference
   _____ (hours) 30 ___ (mins)

3. Is this agreed by all parties? ☐ Yes ☑ No

4. Give dates of any trial period or fixed trial date _____

5. Level of judge   District judge

6. Parties to be served   Claimant

In the	HAZARD COUNTY COURT
Claim no.	HZ000001
Warrant no. (If applicable)	
Claimant(s) (including ref.)	FELICITY ALLEN
Defendant (including ref.)	SIDNEY STEVENS
Date	MARCH 1, 2002

Note You must complete Parts A **and** B, **and** Part C if applicable. Send any relevant fee and the completed application to the court with any draft order, witness statement or other evidence; and sufficient copies for service on each respondent.

Part A

1. Enter your full name, or name of solicitor

  I (We)[(1)] HIGH DUDGEON & CO   (on behalf of)~~(the claimant)~~(the defendant)

2. State clearly what order you are seeking and if possible attach a draft

intend to apply for an order (a draft of which is attached) that [(2)]

(1) the judgment in this action entered in favour of the Claimant on February 20, 2002 be set aside, (2) a re-hearing take place, and (3) execution of the judgment be stayed meantime because[(3)]

3. Briefly set out why you are seeking the order. Include the material facts on which you rely, indentifying any rule or statutory provision

Since trial, the Defendant has discovered the existence of new witnesses who contradict the evidence given by the Claimant at trial. These new witnesses maintain that it was not the defendant who assaulted and beat the claimant, and who removed the Claimant's belongings, but rather the claimant's former boyfriend, Ivor Jackson.

Part B

I (We) wish to rely on: *tick one box*

   the attached (witness statement)(affidavit) ☐   my statement of case ☐

4. If you are not already a party to the proceedings, you must provide an address for service of documents

   evidence in Part C in support of my application ☑

Signed		**Position or office held** (if signing on behalf of firm or company)	
	(Applicant)('s Solicitor) (litigation friend)		

Address to which documents about this claim should be sent (including reference if appropriate)[(4)]

		if applicable	
	fax no.	
	DX no.	
Tel. no. Postcode		**email**	

The court office at

is open from 10am and 4pm Mon–Fri. When corresponding with the court please address forms or letters to the Court Manager and quote the claim number.

Part C   Claim No. HZ000001

I (We) wish to rely on the following evidence in support of this application:

1. On February 27, 2002, the defendant was contacted for the first time by Agnes and Mavis Walsh. They are sisters, aged 75 and 73 respectively, who live at 3 Bleak Road, Hazard, Doomshire, immediately opposite the premises demised by the Defendant to the Claimant.

2. Short statements have been taken from Agnes and Mavis Walsh, which are attached marked HD1 and HD2 respectively. They both state clearly that they witnessed the incidents alleged by the Claimant in the claim form, and that the person responsible was not the Defendant, but rather the Claimant's former boyfriend, Ivor Jackson.

3. The reason that Agnes and Mavis Walsh did not come forward previously was that they rarely go out, and only became aware of the significance of what they had witnessed when they saw a report in the local paper, the Hazard Herald, on February 26, 2002, reporting the hearing on February 20, 2002 and the Claimant's allegations against the Defendant.

Statement of Truth

*(I believe) *(The applicant believes) that the facts stated in Part C are true

delete as appropriate

Signed [   ]   **Position or office held** [   ]

(Applicant)('s solicitor) (Litigation friend)   (if signing on behalf of firm or company)

Date [   ]

Form 154   9.09

Application to set aside order

Application Notice

	In the METROPOLITAN COUNTY COURT

You should provide this information for listing the application

1. How do you wish to have your application dealt with

   a) at a hearing?   ✓ } *complete all questions below*

   b) at a telephone conference?

   c) without a hearing?   *complete Qs 5 and 6 below*

2. Give a time estimate for the hearing/conference

   _____(hours)15 _____ (mins)

3. Is this agreed by all parties?   ☐ Yes   ☑ No

4. Give dates of any trial period or fixed trial date _____

5. Level of judge   District judge

6. Parties to be served Claimant

Claim no.	MT000002
Warrant no. (If applicable)	
Claimant(s) (including ref.)	HOMES2LET LTD
Defendant (including ref.)	SIMON ROBINSON
Date	March 1, 2002

Note You must complete Parts A **and** B, **and** Part C if applicable. Send any relevant fee and the completed application to the court with any draft order, witness statement or other evidence; and sufficient copies for service on each respondent.

Part A

1. Enter your full name, or name of solicitor   **I (We)**[1] Messrs Hunt & Meacham   (on behalf of)(the claimant)(the defendant)

2. State clearly what order you are seeking and if possible attach a draft   intend to apply for an order (a draft of which is attached) that [2]

the possession order made on February 20, 2002 under the accelerated possession procedure be set aside pursuant to CPR 55.19.

3. Briefly set out why you are seeking the order. Include the material facts on which you rely, indentifying any rule or statutory provision   because[3]

(1) the Defendant filed a defence on February 19, 2002 disputing that the notice served by the Claimant was a valid notice under s.21 Housing 1988, and was entitled to be heard on this issue, (2) the court accordingly could not properly have been satisfied that the Claimant had established that it was entitled to possession under s.21 Housing 1988 against the Defendant.

Part B

I (We) wish to rely on: *tick one box*

   the attached (witness statement)(affidavit) ☐   my statement of case ☑

4. If you are not already a party to the proceedings, you must provide an address for service of documents   evidence in Part C in support of my application ☐

Signed		**Position or office held** (if signing on behalf of firm or company)	
	(Applicant)('s Solicitor) (litigation friend)		

Address to which documents about this claim should be sent (including reference if appropriate)[4]

	if applicable
	fax no.
	DX no.
Tel. no. Postcode	e-mail

The court office at

is open from 10am and 4pm Mon–Fri. When corresponding with the court please address forms or letters to the Court Manager and quote the claim number.

Part C   Claim No. [   ]

I (We) wish to rely on the following evidence in support of this application:

Statement of Truth

*(I believe) *(The applicant believes) that the facts stated in Part C are true

*delete as appropriate

Signed [   ]   **Position or** [   ]
         (Applicant)('s solicitor) (Litigation friend)   **office held**
                                                          (if signing on behalf
                                                          of firm or company)

                                          Date [   ]

Form 155

9.10

Claim Form for Judicial Review of County Court

Judicial Review
Claim Form

In the High Court of Justice
Administrative Court

Notes for guidance are available which explain how to complete the judicial review claim form. Please read them carefully before you complete the form.

Seal

For Court use only	
Administrative Court Reference No.	
Date filed	

SECTION 1 Details of the claimant(s) and defendant(s)

Claimant(s) name and address(es)

name

Harry Tennant

address

14 Paradise Gardens, London NE1

Telephone no.

Fax no.

E-mail address

Claimant's or claimant's solicitors' address to which documents should be sent.

name

Greens & Co

address

1 Market Street
Downtown
London NE1

Telephone no.
020-7000 000

Fax no.
020-7000 001

E-mail address
acarrott@greens.co.uk

Claimant's Counsel's details

name

Arthur Brown

address

Allotment Chambers
Corporation Street
London EC4

Telephone no.
020-7999 9999

Fax no.
020-7999 9998

E-mail address
brown@allotment.com

1st Defendant

name

Metropolitan County Court

Defendant's or (where known) Defendant's solicitors' address to which documents should be sent.

name

The Treasury Solicitor

address

Queen Anne's Chambers
28 Broadway
London SW1H 9JS

Telephone no.
020-7210 3000

Fax no.
020-7210 3001

E-mail address

2nd Defendant

name

Defendant's or (where known) Defendant's solicitors' address to which documents should be sent.

name

address

Telephone no.

Fax no.

E-mail address

N461 Judicial review claim form (March 2002)

1 of 5

Crown Copyright. Reproduced by Sweet & Maxwell Ltd

SECTION 2 Details of other interested parties

Include name and address and, if appropriate, details of DX, telephone or fax numbers and e-mail

name	name
London Borough of Downtown	

address	address
Town Hall Downtown London NE1	

Telephone no.	Fax no.	Telephone no.	Fax no.
020-7777 7777	020-7777 7778		

E-mail address	E-mail address

SECTION 3 Details of the decision to be judicially reviewed

Decision:

The failure or refusal of the defendant to attach a penal notice, pursuant to C.P.R. Sched. 2, C.C.R. Ord. 29 r.1(3), to an order of the court dated 14 January 2002.

Date of decision:

14 January 2002 and thereafter

Name and address of the court, tribunal, person or body who made the decision to be reviewed.

name	address
Metropolitan County Court	Justice Road Downtown London NE1

SECTION 4 Permission to proceed with a claim for judicial review

I am seeking permission to proceed with my claim for Judicial Review.

Are you making any other applications? If Yes, complete Section 7.	☑ Yes	☐ No
Is the claimant in receipt of a Community Legal Service Fund (CLSF) certificate?	☑ Yes	☐ No
Are you claiming exceptional urgency, or do you need this application determined within a certain time scale? If Yes, complete Form N463 and file this with your application.	☑ Yes	☐ No
Have you complied with the pre-action protocol? If No, give reasons for non-compliance in the space below.	☐ Yes	☑ No

The decision challenged is a final decision of the county court. The pre-action protocol letter would serve no purpose.

Does the claim include any issues arising from the Human Rights Act 1998? If Yes, state the articles which you contend have been breached in the space below.	☐ Yes	☑ No

SECTION 5 Detailed statement of grounds

☑ set out below   ☐ attached

1. The defendant has failed to act according to law, in that it is a mandatory requirement under C.P.R. Sched. 2, C.C.R. Ord. 29 r.1(3), without exception, that the penal notice should be attached. See R. v. Wandsworth County Court, ex p. Munn (1994) 26 H.L.R. 697, QBD.

2. And/or the defendant's failure or refusal to act according to law is irrational, there being no valid reason for not attaching the penal notice.

SECTION 6 Details of remedy (including any interim remedy) being sought

A mandatory order requiring the defendant to attach a penal notice to the order.

SECTION 7 Other applications

I wish to make an application for:-

An order that this claim be expedited, and that the defendant's time for service of the acknowledging service and evidence be abridged.

SECTION 8 Statement of facts relied on

1. The claimant is the tenant of residential premises at 14 Paradise Gardens, London NE1. The London Borough of Downtown ("Downtown") are the landlords.

2. The claimant brought proceedings in the county court alleging breach of covenant by Downtown in respect of their failure to keep the premises in repair. In those proceedings, the claimant applied for an interim order requiring Downtown to carry out urgent works.

3. On 14 January 2002, His Honour Judge Nice made an interim order against Downtown requiring them to carry out and complete urgent works by 5pm 29 January 2002. A copy of the order is annexed.

4. When the order was drawn up by the county court, no penal notice was attached.

5. C.P.R. Sched. 2, C.C.R. Ord. 29 r.1(3) provides:

 "Where a judgment or order enforceable by committal under paragraph (1) has been given or made, the court officer shall, if the judgment or order is in the nature of an injunction, at the time when the judgment or order is drawn up, and in any other case on the request of the judgment creditor, issue a copy of the judgment or order, indorsed with or incorporating a notice as to the consequences of disobedience, for service in accordance with paragraph (2)."

5. When, on 15 January 2002, the matter was referred to His Honour Judge Nice, the judge refused to make any further order, saying that the attachment of the penal notice was not a matter for him because the county court rule was directed to "the court officer". A copy of the attendance note by the claimant's solicitor is annexed. The claimant's solicitor wrote by fax to the court on 15 January 2002 asking to have the note approved, but there has been no reply.

6. The claimant's solicitor wrote by fax to the chief clerk on 15 January 2002 requiring the penal notice to be attached to the order. A follow-up letter was sent by fax on 22 January 2002. Copies of both letters are attached. There has been no reply.

7. The time allowed by the order dated 14 January 2002 for completion of the works has expired. Downtown have not yet commenced any works, or given any explanation for their failure to do so.

8. The order dated 14 January 2002 cannot properly be enforced by reason of the absence of the penal notice.

9. It is urgent that the works be carried out, because the premises are presently dangerous to the claimant and his family, and to neighbours and passers-by. In particular, the front and side walls of the premises are in danger of collapse. A report dated 20 December 2001 by Apt Ridden, chartered surveyors, is annexed.

Statement of Truth

I believe (The claimant believes) that the facts stated in this claim form are true.

Full name _____

Name of claimant's solicitor's firm _____

Signed _____   Position or office held _____
       Claimant ('s solicitor)   (if signing on behalf of firm or company)

SECTION 9 Supporting documents

If you do not have a document that you intend to use to support your claim, identify it, give the date when you expect it to be available and give reasons why it is not currently available in the box below.

Please tick the papers you are filing with this claim form and any you will be filing later.

☑ Statement of grounds   ☑ included   ☐ attached

☑ Statement of the facts relied on   ☑ included   ☐ attached

☐ Application to extended the time limit for filing the claim form   ☐ included   ☐ attached

☑ Application for directions   ☑ included   ☐ attached

☐ Any written evidence in support of the claim or application to extend time

☐ Where the claim for judicial review relates to a decision of a court or tribunal, an approved copy of the reasons for reaching that decision

☑ Copies of any documents on which the claimant proposes to rely

☑ A copy of the legal aid or CSLF certificate *(if legally represented)*

☑ Copies of any relevant statutory material

☑ A list of essential documents for advance reading by the court *(with page references to the passages relied upon)*

Reasons why you have not supplied a document and date when you expect it to be available:-

The county court has not responded to the request for approval of the claimant's solicitor's note of the hearing on 15 January 2002. It is not known when an approved version may be available.

Signed _____ Claimant ('s Solicitor)_____

9.11   Form 156

Appellant's notice for fast track appeal, with skeleton argument

---

Appellant's Notice

In the	SUMMER COUNTY COURT

Notes for guidance are available which will help
you complete this form. Please read them
carefully before you complete each section.

Seal

For court use only	
Appeal Court Reference No.	
Date filed	

Section 1   Details of the claim or case

Name of court	Summer County Court	Case or claim number	KG000003

Names of claimants/ applicants/ petitioner	Knottmill Limited	Names of defendants/ respondents	Fred Thomas

In the case or claim, were you the
(tick appropriate box)

☐ claimant   ☐ applicant   ☐ petitioner

☑ defendant   ☐ respondent   ☐ other *(please specify)* _____

Section 2   Your appellant's name and address

Your (appellant's) name   Fred Thomas

Your solicitor's name   Rose Budd & Co   *(If your are legally represented)*

Your (your solicitor's) address

12 Cherry Lane, Blossom, Springshire, BL0 0MY.	reference or contact name	Rose Budd
	contact telephone number	033 7222 444
	DX number	42 Blossom

Section 3	Respondent's name and address

Respondent's name   Knottmill Limited

Solicitor's name   Fine Print & Co   *(if the respondent is legally represented)*

Respondent's (solicitor's) contact address

98 City Road,
Centretown,
Middleshire,
MI5 5NG.

reference or contact name   S Smith

contact telephone number   055 6666 333

DX number   Centretown 99

Details of other respondents are attached   ☐ Yes   ☑ No

Section 4	Time estimate for appeal hearing

Do no complete if appealing to the Court of Appeal

How long do you estimate it will take to put your appeal to the appeal court at the hearing?

Days	Hours	Minute
	2	

Who will represent you at the appeal hearing?   ☐ Yourself   ☑ Solicitor   ☐ Counsel

Section 5	Details of the order(s) or part(s) of order(s) you want to appeal

Was the order you are appealing made as the result of a previous appeal?   Yes ☐   No ☑

Name of Judge

District Judge Orr

Date of order(s)

February 1, 2002

If only part of an order is appealed, write out that part (or those parts)

Was the case allocated to a track?   Yes ☑   No ☐

If Yes, which track was the case allocated to?   ☐ small claims track   ☑ fast track   ☐ multi-track

Is the order you are appealing a case management order?   Yes ☐   No ☑

Section 6	Permission to Appeal

Has permission to appeal been granted?

Yes ☐   complete box **A**   No ☑   complete box **B**

*if you are asking for
permission or it is not
required*

A _____

Date of order granting permission _____

Name of judge _____

Name of court _____

B _____

☐   I do not need permission

☑   I   Rose Budd & Co   _____

appellant('s solicitor) seek permission to appeal the
order(s) at **section 5** above.

Are you making any other applications?   Yes ☑   No ☐
If Yes, complete section 10

Is the appellant in receipt of legal aid certificate or a
community legal service fund (CLSF) certificate?   Yes ☑   No ☐

Does your appeal include any issues arising from the Human Rights Act 1998?   Yes ☑   No ☐

Section 7	Grounds for appeal

I (the appellant) appeal(s) the order(s) at **section 5** because:

1.   The decision of the district judge was unjust because of a serious procedural or other irregularity. The district judge acted unfairly and, as a public authority under the Human Rights Act 1998, denied the Defendant a fair trial by persistently interrupting the examination of witnesses and the making of submissions by the Defendant's solicitor, Rose Budd, and by behaving throughout the hearing towards her in a hectoring and intimidatory manner. The district judge's behaviour substantially interfered with the proper presentation of the defendant's case on fact and law. On about 30 occasions in the course of only 25 minutes, the district judge constantly interrupted material cross-examination of the Claimant's witness as to the terms of the defendant's tenancy, and behaved similarly during re-examination of the Defendant, repeatedly refusing to allow proper questions to be put and requiring reasons to be given for each question being put. The district judge constantly interrupted closing submissions, repeatedly stating that he had had "enough of this nonsense".

2.   The district judge was wrong to draw the inference that the Defendant used the premises only rarely, and that accordingly the premises were not the Defendant's only or principal home. The primary fact relied upon by the district judge for this inference was the evidence of the Claimant's manager, Mr Small, that he had failed to get any response to knocking on the door to the premises on an unspecified number of occasions. The inference was not properly capable of being drawn on the facts because there was no clear evidence about how often or when Mr Small knocked at the premises, the district judge preventing cross-examination on this issue. The Claimant's evidence was moreover equally consistent with the Defendant's evidence that, although she spent much of the day visiting friends, she kept her belongings and usually slept at the premises. The district judge should have held, on the evidence, that the premises were the defendant's only or principal home.

3.   The district judge was wrong to hold that the Defendant's tenancy was excluded from statutory protection as an assured tenancy under Pt I of Chapter I of the Housing Act 1988, merely because the Defendant had no cooking facilities in the premises, or any right under the tenancy to the use of a kitchen. The absence of cooking facilities or right to use a kitchen did not prevent the premises being "let as a separate dwelling" for the purposes of s.1(1) Housing Act 1988 (see *Uratemp Ventures Limited v Collins* [2001] UKHL 43). The district judge ought to have held that the tenancy was an assured weekly tenancy, that the Claimant was accordingly required to have served a notice under s.8 Housing Act 1988 and to have established statutory grounds for possession under Sch. 2 Housing Act 1988, and that in the absence of such notice and grounds no possession order could be made.

Section 8	Arguments in support of grounds

My skeleton argument is:

☐ set out below   ☐ ~~attached~~   ☐ ~~will follow within 14 days of filing this notice~~

I (the appellant) will rely on the following arguments at the hearing of the appeal:

The first ground of appeal: unfairness

1.   The defendant had the right to a fair trial at common law and under Art.6(1) of the European Human Rights Convention (see *CG v UK* (2002) Times, January 4, appl. no. 43373/98). The district judge's interruptions substantially interfered with the fairness of the trial, because the defendant's solicitor was prevented from asking questions of witnesses and making submissions, or from doing so in an effective manner. An informed, objective and reasonably-minded observed would say that the fairness of the trial had been substantially impaired.

2.   Accordingly, the conduct of the district judge was incompatible with Article 6(1), and was accordingly unlawful under s.6(1) Human Rights Act 1998. The defendant is accordingly entitled to bring proceedings under s.7(1)(a) Human Rights Act 1998, and to do so by exercising a right of appeal under s.9(1)(a) Human Rights Act 1998. Alternatively, the conduct of the district judge was unjust and unfair as a matter of common law.

The second ground of appeal: inference of fact

3.   An Appeal Court is in as good a position as the trial court to determine the proper inferences to be drawn from the primary facts (see *Benmax v Austin Motor Co. Ltd* [1955] 1 All E.R. 326, HL).

4.   The evidence of primary fact was that on an unspecified number of occasions, which the Defendant's solicitor was prevented from investigating in cross-examination, there was no answer to knocking at the door of the premises.

5.   It was not safe for the district judge to infer merely from this evidence that the Defendant had ceased to occupy the premises as her only or principal home. The evidence did not reveal how often this knocking had occurred, over what period, on what days, or at what times of day. An absence of response to knocking was in any event merely capable of indicating (in the absence of evidence to the contrary) that the Defendant was not present at that particular time. Moreover, the absence of response to knocking was consistent with the Defendant's uncontested evidence that she was rarely at the premises during the day, but continued to keep her belongings and to sleep at the premises.

The third ground of appeal: cooking facilities

6.   The district judge's decision was in flat contradiction of the decision of the House of Lords in *Uratemp*, above. The absence of cooking facilities did not mean that the premises were incapable of being let as a separate dwelling. The district judge would not entertain submissions from the Defendant's solicitor on this.

Relief

7.   On appeal, it is open to the court to determine on the evidence heard by the district judge that the Defendant was in occupation of the premises as her only or principal home and was accordingly an assured weekly tenant of the premises. The court should therefore allow the appeal and dismiss the claim for possession, because the claimant has not served the statutory notice of seeking possession under s.8 Housing Act 1988, or sought to establish any statutory grounds for possession under Sch. 2 Housing Act 1988.

8.   Alternatively, if on appeal the court is not able to reach a conclusion as to the Defendant's status, the case should be remitted to a different tribunal for re-hearing.

Section 9	What decision are you asking the appeal court to make?

I (the appellant) am (is) asking that:

(tick appropriate box)

☑ the order(s) at **section 5** be set aside

☐ the order(s) at **section 5** be varied and the following order(s) substituted:

☑ a new trial be ordered, or alternatively that

☑ the appeal court makes the following additional orders:

The claim be dismissed, with costs.

I wish to make an application for additional orders   ☐ in this section

                                                            ☐ ~~in the Part 23 application~~
                                                              ~~form (N244) attached~~

Part A
I apply (the appellant applies) for an order (a draft of which is attached) that:

1.   The Defendant be granted an extension of time for appealing.

2.   The Defendant be granted a stay of execution on the order for possession.

3.   Expedition of the appeal.

because:

1.   The time for appealing expired, without fault on the defendant's part, while public funding was being secured to enable the appeal to be brought. There is no substantial prejudice to the claimant.

        After the district's order was made on February 1, 2002, an application for an extension of the public funding certificate was made on February 2, 2002. The application was refused on February 9, 2002, but notification of the decision was not received until February 16, 2002. An appeal against the refusal of funding was submitted on February 18, 2002, and allowed on February 25, 2002. This appeal notice was filed with the court on March 1, 2002.

2.   The defendant is a single woman of 67 years, with no relatives. The premises are her only home. She has lived there since November 7, 1997. She suffers from acute angina, for which she is on prescribed medication and subject to constant medical attention. She would suffer serious harm if she were evicted pending the hearing of an appeal.

3.   It is urgent that the right to possession of the premises be determined.

Part B
I (we) wish to rely on:

☑ evidence in Part C
☐ witness statement (affidavit)

Part C
I (we) wish to rely on the following evidence in support of this application:

I confirm the truth of the statements made in Part A of section 10 above.

Statement of Truth

I believe (the appellant believes) that the facts stated in Section 10 are true.

Full name ___Rose Budd_____

Name of appellant's solicitor's firm ___Rose Budd & Co_____

signed _____   position or office held _Principal_____
Appellant ('s solicitor)   (if signing on behalf of firm or company)

Section 11	Supporting documents

If you do not yet have a document that you intend to use to support your appeal, identify it, give the date when you expect it to be available and give the reasons why it is not currently available in the box below.

Please tick the papers you are filing with this notice and any you will be filing later.

☐ Your skeleton argument *(if separate)*

☐ A copy of the order being appealed

☐ A copy of any order giving or refusing permission to appeal together with a copy of the reasons for that decision

☐ Any witness statements or affidavits in support of any application included in this appellant's notice

☐ A copy of the legal aid or CLSF certificate *(if legally represented)*

☐ A bundle of documents for the appeal hearing containing copies of your appellant's notice and all the papers listed above and the following:

    ☐ a suitable record of the reasons for the judgment of the lower court;

    ☐ any statements of case;

    ☐ any other affidavit or witness statement filed in support of your appeal;

    ☐ any relevant transcript or note of evidence;

    ☐ any relevant application notices or case management documents;

    ☐ any skeleton arguments relied on by the lower court;

    relevant affidavits, witness statements, summaries, experts' reports and exhibits;

    ☐ any other documents ordered by the court; (give details)

    _____

    ☐ in a second appeal, the original order appealed, the reasons given for making that order and the appellant's notice appealing that original (first) order

    ☐ if the appeal is from a decision of a Tribunal, the Tribunal's reasons for that decision, the original decision reviewed by the Tribunal and the reasons for that original decision

Reasons why you have not supplied a document and date when you expect it to be available:

Signed_____ Appellant ('s Solicitor)

9.12   Form 157

Grounds of appeal for permission to bring second appeal

IN THE COURT OF APPEAL

Court of Appeal ref. C/2002/1506

ON APPEAL FROM BEDROCK COUNTY COURT

B E T W E E N

MIRIAM MONEYPENNY

Claimant/Appellant

and

BEDROCK CITY COUNCIL

Defendant/Respondent

GROUNDS OF APPEAL

---

1. The Judge applied the wrong test in law in considering whether the Defendants had properly determined that the Claimant became homeless intentionally for the purposes of s.191(1) of the Housing Act 1996.

   a) The critical question under s.191(1) of the Housing Act 1996 was whether the Claimant's former matrimonial home at 14 Hard Place, Bedrock, was accommodation which it would have been reasonable for the Claimant to continue to occupy.

   b) Section 177(1) of the Housing Act 1996 provides: "It is not reasonable for a person to continue to occupy accommodation if it is probable that this will lead to domestic violence against him . . ."

   c) The Judge, in dismissing the Claimant's appeal in the court below, upheld the review decision dated January 4, 2002 of the Defendants which had determined that the Claimant:

      > "failed to take reasonable measures by way of seeking an injunction from the court, and/or assistance from the police and/or [her] social landlord, and could reasonably have continued to occupy the accommodation if [she] had taken such preventative measures."

   d) The Judge and the Defendants erred by failing to address the correct test in law, namely whether as a question of fact it was probable that continued occupation of 14 Hard Place would lead to domestic violence against the Claimant.

e) If the Defendants had addressed the correct test in law, it is more likely than not that they would have determined that it was probable that continued occupation of 14 Hard Place would lead to domestic violence against the Claimant, and accordingly this court should exercise the power under s.204(3) of the Housing Act 1996 to vary the Defendant's decision by providing that it would not have been reasonable for the Claimant to continue to occupy 14 Hard Place, and that the Claimant was accordingly not homeless intentionally.

2. The Judge applied the wrong tests in considering whether the Defendants had properly determined that the Claimant did not have a local connection with the district of the Defendants for the purposes of s.199 of the Housing Act 1996.

a) The critical questions were (1) the date at which the local connection was to be established; and (2) whether accommodation provided on an interim basis by the Defendants under s.188 of the Housing Act 1996 pending a decision and a review on the Claimant's homelessness application was to be taken into account for the purpose of establishing the local connection.

b) Under s.199(1) of the Housing Act 1996, a person has a local connection with an authority's district if s/he has a connection because (among other reasons) s/he is or was "normally resident there, and that residence is or was of his own choice".

c) The Judge, in dismissing the Claimant's appeal in the court below held (in the alternative, if he was wrong on the point appealed under para.1 above) that the Defendants would have been entitled to refer the Claimant to Quicksands District Council under s.198 of the Housing Act 1998 on the ground that the Claimant did not have a local connection with the district of Bedrock City Council but did have a local connection with the district of Quicksands District Council.

d) The Judge erred by holding (1) that the relevant date for establishing the local connection was the date of the Claimant's homelessness application to the Defendant, and (2) that the interim accommodation provided by the Defendants, pending their decision under s.184 of the Housing Act 1996 and pending the review of that decision under s.202 of the Housing Act 1996, was not to be taken into account in establishing the local connection.

e) The Judge ought to have held (1) that the relevant date was the date of the review decision under s.202 of the Housing Act 1996, and (2) that the interim accommodation was to be taken into account.

3. Permission to appeal should be granted by the Court of Appeal, even though the appeal is a second appeal, because the appeal would raise important points of principle as to the correct interpretation and application of central provisions of Pt VII of the Housing Act 1996, potentially affecting homelessness applicants in general. These issues are not concluded by existing legal authority.[1]

SIDNEY MILTON

[1] This is drafted as if the issues on appeal had not already been determined by the decisions in *Bond v Leicester City Council* [2001] EWCA Civ 1544; [2002] H.L.R. 6, and *Mohamed v Hammersmith and Fulham LBC* [2001] UKHL 57; [2002] H.L.R. 7, and as if prior to the amendments under the Homelessness Act 2002.

9.13   Form 158

<u>**Respondent's notice to uphold decision on different or additional grounds**</u>

Respondent's Notice

Notes for guidance are available which will help
you complete this form. Please read them
carefully before you complete each section.

In the	Court of Appeal
Appeal Court Reference No.	

Seal

For court use only	
Date filed	

Section 1	Details of the claim or case

Name of court	Bedrock County Court	Case or claim number	BD000335

Name or title of case or claim   Miriam Moneypenny v Bedrock City Council

In the case or claim, were you the
(tick appropriate box)

☐ claimant   ☐ applicant   ☐ petitioner

☑ defendant   ☐ respondent   ☐ other *(please specify)* _____

Section 2	Your (respondent's name and address

Your (respondent's) name Bedrock City Council _____

Your solicitor's name   G Stone _____   *(If you are legally represented)*

Your (your solicitor's) address

City Hall,
Corporation Street,
Bedrock,
BD1 1AA.

Your reference or contact name	G Stone
Your contact telephone number	022-888 7777
DX number	Bedrock 1

Details of other respondents are attached   ☐ Yes ☑ No

Section 3	Time estimate for appeal hearing

Do no complete if appealing to the Court of Appeal

	Days	Hours	Minutes
How long do you estimate it will take to put your case to the appeal court at the hearing?	1		

Who will represent you at the appeal hearing?   ☐ Yourself   ☐ Solicitor   ☑ Counsel

Section 4	Details of the order(s) or part(s) of order(s) you want to appeal

Name of Judge

His Honour Judge Jackson

Date of order(s)

March 4, 2002

If only part of an order is appealed, write out that part (or those parts

Section 5	Permission to file a respondent's notice

Has permission to appeal been granted?

Yes ☐   complete box **A**

No ☑ complete box **B**

if you are asking for permission or it is not required

A

Date of order granting permission _____

Name of judge_____

Name of court _____

B

☑ I do not need permission

☐ I _____
respondent('s solicitor) seek permission to appeal the order(s) at **section 4** above.

Are you making any other applications?   Yes ☐   No ☑
If Yes, complete section 9

Is the respondent in receipt of legal aid certificate or a   Yes ☐   No ☑
community legal service fund (CLSF) certificate?

Does your appeal include any issues arising from the Human Rights Act 1998?   Yes ☐   No ☑

Section 6	Grounds for appeal or for upholding the order

I (the respondent)

☐ ~~appeal(s) the order~~   ☑ wish(es) the appeal court to uphold the order on different or additional grounds

because:

1.   The Judge was wrong to hold that the Defendants were not entitled or obliged to reconsider on the review under s.202 Housing Act 1996 whether the Claimant had a priority need under s.189 Housing Act 1996.

       a)   The Defendants' original decision dated November 4, 2001 on the Claimant's homelessness application concluded that the Claimant had a priority need because she had two dependent children residing with her.

       b)   Between the date of the Defendants' original decision, and the date of the review decision dated January 4, 2002, the Claimant's former husband and father of the two children obtained a residence order from the Bedrock Family Proceedings Court dated December 12, 2001 whereby it was ordered that the children should reside with their father.

       c)   The Defendants' review decision was accordingly that the Claimant no longer had a priority need, in that the two children neither resided with the Claimant nor might reasonably be expected to reside with the Claimant.

       d)   On the Claimant's appeal in the court below, the Judge held that it was not open to the Defendants on the review to reconsider whether the Claimant had a priority need.

       e)   The Judge was wrong and ought to have held that the review under s.202 Housing Act 1996 entitled or obliged the Defendants to consider all the circumstances at the date of the review so as to consider what duty if any was owed under Pt VII Housing Act 1996 to the Claimant.

2.   If the Judge had held, as he should have done, that the Defendants were entitled or obliged to reconsider on the review whether the Claimant had a priority need, he was bound to have concluded that the Defendants were entitled on the material before them to reach the conclusion that the Claimant did not then have a priority need.

3.   If the Judge had reached, as he should have done, the conclusion referred to in para.2 above, he would not have held (as he did) that the Defendants owed the limited duty under s.190(2)(a) Housing Act 1996 to secure the availability of accommodation for the Claimant for such period as they considered would give her a reasonable opportunity of securing accommodation for her occupation. Instead, the only duty upon the Defendants would have been the duty to provide advice and assistance under s.190(3) Housing Act 1996.

4.   Accordingly, the Claimant's appeal should be dismissed on the further or alternative ground that the Defendants were entitled to conclude on the review under s.202 Housing Act 1996 that she did not have a priority need.

| Section 7 | Arguments in support of grounds |

My skeleton argument is :

☐ set out below   ☐ attached   ☑ will follow within 21 days of receiving the appellant's
                                                                skeleton arguments

I (the respondent) will rely on the following arguments at the hearing of the appeal:-

Section 8	What decision are you asking the appeal court to make?

I (the respondent) am (is) asking that:

(tick appropriate box)

☐ the order(s) at section 4 be set aside

☐ the order(s) at section 4 be varied and the following order(s) substituted:

☐ a new trial be ordered

☐ the appeal court makes the following additional orders:

☑ the appeal court upholds the order but for the following different or additional reasons

The Defendants were entitled to conclude on the review under s.202 Housing Act 1996 that the Claimant did not have a priority need.

Section 9	Other applications

I wish to make an application for additional orders   ☐ in this section

☐ in the Part 23 application form (N244) attached

Part A
I apply (the respondent applies) for an order (a draft of which is attached) that:

because:

Part B
I (the respondent) wish(es) to rely on:

☐ evidence in Part C

☐ witness statement (affidavit)

Part C
I (the respondent) wish(es) to rely on the following evidence in support of this application:

Statement of Truth

I believe (the respondent believes) that the facts stated in Section 9 are true.

Full name _____

Name of respondent's solicitor's firm_____

signed _____ position or office held _____
                                                    (if signing on behalf of firm or company)
Respondent ('s solicitor)

| Section 10 | Supporting documents |

Please tick the papers you are filing in your bundle:

☐ your respondent's notice and any skeleton arguments (if separate);

☐ any witness statements or affidavits in support of any application included in section 5 or 9 of your notice or in a separate Part 23 application notice;

☐ any other affidavit or witness statement filed in support of your arguments;

☐ a copy of the legal aid or CLSF certificate (if legally represented); and

☐ any other documents directed by the court to be filed in your appeal *(give details)*.

Reasons why you have not supplied a document and date when you expect it to be available:

Signed_____ Respondent/'s Solicitor)

Skeleton argument

IN THE COURT OF APPEAL

Court of Appeal ref: C/2002/0160

ON APPEAL FROM THE MARYLAND COUNTY COURT (HHJ DODDS)

B E T W E E N

ELLIE ELING

Claimant/Appellant

and

STRAIGHTOAK BOROUGH COUNCIL

Defendants/Respondents

RESPONDENTS' SKELETON ARGUMENT[1]

SUMMARY

1. The Respondents contend that the Judge directed himself correctly as to the law and the relevant evidence concerning the one issue raised in this appeal (*i.e.* whether the Appellant was "displaced" for the purposes of s.29(1)(c) of the Land Compensation Act 1973 so as to entitle her to a home loss payment).

2. If, contrary to the Respondents' principal submission, the Judge did not direct himself correctly, it is not likely to be possible for this court to determine the issue, and there would have to be a re-trial.

ISSUES

3. The grounds of appeal raise three principal issues, and a fourth consequential issue.

    a) First, whether the Judge misdirected himself in relation to the test under s.29(1)(c).

    b) Second, whether the evidence about the Appellant's transfer application was relevant or irrelevant.

    c) Third, whether the evidence that the Appellant and other tenants welcomed the proposal for redevelopment was relevant or irrelevant.

d) The consequential issue, if the Judge erred, is whether this court can determine as a question of fact whether the Appellant was displaced.

SUBMISSIONS

The Judge's findings of fact

4. The Judge made the following findings, none of which are challenged by the Appellant:

a) The Respondents developed a strategy to improve the MidVale Estate where the Appellant lived, in relation to which they undertook widespread local consultation.

b) During the consultation process, the Respondents gave an undertaking to all tenants that if a bid for Single Regeneration Budget ("SRB") funding was successful, the tenants would be re-housed in their choice of area and type of accommodation.

c) The SRB bid would not have proceeded unless there had been a significant measure of support among the tenants.

d) 85% of the 97% of tenants who responded to the consultation said that they were in favour, and the SRB bid was successful.

e) No tenants indicated an unwillingness to move, provided that the Respondents were able to offer suitable alternative accommodation.

f) All the tenants' preferences were met concerning the location of their new accommodation.

g) There was no compulsion on any tenants to move as a result of the scheme. No deadlines were imposed, and everything proceeded on the basis of agreement.

h) The Respondents, under a "voluntary re-housing programme" approved by the local community representatives during the consultation, undertook to meet all removal and associated costs of the tenants, in addition to paying £250 plus £20 for each year of a tenancy.

i) Conditions in the Appellant's property were not good, and she was anxious to move elsewhere.

j) The Appellant had previously been on the waiting list for a transfer.

k) In August 1998, the Appellant indicated that she still wanted a transfer, and this was not prompted by the Respondents' plans for redevelopment, which were not at that stage finalised.

l) The Appellant said in evidence that she, in common with her neighbours, was delighted to hear that the Estate was going to be redeveloped.

m) On June 24, 2001, the Appellant was offered and accepted a property in one of the areas she had chosen. She liked the house, which was in a better area than the one she had left.

The correct legal test

5. The Appellant's claim was that she was "displaced ... in consequence of ... the carrying out of redevelopment" for the purposes of s.29(1)(c).

6. A person is not "displaced" if s/he vacates voluntarily (see *Follows v Peabody Trust* (1983) 10 H.L.R. 62, CA, *per* Cumming-Bruce L.J. at p.69). The correct test is an objective one (*Follows*, at 69). The Judge clearly applied that test, considering the surrounding circumstances in detail as summarised particularly above.

7. In the present case, the Judge found that there had been prior consultation with the tenants, strong support for the proposed scheme, no indications of unwillingness to move, policy adjustments were made to facilitate tenants' moves, tenants' preferences about their new accommodation were met, there was no compulsion, there were no deadlines, the scheme proceeded on the basis of agreement, and tenants had a real choice. The Judge also found that the Appellant herself had wanted to move, and was happy with her new accommodation in a better area.

8. Accordingly, the Judge made no error.

Relevance of a transfer application

9. The Appellant's wish to move out of her previous accommodation, manifested by a transfer application, was a relevant consideration. A tenant making a transfer application indicates a willingness to give up the existing accommodation in return for new accommodation.

10. In the present case, the Appellant's transfer application had pre-dated the proposal for the redevelopment, and thus could clearly be seen to have been an independent act by the Appellant.

Relevance of tenants' general support for the redevelopment scheme

11. The support from the Appellant and other tenants for the proposed redevelopment, and its subsequent implementation, was a relevant consideration. The fundamental requirement of the scheme was that it should proceed by agreement and involvement of the community, as opposed to being pushed through by the Defendants. There was a substantial history, as demonstrated by the Judge's findings. This evidence was relevant to whether the Appellant's departure was voluntary.

12. The Respondents' tenants doubtless saw that there were advantages for them in giving their support (new homes meeting their preferences, agreed compensation, involvement in the process etc). The same may not be true in the case of every proposed redevelopment, so that generalisations should be avoided.

If the Judge erred, remission for re-hearing

13. For the reasons given above, the Judge made no error. The following submissions are made if any error should be found which requires the Judge's conclusion to be reconsidered by this court.

14. The Appellant seeks a declaration on appeal that she is entitled to a home loss payment. The premise for this is the Appellant's contention that the only conclusion which the Judge could properly have reached was that she was displaced.

15. This court is unlikely to be in a position to determine that, on the evidence which he heard, the Judge was bound to find that the Appellant was displaced. The factual history which the Judge considered was lengthy and detailed. He heard witnesses in a trial lasting a day.

16. Accordingly, if the Judge's conclusion on the evidence is set aside, the case should be remitted for a re-trial.

BART FLEMING

[1] Based on *Ingle v Scarborough BC* [2002] EWCA Civ 290.

9.15 Form 160

Petition for leave to appeal to the House of Lords[1]

IN THE HOUSE OF LORDS

ON APPEAL FROM HER MAJESTY'S COURT OF APPEAL (ENGLAND)

B E T W E E N

STANLEY SOAP

Respondent

and

LONDON BOROUGH OF DOWNTOWN

Petitioners

TO THE RIGHT HONOURABLE THE HOUSE OF LORDS

THE HUMBLE PETITION OF the London Borough of Downtown, of Civic Centre, Downtown, London, praying for leave to appeal SHEWETH that:

1. Your Petitioners (herein after called "Downtown") are, and at all material times were, a local housing authority and freehold owners of the residential building known as John House, Adam Street, Downtown.

2. The Respondent is the weekly secure tenant of Flat 2 in the building, pursuant to a written tenancy agreement dated February 4, 1993.

3. On October 4, 1996, the Respondent commenced the proceedings herein against Downtown for damages and remedial works in respect of noise disturbance from the ordinary use of adjoining flats in the building. By order dated April 25, 1997, His Honour Judge Grey dismissed the claim.

4. By order dated October 20, 1998, the Court of Appeal (Lord Justice Redd, Lord Justice White and Sir Christopher Blew) allowed the Respondent's appeal against the order of His Honour Judge Grey, reversing the judge's decision and awarding damages and making an order for remedial works on the claim, and refused Downtown permission to appeal to your Lordships' House.

5. Lord Justice Redd summarised his judgment in the following words (transcript p.20):

   "The decision of this Court in *Sampson v Hodson-Pressinger* [1981] 3 All E.R. 710, CA, is indistinguishable on the salient facts in this case and is binding on this Court. The building is not fit to be used in a normal way because of the lack of sound insulation between the walls, floors and ceilings of the adjoining flats, and could not be used without interfering with the reasonable enjoyment by the Claimant of his flat. The Claimant is entitled to succeed both in the tort of nuisance and for breach of the covenant for quiet enjoyment."

6. Lord Justice White and Sir Christopher Blew agreed.

7. Downtown submit that the conclusions of the Court of Appeal are wrong for the following principal reasons:

Nuisance

(a) In relation to the tort of nuisance, the Court of Appeal failed to follow clear and binding legal authority that, in order for Downtown to be liable, it had to be demonstrated that Downtown's use of the building, as landlord, was unreasonable user (see particularly *per* Lord Goff in *Cambridge Water Co Ltd v Eastern Counties Leather plc* [1994] 2 A.C. 264, HL, at p.300/F):

> "...liability has been kept under control by the principle of reasonable user – the principle of give and take as between neighbouring occupiers of land, under which 'those acts necessary for the common and ordinary use and occupation of land and houses may be done, if conveniently done, without subjecting those who do them to an action': see *Bamford v. Turnley* (1962) 3 B.& S. 62, 83 *per* Bramwell B. The effect is that, if the user is reasonable, the defendant will not be liable for consequent harm to his neighbour's enjoyment of his land...".

(b) In accordance with the principle of reasonable user, any occupier of land is expected to tolerate the normal, ordinary or day-to-day use of neighbouring land or buildings for the purposes for which the land or buildings are reasonably to be contemplated to be used. Ordinary use of residential premises without more is not capable of being a nuisance. Accordingly, the tenants of the adjoining flats would not have been liable to the Respondent in nuisance in respect of the noise of their ordinary domestic activities, and Downtown are in no different position.

(c) The decision of the Court of Appeal in *Sampson v Hodson-Pressinger*, above, is consistent with the principle of reasonable user only on the basis that the landlord in that case had altered the flat adjoining the Plaintiff's flat with the effect that a significantly increased level of noise disturbance was caused to the plaintiff's flat. The ordinary use and occupation of the adjoining flat had ceased to be "conveniently done", using the language of Bramwell B. in *Bamford v Turnley*, above.

Covenant for quiet enjoyment

(d) In relation to the covenant of quiet enjoyment, the Court of Appeal failed to follow clear and binding legal authority that the covenant is prospective in nature, and does not apply to things done before the grant of the tenancy. In *Anderson v Oppenheimer* (1880) 5 QBD 602, CA, the escape of water from a pre-existing water system in a building did not constitute a breach of the covenant. For the purposes of the covenant, the tenant had to take the building as he found it.

(e) Similarly, in *Spoor v Green* (1874) L.R. 9 Exch 99, the Court of Exchequer held that there was no breach of the covenant when houses built by the purchaser of land were damaged by subsidence caused by underground mining which had taken place before the sale of the land by the vendor. Cleasby B. held (at 108):

"...it ... seems to me impossible to say that there is a breach of covenant for quiet enjoyment by reason of the subsidence of the house in consequence of the previous removal of the coal. This subsidence of the house is a necessary consequence of the condition of the property bought by the plaintiff...".

(f) Furthermore, in *Lyttleton Times Co Ltd v Warners Ltd* [1907] A.C. 476, PC, the plaintiff failed in a claim for an injunction to restrain the defendants from working a printing press. The parties owned adjoining business premises, and entered into an agreement whereby the defendants would rebuild their premises containing the printing press and grant a lease of the upper floors to the plaintiff for use as additional hotel bedrooms. The noise of the press caused substantial disturbance to the occupants of the bedrooms. Lord Loreburn L.C. held (at 481):

"When it is a question of what shall be implied from the contract, it is proper to ascertain what in fact was the purpose, or what were the purposes, to which both intended the land to be put, and, having found that, both should be held to all that was implied in this common intention ... if it be true that neither has done or asks to do anything which was not contemplated by both, neither can have any right against the other."

8. It would be a matter for Parliament, and not for the courts, to introduce a general covenant or liability requiring the improvement of premises in order that they should be fit for a particular purpose, or possess certain qualities. Thus, in *McNerny v London Borough of Lambeth* (1988) 21 H.L.R. 188, the Court of Appeal held that it was for Parliament and not the courts to extend a landlord's obligations to require the remedying of inherent problems of condensation dampness in residential premises. Substantial issues of housing policy and resources are involved in the present context. The required works of sound insulation would cost £5000 in the present case alone, and Downtown have a stock of approximately 20,000 dwellings all of which were constructed or converted prior to the introduction of modern Building Regulations requiring any sound insulation. The Law Commission (*Landlord and Tenant: Responsibility for State and Condition of Property* (1996), Law Comm. No. 238) has recommended substantial statutory reform, including a new implied covenant of fitness for human habitation, to replace the now largely defunct Landlord and Tenant Act 1985, s.8. The Law Commission did not, however, recommend the inclusion of sound insulation within the scope of the new implied covenant (para.8.54 and fn.153).

9. The questions of law raised by the Court of Appeal are of considerable public importance because:

(1) The finding of liability in nuisance potentially applies to all adjoining occupiers across the country, and extends liability to all ordinary activities by adjoining occupiers.

(2) The finding of liability under the covenant for quiet enjoyment potentially applies to all existing and future leases across the country, and extends liability to interferences occurring before as well as after the grant of the lease.

(3) The extension of these liabilities has very significant and widespread financial implications for landlords, particularly for providers of low cost (and often aging) housing in the public and social sectors which would need to be upgraded and improved to modern standards of sound insulation and fitness.

YOUR PETITIONERS HUMBLY SUBMIT that leave to appeal to your Lordships' House should be granted for the following among other

REASONS

(1) BECAUSE the decision of the Court of Appeal was wrong.

(2) BECAUSE the issues are of general public importance and ought to be considered by your Lordships' House.

AND YOUR PETITIONERS will ever pray.

Signed.............................
Agent for the Petitioners

---

[1] The context is taken and adapted from *Southwark LBC v Mills* [2001] A.C. 1, HL.

9.16 **Form 161**

Respondent's objections to petition for leave to appeal

IN THE HOUSE OF LORDS

ON APPEAL FROM HER MAJESTY'S COURT OF APPEAL (ENGLAND)

B E T W E E N

STANLEY SOAP

Respondent

and

LONDON BOROUGH OF DOWNTOWN

Petitioners

TO THE RIGHT HONOURABLE THE HOUSE OF LORDS

THE HUMBLE OBJECTIONS OF the Respondent, Stanley Soap, of Flat 2 John House, Adam Street, Downtown, objecting to the petition for leave to appeal herein SHEWETH that:

A. SUMMARY

1. Your Lordships' House is invited:

    (1) to dismiss the petition; or,

    (2) if you think it right to allow the petition to allow it only on terms that

        (a) the order for costs made in the Court of Appeal in respect of the costs on appeal and at first instance is not disturbed irrespective of the outcome of the appeal, and/or
        (b) in the event of the Petitioners succeeding, they should not ask for their costs of the appeal to Your Lordships' House.

2. Paragraphs 1 to 6 of the petition are not in dispute.

3. The grounds upon which the Respondent submits that the petition should be dismissed are set out in Part B hereof. If Your Lordships are not persuaded by those arguments to dismiss the petition, then the grounds upon which the Respondent contends that the petition should only be granted on terms are set out in Part C hereof.

B. GROUNDS FOR OPPOSING THE PETITION

4. In this Part of the Objections, the Respondent deals in order with the Petitioners' grounds set out in paras 7 to 9 of the petition.

The claim in nuisance

5. The Court of Appeal correctly held below (transcript, para.18, *per* Lord Justice Redd), following *Sampson v Hodson-Pressinger* [1981] 3 All E.R. 710, CA:

    "It is no defence to a claim in nuisance that the premises are being used in a normal way if the premises are not fit to be used in a normal way without interfering with the reasonable enjoyment of adjoining occupiers."

6. The critical element in the present case is the effect which the use of the adjoining premises has upon the enjoyment of the subject premises. The noise of activity which might in other circumstances be acceptable is made intolerable by reason of the condition of the premises, for which the Petitioners are liable.

7. The Court of Appeal's decision was a proper application of the principle of reasonable user, derived from *Cambridge Water Co Ltd v Eastern Counties Leather plc* [1994] 2 A.C. 264, HL, and did not involve any failure to follow that authority. The ordinary day-to-day activities of the adjoining tenants were not "conveniently done", to use the language of Bramwell B. in *Bamford v Turnley* (1862) 3 B. & S. 62 at 83, when they were done in premises which were not fit for that use without interfering with the reasonable enjoyment of adjoining occupiers.

8. Whether or not the adjoining tenants might also be liable in nuisance, the Petitioners, as landlords, have a special relationship with the Respondent to which liability ought to attach. They retained the common parts, walls, ceilings and floors of the building in their ownership (tenancy agreement, clause 2). They also covenanted, among other things, to keep the structure of the building not only in good repair, but also in good condition (tenancy agreement, clause 4). They had moreover been responsible for the conversion of the building into flats, which was likely to have significantly interfered with the sound insulation properties of the structure (judgment, Lord Justice Redd, below, para.10). Finally, they were responsible for letting the resulting flats, and it was foreseeable that the necessary consequence of letting the flats in that condition was to cause disturbance to the occupiers (*ibid.*).

Covenant for quiet enjoyment

9. The Court of Appeal correctly held below (transcript, para.20, *per* Lord Justice Redd), following *Sampson v Hodson-Pressinger* [1981] 3 All E.R. 710, CA, and *Sanderson v Mayor of Berwick* (1884) 13 QBD 547:

    "The noise from the adjoining flats was a substantial interference with the [Respondent's] ordinary and lawful use of his flat. The noise in the flat was caused by the acts of the [Petitioners] or those lawfully claiming under them. Accordingly, there was a breach of the covenant for quiet enjoyment."

10. The use of the building by the Petitioners as flats, with the consequent disturbance to the Respondent from the activities of the adjoining tenants, was continuing conduct for which the Petitioners were responsible. Neither *Anderson v Oppenheimer* (1880) 5 QBD 602, CA, nor *Spoor v Green* (1874) L.R. 9 Exch 99, preclude liability under the covenant in respect of such continuing acts. The decision of the Privy Council in *Lyttleton Times Co Ltd v Warners Ltd* [1907] A.C. 476, depended

on its own particular facts, where the parties had jointly embarked on an enterprise which necessarily contemplated the continued working of the adjoining printing press and noise therefrom.

The role of the courts

11. The courts have been willing to impose and imply obligations at common law on landlords in respect of the condition of premises, without abdication to Parliament. There is no necessary reason why the courts should refrain from a finding of liability in the present case. There has long been an implied obligation on a landlord to ensure fitness for habitation the case of furnished dwellings (*Wilson v Finch-Hatton* (1877) 2 Ex. D 336). There is also an implied obligation of fitness for habitation in the case of a dwelling which is under construction (see *Perry v Sharon Development Co Ltd* [1937] 4 All E.R. 390, CA, involving the relationship of vendor-purchaser but applicable to the landlord-tenant relationship as well). Obligations to repair can be implied on grounds of business efficacy or correlative obligation (*Liverpool CC v Irwin* [1977] A.C. 239, HL; *Berrett v Lounova (1982) Ltd* [1990] 1 Q.B. 348, CA). There is an implied obligation on the landlord in respect of retained parts of a building to take reasonable care that they do not cause damage to the tenant or the demised premises (*Cockburn v Smith* [1924] 2 K.B. 119, CA). A landlord can also be liable in negligence for building defective premises (*Rimmer v Liverpool CC* [1985] Q.B. 1, CA).

Diminished public importance

12. The public importance of an appeal in the present case is diminished because, following the Law Commission report, *Landlord and Tenant: Responsibility for State and Condition of Property* (1996), Law Comm. No. 238, the Government has in any event been consulting on and commissioning a new Housing Health and Safety Rating System as a comprehensive mechanism for dealing with unsatisfactory housing conditions, including a noise insulation standard (see *Housing Fitness Standard: A Consultation Paper*, DETR, February 1998; *Health and Safety in Housing*, DETR, March 2001; and *Housing Research Summary, Housing Health and Safety Rating System: Quick Guide*, DETR, July 2000).

C. IF PETITION IS ALLOWED, IT SHOULD BE ON TERMS

13. The interest, as between the parties, is very one-sided. The effect of the decision of the Court of Appeal, below, is an order for works estimated to cost no more than £5000, and damages assessed at £3500.

14. The Respondent has no interest in the outcome of this appeal, other than in relation to these works and damages, and costs. The Petitioners, on the other hand, are very substantial owners of other residential and commercial property in relation to which (and subject to the prospective legislative changes referred to under para.12 above) the decision in this case has an immediate and substantial impact on the Petitioners' interests. The petition for leave also prays in aid the position of other public and social landlords (para.9(3)).

15. Because of the very substantial inequality of interest in the outcome of this appeal,

Your Lordships' House is invited, if minded to grant leave to appeal, to grant leave to appeal only on terms that

(a) the Petitioners do not seek to disturb the order on costs made in the Court of Appeal as to the costs of the appeal and in the court below; and/or

(b) in the event of the Petitioners succeeding, they should not ask for their costs of the appeal to Your Lordships' House.

D. CONCLUSION

YOUR RESPONDENT HUMBLY SUBMITS that leave to appeal to your Lordships' House should be refused for the following among other

REASONS

(1) BECAUSE the decision of the Court of Appeal was right.

(2) BECAUSE the Petitioners' grounds suggesting otherwise are wrong.

AND YOUR RESPONDENT will ever pray.

Signed..............................
Agent for the Respondent

9.17   **Form 162**

Petition of appeal to the House of Lords

IN THE HOUSE OF LORDS

ON APPEAL FROM HER MAJESTY'S COURT OF APPEAL (ENGLAND)

B E T W E E N

STANLEY SOAP

Respondent

and

LONDON BOROUGH OF DOWNTOWN

Petitioners

TO THE RIGHT HONOURABLE THE HOUSE OF LORDS

THE HUMBLE PETITION AND APPEAL OF the London Borough of Downtown, of Civic Centre, Downtown, London.

YOUR PETITIONERS humbly pray that the matter of the order set forth in the schedule hereto may be reviewed before Her Majesty the Queen, in Her Court of Parliament, and that the said order may be reversed, varied or altered and that judgment may be entered for the Petitioners and the claim herein be dismissed or that the Petitioners may have such other relief in the premises as to Her Majesty the Queen, in Her Court of Parliament, may seem meet.

Signed...........................
Agent for the Petitioners

THE SCHEDULE ABOVE REFERRED TO FROM
HER MAJESTY'S COURT OF APPEAL (ENGLAND)

In a certain cause wherein Stanley Soap was the Claimant and the London Borough of Downtown were the Defendants.

The order of Her Majesty's Court of Appeal dated October 20, 1998 appealed from is in the words following: [set out the entire terms of the order, including the recital]

And Your Lordships gave leave to appeal to Your Lordships' House on March 26, 1999.

LAURA LEADER QC
JAMIE JUNIOR
Counsel for the Petitioners

Form 163   9.18

Statement of facts and issues[1]

Reported	On Appeal: [0000] 2 W.L.R. 566, [0000] 1 All E.R. 237, Times November 11, 0000
Summary	Nuisance – covenant for quiet enjoyment – building converted into flats – noise from ordinary use of adjoining flats – interference with the Respondent's enjoyment of his flat – whether landlord liable in nuisance and/or for breach of covenant
Time occupied	Court of Appeal: 2 days County Court: 5 days

IN THE HOUSE OF LORDS

ON APPEAL FROM HER MAJESTY'S COURT OF APPEAL (ENGLAND)

B E T W E E N

STANLEY SOAP   **Respondent**

and

LONDON BOROUGH OF DOWNTOWN   **Petitioners**

AGREED STATEMENT OF FACTS AND ISSUES

A. FACTS

1. The Petitioners ("Downtown") are and at all material times were a local housing authority and freehold owners of the residential building known as John House, Adam Street, Downtown.

2. The building was originally a three floor, end of terrace, Victorian house.

3. In 1970, Downtown converted the building into six flats, two on each floor of the house. As a result of that conversion, some of the original brick interior walls were removed and the rooms divided up using plasterboard on stud partitions. The original plaster-on-lath ceilings were replaced by skimmed plasterboard. These works had the effect of reducing the sound insulation between the walls, ceilings and floors of the house.

4. At the time of the conversion, there was no applicable building control dealing with a requirement for sound insulation between dwellings. Building regulations requiring reasonable sound insulation when carrying out building work were first extended to Inner London in 1986.

5. On February 4, 1993, Downtown let the front flat on the first (middle) floor (flat 2) to the Respondent ("the tenant") on a weekly tenancy. The other two front flats (ground floor – flat 1, and second floor – flat 3) were already let to other tenants who have remained in occupation throughout the Respondent's tenancy. The three rear flats were vacant at that time, and have since been let by Downtown.

6. The tenant is a secure tenant (under the provisions of the Housing Act 1985, Pt IV), and his tenancy is on Downtown's standard written terms.

7. The following are terms of the tenancy agreement:

    "Downtown retain the common parts, walls, ceilings and floors of the building" (Clause B3).

    "Downtown shall not interfere with the tenant's rights to quiet enjoyment of the premises during the tenancy" (Clause B4).

    "Downtown covenant to keep the structure of the building in good repair and condition" (Clause B5).

    "Downtown shall take such steps as are reasonably practicable to prevent the continuation of any nuisance caused to the tenant having regard to all the circumstances of the case" (Clause B6).

8. On October 4, 1996, the tenant commenced proceedings against Downtown. He alleged that, because of the inadequate sound insulation in the house, mere ordinary residential use of the adjoining flats resulted in noise disturbance which seriously interfered with the enjoyment of his flat. It was alleged by the tenant that this interference amounted to a nuisance at common law for which Downtown were responsible and, further, to a breach of the covenant of quiet enjoyment.

9. The claim was heard before His Honour Judge Grey on April 14–18, 1997. In his judgement delivered on April 25, 1997 he dismissed the tenant's claim.

10. The judge made the following findings of fact:

    (1) The noise suffered by the tenant, as a result of the ordinary use of their premises by the adjoining tenants, constituted an undue interference with the tenant's enjoyment of his flat.

    (2) The undue interference was caused by the interaction of two things, namely the conversion of the house in 1970 and the continuing user of the adjoining flats after the tenant commenced occupation of his flat.

    (3) The resistance to the transmission of noise between the tenant's living room and the room in the flat immediately above fell below the standard now required by Part E of Schedule 1 to the Building Regulations 1991, SI 1991/2768 and Approved Document E (1992), and was "unacceptable".

11. The tenant was given leave to appeal by Lord Justice Green on July 25, 1997.

12. On October 20, 1998, Her Majesty's Court of Appeal (England) [Lord Justices Redd and White, and Sir Christopher Blew] allowed the tenant's appeal.

13. On February 13, 1999, Your Lordships' House granted Downtown leave to appeal to Your Lordship's House.

B. COMMON GROUND

14. The following is common ground between the parties:

    (1) The flats in the converted house are all occupied for the purpose of ordinary residential use by the tenants.

    (2) Downtown have authorised the tenants so to occupy the flats.

    (3) Ordinary use of the adjoining flats results in a significant interference with the tenant's use and enjoyment of his flat.

C. ISSUES

First Issue

15. Can the ordinary use of residential premises, lawfully constructed or converted, for the purposes for which they were so constructed or converted, without more ever be a nuisance and/or a breach of the covenant for quiet enjoyment?

Second Issue

16. If the answer to the First Issue is yes, where a landlord owns adjoining premises which:

    it lets to tenants for the purpose of ordinary residential use, and

    are constructed in such a way that noise made by one tenant in the course of ordinary residential use of his/her premises can be heard by the tenant in the landlord's adjoining premises to such an extent that the enjoyment of the latter premises is substantially interfered with,

    will that landlord be liable in nuisance and/or for breach of covenant of quiet enjoyment notwithstanding that the interference resulting from the condition of the premises and the ordinary use of the adjoining premises existed at the date of letting?

LAURA LEADER QC   **SAMUEL JOHNSON QC**
JAMIE JUNIOR   **SIMON SIMPSON**

---

[1] See the House of Lords' Practice Directions and Standing Orders Applicable to Civil Appeals, directions 11 and 30. The outside margin will carry references to the relevant pages in the Appendix.

9.19   Form 164

Appellants' case[1]

[A]

IN THE HOUSE OF LORDS

ON APPEAL FROM HER MAJESTY'S COURT OF APPEAL (ENGLAND)

BETWEEN

[B]

STANLEY SOAP

Respondent

and

[C]

LONDON BOROUGH OF DOWNTOWN

Appellants

CASE FOR THE APPELLANTS

[D]

INTRODUCTION

1. This appeal concerns the standard of sound-proofing which a residential tenant can require the landlord to provide, under the tort of nuisance and/or under the covenant for quiet enjoyment. Liability under the tort of nuisance affects the occupiers of land generally, whether owners or tenants. Liability under the covenant for quiet enjoyment affects business tenancies as well as residential tenancies.

[E]

FIRST ISSUE

2. The Appellants' submission is that the ordinary use of premises, lawfully constructed or converted, for the purposes for which they were so constructed or converted, cannot – without more – be a nuisance.

[F]

SECOND ISSUE

3. The Appellants' submission is that they cannot be liable under the covenant for quiet enjoyment in respect of matters occurring before the letting to the Respondent.

[G]

NUISANCE

4. Any occupier of land is expected to tolerate the normal, ordinary or day-to-day use of neighbouring land or buildings, for the purposes for which the land or buildings

are reasonably to be contemplated to be used. This is sometimes referred to as the "control mechanism" of "reasonable user", *per* Lord Goff in *Cambridge Water Co v Eastern Counties Leather plc* [1994] 2 A.C. 264, HL, at p.300/F:

> "...liability has been kept under control by the principle of reasonable user – the principle of give and take as between neighbouring occupiers of land, under which 'those acts necessary for the common and ordinary use and occupation of land houses may be done, if conveniently done, without subjecting those who do them to an action:' see *Bamford v Turnley* (1862) 3 B.&.S. 62, 83 *per* Bramwell B. The effect is that, if the user is reasonable, the defendant will not be liable for consequent harm to his neighbour's enjoyment of his land..."[2]

(*ibid.*, at p.299/D-E, comparing [*ibid.*, pp.299/F–300/A] the principle to "natural user" in relation to *Rylands v Fletcher* (1868) L.R. 3 HL 330).

5. This proposition recognises that the tort of nuisance calls for a balance to be struck.

   (a) *Ball v Ray* (1873) L.R. 8 Ch. App. 467 at p.469 *per* Lord Selborne L.C.:

   > "...There are always two things to be considered, the right of the Plaintiff and the right of the Defendant".

   (b) *Sedleigh-Denfield v O'Callaghan* [1940] A.C. 880 at p.903 *per* Lord Wright:

   > "A balance has to be maintained between the right of the occupier to do what he likes with his own, and the right of his neighbour not to be interfered with. It is impossible to give any precise or universal formula, but it may broadly be said that a useful test is perhaps what is reasonable according to the ordinary usages of mankind living in society, or more correctly in a particular society."

6. In the cases where the user has been described as lawful and/or reasonable but has nonetheless been held to give rise to a nuisance, there has always been something more about the facts to suggest that the user was not "normal" or "ordinary".

   (a) In *Ball v Ray*, above, the occupier of a house in a London street had converted the ground floor into a stable.

   > "[I]f either party turns his house, or any portion of it, to unusual purposes in such a manner as to produce a substantial injury to his neighbour, it appears to me that that is not according to principle or authority a reasonable use of his own property; and his neighbour, shewing substantial injury, is entitled to protection. I do not regard it as a reasonable or a usual manner of using the front portion of a dwelling house in such a street as Green Street, that it should be turned into stables for horses ..." (At pp.469–470, *per* Lord Selborne L.C.).

   (b) Mellish L.J. took the same approach (at p.471):

   > "...When in a street like Green Street the ground floor of a neighbouring house is turned into a stable, we are not to consider the noise of horses from that stable like the noise of a pianoforte from a neighbour's house, or the noise of a neighbour's children in their nursery, which are noises we must reasonably expect, and must to a considerable extent put up with..."

(c) *Ball* was followed in *Broder v Saillard* (1876) 2 Ch D 692. See generally at p.701 *per* Jessel M.R.:

> "It is no answer to say that the Defendant is only making a reasonable use of his property, because there are many trades and many occupations which are not only reasonable, but necessary to be followed, and which still cannot be allowed to be followed in the proximity of dwelling-houses, so as to interfere with the comfort of their inhabitants. ... If a stable is built, as this stable is, not as stables usually are, at some distance from the dwelling-houses, but next to the wall of the Plaintiffs' dwelling-house, in such a position that the noise would actually prevent the neighbours sleeping, and would frighten them out of their sleep, and would prevent their ordinary and comfortable enjoyment of their dwelling-house, all I can say is, that is not a proper place to keep horses in, although the horses may be ordinarily quiet".

7. While it may appear that a different approach has been taken in some other cases, they are similarly explicable in terms of ordinary user in the sense above.

(a) The facts in *Sampson v Hodson-Pressinger* [1981] 3 All E.R. 710, CA, concerned the conversion of a roof above a lower flat to a usable terrace for the upper flat, resulting in a noise to the lower flat. Although Eveleigh L.J. refers (at p.713/j) to use of the adjoining property "in a normal way" (summarising the defendant's contention). He continued:

> "The flaw in this argument ... is that the property itself was not fit to be used in a normal way so far as the terrace was concerned. It could not so be used without interfering with the reasonable enjoyment by the plaintiff of his flat. The use of the terrace put a strain on the plaintiff that normal use in a normal building would not have done."

In so far as the decision is supportable, it must be on the basis that the roof was no longer being used in the "normal" way for which it had been intended. None of the earlier authorities concerned with reasonable user were cited in the judgment.

(b) In *Toff v McDowell* (1993) 69 P. & C.R. 535, Ch D, Evans-Lombe J. followed *Sampson*, holding at p.546 (third full paragraph):

> "It is plain, *inter alia* from the decision in the *Sampson* case, that [the transmitted noise of ordinary acts of occupation] does not confer a defence and that ordinary user of neighbouring premises can cause actionable nuisance to an occupying neighbour".

The nuisance, however, was the consequence of the removal of a carpet in the flat above (see p.546 third full paragraph). As in Sampson, therefore, there had been a change which could be said to have altered the reasonableness of the user.

[H] COVENANT FOR QUIET ENJOYMENT

8. The covenant for quiet enjoyment is prospective in nature, and does not apply to things done before the grant of the tenancy. In *Anderson v Oppenheimer* (1880) 5 QBD 602, CA, the escape of water from a pre-existing water system in a building

did not constitute a breach of the covenant. For the purposes of the covenant, the tenant had to take the building as he found it.

9. Similarly, in *Spoor v Green* (1874) L.R. 9 Exch 99, the Court of Exchequer held that there was no breach of the covenant when houses built by the purchaser of land were damaged by subsidence caused by underground mining which had taken place before the sale of the land by the vendor. Cleasby B. held (at 108):

> "...it ... seems to me impossible to say that there is a breach of covenant for quiet enjoyment by reason of the subsidence of the house in consequence of the previous removal of the coal. This subsidence of the house is a necessary consequence of the condition of the property bought by the plaintiff..."

10. Furthermore, in *Lyttleton Times Co Ltd v Warners Ltd* [1907] A.C. 476, PC, the Claimants failed in a claim for an injunction to restrain the defendants from working a printing press. The parties owned adjoining business premises, and entered into an agreement whereby the defendants would rebuild their premises containing the printing press and grant a lease of the upper floors to the plaintiffs for use as additional hotel bedrooms. The noise of the press caused substantial disturbance to the occupants of the bedrooms. Lord Loreburn L.C. held (at 481):

> "When it is a question of what shall be implied from the contract, it is proper to ascertain what in fact was the purpose, or what were the purposes, to which both intended the land to be put, and, having found that, both should be held to all that was implied in this common intention ... if it be true that neither has done or asks to do anything which was not contemplated by both, neither can have any right against the other."

11. There is no general implied covenant by the lessor of an unfurnished house or flat, or of land, that it is or shall be reasonably fit for habitation, occupation or cultivation, or for any other purpose for which it is let (see generally *Woodfall, Landlord and Tenant*, para.13.001). This principle was observed by the Court of Appeal in *McNerny v London Borough of Lambeth* (1988) 21 H.L.R. 188, applying *Cavalier v Pope*, where it was recognised that (at p.194 *per* Dillon L.J.)

> "this is an area where it is from [for] Parliament to extend the duties imposed on landlords of council flats or houses or other low standard accommodation. It is not for the courts."

STATUTORY FRAMEWORK

12. Statute has altered the position at common law, as described above, by several mechanisms to deal with problems regarding the creation and condition of premises. It would be for Parliament to bring about any change in the law.[3] These mechanisms include: planning control; building regulation; statutory covenants;[4] statutory duty;[5] public health legislation;[6] and housing legislation.[7]

13. The Law Commission (*Landlord and Tenant: Responsibility for State and Condition of Property* (1996), Law Com. No. 238) has recommended substantial statutory reform, including a new implied repairing obligation, and a new implied covenant

of fitness for human habitation. Although the Law Commission noted (at para. 4.44) that sound insulation had been suggested for possible inclusion in the standard of fitness enforced by local authorities under s.604 of the Housing Act 1985,[8] they did not recommend its inclusion within the scope of the new implied covenant (see Recommendation at para.8.54 and fn.153).

[J]   ## JUDGMENT BELOW

14. Lord Justice Redd was, with respect, wrong in the Court of Appeal to hold (transcript p.20) that the present case was indistinguishable from *Sampson*. There was no alteration of the premises in the present case after the letting to the Respondent. Moreover, the Court of Appeal's reliance on *Sampson* failed to take into account at all the principle of reasonable user (above).

15. The decision also failed to recognise the prospective nature of the covenant for quiet enjoyment.

[K]   ## CONCLUSION

16. If the Court of Appeal were right, the implications would be very considerable and extensive, not only for public sector lettings, but also private rented accommodation, as well as owner-occupiers.

  (a) The implications for the public sector are considerable, especially in London where the Building Regulations did not apply until 1986. (As a general proposition, the reduction in public spending in the 1980s means that only a small proportion of any authority's housing stock was built in the second half of that decade or later).

  (b) The Respondent's submissions amount to the proposition that many of the Appellants' older flats cannot be used as housing without improvement; that is an end which must be secured by legislation, in order that the appropriate public funds are made available.

[L]   ## SUMMARY

17. The Appellants humbly pray that Your Lordships' House will be pleased to reverse the Order of the Court of Appeal herein, and will direct that the Respondent pay to the Appellants the costs of the proceedings in Your Lordships' House, for the following among other

[M]   ## REASONS

  (1) BECAUSE the ordinary use of premises, lawfully constructed or converted, for the purposes for which they were so constructed or converted, cannot without more be a nuisance; and on the facts the interference complained of by the Respondent resulted solely from such ordinary use.

(2) BECAUSE there is no breach of the covenant for quiet enjoyment in respect of matters occurring before the letting to the tenant.

LAURA LEADER QC
JAMIE JUNIOR

[1] See the House of Lords' Practice Directions and Standing Orders Applicable to Civil Appeals, directions 11 and 30. The outside margin will carry references to the relevant pages in the Appendix.
[2] This was described by Lord Cooke in *Hunter v Canary Wharf Ltd* at p.711/G-H as "the governing principle".
[3] See *McNerny v London Borough of Lambeth* (1988) 21 H.L.R. 188, CA.
[4] *e.g.* Landlord and Tenant Act 1985, ss.8 and 11.
[5] *e.g.* Defective Premises Act 1972.
[6] See now Environmental Protection Act 1990, Pt III.
[7] *e.g.* slum clearance powers in Housing Act 1985, Pt IX.
[8] Also not (yet) adopted.

9.20   PART III: CHECKLIST

Apellants

1.   Be careful to identify correctly the legal provision which creates the entitlement to an appeal/review/re-hearing, because this will determine issues of substance, procedure and accordingly drafting.

2.   Check if permission is required, which will usually be the case in a civil appeal, and apply for it initially from the lower court (unless the appeal is a second appeal).

3.   Check carefully the time within which the appeal must be brought. It may be possible to obtain an extension of time, though some periods are strict.

4.   Identify the court/level of judiciary to which the appeal lies.

5.   Prepare the appropriate notice and supporting documentation, considering whether a stay or other interim relief is required, and whether any applications (such as for expedition) are necessary.

6.   Pay particular attention to the formulation of the grounds of appeal, and the terms of the order which the appeal court is to be asked to make. The grounds need to be sufficiently detailed in order to make clear the error which the lower court is said to have made and/or set out what the lower court has failed to do.

7.   Civil appeals are usually a review, not re-hearing, and it is therefore necessary to identify an error of law or serious procedural irregularity: it is not enough merely to assert that the lower court should have reached a different conclusion on the facts, or exercised a discretion in a different way. The most common grounds are that the lower court misinterpreted or misapplied the law, that there was no evidence to support a particular conclusion, and that the exercise of a discretion was "plainly wrong".

Respondents

8.   Consider whether a respondent's notice is required, to uphold the decision of the lower court on different or additional grounds.

Generally

9.   Perhaps the most important drafting exercise in an appeal is the skeleton argument. The general requirements for skeleton arguments in civil appeals are in CPR 52 PD paras 5.10 and 5.11. A well-drafted appeal skeleton will identify the issues for the benefit of the court and the opposing party, set out all the necessary information which the court needs (both legal and factual), and summarise the reasoning and argument to be used. The higher the level of appeal court, the greater the care required in the content and presentation of the argument.

Index